OUT OF HITLER'S REACH

The Scattergood Hostel for European Refugees 1939-43

Michael Luick-Thrams

Design and Editorial: Nancy A. Fandel for Allied Business Consultants, Inc.
Contributing Editor: L J Dukes
Printer: Goodfellow Printing, Iowa City, Iowa

Cover photograph of Scattergood Hostel guests relaxing at the Cedar
Valley Quarries taken by Helmut Ostrowski-Wilk. All photos in this book
are used with permission of and come from the collections of Camilla Hewson
Flintermann, Earle and Marjorie Edwards, George and Lilian Pemberton
Willoughby, Robert Berquist, John Kaltenbach, Harry Wilk and AFSC.

Inquiries regarding requests to reprint excerpts from *Out of Hitler's Reach*
should be submitted to: Michael Luick-Thrams at www.TRACES.org.

All proceeds from the sale of this book go to TRACES, which is sponsoring
the publication of this third-edition printing. TRACES is a non-profit educational
organization created to gather, preserve and present stories of people from the
Upper Midwest and Germany who encountered each other during World War II.
Many of these stories have lain beneath the dust left in the wake of a World War
most never thought touched the American Heartland. TRACES brushes away
that dust, unearthing an amazing legacy. As we learn about these stories,
may we rise above – and eventually defeat – the prejudices, fears and conflicts
that otherwise demean and destroy us.

ACKNOWLEDGMENTS

I give thanks to all who have helped me in one way or another in this project, from passing on helpful research tips to sharing deep secrets of a lifetime: to former Scattergood Hostel adults Camilla Flintermann [and Peter], Robert Berquist, Walter Shostal [and Ilse], Margaret Stevens [and Ed], Lillian and George Willoughby, Marianne Welter, Earle and Marjorie Edwards, Ernst Solmitz Somers [and Bernice], Ernst Malamerson van den Haag, Pierre Shostal [and Hilary], Hans Peters [now deceased] [and Doris], Lisa Hausen and Robert Cory [and Sally]; to Marydel Balderston, Robert Burgess, Elinor Jones Cloe, Esther Smith Meyerding [now deceased], Ruth Coppock Palmer, Leanore Goodenow, Mary Lane Hiatt and Joyce DeLine Ball; to former "Scattergood Hostel kids" Nicole Hackel, Edith Lichtenstein Morgan, Ilse/Elizabeth Seligmann/Seaman Chilton [and Roland], Irmgard Rosenzweig Wessel, Hanna Deutsch Clampitt [and Phil], Michael Deutsch, Helmut Seligmann/Seaman, Doris Arntal Tabari and Louis Lichtenstein; to "honorary Scattergoodians" Susan Copithorne Robinson, Robert Anthony, Betty Balderston Maurer, Peter Stern, Leola Bergmann, Nona Swope, Rachel Kinworthy and Paul Hagerty; to family of former Scattergoodians Nancy Zimmerman, Sally Zimmerman Weiss, David Zimmerman, Ruth Kaltenbach, Harry Wilk and Peter Curtis; to photographer David Conklin; to advice-givers Barry Trachtenberg, Brenda Bailey and Herr Hohls; to editors Hans Luedecke, Sita Yoder, Becky Calcraft and Lori Dukes; to Mary Bennett of the State Historical Society of Iowa in Iowa City and Jack Sutters of the American Friends Service Committee Archives in Philadelphia; to Josef Keith and Sylvia Carlyle of the Friends House Library, to David Irwin and Christine Patel of the Weiner Library (both institutions in London) and to Dianne Spielmann of New York's Leo Baeck Institute; to Ruth Rauch, Helen Ritter, Cyma Horowitz and Michele Anish of the American Jewish Committee and to David Rosenstein of the American Jewish Joint Distribution Committee (both in New York), and to Gail Farr, Jennifer Coleman and Jeremy Carrion of Philadelphia's Balch Institute for Ethnic Studies; to Frauen Talay and Wagner of Munich's *Institut für Zeitgeschichte*; to Herrn Reese of Berlin's *Luftbrückedank Stiftung* for assistance in funding a first stateside research trip; similarly, to AFSC's Tom Conrad, to Philadelphia Yearly Meeting's International Outreach Committee and to Iowa Yearly Meeting of

Friends (Conservative) for helping provide the financial means to make first in-person contact with numerous survivors in autumn 1994; to Tim Barrett and Jody Plumert, Robert Berquist, the David and Rosalie Braverman Foundation, David Conklin, Howard and Grace Davis, Walter and Vesta Newlin Hansen, Elmer and Lucille Hemingway, Keith and Joanne Hemingway, Elwin and Ada Glee Hemingway Leet, Raymond and Clara Millett, Owen and Doris Jean Newlin and Ed and Peg Hannum Stevens for the material resources to publish this book; to Sally Campbell [and Chuck], Doug Alderfer, Joe Izzo, Mark Dupont and Minneapolis' Omega House folks for providing accommodation on two trips Stateside; to Jane Strange and clan for hospitality while undertaking research in England; to Herrn Pragst and Frau Haselow of Humboldt Universität's *Referat Weiterbildung und Nachwuchsförderung* for guidance in procuring a generous *Stipendium* while I wrote this *Dokumentation*; to Frau Großmann for all her *kleine Bemühungen*; to Herrn Doktor Herbst of Humboldt Universität zu Berlin for overseeing this project, but moreover for having faith in me as a *Doktorand* in *Deutschland*.

Deepest thanks to Monika Ruhnke for encouragement as a special friend; to Wolfgang Wagner for patiently suffering with me for some two years while I was obsessed with and wholly distracted by this labor of love; to INGO Dresp for daring to care.

~ **Michael Luick-Thrams**

CONTENTS

Foreword	A PLACE OF PEACE	*vi*
Chapter 1	AN OCEAN OF LIGHT	*1*
Chapter 2	A HOLY EXPERIMENT	*8*
Chapter 3	IN THESE DARK HOURS	*13*
Chapter 4	SO MUCH AT HOME	*27*
Chapter 5	A GLIMPSE OF HOPE	*40*
Chapter 6	SUCH JOY	*94*
Chapter 7	BROAD TOLERANCES; FIRM CONVICTIONS	*111*
Chapter 8	THE SPIRIT OF THE COMMUNITY	*149*
Chapter 9	FOR THE BENEFIT OF ALL	*168*
Chapter 10	TO ACCELERATE MASTERY	*184*
Chapter 11	AN ELABORATE CELEBRATION	*204*
Chapter 12	A NEW WAY OF LIFE	*226*
Chapter 13	THE MELTING POT	*260*
Epilogue	WHITE STILL NIGHTS	*269*
Appendices		*283*
Scattergood Hostelites		*299*
References Notes		*305*
Bibliography		*319*

This book is dedicated to the memory of those who did not survive and to the hope that those who looked away will be forgiven.

A PLACE OF PEACE

*"A place of peace in a world of war, a
haven amidst a world of hatred."*
~ **Rudolf Schreck**

Open the pages of any serious newspaper and a most dismaying array of
disheartening headlines jumps out, somehow confirming our collective worst
suspicions about the "true" nature of human beings; it too often seems as if
scarcely anywhere in the world exist redeeming stories of acts of kindness or
selflessness on a significant scale. This sobering state of affairs is exactly
why the legacy of the Scattergood Hostel for European refugees provides us
world-weary moderns with refreshing reason for hope. Unfortunately,
though, few people know about the unique events which took place on the
Iowa prairies little more than half a century ago.

From 1939 to 1943, 185 refugees from Germany, Austria, Czechoslovakia, Hungary, Poland, Latvia, Russia, Luxembourg and France found
refuge at Scattergood, a temporary hostel in what had been a Friends [also
known as "Quaker"] boarding school near West Branch, a small town in
Iowa. Among those fleeing Nazi-occupied Europe were of course Jews, but
also political opponents of Hitler's regime, outspoken religious figures, former members of the Berlin city council and the Reichstag, prominent judges
and lawyers, unco-optable artists, journalists and wealthy merchants, families with children, single young male students, elderly socialite ladies and
dejected academics. With the help of the Scattergood staff, these refugees
—or "guests," as the Quakers preferred to call them—sought a niche for
themselves in a foreign culture and to adjust to life in the New World.
Sponsored by Philadelphia-based American Friends Service Committee
[AFSC], the hostel strove to rehabilitate, integrate and assimilate the refugees who came to it seeking assistance. Reflecting their native culture and

the era in which they lived, the Quakers who operated the hostel believed that the best way to help the newcomers was to prepare them for assimilation into the wider American society—in their own words, to "create 'new Americans.'" Friends did so primarily to help the newcomers join American society—thereby avoiding isolation or provoking natives' anti-foreigner sentiment. The Quakers' over-riding goal of Americanizing their guests guided almost every aspect of Scattergood Hostel's program: instruction in American life and institutions as well as the English language, garden and household work, freetime activities, etc.. The refugees, meanwhile, largely sought to adapt to the new environs as a means of basic survival and struggled to juggle who they had been with the new biographies they were building; like other refugees at that time, Scattergood's guests attempted to form new identities and welcomed becoming "Americanized."

The hostel largely succeeded in its efforts to rehabilitate and integrate these displaced persons and serves today as a modest model for contemporary refugee centers. Looking at the hostel's record retrospectively, however, one should keep in mind what a truly unusual phenomenon it was, taking in large numbers of strangers who had recently escaped exceptionally traumatic experiences. In doing so, one can more easily understand the staff members' inadequacies, mistakes and relatively few failures by remembering into what unmapped seas these volunteers were sailing. Scattergood Hostel's most glaring shortcoming—one might say—was its lack of applicable examples.

Prior to the existence of the German Third Reich and the Second World War which it set in motion, massive forced emigration had rarely been in response to such chillingly efficient persecution or had scattered its victims in such a broad swath—one reaching literally around the globe. Certainly, since pre-historic times wars and persecution, as well as natural calamities, caused untold shifts of human populations as individuals, families or communities moved from one place to another. In ancient times displaced persons were likely to move upstream or into the next valley to flee hardship: there, perhaps, they might be accommodated by friends or relatives. In historical times, abbeys or benevolent monarchs and later public charities might have provided refuge and rudimentary relief for those displaced from other lands. Without doubt, throughout history multitudes of unfortunates have suffered immensely: in terms of numbers and duration, however, such episodes of uprootedness were relatively manageable.

The mass-migrations of the 1930s and '40s—spurred first by Hitler's politics of hate and then by war itself—were on a scale and of a duration which made them most difficult to manage. This more recent refugee crisis, then, was an old task made new by the very size of the stream of many hundreds of thousands fleeing Nazi terror. In "receiver countries" like the United States and Great Britain there existed numerous refugee programs, but few attempted to take on their charges' rehabilitation and integration in the manner and scope as did that of Quaker programs; government or Jewish and other private organizations ran many day-time programs with limited services, but few offered round-the-clock, comprehensive assistance. The Quakers, therefore, acted as pioneers, feeling their way into a field in which there were few authorities and even fewer role models. It is conceivable, then, that Scattergood Hostel's was among the first integrated refugee program in modern history. In an intentionally quiet atmosphere, it offered its guests professional and language training, therapeutic social opportunities, varied cultural offerings, basic health care, practical tips for post-hostel life and job placement—all while concurrently providing for the refugees' housing, food and other material needs. Astonishingly, this work was performed largely by idealistic young Quakers fresh out of college and by local farmers—with neither group having direct connections to the people being helped other than their common humanity.

The aggregate list of ordeals suffered and the diversity of stories represented in the biographies of the refugees who turned to Scattergood Hostel for help are ample. To substantiate adequately my view that the hostel's program was innovative and mostly successful in addressing the needs of its charges, however, in certain chapters I will focus on the profiles of a limited number of individuals or families, their flight from Europe to America and how the hostel specifically helped them in this transition—or in the case of staff, what motives brought them to Scattergood and their roles there. These biographical sketches are intended to be representative: the degree to which they are depends on the willingness of the reader to deduce generalizations from specific cases. Regrettably, though, many interesting, indicative stories must be left for presentation in some other historian's account.

A serious difficulty in presenting a social history which has such a subjective thesis is that the historian undertaking such a project must provide enough varied opinions to balance the paper's overall range of views—thereby making her or his case credible. Thus, I have included the contrasting perspectives promised above. Also, speaking for the characters in the story may be potentially distorting: therefore, to as reasonable a degree as possible, I will let the players speak for themselves through liberal use of direct quotes from a wide range of sources—e.g., letters, journal entries, hostel reports and newsletters, newspaper articles and essays, poems or songs written by the refugees. Together, these rich threads of primary sources will weave a colorful, comprehensive account of this important subchapter of the Third Reich saga and of Friends' attempts to create "new Americans" [see my doctoral dissertation, *Creating "New Americans": The Scattergood Hostel for European Refugees, 1939-43.*]

Why must this story be saved from the forgetfulness of our collective memory and why is it at all important whether or not the Scattergood Hostel's efforts at refugee rehabilitation, assimilation and integration were effective? On a practical level and with the world's present problems in mind, because current and future generations could gain valuable insight into how—or how not—to run refugee programs and centers. In this era of disintegrating states and the subsequent displacement of civilian populations, this is no small need. In the wake of the breathtaking, spotfire chaos unleashed in great part by the collapse of the Soviet empire and the end of the Cold War, certain countries have found themselves inundated by—and quite unprepared for—deluges of displaced persons fleeing various forms of turmoil in their lands of origin. As it is, politicians of all stripes in wealthy countries squirm at the suggestion that they "should" accept even relatively small numbers of the current flood of refugees. The Scattergood Hostel, surprisingly, came to life in a country with scarcely any social "safety net" and in an era of unprecedented unemployment, with its accompanying poverty and hardship: if an integrated, effective refugee program was possible in such a country under such conditions at such a time, then we must reconsider what is at all possible to be done today. Scattergood Hostel might provide an important model for contemporary refugee centers and programs: a model, however, does not mean simply positive examples of conditions and techniques to replicate, but also negative aspects and dynamics to avoid. In that light, Scattergood's experience as a hostel might yield lasting significance—through both its weaknesses and strengths.

On a philosophical level, Scattergood Hostel's legacy remains noteworthy by the fact of its very existence. While many millions looked away and tragically few actively interested themselves in the plight of Nazi Germany's rejected Jews and other "elements" seen as threats to the Third Reich, those individuals who participated in Scattergood's efforts to provide refuge were inadvertently adding their names to the finite list of rescuers. True to the Holocaust-related use of the word "rescuer" as defined by the Israeli Holocaust institute Yad Vashem, the volunteers at Scattergood undertook such efforts solely on a humanitarian basis and most received no financial reward for their efforts. (A third defining condition stipulates that the rescuer risked her or his own life—a point made moot by the Iowa prairies' safe isolation.)

As the last wave of the generation of adults who witnessed the Holocaust leaves us, now is our final chance to preserve undocumented cases of those who sensed—on whatever level—the threat posed to Nazi Germany's unwanted thousands and tried to save as many of the imperiled as possible. Scattergood's example of assistance to strangers in need serves us still as proof of how noble human beings can be. Acts of kindness and selflessness are indeed rare, and the heritage of what some inspired individuals among the silent masses achieved at Scattergood ought not become lost. As one grateful refugee wrote at the time of the hostel's closing, through its vision and corresponding actions Scattergood had been a "place of peace in a world of war, a haven amidst a world of hatred."

REFERENCES TO SOURCES
This document refers repeatedly to primary sources—letters, interviews, unpublished reports and memoirs. As of the completion of this project, the American Friends Service Committee Archives (1501 Cherry, Philadelphia, Pennsylvania 19102-1479) possesses copies of all primary sources as well as reports and articles used in this work. In addition, detailed Reference Notes pertaining to this text are included at the story's end. Curious readers or future researchers can consult those Reference Notes for a particular item, located by an identifying phrase from the text in order of appearance. Secondary sources are found listed in the Bibliography.

An Ocean of Light

*"I saw also that there was an ocean of darkness
and death, but an infinite ocean of light and love,
which flowed over the ocean of darkness."*

~ **George Fox**

Without a basic knowledge of Quakerism, its historic peace testimony and its commitment to social justice through personal and collective action, Scattergood Hostel's mere existence can seem baffling—if not incomprehensible. That a group of mostly young Quaker volunteers and a core cadre of local Quaker farmers would go to great lengths without compensation to assist refugees fleeing Nazi-occupied Europe can be understood only in the context of centuries-old, religious-based Quaker principles.

Seen in the long view, the creation of the Scattergood Hostel in 1939 is rooted in events which took place some three centuries previously in the political, religious and economic chaos of Stuart England. At that time large numbers of peasants and small-trades people were forcibly dispossessed of their traditional ways of life. In the century before 1650 the population had doubled to about five million. With the enclosure of what had been common lands, crippling pressure was put on farmers and craftspeople. Unable to support themselves, the disenfranchised turned their wrath on the island's rulers. After Henry VIII's split with Rome, the head of State and the head of the Church were inseparable. Any attack on the power of the monarchy, then, necessarily meant an attack on the vested sacred order: political ferment and religious rebellion were fraternal twins.

A thoroughly privileged aristocracy ruled Britain. Parliament did convene, but without the muscle needed to enact its wishes or to guard against royal excesses. Concurrently, most of the bishops of the Church of England came from the ranks of the landed gentry and the Church sat in Parliament in the form of those same bishops. In addition, bishops held their own courts and enjoyed a wide jurisdiction—including over censorship of morals, charges of blasphemy, adultery, intestacy or the proof of wills, questions related to illegitimacy and the annulment of marriages. Given this inseparable union of crown and cross, the closely-monitored collection of "religious" tithes very much mattered in terms of filling the king's coffers. Expectably, clergy eager to please bosses higher on an entrenched hierarchical ladder prodded the faithful in order to wring the people's pockets.

With this backdrop of the elites' luxuriant wealth and the dominance of the Church in matters social as well as spiritual, common people's hardships seemed only that much worse. Resentments festered freely. Improved farming methods and communications had fueled an increase in unemployment: the accompanying underemployment meant that many were seasonal or part-time farm workers and a sizeable pool of under-utilized laborers flooded the countryside with idle hands. On top of dire economic patterns, several bad harvests in the fifty years preceding the outbreak of civil war in 1642 meant that hunger roamed the land, claiming the weakest and poorest members of an already beleaguered populace.

Nine out of ten people in England lived on the land and, besides London, few cities boasted significant populations. When the spillover of those whom the countryside simply could not accommodate reached London or such regional urban centers as York, Coventry, Bristol or Norwich, a predictable unrest resulted. Idle hands swiftly became idle mouths. Curiously, the people's smoldering dissatisfaction expressed itself above all in spiritual affairs. In a period much closer to the religious fervor of Medieval Europe than to the vigorous intellectualism of a yet-to-dawn Enlightenment, perhaps it can be understood that theological matters were taken completely seriously.

In both province and town in the early 1600s, individuals and groups across England spent endless energy in religious pursuits. The most dominant theological trend which arose out of that intense effort to reform what many saw as a debauched state Church was "Puritanism." This restless offspring of popular discontent cannot, however, be described as a coherent school of thought but rather a disorganized house of contention. In general it would be safest to say that Puritans wanted to purify the contemporary church—often with an eye on the primitive one as a model. Still undergoing the de-Catholicization of Britain begun by Henry VIII, many Puritans were not convinced that the official Church was sufficiently free of Roman practices or that it was fully faithful in its biblical teachings. Most Puritans touted the Bible as the final authority in matters of faith and practice.

A primary pillar of the Puritanical temple could be seen as a profound experience of "grace"—as one religious historian wrote, "an awareness of the reality of God, a confidence in his providence, and a reliance on his illimitable love." Although dressed in supplementary images of sin and salvation,

2

the core concept of grace consisted of the availability of divine experience to *every* individual. Although the Puritans eagerly painted human beings as being wicked, depraved and lost, they equally as eagerly peddled images of an all-powerful, all-wise and all-loving god—an image not common in their day. As "salvation" awaited any who might seek it, the Puritans sought regeneration in all things: their hearts, their families and communities, the church and the nation. In their campaign to attain spiritual "perfection," they also strove to mold the nation into a "godly community."

Of course, movements don't occur in vacuums: individuals attempting to find internal order in the context of external chaos around them grease the wheels of change. One such person was an unsettled and unsettling young man born in Leicestershire, near the Midlands market town where John Wycliffe earlier had launched theological attacks on religious authority. Personifying the age-old happenstance of extraordinary times producing extraordinary personalities, George Fox (1624-91) found himself lost in a sea of spiritual confusion exactly during the height of the unrest wrought by so many changes in a brief time under oppressive conditions. A contemporary of Cromwell, Milton, Bunyan, Wren and Newton, he belonged to a turbulent age. His was an age marked by tyranny and intolerance, but which paradoxically led to parliamentary democracy and religious tolerance.

Born the son of a weaver, Fox served as an apprentice to a shoemaker and livestock handler. His father having been a churchwarden and his mother "an upright woman...of the stock of the martyrs," Fox was no stranger to spiritual matters and as a child "received a tradition of religious seriousness that did not compromise with worldly power." By nature prone to moodiness and melancholy, he suffered periods of depression. In 1643, aged 19 and deeply despondent, he broke his apprenticeship and left his master and village of Fenny Drayton—a Puritan stronghold.

For five years, Fox joined the multitudes and roamed the country—if for reasons other than most. As he did not yet have an inner orientation nor a worldly vocation, it was more stirrings of the soul than of the pocketbook that set the sturdy-built, long-haired young man onto the open road. England was in the midst of civil war, yet curiously Fox's *Journal* ignored the state of the world around him: the only turmoil he seemed to notice was that inside himself. Covering the area stretching from London to the Lake District, Fox desperately sought solace for his troubled self. He approached priests and Oxford scholars, visited countless churches and occupied himself with reading scripture, but nothing provided lasting comfort.

By 1648 Fox reached such a state of dereliction that he could not sustain his forlorn wandering. He had turned to every conceivable quarter for relief —including the established Church as well as various dissenting congrega-

3

tions. To his devastating disappointment, none could offer him the help he sought. After half a decade of nomadic pursuit of release from internal demons which refused to let go, he finally experienced a moment of mystical revelation which would change his life and inspire that of many others. He later related that during a moment of intense searching he "heard a voice which said, 'There is one, even Christ Jesus, that can speak to thy condition,' and when I heard it my heart did leap for joy." This insight of Fox's caught the hungry imagination of other seekers who sought validation of personal experience and continual revelation—in contrast to intellectual interpretation of divine matters and the purported finality of the Bible. His experience gave credence to what others had intimated, yet had not had the confidence to proclaim.

A further revelation of Fox's confirmed what some had come to see as the infinite love of god: "I saw also that there was an ocean of darkness and death, but an infinite ocean of light and love, which flowed over the ocean of darkness. And in that also I saw the infinite love of God..." With these two experiences, Fox solidly established himself as a mystic as well as a reformer. In noteworthy contrast to many other reformers in Christian history, though, he not only claimed to have received divine-inspired revelation, but insisted that everyone else could receive it, too.

It was not only in terms of mystical encounters, however, that Fox differed from his more mainstream counterparts. Whereas the Puritans had argued, for instance, for the substitution of privileged Church elites with lay people and for popular access to external grace, Fox went further. He advocated by-passing the need for any clerical offices, maintaining that each person possessed an internal "Christ" [in more modern terms, an internal "guide"] which could provide spiritual insight. Fox and his later co-religionists coined the term "Inner Light" and argued that every person contained that spark—regardless of racial or ethnic background, gender, professed creed, past deeds or present condition, etc. In this *Weltanschauung* where there existed "that of god in every one," acts of kindness or humanitarian assistance to others were indirect paths to direct contact with a universal divinity. Above all others, it would be this characteristically Quaker tenet which would lead Friends of various countries, at times, to attempt to "speak to that of god"[1] in the disenfranchised, the abused and the suffering.

As with similar groups of the same period such as the Anabaptist Mennonites in German-speaking countries or at present such as Islamic fundamentalists, persecution of self-proclaimed "Publishers of Truth" only fanned the flames of their burning appeal. The number of "convinced" Friends grew quickly—as those in power unhappily noted.[2] In direct measure to the success of the early Friends' message grew a corollary campaign to muzzle

4

it—creating an ironic state in which both king and Cromwell took turns trying to quiet the restless non-conformists. When it became obvious that "Quakers"[3] were not content with pursuing purely religious matters, but also felt compelled to tackle issues of earthly power and justice, alarm soon spread among those with interests in vaccinating an already susceptible status quo against any possible disruptive social viruses. One lone "lunatic" was harmless enough, but as soon as it became clear that others were also willing to take up similar causes, Quakers found themselves bonded for unpaid tithes, booted out of public spaces, banned from publishing and even branded or bored through the tongue. Obviously, they struck a raw nerve. If for no other reason, the Church worried that should this cancer of dissent become malignant, who would fill the pews on Sundays and who would pay the tithes which kept clergy frocked and fat?

Why did the essentially peaceful Quakers seem so utterly threatening? If it weren't enough that they refused to pay state-levied tithes, to swear oaths (for fear that doing so implied a double standard of "Truth"), to stop espousing pacifism and voluntary poverty, to recognize appointed clergy (believing that all persons possess spiritual gifts and therefore are "ministers" of a "living gospel") or to remove their hats in deference to alleged superiors, early Friends simply were seen as queer. They dressed plainly and stubbornly clung for 300 years to the use of "thee" and "thy" as a sign of equality among all people after the formerly formal "you"—once reserved for those above one's social class—came into standard use. Friends observed no outward sacraments nor designated any "holy" places such as churches, as they believed that all of life is a prayer, that every day is a living baptism in and every moment a possible communion with the Spirit, that "that of god" dwells in everyone, that the Church is a community and not a building. They also numbered the months as well as the days of the week to avoid using "pagan" names and actively encouraged the talents of women among them in their collective spiritual quest.

From the beginning, Quakers found it impossible to divorce their daily lives from the mystical, all-encompassing theology they professed. As Penn put it, "True godliness don't turn men out of the world but enables them to live better in it, and excites their endeavours to mend it." Already in the 1640s, numerous Friends left their farms and shops to venture out in pairs across England and share the fresh discoveries of inner renewal that had come to them. Later known as the "Valiant Sixty"—both for their approximate number as well as the tenacity of their zeal to proclaim what to them was a most important message—one wave set out from the Lake District: once they had covered Britain, some of them went on to Ireland, then farther afield to Constantinople, Rome, Malta and the Barbary Coast, the Netherlands and northern Germany, Barbados, Jamaica and—finally—to North

America just as the continent was opening to colonists.

With the arrival in the early 1700s of what Quaker historians call the age of "Quietism," this pitched fervor to publish the Truth subsided; only in the late nineteenth century with the advent of "evangelical" Quaker missions in Latin America, Asia and Africa did Quakerism's global diffusion continue. In the meantime, instead of trying to "convince" the world to abandon its flawed ways, Friends as a group simply "let their lives speak"—as Fox once had exhorted "true believers" to do. Having become intimate with prisons from the inside as former prisoners of conscience, for example, Quakers sympathized with those detained and championed prison reform.[4] Other Friends busied themselves with cause ranging from improved public education to better conditions for women, from the abolition of slavery, a more humane policy towards Native Americans, temperance and disarmament to—much later—respect for sexual minorities and the natural environment. By the 20th century, Quakers earned a reputation for neutrality in places as diverse as Northern Ireland, Israel, South Africa and El Salvador. Friends even landed a coveted seat at the United Nations as a Non-Governmental Organization—so respected were they for their work with humanitarian causes.

Central to Quaker social action since the early days has been Friends' unflinching commitment to non-violence and their drive to find alternative means of conflict resolution. Just as their enthusiasm for social action reflects the idea that any person suffering or in distress is an imperiled "fragment of the divine," their motivation to oppose war and armed conflict arises from their belief that to kill another is to extinguish "that of god." This Quaker conviction was tested early on as, in the confused, paranoid days of the English civil war (1642-60), Friends were accused of having played an integral role in the 1661 revolt of the Fifth Monarchy Men against the recently restored throne, during which the City was occupied for three days. When Charles II regained London he arrested of all those suspected of having sympathies with the rebels—a list which included Quakers as its largest group: some 4,230 innocent Friends were imprisoned. Once most of them were again free, the shaken pacifists issued a statement, a Declaration of the Quaker Peace Testimony which began: "All bloody principles and practices we...do utterly deny, with all outward wars and strife and fightings with outward weapons...the spirit of Christ which leads us into all Truth will never move us to fight and war against any man with outward weapons neither for the kingdom of Christ nor for the kingdoms of this world."[5]

It would be their instinctive opposition to war and their commitment to "speak to that of god" to even the disenfranchised, the abused and the suffering, which would lead a small group of Iowa Quakers—almost 300 years after their spiritually restless ancestors founded a movement which became a worldview as well as a way of life—to initiate an active response to the increasingly desperate plight of Jews and other dejected individuals in Nazi-ruled Europe. Their efforts eventually resulted in Scattergood Hostel—a haven which would prove to be a godsend to many.

1.) This is a basic Quaker premise which seems to have formed early in the history of Friends from a now-anonymous source.

2.) Had George Fox's message not "spoken to the condition" of at least some of his contemporaries, he likely would have joined the countless sea of nameless faces which have rained down upon the Earth throughout the ages. As it was his words found a ready audience, his leadership spawned a movement and his name remains significant in Christian history. Many of those receptive to Fox's message came from other dissenting groups—especially Baptists and Ranters and Seekers. In the early days the larger share of the "convinced" [Quakers feel uneasy speaking in terms of "converts," as they maintain that one can only be "convinced of the Truth" through a process of personal reflection, not swayed to accept new beliefs through external pressure] consisted of North Country shepherds, farmers, craftspeople, drifters and the like. Only after some time were members of professional classes (including Fox's later wife Margaret Fell, a judge's widow) and even the aristocracy (such as the noble-born William Penn) drawn to the people who initially called themselves "the Publishers of Truth." These people wished to differentiate themselves as much as possible from organized Christianity as it had come to be practiced and instead emulated the pre-institutionalized "Body of Christ." In this vein they finally took the name "the Religious Society of Friends," a title which de-emphasized a denominational entity and suggested instead an associated gathering of fellow seekers.

3.) During his restless youth Fox entered many a church during Sunday services and disrupted sermons, often challenged priests' interpretations of "the Word" or accused congregants of lax faith. The people who later embraced his call to radical religion often were equally as irreverent and offensive. Justice Bennet of Derby contemptuously nicknamed the bothersome early Friends "Quakers" upon being told by Fox during a trial of faith in 1651 that he should "tremble at the word of God."

4.) The idea of a "penitentiary" came from Quakers, who reasoned that instead of being thrown into dank and dark collective dens which doubled as effective classrooms of crime, if prisoners were offered clean, lighted individual cells they would use the solitude to pray, study and reflect on their wrong-doings until ready to rejoin society as transformed, productive citizens.

5.) For a scholarly summary of Quaker theology, see Appendix Ia; for a humorous sociological sketch of the Religious Society of Friends, see Appendix Ib.

A HOLY EXPERIMENT

*"... that an example may be set up to the nations,
that there was room there for such a Holy Experiment."*
~ **William Penn**

Although at present the Religious Society of Friends is again growing (albeit incrementally), the number of Quakers in the world seems to have stabilized at around a third of a million—some 180,000 in North America alone. As already mentioned, Friends came to the New World in the mid-17th century. Quakers played an important role in colonial society and provided a lasting model which influenced public life and helped shape national values and institutions as a unified country evolved out of what had been scattered European footholds. Friends' attempts to underscore heavenly hopes with worldly reform resulted in various expressions of their efforts, including the foundation of schools and colleges, mutual-assistance or direct-aid societies, women's rights groups, Native American projects, settlement houses, conscientious objector programs and refugee centers. It would be the marriage of the first- and last-noted which would give birth to the Scattergood legacy.

The Quakers' "Holy Experiment"[1] of Pennsylvania was from its beginning an exception among the thirteen colonies, for it paid the natives for their land and—as long as Friends governed—in turn suffered no attacks. The largest, most prosperous of the colonial capitals, Philadelphia served for almost a century as an early test plot for city planning, which resulted in a clean and efficient urban environment marked by religious tolerance, civic mindedness and thriving business activity. The young, penniless Benjamin Franklin arrived from Brahmin-led Boston and marveled at the predominance of the middling classes in the bustling City of Brotherly Love. The fertile social soil of stable Philadelphia stimulated the growth of groundbreaking institutions, such as the New World's first public hospital, poorhouse, insurance society, lending library and Academy of Sciences—the last of which would break a little ground of its own, with the ever-curious Franklin as its head for a time.

Although they formed a majority in early Pennsylvania, the Quakers remained minorities almost everywhere else in the young colonies. Still, they did establish extensive albeit isolated communities elsewhere. From Maine to Georgia, Friends lived in enclaves where they could cultivate the inner lives of their choosing. Later, however, as historical developments in the wider world around them significantly altered the social climate of the times, Friends in some regions found themselves increasingly in conflict with local values. One such area was the South, where stubbornly anti-slavery Quakers quietly clashed with those involved in the marketing of involuntary human labor. The situation grew so tense that eventually whole communities left Virginia, the Carolinas and Georgia when in 1787 the Continental Congress declared the Northwest Territory open to settlement and closed to slavery. Thereafter, Quakers poured over the Appalachians and re-established themselves in the wooded richness of the Great Lakes-Ohio River Valley area. Mirroring general settlement trends, Quakers often cloned their communities and once every generation extended their reach another hundred or so miles westward, where they grafted new settlements to the fruitful land.

By the early 1840s Quaker outposts spanned the entire Midwest from the headwaters of the Ohio to the banks of the Missouri River. Stretching across Indiana and Illinois, this stream of Friendly migrants seeking a New Canaan came to rest in southeastern Iowa, where Quakers settled in large numbers. One of the major settlements centered around the village of West Branch,[2] ten miles east of Iowa City, the state's first capital city and later home to the largest of Iowa's three state-supported universities. In both the town and surrounding countryside, Quakers comprised the largest religious group in terms of population and influence. Herbert Hoover's blacksmith father and his "recorded-minister" [gifted-speaker] mother—for example—called West Branch home, as did some of Richard Nixon's Quaker ancestors.

From its earliest days, the Quaker community at West Branch continued their earlier tradition of welding "faith and practice"—as collectively-composed spiritual queries and social guidelines among Quakers are called. A station on the pre-Civil War Underground Railroad and for a short time beginning in 1861 the location of the Quaker-run Indian Industrial School, West Branch quickly assumed a leading role in social causes on the frontier. So strong were the roots of spirit-led activism there that the fiery John Brown accomplished the unlikely feat of convincing two West Branch-area brothers to join his futile and ultimately fatal armed insurrection against slavery at the Federal arsenal at Harper's Ferry, Virginia.[3] Later choosing less strident means to let conduct indicate convictions, West Branch Friends sent a dele-

9

gation to the South after the Civil War to assist recently freed slaves.

Once the Quakers in Iowa had overcome the basic hurdles of converting the sea of grass into farms and villages, they turned to the task of taming the soul. As Friends in England, on the East Coast of North America and elsewhere already had been doing for almost two centuries, they, too, concerned themselves with establishing educational institutions to serve their young people—and, by extension, the wider community. It was on this receptive scene that Joseph Scattergood, a wealthy chemist from Philadelphia, appeared in 1873 during a tour of the "frontier." So impressed was he with the vitality of Quakerism on the Iowa prairies that he deemed a school necessary for the advanced instruction of Friends' children. Upon his return to the Quaker mecca on the Delaware, he and his brother Thomas sent some $4,000 to West Branch as seed money for a school fund with which the nucleus of a school could be created.

Since Quakers believe the concerns of all must be taken seriously and addressed, they insist on observing full consensus. They are widely known for the painstaking care with which they undertake corporate social action; they are not known for their speed. Such was the case with the West Branch Friends school. As early as the 1860s, twelve acres of land had been purchased two and a half miles southeast of the village and placed under the oversight of the Hickory Grove Quarterly Meeting;[4] in 1865 its members erected a plain, white-frame meetinghouse—in the tradition of Midwestern Friends —on the corner of the property and planted trees "in anticipation of the campus which was to be." Beyond that, little happened until the last quarter of the century, when additional contributions to the fund made the $9,000-construction of the school a reality and classes began in December of 1890.

Scattergood School started small, with thirty pupils, a superintendent, a matron and one teacher. The following year the managerial-heavy staff grew to include a principal and a second teacher, too. At first local children living near enough to return home at night served as day pupils, but by the turn of the century the school's administrators decided that all who attended classes should live at Scattergood as boarders.

Scattergood consisted mainly of a school for upper-level grades, although a primary school was conducted in a separate building—which later would become the cottage of the hostel caretakers. Attendance hovered at 17, so after a few years primary classes moved to the home of teacher Howard Jones and the schoolhouse was literally picked up and moved to the Scattergood campus, where it served as a manual-training building.[5] Eventually primary-grade instruction was completely discontinued, while a fourth year was added to the high-school-level courses offered and the school secured state accreditation. A further development found the school being transferred in

1919 from the care of Hickory Grove Quarterly Meeting to that of Iowa Yearly Meeting (Conservative).

The sponsors of the Scattergood boarding school aimed to provide an environment where Quaker ideals of "wholesome education, removed from distractions and temptations of crowded areas" could flourish. Each day, for example, brought Collection, when staff and scholars met for Bible reading and "moral instruction." Reflecting the serious nature of Quaker culture at the time, the school enforced strict rules affecting most areas of life. In keeping with Friends' testimony of simplicity, children were not allowed to wear any but the plainest clothes and only subdued colors could be worn. Hair ribbons constituted vanity and buttons were tolerated only as useful—although generally seen as worldly decoration among Quaker adults.

Still, life at Scattergood was not all moral instruction and no play. On Seventh Day [the world's "Saturday"] evenings, the school held its well-received Literary, an excuse for social enjoyment masked as a quasi-cultural event. The surrounding Quaker community also attended these regular programs which consisted of readings, recitations, lectures, debates and moving pictures (of the instructional variety only); prominent speakers visited the school and "some very fine talent...appeared at Scattergood's Literary events." In addition, the school body visited Iowa City to hear lectures such as that given by the Arctic explorer, Steffansson. And while in that town of the gown, Scattergood's charges went on to visit the university observatory and its engineering building. What could have been more wholesome?[6]

With reason, Iowa Quakers prided themselves on the effectiveness of a Friends education: many graduates went on to attend colleges or universities and some became teachers or workers in socially oriented fields. Scattergood alumna Cynthia Embree (Class of 1894), for instance, used her time at Scattergood as preparation to become the superintendent of the Chicago Home for Girls, where she instituted self-government and other reforms among her 70 wards. Anna Dewees (1904) later served as assistant to the head of the Department of Agriculture in Washington, D.C., and Edith Newlin (1905) supervised Friends schools in Philadelphia. Luanna Bowles (1910) taught in Japan for a year, then became secretary to the president of Fisk University, while Emma Hodgin (1911) spent a year working in a hospital in Chalons, France. Chester Emmons (1918) taught as an associate at Columbia University, Theodore Standing (1918) at the University of Iowa and Olive Moffitt (1928) at the Tunessassa school for Native American children.

Despite the noteworthy successes of the little boarding school on the prairie, the academic strength of Scattergood was unable to buck social and economic developments taking place beyond the end of its lane. First the declining birthrate of Quaker couples inevitably meant a decreased pool of potential pupils. Then the economic plague which visited almost every house

11

in the nation with the collapse of Wall Street in October 1929 also came calling at Scattergood, making it impossible for the school to continue to finance its operation. The class of 1931 would be the last to pass through the school's doors for over a dozen years and Scattergood then would sit empty and weather the seemingly eternal Iowa winds until a new use for it could be found—such as providing hope and home to those who recently had been stripped of both in their native, Nazi-held lands.

1.) Penn's quote—here in full—regarded his motives behind establishing a Quaker colony in the New World: "For my country, I eyed the Lord in the obtaining of it, and more was I drawn inward to look to Him and to owe it to His hand and power, than in any other way. I have so obtained it, and desire that I may not be unworthy of His love, but do that which may answer His kind Providence, and serve His Truth and people; that an example may be set up to the nations; there may be room there, though not here, for such an holy experiment."

2.) Named after the west branch of the Wapsinonoc Creek, which flows into the Cedar River about ten miles away, at Rochester, the community's 1940 population was 652.

3.) The two were Edwin and Barclay Coppock. According to an article published at the time of the hostel's founding, "Into the Quaker settlements in 1856 rode John Brown, a fervid-eyed man astride a tired mule. 'Welcome, Friend,' he was greeted, according to Quaker custom. The Negro slaves in his company, with scars on their backs from whippings they had received during servitude, were exhibited. There was strong anti-slavery sentiment among the Friends, and they felt justified in aiding the slaves to escape and in offering hospitality to Brown. Brown went on to Chicago, Ill., but his personality and hatred of slavery left a deep impression on the West Branch Friends. In spite of their strict belief in nonviolence, after Brown's departure they gathered in the small white meeting house and prayed for his success. In the winter of 1857-1858, Brown returned to Iowa Quaker communities and at the William Maxon house, a station on the 'underground railway', trained 11 men for his raid on Harpers Ferry, Va.."

4.) Because the Religious Society of Friends follows no hierarchy, local groups are considered autonomous and conduct their "business" (finances, children's education, social outreach, etc.) once a month in so-called Monthly Meetings, which in other denominations would constitute a parish or a presbytery. Several Monthly Meetings in a given area send representatives every three months to Quarterly Meetings, where larger issues are discussed or bigger projects undertaken; several Quarterly Meetings meet in turn at Yearly Meetings. Various Quaker groups also collect at General Conferences consisting of the annual gathering of numerous Yearly Meetings, which usually draw international attendance. In the case of "unprogrammed" (non-pastoral) Friends, in lieu of clergy a "clerk" acts as facilitator while the community seeks unity on various matters which affect it, and all offices are filled by individual members of the group; "programmed" Friends have pastors.

5.) For an overview of the layout of Scattergood's buildings, see Appendix II.

6.) Being children, pupils did find ways to indulge non-conformist tendencies. One group longed to walk the mile and a half to Centerdale to retrieve the mail, but were forbidden to pass the gate. Ingenuity came to the aid of conscience: the boys removed the gate and carried it at the front of the little entourage all the way to and from the post office. The reporter of the event noted that "obedience had been maintained."

12

IN THESE DARK HOURS

*"We also believe that the personal concern and
Friendliness shown to those coming to us under these tragic
circumstances may be the most effective manifestation
of the Christian spirit in these dark hours."*
~ **AFSC Open Letter, November 1938**

Arising out of their ancestors' 300-year-old concern for social justice and
peace, in August 1938 a conference of young members of Iowa Yearly Meeting of Friends (Conservative) at a camp near Clear Lake, Iowa, wrote a letter
to the American Friends Service Committee [AFSC]. In it they proposed that
local Quakers might cooperate with that organization to bring European
refugees away from the crowded Eastern seaboard's immigration hubs and
integrate them in the Midwest. Based on previous work camps co-sponsored
by AFSC and Young Friends, this modest seed quickly grew into a
significant project.

Originally, the young Quakers planned a summer work camp consisting
of Americans and European refugees. They proposed the project be based at
the closed Scattergood School. They suggested the on-going grim plight of
Iowa's farmers and recent labor unrest at the Maytag Washing Machine
Company in Newton, Iowa, as foci for intended conflict-resolution studies.
Beyond this their ideas remained mostly vague, yet they keenly were
committed to finding some means of action. AFSC secretary Leslie Shaffer
attended the conference and reported that "in considering the social and
economic problems of the times, [the Young Friends] became very
enthusiastic about doing something to help."

Ruth Jones Newlin, secretary of the Young Friends Conference's Refugee
and Work Camp Committee, explained to AFSC-executive Homer Morris
that "most Friends in our Conservative group know of our plans but we have
not presented anything definite," adding that "before we ask permission of
our various groups here, we would like to know the possibilities and some

concrete plans for such a camp." Despite their uncertainty about how best to be of assistance, Young—as well as older—Friends in Iowa were eager to offer what help they could.

The Young Friends' unexpected offer appeared at AFSC headquarters in Philadelphia at an auspicious moment, for the organization's executive secretary, Clarence Pickett,[2] was just returning from a fact-finding tour of Nazi Germany when correspondence from Iowa arrived: one of Pickett's assistants responded positively to their offer on 7 November. Then, Hitler unleashed the vicious *Kristallnacht*[3] pogrom of 9-10 November; Nazi brutality so upset Friends in America that AFSC undertook the rare action of appealing directly to Monthly Meetings for assistance.

In an open letter to be read at local meetings across the United States and Canada the following Sunday, AFSC spoke of a "profound shock to our spiritual life by Jewish and non-Aryan persecutions in Germany." As if anticipating skepticism, the mass communiqué added: "Cables from Germany indicate that American newspaper reports have not exaggerated the tragedy." The letter reported that the U.S. government—in its view—was "acting properly" both with regard to protest and the reception of individuals persecuted by the Nazis, that AFSC centers in Berlin and annexed Vienna were "rendering every assistance possible" (including considering possible food-relief efforts), and that the Committee's main office hereupon would establish a special service for German refugees. The last point, it noted, would be "one of our largest undertakings and will require the assistance of Friends and others on a large scale." Any individuals or local meetings wishing to offer aid in the form of signed affidavits of support or housing or employment for the anticipated arrivals were asked to contact AFSC "promptly."

The missive closed on a religious note, emphasizing "we also believe that the personal concern and friendliness shown to those coming to us under these tragic circumstances may be the most effective manifestation of the Christian spirit in these dark hours." Furthermore, while AFSC would do "everything in its power" as a centralized conduit of service, in the name of reconciliation it was "of the utmost importance that all Friends shall seek freedom from the spirit of bitterness and hatred and will be channels for the expression of understanding and good will within their own communities."

In Iowa as elsewhere, reaction to AFSC's plea was immediate. Levi Bowles, a "weighty Friend"[4] in West Branch, wrote the same day that the letter had been read in meeting and reported that "much interest was manifest and without solicitation some material assistance was offered." He noted: "Public sentiment is very pronounced in condemnation of the great wrongs being perpetrated in Europe at this time" and speculated that "there might be in this community, substantial assistance rendered outside of our meetings." The 82-year-old Bowles—aware that a committee in the meeting was already cooperating with AFSC regarding a proposed project—attached an official photo of the Scattergood School's Main Building and Boys' Dormitory to his letter, adding that he had a "willingness to be of service in any way I can."

As Quakers discussed tangible ways their religious-born concern for the well-being of German Jews—as well as other, non-Jewish victims of the *Nationalsozialist* regime—who fled to America, talk of opening refugee centers spread. The project to which Friend Levi referred involved providing such individuals "a place where newcomers...could go for a few weeks or months to recover a little from the effects of persecution, regain their confidence, improve their English, and, if need be, start re-training themselves for some new line of work before seeking a permanent place in American society."[5]

North American Quakers often take collective social action through the auspices of AFSC and in this case it decided that an extensive refugee-services program most effectively would "speak to the condition" of those in need in Nazi Germany. Such an undertaking, however, would require amazing amounts of logistical planning and not be easy. It also would require amazing amounts of faith.

Following the events of November 1938 and AFSC's subsequent appeal for aid, support for creating a refugee program arose swiftly. In response to resonant replies like that of Levi Bowles, AFSC drafted a letter in which it explained that while one of the main services suggested by its initial letter had been the need for hospitality for those fleeing persecution, it had become evident that "the technicalities of immigration and the refugees' reactions to entirely new modes of life will necessitate a more deliberate placement of individuals and families than was at first anticipated. The problems of readjustment [however] are not to be considered lightly or in great haste, while at the same time, the pressure of the numbers needing assistance makes it necessary to move as quickly as possible."

As they embarked upon a subsequent project, Friends realized that the process of rehabilitating refugees would not be easy. Therefore, AFSC reported that "since social, psychological, and spiritual adjustments come slowly, and often more easily in a group, [AFSC's] Refugee Section has been experimenting with a pattern for re-training which takes cognizance of these two points." If "rehabilitation" meant helping refugees heal the effects of persecution, loss and trauma, it still constituted only part of any program which the Quakers might offer those fleeing Nazi-occupied Europe. The task consisting only partly of temporary relief, it required an additional step in order to be complete—that of helping the refugees integrate and assimilate in an adopted homeland.

From the outset, in establishing a refugee program American Quakers sought to Americanize those who landed in their care. In this respect cultural

15

and political—not just religious—worldviews of Quaker leaders or their supporters played pronounced roles in determining any undertaking's structure as well as ambience.

In the glow of the goodness which eventually reigned at Scattergood Hostel, it would be easy to forget that individuals' lives and identities were being shuffled and traded like so many cards. Without recorded exception, all mention of the refugees' integration assumed that their transition from having been Europeans to becoming "new Americans" would be a positive, welcome development. Friends recognized that their guests faced numerous difficulties in adjusting to life in a new land and culture. Concurrently, however, they apparently blindly accepted that the best survival skills they could cultivate in the newcomers consisted of blanket cultural assimilation.

American Quakers were, after all, Americans. Themselves immigrants to North America some three centuries earlier, they were not immune to the image of American society as a "melting pot" where immigrant groups gradually assimilated and assumed an "American" identity—forsaking or at least diluting the cultural traditions they brought with them. On top of that, in the context of the depressed, distressed and dangerous 1930s, the desire to prove oneself patriotic and "truly American" was particularly strong.

Beyond their own cultural assumptions, American Quakers believed that in the best interest of the persons they hoped to help, conforming to the local milieu would be the most rewarding strategy for finding a satisfying life in the New World. From their point of view "a new community, new work, a strange school, a different standard of living—all require individual adjustments. Such adjustments become great hardships when they must be made in a new country where the language and customs are unknown, when economic security and self-confidence are lacking. Yet 'new Americans,' refugees from political and racial persecution in Europe, are faced with just such problems." Thus, in the opinion of that essay's author, a refugee hostel would make "this period of transition from the old life to the new easier by providing a temporary refuge and center of orientation in American ways and customs for individuals and families needing such assistance before taking their places as self-supporting members of American communities."

Early in its refugee program, AFSC secretary John Rich[6] wrote an essay[7] explaining the main motive behind "Americanization Through Quaker Hostels." He acknowledged that such centers "serve only a small fraction of the newcomers to America," yet at the same time "if the sum of their service was solely the Americanization of the residents they accommodate, they would not be a significant contribution to the solution of the refugee problem. However, the Quaker Hostels intend more than to benefit the group they can accommodate. They are a symbol and the outward evidence of a point of view that is important to all Americans."

16

Although well-educated and "liberal," Rich exhibited the bias that for European refugees becoming an "American" was preferable to remaining a nonconforming foreigner. Based on AFSC-sponsored refugee projects, he held that "living with Americans[8] and talking English, the residents quickly learn the language. Three months or less will polish a refugee without the slightest knowledge of English into a presentable American with an interesting accent. Gone are the continental mannerisms, the clicking of heels, the bowing from the waist. The transformation has been accomplished by good-natured banter and close and constant tutoring. American civics, American history, current events, practical economics are some of the subjects the refugees study with zest and wonder. Above all, they learn to drive a car. Probably this looms more important in their minds than any other accomplishment. It is the mark of an American; proof that you can take your place in society, once you have secured a driver's license."

While ascribing the non-committal adjective "interesting" to the accents with which guests might emerge from immersion in American culture, Rich's use of "presentable" hinted at the indelibility of his bias regarding how "Americans" should sound. Further, he spoke of the shedding of outward expressions of learned, internalized social behavior as one might speak of a habit such as nail biting. What did "good-natured banter" actually entail—cloaked reprimand? And finally, he bestowed the debatable attribute of car-ownership the status of "proof" of fitting into American society.

This implicit disregard for the refugees' cultural backgrounds and specific histories irritated at least one refugee. A future guest, Vienna-born Walter Shostal, would identify what he later regarded as a "very real flaw in the SH undertaking. That it totally ignored and misunderstood the European experiences of these people. As if life had begun for them the day they set foot on American soil. As if their previous life had been part of a previous and lesser incarnation the quicker forgotten, the better for it." Walter admitted, though, that at the time "we, the newcomers, had been a willing prey to that construction and did our best to live up to the expectation of the natives."[9]

In those pre-Vietnam War, pre-Watergate days, America and things American held great appeal. Those already living in the United States, as well as most of those migrating to it, were intent on achieving and maintaining an air of American-ness—even at the price of minimalizing real differences. Given the era in which it existed, Scattergood Hostel largely succeeded in its efforts to excite the desire of the refugees who lived there to integrate and to assimilate. At that time doing so was seen as requisite for survival and therefore a service, not a slight to foreigners.[10]

Besides wishing to create "new Americans," as a group Quakers in the United States thought it best to nudge their guests away from Northeast urban centers.[11] What values or beliefs guided AFSC's coaxing emigrants beyond the Hudson? Presumably they mirrored the sentiments expressed by University of Iowa professor Clyde Hart, who spoke at Scattergood Hostel in autumn 1942. An excerpt from a report about his comments indicates the guiding principles which often went unstated at Scattergood yet determined the hostel's program: "As a method of avoiding the development of prejudice, Dr. Hart suggested that members of minority groups in this country settle in the regions where their numbers are not too large, and that they try to become assimilated as thoroughly as possible in the usual pattern of American life. In this connection he suggested that one of the best places for newcomers to America to settle is in the Mid-West [sic] where conditions will be most favorable to their assimilation."

AFSC's own words—found in a pamphlet it published concurrently in English and German in 1940, complete with a U.S. map on the back cover meant to entice recent European arrivals to move past the lure of Big-City lights—offer further indication of the premises from which it worked: "New York and the other over-populated cities in the East are difficult places for newcomers to America. Many Europeans arriving in the United States often do not realize the advantages that await them outside of New York. Those who try to settle in this great, swarming city must pay high prices for food and high rent for rooms. They must seek employment in competition with thousands of other people, facing hostility and disappointment." Writing on AFSC's behalf, Refugee Section staff member Jean Reynolds then urged readers to "go West and you will find flourishing cities, friendly towns and villages. Living expenses are lower and the people are friendlier. There are as many opportunities for employment as in the East. Because fewer refugees have gone to the Middle West, there is less fear of them as competitors, less hostility against them as foreigners."

The chosen terminology spoke volumes. Words and phrases such as "over-populated," "swarming" or "hostility against...foreigners" clearly indicated that despite being Easterners themselves, AFSC staff had very definite prejudices about immigrants settling in the Northeast. How "over-populated"—for instance—was New York, really? Compared to the centers of pre-war Berlin, London or Paris, the New York City boroughs of the Bronx, Queens, Brooklyn and even more so Staten Island were veritable Garden City-esque paradises. What to an American might have been cramped quarters might well have constituted ample accommodation to a space-taxed German. Also, high urban density could have provided the refugees with the urbane milieu which might have made them feel at home—as opposed to the empty evening Main Street of even the busiest Midwest county seat.

It might have been true that costs of living were high in big cities, but so were chances that refugees might find social-service or other agencies which had more stake in and experience with their plight than those in the Anglo-

Saxon-settled Heartland. Job competition in urban areas might have been fierce, but so was the uninformed prejudice against outsiders of any kind—especially of the Jewish or intellectual variety—which existed in oft-benighted, Protestant-dominated provinces.

In any case, the refugees quickly perceived the very definite anti-East-Coast bias which prevailed at Scattergood Hostel. According to Walter Shostal "it was...made clear that it was not desirable to go back to New York; New York was not really America, not a place where we would quickly and completely become truly American, which was the goal that our hosts had in mind and this was also the goal that we had set for ourselves. We refrained from being nostalgic for the past: we were looking to the future..."

Regardless of its reasons for wanting to draw European exiles to the Heartland, AFSC responded realistically when it admitted how complicated the varied needs of immigrants could be. Of the deluge of applicants for assistance it had received, most had already arrived in the United States and were awaiting urgent help in finding new lives to replace shattered old ones. The pool of people seeking aid contained mostly professionals—physicians, teachers, lawyers, social workers, former government officials, *Kindergarten* pedagogues, business people—yet almost no farmers, artisans or unskilled laborers. This fact only complicated the task of placing new workers in a job market still anemic from the debilitating Depression which had begun almost a decade earlier. If their ironic "over qualification" were not enough of a handicap, some of the fleeing Europeans could read a bit of English, but as French was still the dominant *lingua franca* of international diplomacy, trade, scholarship and culture, few could speak English fluently and several not at all. As a further reflection of pre-war, Old-World culture in contrast to the already automobile-addicted United States, most Europeans did not possess a car (those wealthy enough to do so often hired a chauffeur) and virtually none of the newcomers had valid drivers' licenses or even the training to qualify for one.

Reflecting humankind in general, the aggregate of the dispossessed included individuals ranging in age from younger than six to sixty, men and women, families and singles. Many of the younger single men either had already begun university careers in Europe and interrupted them in order to save their very lives, or were on the verge of beginning their studies but now found themselves in a country where—unlike in Europe—education was mostly self-financed. In contrast, a number of the older men had careers of distinction behind them, but at their age and with rather specific certificates in law or medicine, they faced the humiliating prospect of never again being respected for skill in their chosen fields nor reaching economic self-reliance. In addition, having enjoyed the status as well as monetary rewards bestowed on them for their positions in degree- and title-obsessed Europe, those fortunate enough to have found a still-open escape route from the madness engulfing previously civilized Germany were forced to abandon the fruits of decades of achievement. Combined with namelessness on the American professional scene, such luckless individuals faced a truly debilitating situation.

The Service Committee already possessed active files of several hundred individuals with whom it had been working. Instead of isolated efforts to help each of them specifically, a program designed to accommodate the refugees *en masse* now would be required. Therefore, AFSC quickly commandeered Iowa Young Friends' original idea of a short-term summer workcamp involving some ten to 15 German or Austrian refugees. It converted it into the impetus for a larger, more comprehensive longer-term refugee program intended for 30 or more displaced persons from numerous Nazi-occupied territories.

Once it had decided what its best course of action would be, AFSC moved speedily to realize it. As a model for a larger, all-encompassing facility, it turned to a center for uprooted Germans which it had sponsored for eight weeks the previous summer at Aberdeen on the Hudson, upriver from Manhattan. Homer Morris wrote to one Iowa Friend that it had been a "most valuable experience for refugees who have gone through such difficult times in Europe. A combination of study, physical labor, periods of meditation and lectures on American life proved to be a most valuable orientation period for their introduction to getting settled in American life." The experiment had seemed so successful that the newly formed Refugee Section felt it prudent to integrate the model into its program. At the same time, Morris noted the necessity of providing such a center to which refugees could go as soon as they arrived Stateside—not just once they had become established. He argued, however, that given "so much congestion of refugees in the environs of New York," it seemed desirable that such a center should be located "entirely away from the New York area where there might be greater possibility of the new arrivals finding their way into American life."

Documents available indicate that while AFSC had been in contact for some months with Iowa Quakers regarding possible uses of the vacant Scattergood complex, it had some reservations which gave it pause. In Morris' correspondence with Iowa Friend Catherine Williams, he informed her that AFSC had appointed a committee the previous day to investigate the possibility of opening a refugee hostel at Scattergood, yet confessed "there are actually a great many problems which will need to be worked out in connection with the establishment of such a center." So that "all phases of the problem" could be examined in detail, he deemed a conference necessary in order to personally discuss the matter in depth "rather than to try to settle these problems by correspondence." He added: "We will need to inspect the building, equipment, etc., to determine the adaptability and feasibility for such a center and your group will want to consider the opportunities, obligations and responsibilities that would be involved."

Given a green light, Iowa Friends proceeded to organize a statewide gathering of interested individuals in West Branch on 7-10 January 1939. AFSC representatives attended this ground-breaking joint meeting of the so-called "Conservative" (silence-based worship) and "Progressive" (programmed worship) Quakers. The conference proved significant not only because it gave birth to a structure which would facilitate the hasty opening of the former school as a refugee hostel, but because it brought together two subsets of Quakerdom which had had little to do with each other since the "Great Division."[12] According to a report following the conference:

> *Iowa Friends were united enthusiastically in their support of the proposal for the use of the Scattergood School for a refugee hostel. Seldom, if ever, has any proposal gripped Iowa Friends and fired their imagination as this. They see in it something tangible and near and something in which all of them may have a part.*

Following the well-attended conference, response among Iowa Friends was immediate and almost entirely positive—a development which deeply pleased Morris, who had cautioned Williams that if AFSC undertook the establishment of a center it "would want to have the cooperation of all the Friends groups in Iowa in any such enterprise." By the end of that month both branches of the state's Quakers had committed themselves to the project, with the conservative Friends agreeing to "rent" the property to AFSC for $1 per year, as well as refurbish the physical plant, and the programmed Friends promising to furnish the interiors of the buildings. Each group selected committees to oversee its part of the project and each appealed to its members to donate goods, time and funds.

In her fervor to raise the fiscal resources needed to back such an effort, the excited Williams even wrote to fellow-Quaker Herbert Hoover, who had already responded to an appeal from her for donations to the Scattergood School fund during earlier insolvent times. She explained that the school ultimately had closed, but now was in need of contributions again, this time for a cause near to his heart—the plight of European refugees.[13] Williams diplomatically mused that "Young Friends wondered if thee would be interested in helping them discover at least $1,000 [of the necessary monies]?" and modestly added, "their contact with men and women of means is very limited." In any case, the boy from West Branch who did so well in Stanford and less well in Washington is not recorded as having been moved to give.

Local clergy, the village's mayor and postmaster, a doctor and others more immediate to the developments at Scattergood were another matter, however, and they actively encouraged the creation of a hostel at Scattergood. Support from such quarters rarely consisted of money,[14] but—perhaps more importantly—of psychological sustenance.

West Branch Methodist minister James Gable, for example, initiated contact with the Des Moines rabbi Eugene Mannheimer in hopes of scheduling a visit to the area. In light of the possible establishment of a nearby hostel, Gable thought that "it might be a fine thing both for West Branch and the cause of German Jews" if Mannheimer would speak at the church one evening. Gable lured him with the prospect of "a capacity audience," though more significantly with the assurance that "our people want to be fair, but need information that is authentic." Conceding "there is a good deal of discussion of this project among our people and some strong prejudice or opinion, both pro and con," he reiterated that "public opinion here is yet in the making. We want it to be intelligent and fair." The good pastor knew his flock, however, and understood that "if such a use of [the Scattergood] buildings is not as local people would have it, there is no thought of going ahead, even though the school is not within our corporate limits and cannot be controlled by the town." Mannheimer's rejoinder has vanished, but apparently he did not accept Gable's rather ardent request ["Name your evening and we will do our best to accept it"], for later Gable himself delivered a series of sermons titled "The German Jew: His History, His Present Situation, and His Possible Future." The *Cedar Rapids Gazette* later commented: "the sermons have been non-controversial, and [are] intended to clarify the situation."

Jewish organizations or individuals in Des Moines, Iowa's state capital, and in nearby cities such as Cedar Rapids and Iowa City did offer support—including the financial kind—but AFSC preferred to utilize such aid only after the hostel was open because it feared arousing charges of Jew-coddling. It would not be the last time, however, that the shadow of anti-Semitism would be seen falling across the face of the Scattergood project.

Still, the idea of helping those in need in faraway lands in tangible ways struck a resounding chord in many Midwestern hearts. It resulted in such a voluminous response that—due to the initially adequate funds contributed and the many hands provided to effect much work—the transformation of Scattergood from boarding school to refugee center finally could begin in earnest. That, as the Quakers were to discover, would be no small effort.

When Scattergood School ran out of students, stipends and steam in 1931, Iowa Yearly Meeting did not know what to do with buildings, books, furniture and furnishings. Friends overseeing the institution's mothballing stored much of the school's moveable wealth in the attic of the Main Building, in the simple "gymnasium"—more a cavernous hall, really—and the

Boys' Dormitory, which having been completed in 1916 remained relatively new. The school's caretakers Walter and Sara Stanley—a Quaker couple who had both attended the school as children and had lived there in that capacity since 1930—resided in the Boys' Dorm. All the other buildings, however, went unused and practically uncared for. Iowa's relentless arctic winters and stifling humid summers were not kind to the abandoned school: pipes burst, plaster popped off the walls, windows broke and doors sagged. By the time AFSC and the two branches of Iowa Quakers agreed to breathe new life into Scattergood the place was a genuine wreck, as eight dormant years had given time and nature adequate opportunity to ravage it.

No one doubted that extensive overhaul of the former school would be required before any refugees might occupy the space; the debatable questions included how thorough the repairs should be and how they should be funded. Clearly, in order to set a program in motion, a minimum standard of comfort and safety had to be achieved. At the same time the hostel's visionaries fully expected renovation work to continue throughout the life of the project and play a role in the training as well as rehabilitation of the recent arrivals. As for the monies? To sustain their efforts, it seems the Friends disarmed their *Angst* with the wisdom of the classic Quaker adage, "Way will open."

After more than a decade of depressed agricultural commodity prices and the subsequent near-collapse of the entire Iowa economy, however, such idealism would be hard to translate into practical results. Still, by finding individuals willing to commit to helping with the actual clean-up or reconstruction work and by freeing up solidified savings, most of the money necessary for the estimated $2,500 worth of repairs did surface. Above all, those first monetary contributions were spent on basics: new heating units, complete electrical rewiring, plastering and roof repairs. Despite the difficulty in tapping veins of crucial capital, Friends strove to avoid assuming a primarily materialistic perspective regarding the undertaking. Conservative Friends' annual Yearly Meeting report stressed that the "transformation of Scattergood is, after all, not a business transaction, but a human and spiritual one, and its main object may well be the mutual enrichment of many lives by the mingling of the culture of the Old World with the culture of the New." AFSC echoed this same sentiment: "We are confident that to us, at least, will come renewed religious experience because of this labor of love and fellowship with another minority religious group."

Other early work at Scattergood involved the erection of partitions which divided some of the larger rooms into more private spaces. According to Mary Rogers, acting director of the Service Committee's Refugee Section, it was probable that AFSC would send families or married couples to the center. She reasoned that there "will be older people who are accustomed to living in flats, and are wholly unaccustomed to dormitory life." Thus, she

23

concluded, the partitioning of larger rooms constituted a "must." Further, as she thought it "unwise" for children to sleep in the same room as their parents, "this would mean the provision of a nursery or room for the children." Above all—she wrote in a letter of precise instruction—"we want the group there to realize that the people coming are of cultured background and of professional training and [therefore] the necessity of comfortable living arrangements so as to do away with as much of the tension and friction of daily life as possible."

Some details—despite all the spirituality in the world—simply resisted any attempt to assign them philosophical dimensions. These pedestrian points included the decision whether to use metered gas for cooking and coal burners for heating water or some other combination of energy sources. Which school furnishings could be recycled for hostel use and which ones were simply too worn? What sewage-treatment system would be adequate for the 45 or so expected refugees and staff? How to arrange the purchase of beds direct from a manufacturer in order to receive a discount? Where to find extra funds to buy appliances and bedding, kitchen pots and pans?

A Quaker farm couple who lived at nearby Yankee Corner, Verlin and Sara Pemberton, were to prove instrumental in the organization and later life of the hostel, with Sara performing vital early administrative functions. As *de facto* acting director of the hostel before any appointed staff or guests arrived, Sara also was bitten by the practicalities bug. She wrote to Mary Rogers: "We here are wondering if you could tell us some of the preferences of the German refugees in garden vegetables. Should we plant an asparagus bed?" she asked, but then mused, "of course, that would not produce anything for this year." She inquired if "these people are fond of green string beans, peas, cabbage, tomatoes, sweet corn [of which hardly a single European at that time had ever heard], carrots, beets, spinach, cucumbers or anything else?" Perhaps in embarrassment over possessing so little idea of Europeans' typical diet and tastes, she excused her unworldliness, explaining, "it would help so much in proportioning the garden plot if we knew something about their likes and dislikes." In a later letter she fretted, "Where will you get the money for running expenses? food for the six young men [due to arrive shortly]? potatoes for garden planting?" Clearly, the Quakers were concerned about any possible hitch which might compromise the life-giving fruits they sought to harvest from their efforts. Striving to reach as many of those in need as they could, they also were determined in the process to scatter as much good as they could.

Despite Iowa and East Coast Friends' anxieties over how best to prepare a refugee center in time to welcome the souls they hoped to help, solutions to all the foreseeable—as well as unexpected—difficulties were found. The first refugees indeed were able to arrive a mere twelve weeks after the decisive January conference. Miraculously, they comfortably were able to occupy former schoolrooms which had been empty for eight years. Once they did, it would be the "guests" themselves—not logistical dilemmas—who would command center stage at Scattergood.

1.) The American Friends Service Committee was created in 1917 as a form of alternative service as well as relief to be carried out by conscientious objectors and volunteers. It worked closely with corresponding British Quaker organizations, although remaining fully independent. Following World War I AFSC became a permanent feature of Quaker outreach efforts and found support among the various branches of the family of Friends. Initially, its peacetime program had four components: foreign as well as home service, inter-racial and peace work. Under the directorship of Clarence Pickett (1925-1950), AFSC's activities spread worldwide. In 1947, AFSC and the Friends Service Council of London jointly were awarded the Nobel Peace Prize for their humanitarian and peace efforts.

2.) A press release once described Clarence Pickett as "a very busy man, a leading Friend, an International citizen, a Penn College [of Oskaloosa, Iowa] Alumnus."

3.) On 9 November, 1938, two days of nationwide madness resulted in the murder of 91 and the detention of 26,000 individuals, the ransacking of between 7,000 and 7,500 shops, the burning of 101 and demolition of 76 synagogues, and the ruining of thousands of Jewish homes. This episode served as the final notice to German Jews that it would be best for them to leave the Third Reich. Called the *Reichskristallnacht* in German, the event bears a name which—like the event itself—remains tainted with hate. The same post-war generation of Germans which began questioning their elders' participation in *Nationalsozialist* German culture, daily life and crimes also reconsidered the name which the Nazis had given to this premeditated attack—a name said to romanticize the sight of shards of glass resulting from the night-time raids on Jewish property—and found it unacceptable. I use the name *Kristallnacht* primarily because in the United States and Britain—home to most of this text's intended readers—it remains the most common form of reference to this pogrom.

4.) This Quaker term refers to an important spiritual as well as community figure.

5.) Emil Deutsch attested: "It certainly is hard for many [European refugees], affected in their nervous balance by the horrible experiences and the constant strain of the last years, to fit into new and strange conditions. Moreover, many people, accustomed to regular work and efficiency, suffer from lack of it harder than anything else. Many difficulties, arising among residents of the Hostels [sponsored by the Quakers, of which by the time of Emil's writing there were a few], are based upon this fact. They are hard to overcome before the final goal of everybody's staying at a Hostel is reached, the job, and a new start in American life. But we have to find a way to adapt ourselves to our new life. It is a vital condition of our living in a new country."

6.) During World War II John Rich was in charge of AFSC work in India and China, where according to Robert Berquist "he made important contributions in this work."

7.) In interviews in 1995, three former staff took exception to the tone and content of Rich's essay: Earle Edwards: "That...article...sounds to me like something that might not have been published because it didn't reflect the way the AFSC really functioned. I was astounded [by it. Rich] was a public-relations person. He ended up having his own fund-raising outfit with a staff who were hired by colleges and other institutions in help them in running funding campaigns, so his orientation was always on that side... I was *very* surprised with the way he described things. It just didn't fit in with any of *our* experience or any of what we *knew* was on the minds of people in the AFSC. We were young at that point...but the way in which people functioned—with anything we had anything to do with—was quite consistent with all the rest of our AFSC experience [and] I spent most of my life doing one thing or another with the AFSC [professionally]."

George Willoughby: "John Rich didn't spend much time at Scattergood: he was an organizer, he was a promoter, he had to raise money, he had to sell this: he was a salesperson and so he sold it partly on the basis that a lot of people would say 'This is good.' All the time I was at Scattergood I *never* felt there was any pressure on the refugees to become Americanized. There was pressure to adjust so they could get jobs and begin to take care of themselves, but I never felt any of that and in talking to them I never felt that any of them really felt we were trying to make super-duper Americans out of them."

Robert Berquist: "I felt that [Americanizing the guests] was not [the Quakers'] principal reason: that might have been one reason, but certainly not the principal reason for the educational program... I object to the word 'Americanize' because I think they had a different conception of 'Americanization'—or at least most of them did—than people now would have using that term. And if they were thinking of helping the people to adjust to living here and becoming active participants in this country, rather than just imitating people who were natives of this country. I do think, though, that some of John Rich's statements wouldn't have been fully accepted by many of the staff. I think he overdid that emphasis."

8.) "Compared with any other group of refugees" Emil Deutsch thought "residents of Scattergood lucky in more

25

than one way. They have more opportunity to improve their English than any Americanization school, even in big cities, is able to offer. They have the advantage of being in steady contact with Americans, of imitating and learning their manners, different from European ones, their ways of speaking and approaching problems."

9.) Walter reflected on this theme more than fifty years after the fact, but many basic conditions had shifted since his arrival as an exile. Writing at the time, one of his fellow refugees saw the situation much differently. Lotte Liebman wrote: "The Americans—all of them are young people—are helping us with our work in a real exceptional, nice and friendly spirit. They help us to get accustomed to all American habits; they teach us the language; and many things concerning common life, politics, etc.. But perhaps the most valuable part of their help is that they show us by good example how to live in America. "Keep smiling," "Don't worry," "Take it easy" are the three first commandments in America. Without keeping them, you will never succeed in doing anything in America, whatever qualities and abilities you may have. You have to learn to practice them in this small community in order to succeed in your profession or whatever you may do afterwards."

10.) Staff cooperated with the hostel's Americanization program—once to the point of conflict. When questioned about tensions between refugees and staff, former staff Earle and Marjorie Edwards answered that "relations between residents and staff were remarkably good." Camilla Hewson Flintermann concurred,* adding that "on the whole [refugee-staff relations were positive], except for sensitivity to attempts to 'correct' them, as in the episode...of [staff member Leanore Goodenow] and table manners"—involving "the uproar when she tried with best intentions to 'correct' table manners and have guests hold utensils American style, not European, so they would 'fit in' more comfortably in American society. There were some hurt feelings."**

*Both parties suggested that staff-refugee relations were better than between Germans and Austrians: "This was not blatant, but often conveyed in a subtle way, a comment, or a look. Differences in pronunciation, for example, were obvious, and sometimes referred to slightingly."

**An Iowan and a Haverford College graduate, Leanore had visited Nazi Germany in 1934. She served as a Scattergood staff member in the summer of 1939—only to return in 1944 as the re-opened school's director, a post she held until 1967.

11.) In 1939, sociologist, William Carlson Smith agreed that placing "too many" refugees in one specific area would incite undesired reactions and reasoned that "if the flow of immigrants into an area is slow and gradual they are more readily accepted. They can be absorbed without causing any serious disturbance in the existing order. Immigrants already adjusted assist their compatriots in sloughing peculiarities that might cause resentment. The old settlers of native stock are accustomed to members of this particular ethnic group and an additional arrival now and then causes no excitement. If, however, the aliens come in large numbers, the natives become fearful; they fear competition and a lowering of their standard of living; they fear their institutions cannot digest so much new material and will be destroyed in the attempt; and they fear that everything for which they have struggled and sacrificed will be trampled under foot by inferior peoples.... The fears, due to causes real or imagined, raise impassable barriers of prejudice against the newcomers, and they are denied all wholesome contacts with the old residents. This attitude tends to solidify the immigrant group, and they become more interested in continuing their old ways of life than they would be otherwise. The prejudicial attitude of the natives is no solvent that will tend to reduce the old-world customs of the immigrants." (Smith, p. 154)

12.) That split over divisive theological differences and modes of worship some five decades earlier resulted in programmed Friends adopting ministers to oversee their "churches" and a format similar to mainstream Protestant services. Their more traditional counterparts conserved the silent, unshepherded "meetings" of earlier Quakers.

13.) Following both World Wars, Hoover oversaw the implementation of large-scale feeding and relief programs in war-torn Europe, for which he received grateful recognition as a "great humanitarian"—despite the lingering shadows of his presidential shortcomings.

14.) There were, however, individuals who indeed did contribute monetarily to the project. One man—"not a member"—stopped in What Cheer, Iowa, and asked Friend Wilson Emmons about the proposed hostel. The man explained "I want to help with that. I think it a very worthy cause. I am not in favor of sending an army over there to lick those dictators but it is our duty to help take care of the innocent victims." He left a check for $25 and departed.

So Much at Home

*"We are so happy and feel so much at
home that we hardly believe that we
have been here only a short time."*
~ Heid Ladewig

At first, AFSC selected five men—two Germans, two Austrians (both Jews)
and a Czech—to continue the extensive remaining renovation work thought
necessary before women and families comfortably could live at the emerging
hostel. Four of the five, plus a young American Quaker, John Kaltenbach,
drove in a borrowed station wagon from Pennsylvania to Iowa, only to be
greeted at Scattergood's driveway early Saturday afternoon on 15 April 1939
by four carloads of reporters and photographers. They found "so many press
men that we couldn't find our friends at first" complained John,[1] the chaperon of the group and a head staff member for fifteen months.

   The travelers—John called them "little Daniel Boones"—arrived in Iowa
worn by the three-day drive behind them. On the first morning of their journey they had been met in the Philadelphia YMCA's restaurant by AFSC's
Mary Rogers, the hostel's director-appointee Albert Martin and his wife
Anne. The little band was to be "introduced as a group to the anticipated
pioneering à la 20th century" and enjoy a launching-off breakfast. With their
stomachs full, the troop set off—only to pause early on at Gettysburg, where
John told the men something about the Civil War. Once back in the car, that
stop provided many miles' worth of discussion of American history. Their
initial ebullience suffered somewhat, however, as their modern-day "Conestoga"—again, John—struggled its way over the Alleghenies in snow. At
times they drove to the lively *a cappella* accompaniment of muezzin calls
provided by Karel Gam, the Czech geography and anthropology professor
from Moravia who had traveled in Africa as well as the Middle East and
whose tongue could "vibrate like a bee's wings in a Model T exhaust pipe."
By the time they reached Illinois, though, some of their party had become

downright testy. At Rick's Restaurant in Joliet the little band found "a full course meal for 35 cents and a nice waitress in the bargain" and most were impressed with "the friendliness of the mid-west [sic] as contrasted to the east." Kurt Rosegg—one of the two Viennese and a goldsmith with a law degree—however, found the server's informal demeanor and amiability "appalling." Back on the road, all were "happy that the major grind" was over—albeit by then also "dog-tired."

Reaching their destination mitigated the ensemble's travel-induced fatigue. The barrage of photographers' flash bulbs and the storm of questions posed by curious Main Street journalists slapped them back into life. Karel exclaimed, "I've never received such a welcome since the king of the Felater tribe in the jungles of Anglo-Egypt welcomed me when I was on a research expedition." The carefree Czech teased the reporters with his assessment that "Hitler is the essence of force and brutality" and "everything went well until I wrote articles against Nazi-ism." After the German dictator took over the Czech forces, Karel was among the first to abandon that emasculated army. The other refugees remained more cautious. A former Berlin *Senat* statistician, quiet Kurt Schaefer only would offer, "I have nothing to say...but wait until all of my relatives get out of Germany and I'll tell you a lot." Relenting a bit, he did explain that he was not a Jew, but when he had spoken of his opposition to National Socialism, he soon was told that one of his grandparents "carried Jewish blood." The circumspect numbers juggler claimed—in "perfect English," said one reporter—"I never knew it before." In contrast, Kurt's travelmate Fritz Treuer of Vienna would speak only of his musician wife and 13-year-old son, Robert, both of whom stayed in New York. The former bank and export-firm employee scouted for a farm and a new livelihood on the Iowa prairies, having failed at finding any work in Manhattan other than as a janitor at Radio City. Green-thumbed Fritz then "burst into a lecture" on what fine flowers and vegetables he would grow in the highly fertile Iowa loam. He mused that he wished his family could have joined him to see it and "hear the wind whistle in the tall trees." Cheerleader Kaltenbach avoided political issues altogether, choosing instead to smoothtalk the locals with assurances that the newcomers were "thrilled with the open country in Iowa." Pressed for details, John conceded: "As to Iowa roads—well, we spent half an hour in a side road mudhole after we left paving to come out here."

Calling Hitler a "onetime Austrian paperhanger," the reporters refused to be led down a false path by the cunning kid from Smalltown, Pennsylvania. They trailed the young Friend and the newly arrived refugees the whole afternoon around the Scattergood campus and even that evening to a potluck sponsored by local Quakers, striving hard to produce a story they thought their readers would want to read. Under the bold headline "Strong Story Told in Faces of 4 Refugees," heavyweight *Des Moines Register* reporter Howard

Dobson painted a dramatic picture, asserting "history gone insane has written strong stories on the faces of four men who have come to Iowa to find peace." He developed this image, maintaining the stories were products "of the nightmares of mental and physical Hells that man has made for man on earth, and of the cruelty in a world where men yell 'Heil' at each other with arms stiffly upraised and persecute their brothers...[and where Hitler and his thugs] mocked civilization in a thunder of goose-stepping army boots."

True to form, West Branch Friends had little time for public relations—especially when feeding the stomach might be an effective first step toward feeding the soul. That evening found the excited Europeans fully torn between "balancing on their knees trays of Iowa farm food which Quaker housewives offered to wanderers far from their homes" and answering the myriad queries posed them by curious natives. Quaker "dignitaries" such as Taylor Guthrie, pastor of the West Branch programmed Friends church, were sure to attend this not-to-be-missed reception for the long-awaited "guests." They listened intently as Kurt Rosegg—who'd left annexed Austria with a ticket for New York and a mere ten Reichsmarks—and Fritz Treuer spoke of life in the contemporary Old World, of gardening and *Autobahnen*.

Between "heaping plates of Quaker meat, bread, cake and pie," the first four refugees to arrive at Scattergood spoke to Friends and reporters alike, not quite sure what the difference was. From the impressions they gave, Dobson concluded that "these four men carry no overtone of revenge. There is little room for revenge in a heart full of dejection and sadness. You have to watch for the stories, and catch Fritz Treuer looking out a window—see Kurt Schaefer sit with his hands folded, smiling automatically behind his glasses—see Kurt Rosegg's quick gestures and nervous glances—notice Karel Gam's restless pacing. These are small signs, and they disappear quickly in conversation. Maybe Rosegg is thinking of the night in Vienna when he took his 71-year-old mother through a Nazi gauntlet, but he doesn't tell of this. He is busy telling a Quaker friend about the new high-speed highways in Germany." Dobson reported, however, that after some time "they could hold it back no longer. [The refugees] fell to talking of Hitler, the Nazis, and fleetingly of their separate stories. Once released, the flow rushed past bedtime, and into the hours of the morning."

While the Europeans eventually found the evening an outlet for the airing of long-stifled stories, their 22-year-old chaperon experienced it otherwise. John wrote a tellingly terse entry in the spanking-new *Book of Scattergood*: "In the evening Friends came in for supper and we had a small meeting in which the spirit moved deeply and friends rested in loving fellowship. We feel," he said, "at home."

Sunday came, accompanied by questions of faith. In the sect-sensitive

Midwest, the newspaper reporters were sure to note for their nosey readers that of the first four, Karel Gam was Catholic and Kurt Schaefer Protestant, but "neither Jew is of the orthodox religion." John had stressed the night before that come Sunday morning the guests would be taken to any church they desired; they would be welcome at Quaker meeting but not be "compelled to attend."[2] As it turned out, the four sat next to their hosts in the quiet of Friends' silent, expectant waiting. Afterwards they were invited to Sunday dinner by local farm families. That evening a fifth individual—26-year-old George Laury, a Hamburger (John joked, "without onions") and former radio exporter—arrived in Iowa City aboard a bus and completed the ranks of the first contingent of guests at the Scattergood Hostel.

The first weekday morning at the site found all of the men busily engaged in repair work—their various projects punctuated by the last efforts of an assortment of plumbers, electricians and carpenters. Kurt Schaefer later described their efforts in detail—characteristically, all in good humor:

We had to scrub many floors (it is surprising how many floors there are in that little building). We scraped wallpaper off walls, painted, plastered, carpentered and dug in the garden. I was expected to weed the strawberries which did not look nearly as pretty as the weeds. John Kaltenbach was the worst foreman there has ever been in the history of the laboring classes. The worst was that he seemed to be able to do any odd job. We found each other driving everybody else. Ugly calluses developed on our hands. At supper the boys fell over their meals in the most disgusting manner. Kurt Rosegg, a delicate intellectual from Vienna, had a hungry look in his eyes after having finished three plates with a mountain of potatoes on each. Our bodies grew so strong that we became afraid of our brains. Since my childhood I had not gone to bed by eight or nine o'clock, and since my childhood I haven't felt so ridiculously fresh and rested in the morning. Change had come over us newcomers; working feverishly without asking time and a half for overtime; Iowa farmers contributing thousands of dollars to build this home for some strange, odd-looking foreigners; American boys and girls trying to teach us newcomers how!

On one hand, their excuse for being at Scattergood some three weeks before the next guest would arrive consisted of completing important renovation work, yet on the other the six men found that their "work" involved as much petty organizing and community outreach as actual hammer swinging and spackling. Already on Tuesday local Friend Emery Hemingway whisked Kurt away to Tipton to hear AFSC's Raymond Wilson speak and to talk to a discussion group. And, as the hostel's kitchen was nowhere near useable, the men had a convenient standing excuse to accept endless invitations from area Quakers to dinner. At one such outing to the Edgerton home, the well-traveled Czech discovered an old violin, assembled the various pieces and "drew forth music of his native Moravia, his adopted Arabia, and the swing of his present America." Multi-talented himself, John "jammed in on the piano." Perhaps this impromptu gig set the toes tapping of even the most somber of Quakers on hand.

When not socializing with locals or pretending to work, the men engaged in informal "educational instruction." By day, in spare moments John offered English lessons and, by night, occasional tours intended to instill in the guests some of the specialness of the world that is America. One evening he took some guests on a "moonshine walk, leading the whole tribe through the happy (but pathless) hunting-ground of...Indian fantasy and demonstrating how to climb fences." He told his attentive audience about the Native Americans who used to roam the plains, but he "watched them file along fence-rows with nothing but rolling fields and wide sky and silver frost behind their trudging shadows." His thoughts dwelt not "on Indians, but far back in the period of our religious heritage to a time when our spiritual forefathers wandered in small bands over the land between the Nile and the Jordan."

Given the close quarters he kept with his charges, John quickly formed intimate impressions of the five men—both as a group and as lively individuals. He wrote at length to AFSC and the Martins about them, at first congratulating the Service Committee for "picking a group for our initial effort that is representative of nearly every kind of refugee, geographically and temperamentally." He maintained that such a composition would "help in the future for these people around here to meet the newcomers and recognize in them types they have met before." He also crowed that "clashes have been few." In the next breath, however, he confessed that those were "cases of individual temperament...accentuated...by racial and geographical differences." John pointed out that both Jews hailed from Vienna and "talk a lot about Vienna, more than the rest do about the rest of the world." He lamented that this tended to alienate the Jews from the others, which was "not so hot." Therefore, he requested in the next assignments—for example—a Jew "from the north" and "a stolid Protestant from Austria if thee has any," because at present "the two groups are as hard to reconcile as a Prussian and a Frenchman, Bismarck and Chopin."

It so happened that the Viennese were the only ones in the group who had "any particular manual skills," which meant that they were needed for separate, specialized jobs, leaving "bull work" for the other three. John fumed in frustration: "I have had to adopt a kind of three day shift in my own mind, in one sacrificing temperament for efficiency, and in the other slowing down for the sake of group spirit, first three days one way, then three the other."

The fledgling hostel's *de facto* leader found Kurt Schaefer "the best of the group," with "more experience, more discipline" and the best English skills. He also thought that the bookish Berliner was more "clear headed about things here and about what goes on in Germany." The young Quaker said he would recommend Schaefer "without reserve for any work the committee might have with refugees"; in fact the husky bachelor's trustworthiness soon won him appointment as the first financial secretary of the hostel—no small act of confidence. A social democrat and a pacifist "with an immense amount of information of internal [German] conditions, business methods and political possibilities," Kurt had spent five years in exile in England and—in connection with British trade unions—had become active with refugee-relief efforts before finding a slot at Scattergood. On a practical level, though, he remained very much a *Mensch*: "the slowest to get up in the morning" John remarked, adding "but when he gets down[stairs] he is good for all day."

Less easy to work with was the short, slightly stooped Fritz Treuer, who, although "in fair shape and delighted with the country" despite missing his family, was "considerably handicapped by his deafness and preoccupation with the exact method of suckling pigs, finding out where doves nest, and magnetic storms on the face of the sun." He once told a flabbergasted John "in all seriousness that the sunspots were bad" and therefore he couldn't work. If that weren't enough, the idiosyncratic Austrian once explained that he spent a lot of time outside digging because it was the most effective laxative he knew. Nonetheless, John allowed: "Withall [sic] he is delightful, and I have him for [a] roommate because few of the rest of us like to shout all the time, but we all have been shouting at each other anyhow so that Fritz can be in on everything. It has gotten so that we raise our voices out of habit" he realized, "even when [Fritz] is not around."

John noticed that kid-faced George Laury—formerly "Heinz Lurie"—kept to himself much of the time, "eternally writing at something or other." He seemed most afraid of talking about Germany, although he did accept a speaking engagement at the West Liberty Rotary Club at one point. George seemed "a willing worker," albeit "used to a rather high standard of living." In contrast to the German loner from the mouth of the Elbe, the congenial Czech from that major European river's headwaters appeared to be the "most volatile one, impetuous, up or down." John speculated that Karel had only begun "to realize what has happened to his country with the recent receipt of mail that has been cut and elided." On a lighter note, Karel's use of English was a "perpetual marvel," as he could use "more wrong words at the right time than anybody [John had ever] heard." The endearing man from Moravia brought wide smiles to Quaker faces when he fell asleep under a shelf in the pantry, only to be rudely awakened when an intruder unknowingly dumped a stack of newspapers on his head.

Kurt Rosegg posed perhaps the most trouble—according to John—because of his "perpetual tongue motion." The others had all complained about their wild-haired fellow exile and "at one point threatened that their patience was wearing thin. He is the smartest of the crowd and the best linguist" John granted, "but his manner is rather difficult sometimes." One night he called Kurt aside and "talked the whole thing out...most favorably." Later it seemed the sensitive goldsmith from Vienna "improved a lot" and Kurt Schaefer mentioned a difference in Rosegg's behavior, owning that he had "swung for the better." Clearly, each of the men had his own cache of bothersome ghosts from less happy days in Nazi-occupied "Greater Germany." Perhaps it is a wonder not that conflicts broke out, but that they did not appear more frequently and in less resolvable forms. In any case, there would be plenty of other problem-prone guests in the future; it would be only a matter of time until they came onto the scene, too.

Some three weeks after the first set of guests arrived at Scattergood, others began to join them—although initially in a weak trickle. On the 5th of May a '36 Chevy with Pennsylvania plates pulled into the driveway carrying a woman and three male co-travelers. The woman turned out to be Anne Martin—the wife of the appointed director, who would not appear for almost another three weeks—and the two Martin boys, Joe (age 17) and Dick (11). The other young male (and owner of the car) was a 17-year-old rebellious youth who already in his vernal life had met his share of trials and tears. Erhard Winter[3] had been born in Lüneburg to a rich, well-known half-Jewish family, but fled first to Berlin, then to England and finally to Philadelphia with his mother, younger sister and two older brothers. The family left Lüneburg after the Gestapo took Erhard's father Friedrich—editor of a left-leaning newspaper—to the Fuhlsbüttel concentration camp near Hamburg in spring 1933. There they beat the helpless man until he finally died. Erhard later held that his father was not beaten to death all at once, but "gradually over five days as a kind of training exercise for young aspiring stormtroopers. It's like in the Mafia," he would explain darkly: "you have to make a 'hit' before you're a soldier. So with the S.S. you had to beat a Jew to death before you're a full fledged trooper."

Stripped at age of 11 of the stable childhood home which he had known, thereafter Erhard struck out blindly—a lost, wounded boy forced by an unhappy fate into early manhood. Predictably, he became a proverbial "problem child." His story, unfortunately, would not be the only one of its kind at the Scattergood Hostel for European refugees; it would be only too normal.

Having become active with Quakers upon reaching the German capital and having become acquainted with the Martins while they served as AFSC representatives in Berlin from 1936 to 1938, Erhard's mother Katrin contacted Friends once she arrived in "Quaker Town." With their help she established a boardinghouse in a Philadelphia suburb where AFSC later accommodated newly arrived refugees. Busy caring for other uprooted souls assigned to her, she not always could watch Erhard as carefully as needed, so, when he decided that stoking the boardinghouse's coal furnace and mowing the lawn were beneath him, he sneaked off unnoticed to Philadelphia's docks and stowed away for England. He got as far as New York, where once put ashore he simply scoured the *New York Times* for the schedule of ships' departures and tried again—this time buried in a root cellar where he lived for four days on raw potatoes. Confident that the ship was too far at sea to be put ashore again, he surfaced—only to land in Liverpool's Walton prison once the steamer reached Britain. As the lad had no papers, money or friends, authorities there decided finally that it was the Cunard-White Star Line's responsibility to return him Stateside. That was supposed to be that.

The only thing was, the slippery knave escaped in transit to the ship, ran off and roamed England for a month—*sans* official identity or money and with only the clothes he had been wearing upon his unannounced departure from suburbia. Finally re-arrested, the Brits forcibly bid him *adieu* at the docks and within good time he found himself at Ellis Island. As he soon discovered, however, the former stepping stone into America was by 1939 no longer the main immigrant funnel for the U.S. labor market. Rather, as he saw it, it had become "a holding place for undocumented aliens, anarchists, Communists, suspected terrorists and bomb throwers, people with horrid sexually transmitted or other infectious diseases and other assorted riff-raff." Erhard qualified under several categories.

While there, Erhard had relatively few roommates, although the detained weren't confined to cells but lodged in big open dorms. Erhard found the food "great" and, compared to the English jail, his stay on Ellis Island was like a "rest cure." This camp-like accommodation didn't last long, however, for in April 1939 a judge called Erhard before an immigration court. As an adult, Erhard would see the event in very dramatic terms, later writing that the official "yielded to the pleadings with many tears of Katrin for forbearance and mercy for her wayward and misguided son Erhard, while Erhard judiciously for once kept his mouth shut. And so he was released back into the good old U.S.A. to the care of his mother. However, during the proceedings suddenly he felt terribly sad and filled with anguish and his eyes filled with tears as it came to him like a hammerblow—the realization how unspeakably much she loved him and how much suffering and woe his vagaries had caused her, who had suffered so much and so deeply already in the preceding six years."

Not surprisingly, Erhard's penance proved only partial at best. True, he surrendered his dream of sneaking back to Europe, but he could not befriend the idea of playing boardinghouse schlep. So, he decided to head west—the direction of all great tales told by Karl May, the German writer who despite having never set foot on North American soil impressed Erhard with his wildly successful serial accounts of Western lore. How convenient that his mother knew of the Martins' intended move to Iowa! Erhard finally had found a legitimate alibi whereby he could escape the suffocating safety of the East Coast's white-collar suburbs: he would chauffeur Anne Martin and her sons to Scattergood, help finish the renovation work and...well, what Katrin didn't know beforehand—he thought—would not hurt her. Yes, he'd "make himself useful" at Scattergood for a while, but—as usual—Erhard ultimately would do what he wanted anyway, which in this case consisted of busting out of the confines of all imposed structure and heading off on his own, past the pitfalls of a known biography and away from authorities—Nazi, Quaker, parental or otherwise.

Not the only refugee to do so, Erhard arrived at Scattergood with a sizeable chip on his defiant shoulders. For one thing, he did not regard himself as a refugee because—according to him—the term "entailed passivity, dependency, being a victim." Likewise, he did not consider himself a Jew, although his father was a Jew (and an agnostic); Erhard was uncircumcised and had no religious training nor inclinations. "For the most part" he would later admit, he found the Jews at Scattergood "a whiny, complaining, smartalecky bunch who were never satisfied" and with whom he felt he had nothing in common, whom he disliked and with whom he "wished to have nothing to do. They were," in his opinion, "shirkers." He claimed: "Whenever...a tough or dirty job needed to be done, all the Jews disappeared and it ended up being done by staff or by one of the non-Jews." Further, he purported that "many of the Jews at S.H. found its simple lifestyle and accommodations somehow demeaning; some expected staff to wait on them; few expressed gratitude, mostly they expressed irritation and self-pity." Erhard found the pronounced personality of one of the other guests—for example—particularly offensive and he later labeled him "a greasy Jew," referring to the man's attempts to straighten his naturally wavy, dark hair. Something about the Jews at Scattergood evoked questions too unsettling and overwhelming for a deeply traumatized 17-year-old to even attempt to field. At least, so it was for him at that time, but even 55 years later he recalled: "I found Scattergood Hostel a rather tiresome affair and stayed there no longer than I had to."

Still, Erhard Winter's days at Scattergood weren't completely filled with disgust. Even though he had deemed the work his mother needed done much too common for him, Erhard enjoyed the rigorous outdoor workout available at Scattergood. Before suddenly setting off one day and hitchhiking to a

Bruderhof community in South Dakota, he undertook various self-selected projects—such as demarcating the driveway with big white stones so as to save the lawn which he so lovingly mowed sitting behind a horse hitched to a series of rolling blades. Meanwhile, others—perhaps less wounded and thus better able to focus on more pressing collective needs—busied themselves with finishing basic tasks, so that by July 1939 the hostel seemed settled enough for the first family to arrive, accompanied by the first full-time staff besides John Kaltenbach, the Martins and the ever-present, completely winning Stanleys.

The Deutsch family from Vienna—Emil, Regina and their two red-haired children, Michael (age 9) and Hanna (6)—brought a new presence to the hostel, as had the arrival of the first female guest at Scattergood, Adelheid Ladewig. "Heid" and her husband Hans came from Berlin and preceded the Deutsches by a month. In contrast to the devoted Scattergood fans which the Deutsches were to become—to the point of spending their holidays there after having established themselves elsewhere, becoming Quakers and sending the children to the re-opened school after the war[4]—the Ladewigs were to have a decidedly mixed experience there, one which mirrored the complexity innate to most human endeavors.

Having "fought for Germany on all fronts" in World War I, the stocky Hans had been a lawyer for 25 years in the German capital when the couple decided to flee the Nazis' terror. They did not do so lightly, as at 53 it remained unclear if Hans ever again would be able to practice law and Heid's training as a linguist also would not be automatically transferrable to a new country. Still, despite their anxiety, at first the Ladewigs felt mostly relief at having found some welcome quiet among Iowa farms. After little more than a week the motherly, likeable Heid wrote to an AFSC staff member in New York, "we are so happy and feel so much at home that we hardly believe that we have been here only a short time." Stating that Scattergood was situated in "most beautiful surroundings," she gushed, "we would not have dreamed that there still exists such a peaceful spot in the world." Delighted that they had "a very cute room" and a bathroom "just next door, so that it could not be nicer," she raved as if the pair had chanced across an ideal holiday destination. Granted, they did have reason to sing songs of celebration during their first weeks among Friends, for on the night they arrived the university in Iowa City awarded Hans a scholarship to attend a lecture course on legal accounting six times a week. In the afternoons he could work "with great pleasure" in the garden and fields, while Heid worked mostly in the kitchen—which, with now 23 mouths to feed at every meal, was a pressing necessity. Moreover, the Ladewigs found the "young helpers" to be "very nice," with the blond, lively Heid confiding that "their consideration for my bad English is touching."

If this love feast were not sumptuous enough, shortly after their arrival the seemingly charmed twosome appeared in articles about Scattergood which ran in two Iowa papers with "fabulous curriculums." They also attended a Methodist gathering some 50 miles away in Anamosa, where Hans spoke "on the refugee question" and both were "swamped with questions." Two days later they attended a faculty reception at the university; Heid found it surprising, however, "how interested people are in our fate, and how intelligent their questions are. All of them are very nice to us" she reported, adding :"We are constantly having callers." She explained that many "farm families come to see us in the evening, and then we have much fun together." This happy combination of cozy accommodations in tranquil surroundings, further educational opportunities, work which made at least Heid feel "to be of some use" and sudden fame promised to be a hopeful omen for the Ladewigs that they indeed could find a home in a new, adopted land. As with many good things, however, this enchanted existence was not to last, either.

The records do not provide adequate explanation for the turn of events which shattered their lucky streak, but various secondary sources indicate that the longer the Ladewigs stayed in what was to become a four-month sojourn at Scattergood Hostel, the less agreeable they found the place, its people and the program. Regardless of their status as "refugees," Hans and Heid Ladewig were, above all, people—with all attendant strengths and oddities. At the time of their stay at Scattergood they were facing as individuals and as a couple what well might have been one of the biggest challenges of their lives: the loss of life-long cultural as well as personal identities. In that context any personal or interpersonal conflict perhaps could be more easily projected onto an external environment than confronted as one's own internal turmoil. Thus, it would not be hard to believe the explanation of one former staff member—who requested anonymity regarding this point—that Hans thought one of the male "young helpers" was being a bit too "nice" to Heid. Certainly, something serious in their marriage was amiss when even the 16-year-old volunteer Camilla Hewson could sense that their union was "difficult." And, Hans appeared to that same young Friend from Des Moines to have had "difficulty adjusting to his changed status." A *Register's* reporter also could feel the couple's underlying *Angst* and noted in a caption of a photo showing a napping Hans that "he's afraid he's too old to practice law in this country," and in one under a photo of Heid hanging Scattergood laundry outside to dry, that the couple "wonder about the future."

In any event they did find a position, working with Native Americans on a reservation near McCloud, Oklahoma—which according to Hans "with the best of will cannot be called a 'placement.'" Hans wrote to friends in Philadelphia that he and Heid were "very enthusiastic of the idea underlying Scattergood and went into it therefore with all our intensity. However," he

37

added soberly, "we must state now that Scattergood essentially meant for us a beautiful and very inexpensive summer resort." As partial explanation he said that "the person in charge is a young man of 23, the placement officer 25. Both are excellent people, who endeavour to give their best" he conceded, "however both lack the experience so necessary for such [a] difficult task."

Apparently an acquaintance of the Ladewigs had inquired about also participating in the refugee program at the hostel, for Hans made it clear that "as to Scattergood, we cannot with our experience advise [Dr. Katz' son] to go there." In his assessment, "in the main one may say that the project has not fulfilled its idea as such cases for which it was thought, who are difficult to be placed [and] could be placed just as hard as in New York." Hans' one-page letter did not offer much further grounds for their acute disappointment with Scattergood. Apparently, though, they felt justified in making this rather sharp critique, for a translated copy of this private missive reached Mary Rogers at AFSC's head office. She relayed the issue to Clarence Pickett via memo: "We know how [the Ladewigs] were treated at the end of their stay and why they feel critical but I believe that there is some basis in their criticism that the staff is too young and, secondly, that we need on it some people with rather definite skills." She maintained, however, that "their criticism regarding the placement is not justified."[5]

Because Scattergood Hostel was run by amateurs attempting to found an institution scarcely like any other of its kind, without doubt opportunities were missed, mistakes were made and people were offended—but concurrently some lessons were learned, too. Like Quakerism itself, Scattergood was an experiential process. Still, journal entries, letters to friends and family, in-class reports and other documents left behind attest to a largely positive, relaxed atmosphere at the hostel. Most guests were extraordinarily grateful, not to mention relieved to have discovered a quiet refuge where they might reassemble fragments of their road-worn lives. Unlike Hans and Heid Ladewig, it seems the great majority of guests left the hostel with feelings akin to what one might feel toward a familial home or a beloved relative.

With some hard knocks under its belt, then, the hostel continued to grow rather rapidly, so that by August 1939 the targeted population of thirty guests and ten or so staff was mostly in place. At that point daily life there began to more closely reflect the AFSC's vision of providing a place where refugees "could go for a few weeks or months to recover from the effects of their recent experiences, regain their confidence, improve their English, learn to drive a car, and if need be, start retraining themselves for some new line of work before seeking a permanent place in American society." And, true to Friends' aversion to organized hierarchies, from the beginning attempts were made to run the project as consensually as possible, with continual input from those being helped. This unorthodox style of management had the desired effect of helping the up-rooted Europeans feel that they again received respect and had some power over their own destinies. Psychological dynamics were not inconsequential, as many guests had suffered emotional trauma before reaching America's safe shores. Several were known to pace the upstairs hallway of the Main Building late at night and most eagerly scoured newspapers or radio bulletins for news from "home." A few were seen "wolfing their food" at mealtimes or even swiping lard from the pantry after bedtime, having too intimately made acquaintance with hunger in one of Nazi Germany's many concentration camps—and all had tales of narrow escape.

1.) It seems John Kaltenbach initiated the keeping of *The Book of Scattergood*, an almost-daily log of events and impressions regarding the hostel which staff and refugees took turns recording. On the first page presumably Kaltenbach wrote: "This book is dedicated to the friendships found in Scattergood between men and women of all nations, races, and creeds."

2.) John's were not mere words but actual—if unwritten—Quaker policy. Walter Shostal of Vienna, who became a guest at the other end of the hostel's life, described the state of religious affairs there: "Sundays were quiet at Scattergood. There were no English lessons and no unnecessary chores. There was, though, a standing offer to provide transportation to any place of worship within reach; I can't remember anybody accepting the offer. We mostly went with the staff and a few neighbors to the Quaker service [sic] on the grounds. There was no pressure—not even encouragement—to attend, but we felt it was the polite thing to do and it did not hurt, even if in our case the spiritual need was lacking. And, it was pleasant enough, this quiet hour, to sit in the cool of a summer noon with no sound but the humming of a bee and to spin one's own thoughts. Nothing could have been more peaceful than this hour."

3.) The names of the subject, his hometown and parents have been changed per request.

4.) When Emil found an accounting job with Scattergood Committee-member Jay Newlin's Pioneer Hybrid Seed Company and the Deutsches moved to Des Moines, they joined the Friends church there and became lasting friends with Cornell and Estelle Hewson, parents of Scattergood-volunteer Camilla. Emil and Regina volunteered at AFSC's regional office in the Iowa capital and contributed financially, too. After Regina died Emil married a Quaker, as did daughter Hanna—Phil, brother of Scattergood summer-volunteer Amy Clampitt.

5.) Despite a less-than-ideal end to their stay the Ladewigs evidently left with a positive impression of Quakerism, for friends of former Scattergood staff later reported that Heid attended an East Coast Friends meeting for a while.

39

A GLIMPSE OF HOPE

*"Amidst the dreadfulness and the distress of foreign
refugees in the European concentration camps,
there is from time to time a glimpse of hope."*
~ **Mariette Shumaker**

Who were the "guests" at Scattergood Hostel—what were their names, gender and ages, and what had been their professional as well as social backgrounds in Europe? Moreover, from where did they come[1] and under what conditions did they leave their homes? Although each of the 185 individual refugees at the hostel had a unique tale of increasing misery under the Nazi regime and of eventual escape, it must suffice to examine the telling experiences of a few and see them as representative of both the general travails and particular problems facing the whole.

The creation and dispersion of refugees began early in the Third Reich's existence. Soon after the Nazis' *Machtergreifung* in spring 1933, for example, Grete Baeck[2] received a telephone call late one evening. The caller told her to catch the next train for her native Vienna. She did—the last one before Hitler ordered the borders closed. A Jew and a leading actress at the German capital's left-leaning *Volksbühne* theater, had she remained she likely would have landed—and just as likely died—in a concentration camp. As it was, Grete fled so swiftly with a single bag that she had not even time to locate and warn her "Aryan" army-officer husband of three years of her going.

According to a writer at the time, "leaving Berlin for her native Vienna was a blow but there were some compensations. She had some money and she was back home again. Grete [had always been] a foreigner in Germany; she was always made to feel it. Austria was home... The Vienna theater was still prosperous and it welcomed [her]. In her work she could forget some of the heartaches. She got word from her husband. Could she meet him at the border near her old house in the Tyrol? She could and did. It meant an eight-hour climb, alone, to the mountain peak where Austrian and German border guards faced each other. He stood in Germany, she in Austria. They talked for an hour while German soldiers listened to every word. It was hopeless, they agreed. [An *Oberleutnant*, he] could not get out. It was suicide for her to return. Their marriage...was to end in annulment, a solution that was satisfactory to no one save Hitler."

With the German *Anschluß* of Austria in March 1938, Grete lost even more. The three-story mountain home she renovated after coming from Berlin and all her money remained behind when she fled to Prague, where "the flame of the theater still burned brightly." A new member of the growing list of exiled Germans and Austrians in the Czechoslovak capital, she found herself amidst numerous dramatic greats. Others with whom she had performed, though, had already removed themselves to America—Peter Lorre and Lionel Royce to name two. Grete resisted following them because she "had never learned to speak English for no other reason than that she just didn't care to. She knew French, German, Italian, Czech and Hungarian well. Not a word of English." Soon enough, however, her decision would be made for her.

In September 1938 Britain and France sacrificed Czechoslovakia to Hitler and Grete caught the last plane out of Prague for Paris, where after a fortnight she secured passage to New York. Landing with $3 in her pocket and no knowledge of English, the salt-and-pepper-haired woman desperately turned for help. She found it among the Quakers, who sent her to Scattergood Hostel, hopeful she could more quickly find the keys to cultural assimilation living among settled rural folk in Iowa than running among displaced urbane Germans in Manhattan.

The Nazis' political enemies fled persecution, imprisonment or possible death through various routes—two early primary ones being via Prague—as ultimately in Grete Baeck's case—or via Paris, as with Ernst and Ilse Stahl,[3] who according to Ilse "were black sheep...political refugees and from the *very* left side." A Breslau native, Ernst had supported in the Spartacus movement in the days following the collapse of the Hohenzollern dynasty and served time in a *Weimarer Republik* prison for gun-running during the Communists' attempt to plant a Soviet republic on German soil. His and Ilse's leftist political convictions and activist past provided amble reason for the Nazis to want to persecute both of them. Ilse later explained,

After the Reichstag burned, Ernst had to disappear because the very day before the Reichstag burned, [the police] came to our house...to the landlady, knocked on the door [and] wanted to arrest Stahl. Since we lived downstairs, Ernst went into the bedroom of the owner of the

41

apartment...and he could go out through this window into a courtyard. And the courtyard was from a big, big angle of houses surrounded. And he could go in this house and this house and run through all the attics because they were open, and could disappear. So he disappeared; the police didn't get him. The police came to me with a big dog. I was laying in bed because I had something [wrong] with my neck... They said, tomorrow I have come to the police and if I don't come they will arrest me and so on and so on... I did not know [where to find Ernst], but at this time I was informed that nobody knows me. All people, all our friends—they are not to know us, because [the Nazis] search for Ernst. So when I saw somebody approaching, I would not make "hello": I would look straight and sometimes even a little bit to the other side in order not to be tempted. Other friends did the same—that was our rule: that we would not give one friend through another friend to the police. So, I was totally isolated by choice, more or less. Because that was our rule and we followed our rules.

Unbeknownst to Ilse, Ernst set out for France by walking over the Thuringer mountains to Czechoslovakia, using a false passport. He and a companion were detained on the border for some four weeks by the Nazis and charged with espionage and other "crimes against the state," even though the authorities were unaware of whom they had in their custody. Although Ernst could not drive and spoke "very bad French," he eventually won his freedom by posing as the *chauffeur* of the mayor of Strasbourg, who cooperated by writing a letter of inquiry and support on his behalf. After Ernst fled Germany, the Nazis concluded that he actually had gone underground and searched for him. In the process they arrested Ilse's mother and two brothers in Jena and kept them for a week. In the meantime, Ilse lived a precarious life in Berlin in danger, constant fear and without means of economic support. The police ordered her to register her whereabouts daily and she simply bid her time until she received word of Ernst and could leave the German capital. The British chapter of the Salvation Army often fed her, as she was undernourished and "just was tumbling over...and weighed less than 80 pounds and had to walk three miles to work every day." Despite being marginalized professionally—and thereby economically—as an "enemy of the people," Ilse found a job washing car windows until receiving retraining and finding employment as an apprentice in an "Aryanized" Jewish-owned lithograph-picture plant. Through legal trickery, she eventually got forged papers and made her way to the Rheinland, where she arranged illegal passage into France via a valley along Germany's western border. Decades later Ilse explained her flight in detail:

Since I did not know French or the border situation, [communist friends] fixed a place in Ober Elsaß because Ober Elsaß is swampy and it's wide and you can see from here and the river is in some places in many arms and also shallow and you can see there's a frontier running in this valley: you can see the [train] station from the French from the German station. And this place we wanted to come. They fixed a man to pick me up. I had to go to a certain station—then go out of the train that nobody followed me—a very tiny station and walk to other station, maybe fifteen miles [away]... I had to dress in a certain way so that I didn't look like a communist, because [laughing] we had straight hair, strange clothing, strange shoes. And before I went, I got first some shoes—you can laugh now, [but] that was difficult. That was a disguise. The kommunistische Frauen *had straight hair—I had a little wave, but all straight, straight, straight: no makeup whatever, flat shoes...all this had to go...* [A friseur *created a special hair do] and put false eye lashes in the eyes and also made my fingernails pink... They gave me shoes with such heels which I had in a net [bag to carry them in] because I could not go in [them] and I now had to go to a certain train station...and meet a fellow I'd never seen....and I should stay on this little train station till the train had gone: I should exactly use this and this train at this and this time. I should come the 2nd of May and since [on] the 2nd of May the whole population of the Rheinland in France sells [Ilse assumes a shrill voice and an affected French accent]* "Bouquet, bouquet!"—*these May flowers—I should have a big May flower on the side so that this fellow would recognize me and I should wait till the train is gone and walk all time up and down, not on the train but on the house wall where the coffee houses are and this fellow would pass me by and would say* "Coffee?" *and [Ilse whispers] I would say* "Satz"—"coffee ground"—"Kaffeesatz." *May came and this fellow could not go... So they postponed it and I could not go with my May flowers and it became difficult to make something else out, but* "Kaffeesatz" *stayed. So I was dressed, went on the train, changed the train four, five times—even though I didn't have to, only to get rid of whoever followed me. Then I went out on this station and nobody was on the train anymore and I walked up and down. And I saw a man smaller than I, with such a nose and only one tooth in the mouth—also dark-skinned, very boney. I walked up and down, he walked up and down. And I didn't dare to say,* "Kaffee" *because I thought,* "That is the police; that is a gangster from the police!" *Then I turned around and on the opposite from this place, I looked and pretended I looked for the coffee shop and he came and said,* "Coffee?" *and I said,* "Korn" *and he said in very heavy-set German,* "Follow me." *And I followed. I had only a net [bag], one sandwich with pork fat and [laughing] the shoes. I took the high shoes off and put the flat shoes on again... And this fellow told me [so as not to walk together] "Try to do something that you have to stand, too, or walk a little slower," and so on... All the time I was afraid [Ilse's voice breaks] in these little villages to lose him! But I followed. And it took hours and hours—out of the little villages, through a little woods, through this, over meadows, through fields. And we walked and walked—nearly two and a half hours. And then came a broad valley: I did not know the landscape, I did not know the situation... Then, on the edge of the valley, he all of a sudden stopped and I stopped, too. Then he said to me, "In 50 meters or so we will stop just on the edge of the woods and I will talk to you: there we can come together and talk. And in this 50-meter stretch came all of a sudden a bull running against me and a peasant behind him and he hollered in German dialect, you know: "This dumb Vieh is not satisfied with a German woman; he has to go to the French woman—he all the time goes to the French woman." That's what he hollered! Because on the other side was the French, where there were no animals—except this bull. Where he came from, I don't know. And "Go out of the way, stand behind a tree!" he hollered, because he ran with a whip behind... He came a little later, this little man... Then, after this bull affair, he came out and [we] talked to this peasant in French, because on the border they speak French and German. But I didn't come from this part—I could not understand either or: the dialect of the Germans [was] not very good... So, he said "Settle down..." We then came to a place where the valley got a little smaller and very easy to be overlooked and he said "Look here, that's our crossing point and other there—far, far down there, see?—these are the French and that's our goal, to go over there." There was a small, small bridge...and we were sitting there and resting because we had really walked, walked, walked—and through the swamps—and was wet up to here! Everything was soaked. And so, he said, "See—come here, come here!" In the middle...of this was the frontier and from this station [the German guards] came... He said: "We have to go through this swampland; we have to figure out a time when they go this way and turn against us. Don't fear the French, don't fear the French: only watch the Germans! When they are over the point that they cannot see here on this place, we start and you go as quick as you can. And if you realize you cannot make it"—there was reeds going quite a bit, so high—"then lay down and keep still. And when I whistle [Ilse whistles faintly], then you can come out. When we are over this middle line, don't fear the Germans: then we are in France and you don't need to fear anything. Okay?"*

And so we walked—with a few interruptions—and when I was about a
quarter of the end of this frontier place to the French, they came out
and they all [yelled greetings]. And you know, they did not know that
we came for political reasons or whatever. It was, of course, because
the French men liked German girls... [The guide] had told them—he
looked like a man who never fancied a woman, really—"I bring my
future bride illegal over here" and so, when I came...on this place was
a dress for me, fresh shoes, fresh underwear—because I had to walk
through the swamps—and a car! The limousine from the mayor from
Strasbourg was there—so you see! From there on, straight through to
the mayor of Strasbourg and they all congratulated him and—they
spoke French—I didn't understand anything. I only know that they
said, "My goodness, where did you get this nice girl, you old [Ilse
laughs]...." When I came [to Strasbourg] there was—surprise, sur-
prise!—a big banquet in the mairie *and here was sitting Ernst! I was so*
excited.

Once in France, the couple spent six months in Strasbourg and a teachers' union took "good care" of them until they moved on to Paris. When the
Wehrmacht rolled into France in spring 1940, they fled once again and kept
running—till they reached the unlikely destination of Iowa."[4]

Some of the stories of flight to be told are considerably more tragic than
others. That of Boris Jaffe, for example, can be seen only as one of ongoing
suffering. A rather tall, slim, "handsome man with a military bearing and an
immense pride," Russian-born Boris had served the Czar as an army officer
in the first World War until he was wounded, captured and interned as a
prisoner of war in Stolp, a small town in northeast Germany. Later, after the
Bolsheviks overran the Romanovs' imperial government, he chose to remain
in chaotic post-Hohenzollern Germany rather than face the Reds back home.
After some time black-haired Boris married doe-eyed, Lithuanian-born Ida
Pochumenski and through good fortune became a regional distributor of
American films in Germany for Warner Brothers. So settled, the couple
moved into a comfortable home in a residential section of eastern Berlin[5] and
by 1933 had three young children—Alexander, Tamara and Jascha.
This enviable life could well have continued, except that with the advent
of Nazi dictatorship Boris found himself increasingly persecuted. Although
the son of Jewish parents, he had always claimed his religious affiliation as
"Greek Catholic" and therefore should have been spared the stupidities of
Nazi legalism due to questions of confession. Having a self-identified Jewish
wife, however, meant that he was the father of three children unescapably
held in contempt by those in power and as a Russian he himself always would

45

be seen as an *Untermensch*. On top of that, given that he peddled "decadent" and utterly *unpassende* "Jewish" films from that Mecca of "frivolous debauchery" known as "Hollywood," Boris' career was slowly wrested away from him by a series of Nazi decrees. Warner Brothers soon discontinued its operations in Germany due to the hostile Hitler regime, but sent Boris a stipend for several years anyway, although he had begun work with smaller firms—and then later sent money to his wife in his absence.

Boris received the first notice from the Berlin police ordering him to leave the country in 1937 but somehow lingered on eighteen more months, leaving on 27 October 1939—five days after his daughter turned seven and only two days before his visa expired. Riding a train to Copenhagen and then a steamship to New York, 47-year-old Boris took a prized photo album with him but left his family behind—likely either because of the prohibitive $200-per-ticket trans-Atlantic passage or due to successfully restrictive immigration laws. The album was filled with "crinkled-edged, black-and-white pictures of picnics and parties, boys dressed in *Lederhosen* and a dimpled, curly-haired Tamara clad in ruffles." As one biographer later put it: "For more than six years, [it] would be the only family he had."

Landing in New York, Boris discovered that his difficulties with English would preclude any meaningful employment. This in turn rendered him unable to pay passage for his family out of the Third Reich or to persuade hard-to-please American consular officials that he could keep his family from becoming public charges if permitted into the country. At first he lived with his brother-in-law's family, communicating with them only in Hebrew and some German for he knew "no English whatsoever." After several months he found the situation "very trying," as he saw himself as a burden on his hosts and he did not like feeling dependent upon them financially. He acknowledged that he also was "not developing any understanding of America." According to the first job-placement director at Scattergood, Giles Zimmerman, Boris saw "the necessity of a complete understanding of the language and customs" of his adopted country, so accepted an AFSC offer early in 1940 to travel to Iowa to "learn these important factors as quickly as possible." Zimmerman reasoned that "since he had been a refugee from Russia to Germany following the last war," Boris realized that he had to get to know "the common man on the street" before he could successfully enter American society. To illustrate how little the Saint Petersburg native knew about the New World, Zimmerman related that "he thought Florida was a city and Miami, Florida, was a hotel." Boris did not discover his error until he had been in the United States for nine months—and then only when he and John Kaltenbach had a geography lesson "in the real heart of America," under Scattergood's big maple trees.

Very much a man on the run—if not from hunting authorities, then from haunting memories—Boris did not have an easy time of it at Scattergood. "Our mysterious Russian"—as the peppy young Quaker volunteer Camilla Hewson called him—moved around the place at times almost ghostlike, apparently being visited by some internal ghosts of his own. He lost weight, by day brooded and by night walked the upstairs corridors of the Main Building. Giles Zimmerman's wife Lynn later recalled: "In the dead of night, I would hear him walking back and forth," adding, "I would go and walk with him." She noted that "he would talk about Tamara and his boys" and show her "pictures...the same pictures, over and over again." He most often shared with her one particular photo of Tamara on the first day of school with "all those presents... The pictures he always dwelt on were of her," she said.

The hapless man worked heartily outside on projects such as clearing the garden in spring of debris left from the previous fall's harvest, but his thoughts were so restless that he could not study and his English remained "impenetrable." Although his body was on the Iowa prairies, Boris' mind was on the Prussian plains and he could not cope with the thought that his family was in danger. In a communiqué of February, 1941, Ida Jaffe wrote that the Nazis had sent one close friend to a concentration camp and murdered another on the street. Further, Berlin officials demanded that the family surrender their home. Although the money Warner Brothers continued to send kept them alive, it came mostly irregularly and food had become difficult to find. According to a letter an AFSC worker wrote to the Jewish Joint Distribution Committee (JDC),[6] Boris feared that "danger is closing in on his wife and it is only a matter of time until she herself becomes a victim of persecution." Having started seeking visas for his family upon arriving in America, Boris finally found an Iowa farmer and a businessman "moved by his plight" who were willing to sign the vital affidavits of support. And, Quakers wrote "countless" letters on his behalf. Despite these developments, however, the visas remained beyond his reach.

Desperate, at the end of that month Boris drafted a personal appeal to the American consul general in Berlin. "Honorable Sir," he pleaded, "this is a request made by a husband and father on behalf of his wife and three small children...I am most anxious to have my family join me in the United States. The reasons for this I know you can well understand... Their life in Berlin has not been easy during these months, [but] they have borne it with fortitude and courage. I would like to relieve them of this as soon as I can."

Just then a cable from JDC's Berlin office informed Boris that the counsel had agreed to award his family the visas—if their passage were paid in-full in advance. The staff at Scattergood had not abandoned his case, although Boris already had left the hostel some six months earlier to accept a menial job as a porter in a Cedar Rapids, Iowa, department store at the measly salary of $14 per week. They rushed to raise the $600 through direct appeals to

47

civic groups and, according to one source, by "buttonholing friends as they were depositing their paychecks in local banks." Combined with funds from JDC, the sum was collected and sent to the appropriate official. Boris had been "close to a nervous breakdown," but once the money was underway and the myriad bureaucratic requirements seemed met, he relaxed. He also decided—despite his miserable English—to return to New York and find a job in order to "do something to aid his family." Once on the East Coast, however, the scheme collapsed—although records don't explain why —and Boris was back where he began: terribly sad and anonymously alone in the midst of millions.[7]

Technically a Jew, a Slav and a "dealer of decadence," Boris Jaffe in Berlin failed the Nazi test of acceptability on three counts. On the other end of "Greater Germany" in Vienna—the former capital of a former country—Viktor Popper failed the test on only one count. One, however, sufficed.

Born in "very comfortable circumstances" to a wealthy family, as a child Viktor enjoyed the amenities of having an English governess—and thereby learned to speak her language "without accent, and very nearly perfectly." He passed through *Hochschule* and *Technische Hochschule* to the *Universität Wien* with plans to be an engineer. A serious illness and the handicap of a nearly hunched back, however, made him change his mind in favor of a career in music, "less because it was necessary...to earn a living than because [he loved] music, and...wanted to make others love and understand it, too." Viktor initially experienced difficulty, but then more and more pupils sought him out, plus a circle of older students gathered around him, profited from his teaching and admired his compositions. In turn, he became the pupil of two renowned psychologists who shared his interest in music. Thus he began dividing his life between these two interests, with four or five evenings a week spent at the opera or in concert halls and Sunday afternoons at a gathering of amateur but "nonetheless competent" musicians. He also visited great musical festivals such as those held in Bayreuth and Salzburg, and began a doctorate degree in music at the *Universität*. All seemed set.

Then the Nazis appeared and Austria disappeared—along with Viktor's dreams, for he was a Jew. First, he could no longer instruct "Aryan" pupils, then the *Universität* closed its door to him, as did the opera and concert halls soon after. Finally, more public spaces became off-limits to Jews till the situation degenerated to the point where even in ordinary conversation with an American, Viktor had to admit "oh, yes, I know the movie of which you are speaking; I read reviews of it. But, I didn't see it, for it appeared in Vienna after the moving-picture theatres were closed to non-Aryans."

And, as Peg Hannum—the Scattergood staff member who related this story—put it, "to complete the series of indignities and discomforts" Viktor

48

had to move from his comfortable flat, "furnished with taste and care." He took his mother to live in a smaller one in a poor quarter of the city, but "as it would be too great a concession" to have let him stay there he had to move yet again, to an even smaller accommodation. In the process Viktor had to part with many cherished possessions until he was "stripped of nearly everything [he] once owned" and obliged to live as best he could, sharing one room with his mother and trying to "give her the few small comforts still within [one's] power to obtain." Hannum protested: "So hidden and removed from observation, can you hope to be let alone? By no means, for there is a decision on the part of the government to remove as rapidly as possible all males to Poland (and transportation to Poland...meant slow starvation under unthinkable living conditions)."

Nazi officials were not averse to bribes, however, nor—according to Hannum—"too far removed from humanity to forget former friendships," so Viktor escaped that fate and wrote letters "by the dozens" until he secured an affidavit from someone in America willing to be legally responsible for his maintenance. Once he received his quota number, he packed his belongings—"music and books and a few personal effects"—but to conserve space even tore apart some of the books, removed the bindings and whole sections in order to keep only what he could not part with. As he was forbidden to take money with him, he made sure to carry a few pieces of silver—but "not many, for it weighs so heavily." Viktor also had to leave behind his library of opera scores, manuscripts of compositions, symphonies and chamber music, etc., "making a careful and totally unsatisfactory selection." As for his grand piano, that had "already been abandoned."

While making these preparations to leave what once had been Austria, Viktor read in the newspaper that the ship on which his brother, sister-in-law and their children had been sailing to Palestine was sunk in the harbor of Tel Aviv—within sight of land. He had not seen that brother for more than a year, as when he left for Czechoslovakia it had been in a sealed train. Despite that the desperate Viktor had stood "for hours" at a station through which the train was to pass in the middle of the night "in the faint hope of catching a glimpse" of the brother from behind locked windows. Viktor chose not to tell his mother about the loss of her other son, thinking that his own departure was enough for her to bear—although it was she who had begged him to leave, reasoning that he was in greatest danger. Just before his departure, though, word out of Switzerland had it that the brother and his family had "miraculously escaped drowning [and were] among the very few to save themselves by swimming ashore"—only to land in an internment camp. The news reassured Viktor and with it he allayed part of his mother's anxiety. His own leave-taking, though, remained dramatic enough given that he himself had to travel several days in a sealed train from Vienna through Berlin and

Paris to Madrid, then later on to Lisbon. After several days of impatient waiting there and trying to arrange the shipment of the trunk carrying his music and books, he finally secured passage to New York. To his amazement he found the Ellis Island officials—in pronounced contrast to the Nazi ones with whom he had painfully too much experience—friendly. Thereafter, he discovered to his surprise, he was simply "free to begin a new life. But how?"

Speaking as if she were he, Hannum argued Viktor's case, commenting:

> *With twenty years of adult life behind you, you must make a new start, among strangers, and deprived of the tools of your trade; deprived, moreover, of the means of acquiring them, shut out from the atmosphere in which you had been accustomed to live, cut off from everything which had been your life. You almost regret your personal safety, for your trunk full of books and music has apparently been lost, or confiscated by the trans-shippers who make enormous profits on such transactions; you worry about your mother, your relief at each letter being swallowed up by almost immediate reflection that much may have happened since that letter was written and posted. What can you do? You make friends who will try to help; contacts are made, people take an interest in you, invitations multiply. A job? Pupils? Not yet, nor any signs of them. But you call up your reserves of courage; you resolve to try.*

Others among the Scattergood Hostel's almost two hundred guests fared far better than the luckless Boris Jaffe or the disenfranchised and dispossessed Viktor Popper. Karl Liebman of Frankfurt-am-Main—for example—had been gassed by American doughboys at Verdun in 1918. Unexpectedly, his brush with death in the armed forces would save his life some two decades later.

A former lieutenant of an artillery unit who was blinded for a week after that dramatic mishap, following the first World War Karl "tried his hand at several business enterprises" before passing law exams and being accepted into a firm. On the first of April 1933, however, he went to work in the morning to find a boy Brown Shirt standing beside his office door. Neither said a word, "but that was Liebman's introduction to the fact that Adolf Hitler had come to power in Germany." The 49-year-old professional told a reporter: "At first I didn't think [Hitler] would be able to put over his program. It sounded too crazy" he thought, expecting that "farmers, the army and the big industrialists would stand against him. Anyway" he mused, "the average German doesn't think about politics—or didn't."

Soon thereafter the law firm received rules to follow dictated by the central powers. Subsequently some members of the firm were forbidden to practice at all because they were Jews. Karl, however, "was shown special consideration." For one thing, although his father was a Jew, his American-born mother was a Christian—as was he. Moreover, as a bemedalled veteran, the compactly built, now-bespectacled Karl "had friends in the army" so that even after being deprived of the legal right to practice law, he remained employed as a law clerk. Thankfully, due to his military connections he "never saw what the inside of a concentration camp looked like."

Instead Karl "only felt the fear, the ever-present, gnawing, looming threat of violence, of nameless terror reserved by the Nazis for the Jews." At night in the apartment house where he and his diminutive wife Lotte lived he could hear "the tromp of hobnailed boots" and knocks on his neighbors' doors, followed by "the screams and protests of the women" as his neighbors were dragged off by storm troopers to concentration camps. "They came to every door in our apartment house but mine" he recounted, adding "maybe they forgot me."

It took more than a year before the childless Liebmans could secure the papers necessary to flee Nazi Germany. By the time they did their remarkable luck had been stretched to the eleventh hour: the ship they finally boarded for America arrived in New York on the last day of August 1939—one day before war broke out in Europe.

Not all of the refugees who made their way to Scattergood came because of "racial" or religious persecution—politics also made some individuals wholly unpalatable to the Nazis. Several such people arrived at West Branch, but perhaps the most notable was Marie Juchacz, a staunch Social Democrat, founder of the *Arbeiterwohlfahrt* (a workers' welfare agency) and the first female member of the post-Hohenzollern Reichstag—active in that contentious house from its inception under the *Weimarer Republik* till its emasculation in 1933.

To avoid likely persecution and internment under the brutal new Nazi regime, Marie left Berlin soon after Hitler seized power. She retreated first to Saarbrücken, a western border town relatively far removed from the horrific events taking place in the Prussian capital. There, in the home she established in the Bahnhofstraße, the placid, gray-haired woman provided a refuge for former party and Reichstag members. When a plebiscite returned the Saarland to Germany in 1935, she then moved just across the German border to Mulhouse in Alsace so that "the connection with the homeland through personal contacts could be maintained." Once on French territory the 56-year-old activist found herself running a household full of fellow emigrants. With the outbreak of war in late summer 1939 she had to pack her suitcases again and move on to the next station of her involuntary journey —this time to a small village in the officially unoccupied South of France.

When it became clear, however, that the German *Führer* wanted to make the tenancy of Vichy territories official, she and her little band planned to flee once more, this time over the Pyrenees. Meanwhile, the Vichy government finally granted her an exit visa, so in March 1941 Marie sailed to the French Antilles island of Martinique, where she waited several months before receiving permission to pass on to her next destination, New York. There she quickly set about her on-going, self-appointed task of helping others.

While she engaged herself with volunteer work on behalf of other refugees, Marie herself struggled to adjust to her own plight. She wrote that "in the course of time the situation became relatively pleasant and bearable. At the beginning [however] it was really meager and torturous for me here in New York." While her mind stayed occupied with the unending difficulties she faced in dealing with her immediate environment in America's First City, her heart remained attached to the unending difficulties her loved ones and friends faced far off in Germany's Third Reich. She explained to a friend that "[thoughts of] the Homeland pull me back, exactly because things aren't going so well over there. And because I don't hide this feeling, but rather quietly and trustingly show it, you shouldn't push [me]. As soon as it is possible, I will come."

Surely, though, it would take time before the 1,000-year Reich would fall: to some degree Marie realized that she had to accept facts as they were and cope as best she could. Although grateful for a safe haven from persecution, life as an exile was not easy for this divorced mother of two. In a circular letter to friends she confided "I did not arrive in this country light-hearted. But, it would be a great injustice, did I not thankfully acknowledge the friendly hospitality with which one in this country approaches political refugees. When the U.S.A. itself was at war, hardly anyone made us feel from where we came. Despite that, it is not easy for a no-longer-young person to sink new roots in a foreign-tongued country with other morals and customs, with other perspectives and conditions of living. That is the case for me and very many others who share the same fate."

Despite her personal hardships, the eternal advocate of better living conditions for all continued doing whatever she could to be of assistance. According to one biographer, "in the years of emigration, Marie Juchacz had been tirelessly engaged—within the framework of the given possibilities—to lighten the lives of her companions in fate." In that same vein Marie's friend Hans Hirschfeld of Berlin reported that "without many words" she gave an example to others of "how one had to try, even under the most adverse of conditions...to work, to help." Often, in addition to intangible encouragement, she provided her dejected visitors with something to eat or drink, which also soothed restless minds and strengthened wearied bodies. "In the kitchen, at the sewing machine, in the household, but also amongst the gatherings of groups and circles of emigrants—whether in France, Switzerland or in the United States—Marie Juchacz was always the same: always the strong one, the giver and the listener. Here is a person who through personal pain and inconveniences never forgets that we human beings are there to help, support and give counsel."

In Europe, Juchacz had felt at home: she understood the culture—and the language—and used this familiarity to campaign successfully on behalf of the plight of women in general and mothers in particular, of children, workers and others unable to champion their own most-pressing interests. In America the opposite was true: none of her training nor experiences prepared her for such an alien environment. Unlike the majority of immigrants in saner times, she had not chosen to begin life anew in a new land, but rather, as a political refugee, she had arrived through no choice of her own. She found herself, then, in effect as debilitated as the Nazis might have rendered her—short of execution. In this state of despair, she wrote on her résumé—apparently to AFSC—that "I still speak no English, but attempt with all energy to be done with all the difficulties of the language and seek a livelihood." She emphasized "I am healthy," but then conceded that "my 62 years and being decades-long accustomed to organizational and office work make it very difficult, almost impossible, for me to feed myself through physical labor." The Quakers understood her plight and took Marie in at Scattergood for most of a year,[8] until the usually independent woman opted to return to New York "to be with friends and relatives."[9]

Despite years of necessary nomadic wandering due to the occupation of her *Heimat* by armed fanatics, Marie Juchacz somehow avoided landing in one of the various refugee camps where so many other future Scattergood guests would sojourn. The internment of various individuals who later would turn to the Quakers for assistance deeply affected their psychological as well as physical conditions upon arrival in Iowa; their assorted experiences would mark and remain with them for years to come.

The initial camps were established to *help* refugees, while later camps most often were created to *detain* them. Of the former, the young Austrian Irwin Blumenkranz explained that "when the mass of people who were forced to leave Europe grew bigger, the English government did a great thing to help persecuted and exiled refugees": in January 1939 Parliament passed a bill offering additional numbers of emigrés the chance to stay temporarily in Britain. Those who already had a possibility to migrate to third countries were allowed to spend their time in mass-accommodations until the final leg of their respective journeys. To take advantage of this Friends Service Council in London joined with other refugee-service agencies to create Bloomsbury House, which operated "independently of all other social organizations" and sponsored the Kitchener Camp near Richborough in Kent. While generally quite accepting of the diversity inherent in the sheer numbers fleeing Nazi-occupied central Europe, the camp did implement some discriminating conditions: only men between the ages of 18 and 45 could reside there and each man had to provide proof that he would leave England at some point during the next three to nine months—as well as pass a medical exam. A prospective medical student, Irwin found it "very difficult" to get into the Kitchener Camp due to the "many thousands of applicants," yet received a slot anyhow, as "always when some members of the Kitchener Camp had left England, new people...were admitted."

At the beginning, "when the first refugees entered the Kitchener Camp they found nothing but an old ruined military camp. Then" he noted, "the hard work of rebuilding began." Two staffs directed the camp: an English executive staff—an arm of the Bloomsbury House's Kitchener Camp Committee—and a German staff which acted as a liaison between the camp's administration and the refugees. Next in line in the camp's administrative hierarchy came various departments: employment, accounts, education (which also attended to religious matters), postal, etc. To illustrate that "all these departments had to fulfill a lot of work," Irwin described his own job in the postal department: "It had a much bigger business than any little town with the same population. Some days there was an incoming mail of nearly 6000 letters and 300 parcels. This mail had to be distributed and delivered to the receivers as promptly as possible. The daily sale of stamps sometimes amounted to $110. The customs duty on parcels from abroad amounted to $50, some days. Every day a lot of registered letters were delivered and forwarded." Irwin was sure to add that "all this work was done with greatest reliability. You could find the same scrupulous work in any department of the community. From ruins, thus, arose a town under the hands of the refugees. Huts and roads were built and a lot of craft work done. Many worked in the fields getting from this work recovery for their nerves after the terrific experiences they had to undergo before their arrival in the Camp. Everybody had to work according to his knowledge and ability."

Not every moment, however, was consumed with labor. The conscientious Irwin explained that "having done the work of the day we spent the evening entertaining and conversing." While the camp's cinema accommodated 400 each evening, he calculated that "at least once a week 1500 persons took part in entertainments in the big gym." The refugees also enjoyed such events as theatrical performances, concerts and "speeches of prominent persons." In their free time the uprooted, distraction-hungry men had radios, books and newspapers at their disposal.

The virtual holiday-resort atmosphere of the Kitchener Camp would not last, though, for "with the outbreak of the war the gradual disbandment of the camp started"—primarily because immigration from the Continent virtually stopped. Thereafter "many members got their visas for the United States and a considerable part joined the British army." Irwin left the camp in May 1940 "when...the dissolution of the Camp was nearly completed, after having fulfilled a great task in the problem of the emigration from Germany."

Once hostilities broke out between Nazi Germany and the Allies, the nature of refugee camps in Britain changed completely—and literally almost overnight. From the *Kristallnachtpogrom* of November 1938 till world war erupted in September 1939, the British government acted quite generously in its expanded willingness to show an open door to those fleeing Hitler's Germany. Even in the period of the so-called Phoney War refugees as well as bona fide Nazi supporters stranded in England due to the outbreak of war were allowed relative free movement. As the *Wehrmacht* almost effortlessly rolled over the Lowland Countries in May 1940, however, the nation's mood shifted to one of pronounced alarm. Then, when France swiftly fell to Hitler's pounding onslaught and Britain's troops had to evacuate the Continent via the port of Dunkerque, the Brits panicked. Winston Churchill growled "Collar the lot!" Public sentiment echoed his and within days first German and Austrian men between the ages of 16 and 60, then women and even children were subjected to arrest, questioning and imprisonment—this time, though, not at the hands of a totalitarian dictatorship but a "liberal democracy." Even if Whitehall meant most of those interned no harm, the fact remained that thousands of lives ground to a halt and those individuals were denied their freedom. And, their lives would never be the same.

The 50-something lawyer Martin Kobylinski, for example, had fled Berlin for London, where he passed what he called the "British Tribunals" and promisingly was awarded "the best note: 'Friendly Alien. Refugee from Nazi-Oppression.'" Thus, he happily expected to settle quietly into English society. After France's defeat, though, "one day a nice gentleman stepped into [his] room saying, 'I am very sorry, but you must be interned.'" A London police-department "Black Maria"—as the force's cars were nicknamed—waited outside and whisked the confused German exile away from what he had concluded would be a safe haven. Although he understood that with the collapse of the French front all male non-Brits immediately had become suspicious, he did not understand why he should be considered a threat to national security, as he had been granted favorable legal status. Still, cooperate with the authorities he must. And did.

In proper British fashion, Martin and other aliens apprehended in his adopted neighborhood first were provided with cups of tea and only *then* sent packing via Liverpool to the Isle of Man in the Irish Sea. Arriving in the island's largest port, the men disembarked. Martin later recalled: "On the

55

way along the beach, the people of Douglas watched in astonishment this procession of nearly one thousand men, carrying their luggage, tired by the long way and apparently not very happy to be marching between soldiers with fixed bayonets. [This contingent plodded on for 40 minutes, the whole time passing] the ranks of men, women and children of Douglas. Then the gates of Hutchinson-Internment Camp between the high double fence of barbed wire were opened to receive their first guests."

In retrospect Martin assessed that the "treatment of us in the camp was absolutely fair." The men enjoyed relative self-government, complete with their own self-elected leader. The military guards—"a staff of several officers and a small detachment of soldiers"—usually remained outside the compound and the camp's commander even dubbed his charges "a happy family." Still, the spooked German detainee said "we passed always the high gates of the double barbed wire with a strange feeling." He did note that this "family" consisted of "the most interesting people ever rounded up—famous scientists, professors from Berlin, Vienna and many other Universities, poets, sculptors, painters, musicians." The men organized concerts "so fine that one could forget where [one] was listening to a singer of the Opera of Vienna." They also sponsored their own "University of Hutchinson-Internment Camp with daily lectures in languages and all branches of science." Martin found it an "honor" to be one of three judges in the camp's court of arbitration, as each had to serve in some sort of capacity in the daily functioning of the place and "all of the work in the house was done as a matter-of-fact by ourselves." The men continued to be prisoners, however; keeping them under constant watch, the camp's administration subjected the internees to twice-daily roll call.

For the four months that Martin stayed at the camp, the situation remained more than bearable. The diversity of internees also provided endless distraction from the sobering fact of forced incarceration or the horrific scenario of wholesale slaughter should the Nazis conquer Britain and the Isle of Man. "You could see there monks and other clergymen in their official robes"—for instance "a Jesuit-Pater and many Rabbis." Also, each "boarding house" boasted its own front garden ornamented with flowers. And sometimes, "in the midst of guards," the men could go for a walk or even "a bath in the sea. But," Martin confessed, "we all longed for release." Freedom eventually did come, albeit painfully slowly, given that—as the tolerant Jew acknowledged—"England was fighting for her life and there was the usual red tape besides." His time there could not have been only traumatic, though, for he later reflected that "as I look back on those months spent on the Isle of Man, my most pleasant remembrance is the hour each day, when guarded by our sentries, we could walk through the beautiful island."

Britain was not the only site of camps intended to detain refugees. Across the Channel on the Continent existed others—created either by the Nazis or collaborationist puppet regimes in quasi-German-ruled territories—and displaced persons frequently found themselves in one of them. The story of Alfred Adler, for instance, provides a striking example of medical conditions prevalent in such detention centers.[10]

A French-born, German-educated Jewish physician, Alfred practiced medicine in Frankfurt-am-Main for a decade before things got "a little hot for him in Germany" and he fled back to France, where he obtained "all the proper credentials and papers which were supposed to keep him out of the concentration camps." Despite that, eventually he was summoned to appear with several hundred others to have his papers "examined"—he never got them back. Instead, he was sent to Gurs, a camp in the South of France where "12,000 hostages" were being held. Because he was a doctor, the camp's administration put him in charge of one of the facility' s 30 blocks, with each block containing 25 barracks so dirty—handsome young Alfred later would claim—that "an Iowa farmer would refuse to drive his hogs in them."

Sanitary and general health conditions in the camp continually worsened. During the winter of 1940-41 more than 1,000 internees were said to have perished from starvation and the cold. According to a reporter's account, "an epidemic of disease started in the camp and was never stopped." Alfred's daily ration consisted of three slices of bread and a bowl of Spanish pea soup—food one could eat immediately or stretch over three meals, for that was all each prisoner received. "The water simply gave out during the winter," Alfred recalled, "and not a drop was allowed for washing. No soap was to be found." To administer hypodermic injections, he had to climb onto the roof of the barracks to gather snow and melt it "in order to obtain enough water for treatment." Women and men were separated, and over-crowding became such a problem that "it was impossible to keep down disease."

After almost a year of somehow surviving in the camp, some "influential friends" of Alfred's were able to secure his release, and he was put on a freighter headed for northern France carrying 150 men in one room and 150 women in another. In route he delivered two babies in the women' s quarters, but the throng of women hindered his work, with "all of them trying to help and all of them getting in [the] way." Once at his destination, however, Alfred found camps in northern France to be "much better than those in southern France" and that the "French officials in charge of the camps were as kind as possible to their hostages." Understandably, though, the refugees struggled to do everything possible to better their miserable lot.

Various relief efforts in France attempted to assist as many of the displaced as possible—a struggle complicated by the fluid political situation which reigned in both the German-occupied northern and the marginally autonomous southern parts of the country. Middle-aged Kaethe Aschkenes, a Viennese Jewish socialist who later would spend nine months at Scattergood, was among those in the South of France in summer 1940 who scrambled for any available escape route. In the process of fulfilling the seemingly endless paperwork necessary not only for an American visa to enter the U.S., but also for French, Spanish and/or Portuguese transit or exit visas, she had ample opportunity to visit Marseille's Quaker refugee-services office. Her subsequent report shed much light on the overwhelmed office as it tried to assist pitiable individuals who otherwise had little or no hope of survival.

Right away in her account Kaethe emphasized that there were not only the "thousands and thousands" of refugees from "the various countries of the north and east of France, those victims of Hitler's invasions," but "first of all the unfortunate Spanish people who have come in large numbers directly from the war zone." The sympathetic social worker noted: "many of these poor cripples are without arms or are supported by crutches or are blind." She observed them in summer, but asked herself uneasily "how could they survive the winter and be re-adapted to a normal life? Every passerby is affected by these dreadful pictures of the consequences of the war [and for example] the Spanish women with their children who fled with their husbands when total collapse came in Spain. They all are so indigent, no clothes, no shoes—even their espadrilles are in shreds. [And there was] hunger and resignation...expressed in their eyes." In response, Kaethe wrote, Friends imported flour, canned milk, lard and other "essential foodstuffs." They also installed a kitchen in a barn, but there was not room enough for serving 300-400 individuals concurrently, "so it [was] done in three shifts." She stated that from 11:30 to two o'clock every midday and from 5:30 to seven o'clock in the evening, "one [recognized] the location of the dining hall by the crowds of people waiting for food." She noted that Quaker volunteers had established workshops for repairing shoes, garments and underclothes; the refugees also altered old dresses and coats for each other.

Friends operated about 75 "children's colonies in the whole of France," where young people from age five to 14 and "of all nations and all religions are boarded." In the Quakers' hectic Marseille office Kaethe saw exhibited "wonderful needlework, puppet-shows, designs to show how the children are occupied." In the next breath, however, she complained that the prospect of getting the children away from danger was much less promising: "The great difficulty was to get the boat. Every week there was another promise, but the phantom ship did not arrive. The poor children dreamed meanwhile of a wonderful journey, of butter, milk and enough bread. After months of waiting, the ship arrived."

Friends offered women with children a separate hostel in a former Swedish rest home for sailors which came fully furnished—a fact which made the Quakers "especially glad." American doctors ran the center and they provided about 60 persons with accommodation for up to one month, during which time they intended that the women find other, more long-term shelter. Kaethe thought that "most of these women with children came from the concentration camps in France" and that the invitations to a consulate which they had in hand inspired "again self-confidence and hope."

To better convey the atmosphere of the center, she offered a "tour":

Let us look in upon the office work of the Friends in Marseille. In the waiting room, a big hall, there are never enough chairs for the applicants. There is, for instance, a family with three children. Since 1938 they have been in Paris. When the war broke out, the father became a soldier in the French Foreign Legion. He is now somewhere in Africa. The oldest boy, only nine years old, is the interpreter for his mother. She tries to explain that they need a home. Fortunately there are several members of the office who understand German. The case worker gives them some addresses. The next is a refugee from Alsace Lorraine. He is only fifty years old but seems to be much older. Two of his sons are prisoners in Germany; one died in battle some months ago. This man couldn't bear the terror and fled to unoccupied France hoping to find a job. The lady at the desk keeps the newspapers for him and marks the advertisements which may be of interest to him. Two sunburned young women are waiting for the case worker who takes care of those from the concentration camps. These two have already their United States visas but not the transit visas for Spain and Portugal. The camp office has only allowed two weeks for the formalities but this was not sufficient at all, and they are obliged to return to the camp. Time passes quickly. It is getting late; there are still many people waiting and the new clients can only have appointments for the next day or even the day after that. The cases are varied—every one is a cry of distress and the Quakers make all efforts to bring help.

Kaethe—who after the war's end migrated to Israel—had more luck than the two sunburned young women: she eventually succeeded in jumping through the myriad hoops put in place by the U.S. State Department to effectively throttle immigration to the United States to a mere fraction of all those hoping to flee beyond Hitler's reach. In time she, too, sailed for America. It seems that before departing from overrun Marseille, however, she became acquainted with a lass much less lucky than herself, for in autumn 1941 a translation of the melancholy girl's letter to her appeared in the monthly

Scattergood Hostel newsletter:

Dear Miss K: June 27th, 1941

Soon three months will have passed since you started to write your letter. You wrote it on a steamer that would take you to a world where—I at least hope and wish—you will not know the sufferings which will be our fate, our calamity still for a long, long time. It will be August when you get this letter. Such a distance is a great affliction, but I am saying to myself that even the widest distances cannot separate two beings united by a deep friendship and a faithful mutual thought. There are harder blows than material separation, namely to live closely with another and yet be separated by abysses of bad will and misunderstanding.

I never before received a letter written on a ship. Your letter gave me the impression of a wonderful thing coming out of a fairy story or of a fancied report of unusual adventures. It was spiced by sunlight, by sea air and, above all, by freedom, by the freedom which lives beyond the chains by which we are strangled. And then I was happy to read on the last page that you are finally arrived there. In my soul I felt that the high tension left me at the idea that from now my thoughts could wander to you as to somebody who had reached the port with the tranquil waters for which human beings long. Old Europe, tender and sympathizing to those who were loving grace more than force, dreams more than the material, tenderness more than cold reason, art and beauty more than profits—this Europe is dead, dead for she has been killed. Certainly there is one consolation for hearts too tormented: the smallest fatherland, the native house, the surrounding fields which human will could not change—God be praised! And this is a refuge for the too dark days, when one is sighing inwardly because the burden is too heavy.

Oh, that I cannot enclose in this letter all you loved. If there should be needed only my good will, it would be done suddenly. When this letter will be read in America, certainly one will say: not everything is so sad in poor France that one couldn't love something. Well, without any doubt this is true. One can love it with such a force that one never forgets its charm. Above all: never forget the little lonely French girl who writes to you.

Perhaps the plight of children during the chaos which spilled over Europe during Hitler's 12-year reign remains to this day one of the most tragic of the too-numerous pathetic aspects of the Holocaust. Hundreds of thousands of them perished in internment, in transit or in the gas chambers of Nazi death camps—where they thereafter were rendered into mere ashes. Already during the rule of the Third Reich, however, at least some individuals took an interest in the welfare of the young—of the following generation.

The Shumaker family of France witnessed its share of the calamities taking place all around them. With a multitude of other desperate refugees, Jack and Mariette and their young daughter Monique (age 6) made their way to Marseille, where they eventually found the Quakers. Unlike so many others, though, they were able to find a way not only to help themselves but to actively assist others in need; they chaperoned the fourth convoy of children which AFSC sponsored to leave Europe for the still-peaceful United States.

Of their experiences Mariette later would write at length, testifying that "amidst the dreadfulness and the distress of foreign refugees in the European concentration camps, there is from time to time a glimpse of hope." She supported this claim by referring to the evacuation of helpless children "of all origins and all nationalities" who through good fortune "have found again in this country the cheerfulness of life, and the quietness of a home with a family." The convoy which they accompanied consisted of 54 youngsters, of whom 22 were Spanish children "driven away by the revolution with their whole family. Most of them lost their fathers or brothers in the civil war. The mother and the children escaped from one town to another under the bombs and finally reached France, where they were interned in camps."

According to her, AFSC "succeeded in liberating a great many of them who were sent to homes and colonies." As an example she told of "family L. composed of Felipe, Julian, Rogelia and Sarita fled from Valencia, where their father was killed by a bomb, with their mother and two of her sisters." While the oldest son continued to fight against Franco's army, the rest of the family drifted to the colony of Los Caillols, outside of Marseille. Three members of the family found lodging with the Shumakers and two stayed with the mother, who was a cook. Mariette had read "the farewell letter addressed by the eldest brother to the children leaving for America: it was a masterpiece of pathetic and sensitive feeling." In it he encouraged his brothers and sister to "be proud and strong and good; they should never forget that their father died for freedom and the love of democracy."

On 14 May 1941 the entourage left Marseille aboard the *Marechal Lyautey*, which took them as far as Casablanca. As they settled into their temporary home the children impressed Mariette with their selflessness: "The girls unpacked first their own things and then went to the boys' cabins, where their brothers were, and put away their clothing. We appreciated the kind way the girls took care of the boys, even those who had no brothers, sewed and mended for others." This nobility seemed even more extraordinary, given that the children were all between the ages of 7 and 14.

61

Although the first day in transit was "rather bad," Mariette reported that "the second morning was a glorious spring day, with the sky as blue as the Mediterranean. The ship was sailing along the Spanish shore, and our little Spaniards were shouting with joy. For three days and a part of the evening the Spaniards lay along the deck's guard-rail watching their country, which they had left years ago and were seeing for the last time."

The trip to Casablanca required eight days. To break the monotony, not to mention to use the seemingly endless time to profitable end, the travelers "established a schedule: games alternated with English lessons and short lectures on subjects in which they were interested." Unfortunately "food was rather poor, but the Friends Service Committee, always provident, gave us chocolate, biscuits, dry milk and sardines."

These industrious little castaways impressed not only their chaperons, but other passengers aboard the lumbering ship, too. As proof of the children's enviable ability to cope in a most trying situation, Mariette related that "after a few days our children were the most popular on board and passengers of every class came to visit them. We were greatly helped by a French boy scout; he came every day and taught them French songs and games. Finally the whole convoy had a complete repertory of songs and they could perform like professional actors. The day before we landed in Casablanca, we had a little ceremony when they gave the Captain of the ship a beautiful drawing made by one of our little talented boys."

On 21 May the convoy arrived in the African port, tense and teeming with Europeans desperate to leave for points beyond—for *any* point not in the direction of Berlin. The Shumakers had to content themselves with an 18-day stay in Casablanca, "but the time seemed short [for there] were plenty of walks, the beach was near, people came to see them and brought candies and clothing." For a change "food was abundant"—perhaps too much so, however, as "almost all the children suffered a little indigestion."

On 7 June the group again sailed on, this time aboard the *Serpa Pinto*, a Portuguese vessel where the relatively luxurious conditions pleased them immensely. For Mariette, "one of the most strong impressions was the outcry of the children when they saw the white bread and the butter on the table. The meal times were one of the best moments of the day, because the children were allowed by special favor to eat in the second class dining-room." Anticipating her readers' possible skepticism with this rosy picture, she intentionally blemished the mostly positive portrait she had painted, adding: "Don't think they were always nice little lambs," for "we had more than once to scold them."

Still, the voyage passed mostly pleasantly, till eight days later the ship docked in Bermuda, "a fairy dreamland. A gorgeous sunset made the scene most beautiful, and the children would not go to bed that night." Early the next morning delegates from the Bermuda Women's Auxiliary came on board, looked at the children, noted their size and in two hours returned with "lots of clothes, underwear, shoes and socks." Then they invited the little exiles to a party at the summer house of the island's governor: "Very poorly dressed in their old European clothes [the children] worried about their costumes for the party. [By noon, though, they were] all dressed up; the girls had ribbons in their hair, the boys white collars. They were like foals pawing."

The governor's private launch came for his honored guests at three o'clock that afternoon, then shuttled them to the official residence where "all the Bermudian authorities were present and ten Sea Scouts who were in charge of games." The hosts distributed toys and books, then served the little ones ice cream, cake and fruit juice—delectables which most of the children savored for the first time in several years. So thoroughly partied were they that "the children came home half dead, and the ship's doctor wondered how many of them would be sick the next day." One of the boys excused their less than fit state, explaining "it is the first time since we left our parents that we were so spoiled." One dutiful girl, however, countered guiltily, "I can't enjoy these good things because I think of my poor mother starving in camp."

The next day found the colonial secretary's wife hosting a party for "the smallest ones" in the convoy. Afterwards they returned to the ship "once more with toys, candies and cake." The generosity, however, didn't end there, for "the whole day long people came on board and brought clothes and toys." The British military commander's wife came, noticed the pathetic state of the children's shoes, disappeared and half an hour later reappeared with 18 pairs of new ones. In appreciation of this outpouring of support, the children "sang and danced for them; the Spanish girls were very graceful dancers." Later the governor's wife came and watched a dance performance.

Like the agreeable sojourn in Africa, however, the convoy's stay on the idyllic Caribbean island also came to an end. "At last" Mariette lamented, "the heart full of regret, we left Bermuda. The departure was a real climax. All the authorities came on the pier and bade us good-bye. The Sea Scouts sang together French and English songs and slowly the ship left this hospitable shore." Two days later, on 28 June, the celebrated party of hopeful children and their chaperons sailed past Staten Island. Mariette later recalled that: "there was a general victory cry when the children saw the skyscrapers and the Statue of Liberty. The excitement was so great that eighteen of them had temperature and instead of landing had to go for several days to Ellis Island. The others, soon followed by these, went for a few days to a colony in the Bronx, New York. After which each of them went to a family who will take care of them and where they will know again the sweetness of life."

The majority of Scattergood's guests fled Nazi-held lands before open warfare could disturb their lives even more than creeping social stigmatization and later persecution already had. Records indicate, however, that half a dozen actually witnessed armed conflict—one of that number being Magdalene Salmon of Warsaw. She chose to remain in her hometown on the Vistula even while the *Wehrmacht* pounded the Polish capital to dusty rubble during the Poles' valorous but vain attempt to stave off the on-coming German colossus, against which they simply lacked serious firepower.

A social worker in the municipal office of family services, Magdalene used her post to keep abreast of developments—as far as the city government had an inkling of what was happening, given that the situation changed so quickly, without warning and in a vacuum created by the crippling lack of functioning infrastructure. Still, she knew too well the basic sequence of events following the Nazi invasion of Poland on 1 September 1939.

Already on 4 September, as German troops approached Warsaw, the utterly defeated Polish military command decided to capitulate, then withdrew in the direction of Lublin. Magdalene later recounted that "contrary to this decision the civil government of Warsaw decided to defend the town and created the Committee of Warsaw Defense." Lingering soldiers and "workers' battalions formed by civilians" under the command of Mayor Starzynski were to protect the besieged city—a noble if quixotic assignment. Magdalene held: "This decision to defend Warsaw expressed the will of the population. In the besieged city the people didn't know that on the 17th of September the Polish government had left Poland, that the Russian army had occupied the east part of Polish territory and that all Poland was a victim of aggression. On the contrary the people hoped that the English and French armies would attempt to invade Germany. In the month of September nobody would say that the bombardment would be too strong to stand, but despair after the surrender was universal."

Pointing out that the Germans "regularly" bombed Warsaw's industrial quarter, Magdalene conceded that "the civil defense was not well prepared...Before the war there were many orders in the matters of the gas defense. In each apartment one room was especially compact against gas, but we forgot that with the first bombardment all the windows would be broken. We had not enough wells. In the first several days the bombardments had destroyed the water system and the city was without water. This increased the danger of fire in the time when the city burned. All cars were mobilized for the army and with no cars available it was impossible to transport food from the train stations and storage houses and to distribute it among the people."
This city employee openly admitted that to worsen matters, "the staff of administration was not well instructed. All the preparation was a military secret. The directors told us that at the proper time the right men would come

and give explanations, but in the dangerous days of bombardment nobody gave the instruction, because the municipal staff was incomplete as a result of bombardment and panic. We had not had experience with modern war at this time."

The mother of an infant daughter, Magdalene lived in a neighborhood where the inhabitants "were those who had lived there before the war. They lived in small workers' houses without cellars, and were taking refuge in the big cellars of factories and churches. In calm hours they could go home to change their clothes, to sleep and to eat. Besides these people in the cellars were those who had come to Warsaw from other bombarded Polish towns and those who were coming from destroyed or burned houses. They had nothing: no clothes, no money, no food.

In Magdalene's district, most people found housing in "four big shelters. Each of these created its own organization." One shelter consisted of a factory shelter containing several thousand people, where "the workers organized the life and gave the food from their cooperative. Each person who came had to obey the very strict discipline, to wash, to cook and to clean. The second shelter, as big as the other, was under the church. Chairman of this place was an old hunchbacked monk. Each family had its place on the floor. The old monk, going from one family to another, organized public prayers. In the third immense factory shelter were many refugees. The people there were very tired, unprovided for, frightened and inert. The fourth shelter was under the big slum inhabited by the criminals of the city. Before the war several policemen stayed there day and night. Now one young woman was sufficient to organize this shelter. On the 20th of September the slum was bombed and burned, and most of these people were killed. This was autumn and in the fields near Warsaw were the vegetables, but each man who was seen in the field was shot down by the German planes and machine guns. Only the people of the slum had the courage to go into the fields." Magdalene went on to describe how "Warsaw was bombed now by plane, now by artillery, and during the last several days by both planes and artillery. This was hell on earth. Those people who did not die during the first hours of the bombardment were transported from the shelter to the hospitals. From day to day were fewer hospitals remaining undestroyed. From day to day the transport through the bombed streets became more difficult. People were trapped under the ruins. The wounded lay one next to another on the beds and on the floor. The wounds were very painful; often the bones were crushed, and the wounds were dirty with blood and soil. The doctor could do nothing without water and light, so the victims died without help."

It was winter when Magdalene took her little Krystine, left her work and made her way to Russia, which she then crossed on the Trans-Siberian Railroad enroute to America. In the weeks before she left Poland, however, she watched as "Germans governed the town and with them came hunger and misery. In Warsaw there was no coal; all the windows had broken panes. In the night began to assemble outside my office the people asking for help. We gave them the money for one kilo of bread a month. To receive this amount of bread hundreds of people would stand for hours in the cold and rain. And this—to see the people starve—was the worst of all."

Magdalene Salmon was not the only Polish guest at Scattergood to see firsthand the ravages of war. Unlike Salmon, however, Stanislav Braun was not living in Warsaw at the time of the invasion and subsequent destruction of the Polish capital, as he had been living in Paris since his graduation from what Americans would call "high school." Once his native Poland had been attacked, though, he enlisted in a Polish division of the French army and moved to the French front, on the western edge of the Nazis' intimidating Reich. Said a reporter who retold Stanislav's story: "He and his fellow Polish soldiers were in military service to kill Germans, to avenge the honor of Poland." This angry young father, however, would be disappointed.

"The first day we were up at the front" Stanislav later recalled, "we took our guns and started shooting at the Germans. Then the French hurried to us with their protests. 'Please, please do not shoot at the Germans...If you do, the Germans will shoot back!' [Which they did, killing four French soldiers.] After that the Polish soldiers were very unpopular with the French."

Stanislav then began to view French military operations with growing suspicion and asked his "hosts" why the Maginot Line contained a "gap" where they "happened to be stationed." The French explained it had been left there "so that residents of the Saar would not be offended and thereby encouraged to vote to go back to Germany." The reporter noted in parentheses: "They were not offended but voted to go over to Germany anyway."

When the Germans later burst into Belgium in a spearheaded action centered at that very gap in the Maginot Line, Stanislav helped the French "try to stem the attacks with mule-drawn equipment, inadequate to hit the low-flying German planes." Not surprisingly, the French front soon collapsed.

Stanislav fled first to Paris. Learning that his wife Sonia and their six-year-old son André had preceded him to the South of France, he pushed on through the chaotic French countryside until he reached them there. Officially, German demands issued at the time of the Nazi-dictated armistice stipulated that all foreigners who had fought with the French were to be placed in concentration camps. The clever Pole, however, found a friend—an officer in the French army—who drafted a fictitious certificate claiming that Stanislav was "in the process of being demobilized." As foreign-born soldiers could not be interned until they had been demobilized, the endangered Stanislav thus possessed technical immunity. Amazingly, the puzzled French officials who stopped Stanislav for questioning honored the order, allowing the trained economist-statistician to reach the still-unoccupied South, where he eventually secured American visas for himself and his family.

It was not easy for families to flee the Nazi menace. Individuals could be more flexible in exploring or selecting possible options and had fewer bureaucratic nightmares to suffer than did couples trying to arrange complete sets of endless forms, certificates, tax receipts, affidavits, visas and —finally—tickets for passage. Also, flight for one cost much less than flight in quantity. At the same time, however, spouses and perhaps children, too, could provide not only comfort but on-going motivation to endure the often heartbreaking, defeating tribulation of trying to arrange one's own survival.

The impetus to emigrate from the Third Reich arose within the first days of the ascendance of the Nazis in March 1933. Over time and with the expansion of anti-Jewish decrees aimed at both expelling the Jews from Greater Germany and milking them of most of their wealth in the process, the push to escape increasing peril became much more urgent. Still, maybe a majority of those threatened rationalized that—being a "civilized" land—Germany was their rightful home and they could count on a liveable future there. For such people, only after the devastating *Kristallnachtpogrom* of 9-10 November 1938 would it become unmistakably clear that their hopes for a return to saner days were illusionary and that the need to leave was real.

Louis and Grete Rosenzweig of Kassel were two of the many German Jews caught unawares by the political landscape's rapid deterioration under Adolf Hitler as "changes which nobody ever had anticipated came about." As short, spritely Grete later would explain, they had always considered themselves "German citizens in the first place, Jews by religion." She maintained that even though there "had always been a slight anti-semitism in certain circles, it had not been a general feeling or action towards an individual Jew." She further noted: "We had just as many close non-Jewish friends [as] Jewish ones." Herself a trained goldsmith and master needleworker, she had been the only Jewish student in her class and her husband had been the vice-director of a steel plant, as well as the president of "local citizens' organizations in the city besides having received medals for war and peace activities."

Initially the shift of political winds in Germany was barely perceptible and—according to Grete—was "only felt as a bad undercurrent creating uneasiness among the Jews and forcing Gentiles into organizations and actions." Eventually, however, the Nazis' presence became pervasive. The first "upsetting sight" Grete caught of the frightful new social order came when she met daughter Irmgard's teacher in full Nazi uniform—and that "at a time when not all people were yet forced into uniform and organizations." Then, as it became increasingly "difficult for a Jewish boy to attend school and not be able to associate with his classmates," the Rosenzweigs decided to send their older child, Ernst, to a Swiss boarding school. Later, Ernst went to England to attend a Jewish agricultural school for boys "who were going to emigrate"—but then was interned as an "enemy alien." Meanwhile, Louis' firm soon dismissed him due to "race"—an act which Grete saw as ironic, given that a Jew had founded it. Tall, stately-looking Louis subsequently opened his own tax-and-auditing consulting office. This whole time "life for a Jew got harder and tenser by the day. Jews in small country communities felt the pressure of the Hitler system sooner and harder [and for them] it began very early to be unbearable... Jews looked for chances to leave Germany where they were not wanted and finally were in danger."

As the emigrés needed financial advice, Louis' business flourished. He quickly became knowledgeable with the plethora of new anti-Semitic regulations and even earned the title "currency lawyer" under the new legal system. As his wife noted, he was "the only one in the whole area, officially named to help only Jews. It was a dangerous job," as every morning he had to report to the Gestapo and "he never knew if he would be able to come home again or would be sent to prison." For that reason his suitcase was "always packed." Grete appreciated her husband's tenuous status because of his being in a "leading position among the Jews": as chairman of the Jewish orphanage and president of the congregation, he was in "a very exposed situation."

The first drastic development to occur in Kassel involved the Jewish orphanage. On 6 November 1938 Nazi supporters attacked the building and broke the windows; by the time they had their fill of destruction, "much damage was done." They confiscated the wrecked structure anyway, and the traumatized children had to find shelter in private homes or in "primitive quarters" hastily outfitted in the Jewish grade school. Until the time that the children were provided with opportunities to emigrate, the Rosenzweigs offered accommodation to a "very nice, little boy" in their home.

Soon after the destruction of the orphanage, the Rosenzweigs received a phone call in the night with the message: "The temple is burning!" Leaving the adolescent Irmgard in the charge of her maternal grandmother, Louis and Grete rushed to the city center. There they came across "an overwhelming sight: the synagogue in flame, a huge fire outside on mainstreet, all the books from the temple...carried outside and thrown into the flames and burnt up." As they had no chance to intervene nor to rescue anything, they stood aside—"terrified." Grete said that they were "fortunate that the Nazis did not pay any attention to us and that we got home safely." The next time, however, they would not escape Nazi thuggery so unscathed.

As Grete walked through the park across the street from the Rosenzweig residence on her way home at dusk in the late afternoon of 9 November, she saw obscure shadows "of human beings jumping into the bushes" as she approached. The incident gave her such an "eerie feeling" that she went inside and "watched all evening from a dark window, but seemingly all had calmed down." The Rosenzweigs retired to bed, but—as she well would remember— "it was not long that we heard a terrible pounding on the entrance door —crash—it gave way and a horde of Nazis came tramping up the stairs and rang our door bell. It was the night which no German Jew will forget."

The intruders came to haul the entire family to the police station, including Grete's elderly mother: "Grandmother Hedwig[11] was sick in bed. No excuse! She had to go." Then, when the Nazis demanded the house keys from Grete, the scene turned ugly: she answered "How did you get in?" and for her daring insubordination they began "beating down" on her.

Even in this shaken state, however, the intelligent woman considered possible troubles. Knowing that Louis possessed arms and some ammunition "left from his service with the citizens' guard which he had not turned in," Grete slipped away, put the ammunition into her pocket and hid the firearms "way back in the linen closet." Then—with Louis *sans* dentures and Grandmother's silk slip draped over Irmgard's arm—they rode in a truck to the busy Kassel police headquarters, where "after waiting and having been questioned the men were kept, the women and children dismissed." After the formalities, Grete admitted Grandmother to the Catholic hospital where "her doctor sent his patients." Then Grete took Irmgard to some friends' house where she thought "no man was home." To her surprise "one of the sons opened the door." As she assumed "that meant the Nazis would come to that house too to get the boy," she decided to keep Irmgard with her. In any event "the boy had enough warning that he could escape and go into hiding."

Grete realized that "the next step was to get rid of the ammunition. What could I do?" As there was a "quiet lake way up in the forest" where "no one would watch us," she took Irmgard and "started out on [a] long hike from downtown through the suburbs—ever so often passing Nazis leading Jews [to police headquarters]—up the mountain into the woods." When they reached the lake, Grete dumped the whole package into the water. Then, the two made their way to the house of Louis' mother.

By the time Louis' office was to open the next morning "women and more women came who wanted help." Grete discovered that "ALL the Jewish men had been taken away including the rabbi." Stating that she could "tell for hours about all the happenings during these days of horror," Grete mentioned as representative that in the Rosenzweig home "most of the windows, all the mirrors and lamps were broken, the floor soiled, furniture ruined [and] the little bird which we loved, was gone."

On that first night of what would be a two-day nationwide pogrom, Grete learned that Louis had landed in army barracks, where she managed to have his dentures delivered. As they waited for his return she and Irmgard "stayed together day and night," only to find that the tormented Jewish men had been sent to concentration camps. Unexpectedly, however, Grete later could say that "in all those bad times...a good fate was with us," for she found a way to ensure Louis' return. Louis' doctor—"despite being a Catholic"—used his influence to convince the Nazis that "deportation would be fatal" due to a previous condition described as "spontaneous pneumothorax." Upon his release Louis returned to Kassel, where he remained bedfast for the next few weeks. Grete later lamented that although they did not own their home, they had to restore it at their expense and "after all the repairs were done we were forced to move." She noted: "from then on we had to move and move."

After the minutely planned and cynically orchestrated "Night of Broken Glass" pogrom, the only contemplatable course of action for the Rosenzweigs consisted of leaving Germany as fast as haste flung at rigorous bureaucracy would allow. Like them, the Seligmann family of Heidelberg also concluded that the only option left for them was to abandon the entire locus of their lives and begin again abroad. This decision could not have been easy, for like the beleaguered couple in Kassel, Sigmund and Friedel Seligmann were both about 50 years old and had two children—Helmut (age 9) and Ilse (5). Also like their fellow dispossessed to the north, they would find the process of arranging leaving Hitler's Germany discouraging and exhausting—an emotional as well as financial gauntlet. Although they already had explored several emigration possibilities and had resigned themselves to remaining in the increasingly hostile Third Reich, for the Seligmanns "with the events of November, the slow and merciless death of existence [as they had known it] came to a sudden and final end."

As early as 1937 the brown-haired, erect-standing Sigmund realized that "the fact that my wife Friedel...was of 'Aryan' descent and both children...were raised Christian didn't change the increasingly critical situation. On top of that, the children were at the age where they had to suffer from the regression of the system in and outside of school." Being by heritage a Jew and by profession a seller of chemical fertilizers as well as a self-employed horticultural consultant, with the implementation of a general anti-Jewish boycott Sigmund lost more and more customers, to the point that he had to declare 1937 a *Verlustjahr*—a "year of losses." As his business had been a thriving one—serving farmers and gardeners, retailers and co-ops, municipal, city and state agencies in a 50-kilometer radius of Heidelberg—this strangulation of the family's livelihood had devastating effects.

As of spring 1938, then, the Seligmanns sought to relocate. "All attempts to enter another European country failed" Sigmund later recalled, which he owed was due to "my occupation [being] neither important nor my wealth great enough to open a door somewhere." Thus, "there was nothing else left but to think about [moving] overseas." Sigmund's sister had migrated to Australia, so for a while he and Friedel considered joining her—until they received the reply that "we were no longer young enough and we didn't have enough children!" So next they turned their attention to America, where the husband of Friedel's cousin signed a crucial affidavit of support. Unfortunately it was a non-transferable one, which would have meant that Sigmund would have had to leave his family behind—understandably, at first an unacceptable option.

Separating the family remained unacceptable, that is, until the pogrom of November 1938. The Seligmanns were not spared a house search and "the destruction and confiscation of the apartment by the SS," nor Sigmund the "subsequent abduction to Dachau," where he languished for five weeks as "prisoner #21,832"—complete with standard-issue, gray-and-white-striped pajamas. He later avoided disclosing the details of his life there, other than tersely asserting that "the name 'Dachau' alone suffices to evoke the treatment—or better, the mistreatment—to which I and the other internees were exposed."

Happily, Friedel managed to arrange Sigmund's release. What should have been a joyous return home, however, was dampened by the ugly realization that "the family of a former Dachauer [inmate] could not remain in the Franz Knauffstraße housing estate of the Associated Union of Employees, where we once bought the right to live with the help of matching public-aid monies." Although they did so voluntarily, the Seligmanns forfeited their investment and abandoned their single-family apartment, moving instead to the Brückenstraße quarters of a certain Herr Leiser, the non-aryan brother-in-law of the place's proprietor. The Seligmanns did not know that the two children and their mother (who as an "Aryan" easily could have divorced her husband and thus avoided all difficulties)[12] would reside in such cramped conditions until their own departure from Germany almost two years later.

"After the return in December" Sigmund acknowledged, "only the liquidation of my firm remained," a task which promised to impoverish the company's cash-strapped accounts. He sold the stock at clearance prices to a concern in Worms—which in turn simply absorbed his customers without compensation. Friedel already had sold the company car at a bearable loss during his incarceration in Bavaria's infamous concentration camp; these additional forfeitures, however, along with other "expenses and obligations"—such as circa 2,000 Marks in the form of a *Judenabgabe* (Jew tax)—exhausted the family's finances.

After realizing the Nazis' intentions, Sigmund understood that he had to undertake all possible actions until he could find an exit from the intensifying Hitlerite Hell. Thus, despite all discouraging failures, he pressed on with efforts to flee Germany until, finally, way opened. A local pastor by the name

71

of Maas, in conjunction with Robert Balderston—a visiting American Quaker and the husband of a woman who later would serve as director of a refugee hostel in some obscure province called "Iowa"—came to his aid.[13] The pair granted the grateful agronomist a decisive favor: they vouched for his character, i.e., that he was a worthy and fully acceptable candidate for life in America.

Only then did the American consulate in Stuttgart issue Sigmund a visa. The hitch? It provided entry for him *only*. "It was a heavy shock to have to come home with the decision that although I provisionally could emigrate alone, the family had to stay in Heidelberg despite the state of war." Sigmund somberly added: "Through this separation and its accompanying uncertainty over fate and complications—which I saw connected for the first time in the USA—the persecutions had an effect across time and space."

As Sigmund soon learned, with the granting of a visa his work had just begun. The necessary "last transactions" involved tremendous expenditures, such as requisite exit taxes to be paid at the *Landesfinanzamt* in order to receive permission to take property with him. In addition he had to post bonds assuring his solvency for possible debts at the local Heidelberg *Finanzamt*—where officials found "reason" for levying a tax of again circa 2,000 Marks. Following the payment of all compulsory taxes and fees Sigmund still had to trek to Karlsruhe, Stuttgart and Berlin in order to retrieve corresponding documents from the Imperial Union of Jews or similar social-service offices—not to mention the tickets for passage aboard the Dutch steamer *Volendam*. During a visit to the Imperial Insurance Institute of Employees, the harried man discovered that his claims for compensation for previously made self-employment insurance payments were "resultless"—as were those regarding some life insurance policies for him, his wife and their family. So arbitrary and exorbitant were the costs involved with leaving Nazi Germany that by the time he actually reached Rotterdam in February 1940 for the long-awaited voyage, Sigmund had the equivalent of 10 Marks "in the pocket."

Sigmund safely reached America, but what of the rest of the family?[14] His wife and children remained behind, suffering a less-than-choice living arrangement and the barest of budgets, given that their husband and father had been able to leave very little money with them. They were to survive until their own trip across the Atlantic through the support of relatives, friends and Pastor Maas of Heidelberg's 14th-century Heilige Geist Kirche.

Away from harm in the United States, Sigmund struggled to secure his remaining family's passage as soon as possible. Given the handicap of his age and rather specialized training, he thought himself lucky to locate work on a farm in Maryland where he worked for room, board and $10 "pocket money" per month. This meager situation lasted until spring 1941, when he moved to Iowa to take a considerably better position at Shenandoah's Earl

May Nursery at the promising wage of 30-cents an hour—or, "sometimes at a weekly salary of $17.50." At that rate, however, such minimal income made it impossible for him to save any adequate amounts to apply toward the $950 tickets necessary to—in effect—ransom his family.

Meanwhile in Germany, Friedel did not waste any time before chipping away at the massive obstacles blocking her joining her husband in the New World. Mimicking Sigmund's earlier carrousel of errand-running to Karlsruhe, Stuttgart and Berlin, she organized all the respective details for herself and the two children till they, too, were set to leave. They departed on August 1941, first via Berlin to the Spanish border in a sealed Gestapo-escorted passenger train, then to Lisbon, where with minimal belongings they set sail for New York aboard the Portuguese-registered *Mousinho*. Had it not been for a squirreled-away Swiss bank account which Sigmund tapped for the fare or for the Maryland farmer and his relatives who signed affidavits of support, Friedel, Helmut and Ilse would not have had occasion to suffer the ship's "primitive conditions" in exchange for the chance to survive.

Whether they departed from Rotterdam or Lisbon, the Seligmanns—who in America altered their name to "Seaman"—enjoyed direct and relatively brief passages to the New World. Other future Scattergood guests, in contrast, did not. The Weilers, for example, were made to travel a total of 27,000 kilometers in order to end up on the Iowa prairies. As one reporter put it: "The man went out the front door, his wife and little daughter departed by the back way and they were reunited on the other side of the world."

Like almost all other German Jews, with the ascendancy of the Nazis, fair-haired Gus Weiler of Neustadt could no longer continue his profession-by-training, so the former butcher took to trading livestock—a livelihood which the regime eventually also forbade him to pursue. At that point he and his wife Rosl—both in their 30s—decided they had no future in Hitler's Reich. With the help of AFSC they were able to secure a visa, but as with the Seligmanns only for the head of the family. In this case, too, the man of the family grudgingly fled solo—on 1 May 1940, aboard the last Italian passenger ship bound for the United States. Upon landing in New York he visited his fellow-refugee brother before heading to Iowa to wait anxiously at Scattergood until his wife and their five-year-old daughter, Bertel, could join him—a reunion he was not sure ever would occur.

In the meantime, before Rosl and Bertel could follow, the war in Europe intensified, so that Rosl decided to undertake what the reporter covering their journey sensationally would proclaim made "Mr. Weiler's jaunt...a street car ride in comparison to that taken by Bertel and her mother." First, the two went to the East Prussian city of Königsberg to board a train bound for Lithuania, which had not yet fallen prey to Nazi Germany's unsatiable ap-

73

petite for *Lebensraum*. On the border, however, German officials forced them to forfeit their money, "promising it would be forwarded [and then] forced donation of small change to the Red Cross and also forfeiture of German food stamps. Thus, two-thirds of the Weiler family entered Lithuania and headed for Russia with their passports and tickets and no money."

Initially, the Russians refused Rosl and Bertel admittance when a soldier discovered that the routes outlined in their passports did not jibe with that of their tickets. After a night "in a bare room without food or water," however, the next morning the two were granted permission to proceed to Moscow. There, upon a guarantee by AFSC that the German government would be repaid, the Moscow consulate of the German foreign office provided Rosl with money—"after three days of red tape had delayed the journey."

For eight days and nights the solid-built, usually jolly Rosl and her curly-haired daughter rode a trans-Siberian train "bearing many refugees" and in which "everyone was sick." There they changed trains and proceeded to Pusan, in occupied Korea, where they secured a two-day passage to Japan. The duo then continued on to Seattle—a trip which required 12 more days. From the Pacific Northwest Rosl and Bertel rode a bus literally across more than half the North American continent in order to rejoin Gus—some four months after the family first had separated.

The themes of separation—due to authorities' intransigence, disruptive political events and lack of funds or luck—as well as reunion would appear and reappear among Scattergood's guest families. Some would find their way back together shortly before embarking as a unit to Iowa to recover on the tranquil prairies, some would surface while relatives waited at Scattergood for them to make it to America and still others waited at the hostel in vain—only to learn than their loved ones had been annihilated at Auschwitz. Perhaps the most dramatic of these amazing when not tragic stories involved that of the Shostals. Originally from Vienna but later of Paris and Marseille, they were seemingly always one step ahead of the Nazis.

Walter Shostal did not want to go to America[15]—and he told his visiting Aunt Meta so. He and his Hungarian-born wife Magda—or as Scattergood renamed her, "Theresa"—had left Austria in 1933 for economic reasons, given that the photo-agency which Walter shared with his brother Robert could not support the family in Vienna alone. Besides ready customers, the resettled young couple found an agreeable life in the French capital. They became fluent in the language, immersed themselves in the vibrant cultural scene and gave birth to two sons, Pierre and Claude—both French nationals.

Feeling so much at home in the City of Light, Walter did not think twice in summer 1938 before declining his visiting Aunt Meta's offer to provide the affidavit of support necessary to obtain immigration visas to the United

74

States. He dismissed out of hand that faraway country to which she and his Uncle Gustav had gone many years earlier, where they had done so well economically and which, in her opinion, was "a much better and safer place to live than Europe." Facing the elderly, "somewhat stout, rather stern yet friendly looking woman" in the sitting room of her suite in the Hotel George V, Walter was more impressed with the "quiet elegance" of her accommodations than with her proposal. He understood the concerned woman and her husband had returned to "find out how their respective families were faring in all that turbulence, [given that] Hitler had marched his troops into the Rhineland in violation of the terms of the Versailles peace treaty; he had gobbled up Austria, threatened to eliminate Jewish life from German lands as well as maybe all of Europe, and he made all sorts of noises threatening his neighbors."

Despite the various reasons why Aunt Meta might worry for his safety, however, Walter did not feel "personally threatened." He did acknowledge: "Yes, I had lost my nationality: a pusillanimous French government did not recognize any longer my Austrian passport, so as not to displease the German dictator." Instead it issued him "a French piece of paper" which specified his nationality as *Exautrichien*—"former Austrian." The government in Berlin would have supplied him with a German passport and stamped a big "J" in it, which would have identified him as a Jew—"a second class citizen, but I did not like that." Although he had become in effect stateless, he felt content, thinking, "I could travel nonetheless."

Walter did have valid reasons to feel secure in his adopted hometown on the Seine. The government of the French Third Republic—in contrast to that of the German Third Reich—had granted him permanent residency and even the *carte de commercant* which carried the right to exercise a profession and was "so difficult to obtain." Moreover and according to him most important, Walter "loved France, the French language and...French literature." He declared that "if war came, I would take my chance with the French people, as I had confidence in the French army. They had held back *less Boches* [a hateful French term for 'the Germans'] once before" he reasoned. As fate would have it, he soon got his chance.

War erupted a year after Aunt Meta's memorable visit, but initially it seemed to be *une drôle de guerre*—the "phoney war." Walter complained that "France did nothing while the Germans annihilated Poland and divided it up with its new-found Russian ally." Instead, the Paris government demanded that all Germans and Austrians—including Jewish refugees—report to a large suburban football stadium in Colombe for internment, where Walter found conditions "bad." He held that the French "were just as distrustful and jittery with regard to these people as a little later after Pearl Harbor the

Americans were of their people of Japanese ancestry, and they treated them just as badly. They feared a 'fifth column' as they called it—a term taken from the recent Franco war in Spain."

The authorities "had nothing prepared and were at this moment not good at improvising." The only food available consisted of *Pâté de Foie*—liver paste—and bread. It was "very good *Pâté de Foie*" he conceded, "but if you eat nothing but that for weeks you get nauseous even at its looks." On top of the monotonous fare, the hygienic conditions were "deplorable, with four or five big drums for perhaps 10,000 men. The regular toilets were outside of the stands and not accessible. I could not bear to get near these drums and simply did without. How I could survive this without permanent damage to my health is a piece of good fortune."

After two weeks or so the authorities emptied the stadium and sent the Austrians—or "ex-Austrians," rather—to Normandy, "a night's train ride away"; Walter was not sure where the Germans were sent. "The new place was a slightly sloping meadow surrounded by barbed wire. Nothing else." His first night in this setting was "miserable. There was a slight rain." After a few days, however, the situation improved. "Cesspools were dug, a kitchen built, barracks with cots inside erected and camp life began to get organized." The men distracted themselves from the pervasive stress and boredom inherent to forced captivity with lectures and bridge games; they "played soccer and waited." A few weeks later they were informed that those with *attachés Français*—"French family relations"—could return home. Walter had such an *attaché*—his two-year-old son Pierre, a French citizen.

Under the pale of the "phoney war," Walter discovered that "Paris had changed. [For one thing] the lights had gone out for fear of aerial attacks which had not yet come. All able-bodied men were gone—all in the army manning the Maginot Line...or standing guard elsewhere." He also found that his business had "shrunk considerably," necessitating that the family live on their "small savings." Walter saw that "things were difficult both practically and morally: could I sit home and let the French fight their war as if it did not concern me? When all was over and victory won whom could I look in the eye and say 'I want to be a Frenchman?' There was only one answer: I had to enlist and be one of them." His loyalty to his adopted land, though, was to be severely tested.

Walter went "to the right place, signed a certain paper, got a receipt for that noble act and was sent home," having been told that he would be summoned in "due time." After a while he received notice that there had been "a certain change" in his enlistment: "It was not any longer simply for the armed forces. It was *á titre de la Légion étrangère*. What did that mean?" He trundled back to the place of his enlistment, where "a friendly captain explained this measure was taken in the interest of people like me," for if taken

76

prisoner by the Germans "in all likelihood they would shoot me immediately as a traitor to the *Vaterland*." If the French sent Walter and other similarly situated individuals to Africa—their reasoning went—he would if at all stand against the Italians "who in a similar case might be less ferocious." Walter thought "it sounded reasonable enough. And anyway" he figured, "I had no choice if I wanted to serve."

Furthermore, the officer in charge gave Walter the spurious explanation that "it was not really 'the' Foreign Legion" but "only *a 'titre de la Légion*"—special units for those enlisted for the duration of the war. As the wily representative of the Establishment maintained: "There would be no mix with the real Légionnaires who had to enlist for five years. The truth of the matter was...the government did not fully trust us. They feared spies, saboteurs and the 'fifth column.' They preferred to have us out of the way; we were less dangerous in Africa than on French soil."

Walter received his call to duty and left Paris on Christmas Day 1939. While he finally could satisfy his sense of obligation to France, Walter's wife saw his departure differently and later said that "it was a very sad Christmas, the first and only one in my life without a Christmas tree." The pregnant Magda expected to give birth soon and hoped that Walter would stay "until Claudie was born"—but that would be another four weeks. In the meantime the trained teacher and one-time cloister candidate had to oversee her family's business matters, a role she was able to fill as she had worked with Walter in the office. At least in his absence she did not feel "very lonely," as her mother-in-law—who already had obtained a visa for America—waited until after Claude's birth and left for the United States the following March.

In a report which she wrote once her family had reached Scattergood, Magda explained that "all our male employees joined the army but it didn't matter [as] business was very slow and I worked with a secretary and a young apprentice. I had all the advantages the Frenchwomen had whose husbands were mobilized [by which was meant the legal forgiveness of rent payments and a monthly 700-Franc government stipend]. It wasn't enough to live on, but it helped a great deal toward supporting us."

Referring to the seemingly endless time following Walter's abrupt departure, Magda said that "in all these months we sometimes had air-raid alarms and we heard the shots of the anti-aircraft guns. This was a sign that enemy airplanes were over Paris, but"—to her relief—"they never dropped any bombs." The frightened citizenry of the French capital—at least those souls remaining after so many already had left for the front or fled—could not know that so little firepower would be needed in order for the Germans to conquer the city. In the beginning, then, Magda and her family always went to the cellar "as we had orders to do." Magda said "it was very hard for the

77

children...especially for Claudie who was only a few weeks old." On such occasions, at least, the dutiful wife could knit "many pairs of woolen socks for Walter during those nights in the cellar and we joked often, saying if only there would be more alarms. I was so busy during the day that I never had time to knit and Walter needed so badly woolen things for the night."[16]

While Magda was knitting the nights away in Paris, Walter marched south through France with the other suspect foreigners, moving "in several slow stages, from encampment to encampment, which were most uncomfortable." He would remember one in particular where he and the others spent several days. "It was an airplane hangar: no heat, no blankets...a thin layer of straw on the floor was all; no water, either. Two water spouts were frozen solid." At least he still had a warm "civilian coat; others in [the] group had nothing." Recalling a Spaniard who came out of "a camp for remnants of the Spanish Republican Army" and had fought Franco in vain, he sneered: "The generous French had interned [him]. That Spaniard had not even a shirt under his thin jacket."

Finally, the cold, ragged men reached their "last stop in Europe...Fort St. Jean, overlooking Marseille. It was a magnificent spot on a promontory high above the city." In centuries past the fort's cannons had protected the entry to "its vast harbor, which had already been used by the Phoenicians." Walter held that "there are few spots in the world with a view equally dramatic."

Once at St. Jean, Walter and the others had "a little foretaste" of the future which awaited them. "We were treated to a welcoming speech by the commander of the fort, a gray-haired captain with only one leg. There was much in his speech about glory and valor and all about the Legion and what an honor it was to serve in its sacred ranks." Walter supposed that this tough character had lost his leg "on some *champ d'honneur*"—"field of honor"— such as Verdun or Chemin des Dames. In any case, "he was heavily bemedalled, so we had no doubt." The officer ended his address with the "somewhat chilling words: *là bas vous servirez la Légion d'abord, la France ensuite*"—"Over there you will serve first the Legion and then, also France." Walter thought: "It was not exactly what we had in mind when we enlisted." The "recruits" had time to ponder the testy commander's message, as they would spend four or five more days at St. Jean, of which Walter later could attest "never did I meet with bedbugs as ferocious as [those] at St. Jean!"

It was still daylight when the new inductees finally embarked on a ship bound for Africa, but the vessel ventured out of the harbor only after sundown—and then "with all lights out, with even no smoking on deck, as there might have been enemy U boats lurking in the dark." As he sailed to an uncertain destiny Walter lay on his back, "looking up as the top of the mast drew circles against the incredibly starry sky. It was most romantic" he

78

thought, bidding "'*Adieu*, Europe, *adieu* family'—but toward what fate?"

When the sun reappeared Walter found himself in Oran, where he and the others boarded a train bound for Sidi Bel Abbés—the headquarters of the French Foreign Legion. It did not take long for him to discover that "it was the Foreign Legion all right. 'Special units, special treatment?' What was that nonsense? We were in the Foreign Legion, weren't we? Those gentlemen in Paris could say and write whatever they wished: the Legion made its own laws." To illustrate this sudden loss of virtually all rights Walter referred to Claude's birth: "I received a wire announcing that I had become the father of a second healthy boy." As he knew that gave French soldiers the right to a one-week furlough, he went to the company officer and proudly produced the telegram: "I did not even get to see the lieutenant. I was laughed off the premises. 'Furlough at the Legion? Who ever heard of such a stupid thing?' If I knew what was good for me, I would disappear—"and on the double!"

Walter would find his new incarnation a "hard but healthy life." He doubted that he and his comrades became Legionnaires "worthy of that name," but it soon began making soldiers "out of that bunch of civilians." Fortunately the men saw no fighting, but "that was good," as their equipment was "miserable. Our guns dated from the First World War, our ammunition—which had to be used most sparingly—came in boxes which were stamped '1917.' Every fourth shot was a dud. [So poorly armed, at least the troops saw no sign of the enemy.] Once in a while a small Italian plane—an observer—would come our way to look us over, but he stayed at a respectable altitude; he did not know that we did not have anything to hit him with."

An occasional Italian flying overhead, however, would not be the only soul Walter would encounter in the middle of the desert. Sometimes he was responsible for leading one or both of the company's two mules to the Wadi, an undulating rivulet about half a mile from the camp and the men's water supply. Sometimes as he approached the water's edge Walter would witness what he described as a most "impressive spectacle." A unit of Spahis—"Moroccan horsemen whom Parisians used to admire at military parades because of their splendid uniforms and magnificent mounts"—encamped not far from the Legionnaires' camp. Periodically "a few of those Spahis were down at my Wadi with 30 to 40 horses or more—the animals getting their baths and drinking their fill and frolicking in the cool water—manes and long tails flying in the air and spray surrounding it all. The neighing of the horses and the guttural joyous shouting of the men trying to keep some order in the melee completed the picture. If a movie maker had been able to watch that scene, he would have made it the center piece of a *beau geste* movie. Yes, there were...moments of beauty in the Legionnaire's life."

To Walter's consternation, nonetheless, there were also moments of extreme frustration—namely, at the banks of that same rivulet. The compactly built, previously office-bound professional explained: "Quite a few times I had to bring up the water supply needed by the kitchen. If we were two with both mules, no problem; if I was alone with one mule only, it became more difficult. Each mule was to carry two smallish barrels attached to its wooden saddle. If these barrels were only partially filled, I was severely criticized as a 'damned weakling'; if the barrels were completely filled, they were damned heavy and I could barely lift them." To get them onto the mule, he had to heave them to shoulder height. "This damned beast" Walter swore, "knew how heavy that barrel was. If it was only partially filled, it would let me do it, but if really full, it would gingerly move a couple of steps sideways as soon as I had that barrel shoulder high. I could not reach the saddle and the mule would look at me with an expression like a diabolic grin—the upper lips lightly raised, exposing its teeth. [When two men undertook the job] there was no problem and the mule was the loser; one would hold the mule, while the other handled the barrel." On his own, however, Walter found the "Battle of the Wadi" to be the most trying test of his military career.

Such an amicable state would not last, though. The men "knew little of what was happening in the outside world," as none had a radio and the newspaper which came from Oran carried "only a little news, heavily censored as it was." Still, with time the men understood that the "phoney war" "was not so phoney any longer. The real thing had started and it did not seem to go so well"—which was clear, as in passing they picked up words like "strategic retreat" and "regroupments," as well as jargon involving "shortening the front" and "the establishment of new lines." Eventually "the blow came; the truth could not be hid any longer. The Germans were in Paris."

Stunned by the news of the German victory, Walter mourned: "It was the saddest day of my life. Never had I felt similar despair and utter hopelessness"—for from his perspective it seemed as if "our life had come to an end: the Germans parading on the Champs Elysées!" Later, as night fell, "*les anciens*—the true Legionnaires—sat around at the canteen, more or less half drunk, bawling the *Horst Wessel Lied*—the Nazi hymn." Walter only could repeat: "It was the saddest day of my life."

Indeed the Germans had captured Paris—and with a flourish! Their sweep into the French capital, however, had been predictable as early as May 1940, when the *Wehrmacht* overran the Netherlands and Belgium effectively unopposed. The French could not imagine that their ancient foes would so easily trounce what surely would be staunch resistance. As Magda saw it: "We began to feel uneasy but we never thought that the Germans would reach Paris." As the hated *Boches* advanced toward the French capital, though, she watched the refugees come through Paris—first the Belgians and

80

later French from the North of France: "It was heart-rending to see those tired children in the halls of the stations where the refugees assembled." Most of the refugees had come on foot; their clothes were torn, their faces distraught. "They had had no time to save anything and if they had a few things, they had thrown them away on the roads [as] they were too tired to carry them." Offering "whatever we could spare," Magda helped as she could —but the need was overwhelming.

As Magda worked among the displaced, she heard stories "of how they had been machine-gunned and bombed during their escape and that many had died on the roads either by guns or from exhaustion. We were shocked and frightened, but...down in your heart you can't believe it, you simply have not the imagination to feel it. We felt so secure in Paris, we always thought it would be as it was in the other war," that the Germans would be stopped before reaching the city. Despite all denial, though, on 23 June Hitler rode down Paris' most famous boulevard and to the Arc de Triomphe enroute to pay tribute to an earlier European conqueror—Napoleon Bonaparte.

Before the haughty *Führer* could strut around the deserted French capital, however, his men had to take it—an assignment which proved to be embarrassingly easy.[17] Initially, with the collapse of the Belgian army and "the tragic days of Dunkerque," the first *Luftwaffe* planes laced the skies over Paris. On Sunday 2 June 1940 those same skies carried broadcasts from Greater Germany aimed at the population of Paris: "Parisians" the speaker squawked, "this was your last quiet Sunday." At noon on the next day German planes returned, as Magda laer recounted: "the sirens began to scream, we knew this time it was serious and we went down in our cellar. It was horrible. We heard the usual anti-aircraft guns and besides that there was the thunder of explosions. The walls trembled [yet I tried not to show fear] because of the children [and so told Pierre a story] to divert his attention from the terrible noise, but my lips trembled. When I looked around I saw white faces and eyes full of fear. In an hour, all was over."

Just before Paris fell, Magda decided to remove the children to the family's summer apartment in the suburbs, "thinking that...Paris would be bombed every day." She intended, however, to remain in the city and visit the children twice a week. A true mother, she stressed that Claude's nursing "was no longer a problem; all the troubles and especially the bombing had affected my ability to nurse him." With the family's Alsatian nanny Catherine in tow, Magda hired a taxi and the four left for the suburbs, where they saw the effects of the bombing: "Not far from our house a bomb had fallen in the street, leaving a big crater [and] all the windows in the street were broken, but there were no victims [in the neighborhood]." The apartment she had rented was located on the estate of friends who "once had money and had lost it," so "all looked a little neglected but there was a large garden once cultivated but now a wilderness." Regardless of explosive events past the gate, "Pierre liked it very much and was happy. It was so peaceful and quiet." Then came the first night—and "it was hell." Sirens wailed, anti-aircraft guns fired and bombs fell just outside the village, so that Magda could see fires from the windows. "It was worse than in Paris. I regretted having left, but it was too late." The next day Magda returned to the city, but because she was anxious took the train nearly every evening and spent nights with the children in the country. She discovered, though, that "it was the same hell every night and often even during the day time."

On the Sunday before the occupation Magda was in the garden as Pierre picked strawberries, "which grew wild everywhere." Suddenly she spied several German airplanes overhead, anti-aircraft guns began to shoot and they "saw the explosions in the sky." She called Pierre, who was "angry at the interruption of his picking" and the two ran for shelter under a tree, as it was too late to reach the house. Then French planes arrived and for half an hour Pierre and his mother "could observe a battle in the air, which excited us like a sport game. [Eventually] the planes disappeared in different directions and Pierre went back to his strawberries. There wasn't even an alarm during this battle [as] they had no time to give it."

The leisurely child's play of collecting stray fruit, however, soon ended, as over the following days "the situation became more and more confused" and "thousands and thousands" left Paris with cars and trains in an effort to go to the South of France. "Most of them didn't go very far" Magda recalled, for "there were fewer and fewer trains and no more gas for the cars." The French authorities had begun blowing up bridges over the Seine and it became nearly impossible for travel between Paris and some of its suburbs. In general, "an atmosphere of fear and panic came over us. There was no order any more. The Governor of Paris made a speech over the radio saying that Paris would be defended house by house and stone by stone, [an action which Magda claimed] was one of the most horrible crimes of the war, because everyone became sick with fear and millions began to leave the city on foot. It was an indescribable chaos." Because of the resulting pandemonium, in her mind "the last chance to stop the Germans was taken away by this exodus," as the roads teemed with masses of refugees and soldiers who "moved without order."

Black-haired Magda, however, was in similar straits and made "desperate efforts to find a possibility to go south." As she would find, though, no one would accept four extra passengers—even if "one person could find a place in a car or even try to escape on foot. People paid astronomic prices for a place in a car," but "for us it was hopeless." So, she resigned herself to coping with the chaos, based in the little village which by this time had become "completely deserted. All civilians were gone and the shops closed. We couldn't even buy milk" Magda recounted, as "the milk-man was gone, too." She realized then that it was "no longer possible to stay," but since it was equally impossible to find passage to the South, "the only possibility was to go back to Paris." Incredibly, that's what the little troupe did.

The loyal Catherine pushed Claude's carriage and, as "Pierre could not walk fast enough," she and Magda put him in alongside the baby and set off through a "strange atmosphere...a kind of smoke or fog." One rumor purported that it was an artificial fog emitted "in order to hide the retreat of the French army," while another held it was the smoke from huge gas reservoirs which the French had blown up to keep from falling into Nazi hands. Magda noted that they "never knew what it really was but the last explanation seemed...the most probable, because we heard explosions far away." Periodically out of this "fog" emerged small groups of retreating French soldiers: "To see their faces made us cry." Magda remembered pitifully that "most of them were drunk and they had no officers with them. It was a retreat without order [as] nobody knew where to go."

As they plodded down a road swirling with "soldiers moving in the direction of Paris and cars and people on foot who were coming from Paris and going [Magda] did not know where," Claude began to cry from hunger. Stopping for a few minutes at an inn to have his milk warmed up, they had just left the inn when Magda heard "a strange noise" which she did not recognize until she heard "some soldiers calling and...running to bushes." Then it struck her: "we were being machine-gunned and at the same moment the plane was only a few yards above our heads. I could clearly see the faces of the pilot and the gunner. I screamed and was headless for a second, but Catherine was already in the bushes with the children. [Falling into the ditch beside the road, somebody pulled Magda into the bushes, too.] I remember they were currant bushes and the berries were red and ripe. Pierre was hungry and began to eat the berries. We remained [there] for a long time [and heard] many planes...but saw only a few which dived low because of the strange fog." None of the civilians was hit, but as they resumed their trek into the city they saw several dead soldiers in the ditches.

After another hour of pushing on down the congested road, they reached a town with a station where "a train was waiting. Hundreds tried to go in, but it was hopeless." When the station master saw Catherine, the children and Magda, however, he pushed them in. Claude's carriage "remained there," however, as did "many...who couldn't go in."

The fog worsened in the city—which in any case seemed a bizarre version of its usual self: "It was hard to breathe. There was soot in the air and...clothes became greasy. The streets had a strange aspect [as the shops were closed and] groups of tired looking people moved in the direction of the different *portes* pushing all kinds of vehicles with their personal belongings.

There were no cars at all." Oddly—yet fortunately—the Metro was operating, so the little band hurried home and "went to bed. I had a strange feeling [as] everything seemed to me like a dream. A few hours ago we were hiding in bushes from the firing planes and now I lay in my bed at home."

At least partially recovered from the previous day's exhausting events, the next day found a determined Magda planning an escape from harried Paris.[18] First she "ran around looking for a chance to leave Paris by car," but soon realized "there was none and...gave it up." She tried to buy some food, but as she found a neighborhood pharmacy was open, all she could find was evaporated milk—which she combined with "some fruit preserves and cookies at home and we lived on them." That afternoon the druggist told her that the city had been declared a *ville ouverte*—an "open city"—which meant it would not be defended, so "there would be no battles in the streets, no bombing. In one sense it was good news" she thought, "but in the other there was no hope any more. It was perhaps a question of hours and the Germans would be here"—and she was right.

Writing about her experiences, Magda remarked that if the decision to surrender the city "had been taken two or three days earlier, most of the people would have stayed at home and many lives—especially those of children—would have been spared and a great deal of misery avoided. [But] the fact that we couldn't find any possibility of leaving Paris was good luck and probably saved our lives, at least the lives of the children. Besides the soldiers, thousands of women and children died on the roads. Our adventure was short, but I can imagine the hardships of those who were out for days and even weeks."

Despite the obvious threat of venturing onto the dangerous roads, Magda continued to contemplate possible means of reaching the South. She almost had given up her search when a neighbor mentioned the possibility of finding passage on a truck scheduled to leave the next morning for Orleans. The driver agreed to take the three Shostals with him and said they should meet him at Place Pigalle at seven the next day. At this point Magda had begun already "to understand that it was foolhardy to leave without knowing where to go, as millions did." The thought that she could send post to and receive letters from Walter in the unoccupied South, though, had made her change her mind—so she packed "once more" and waited.

All that night Magda could not sleep: "I was too excited. I sat down at our window and waited. The last two days had been relatively quiet, we had no more air-raid alarms. But that night was hell. Heavy guns—not the anti-aircraft guns to which we were already accustomed—fired all night and they were not very far away. The walls trembled [and the sky] was red and from time to time huge flames rose [and her eyes watered because of the smoke and fog]."

Then, nothing. "At dawn the guns suddenly stopped firing. The quietness was strange." Magda woke the children and prepared to leave. Catherine carried Claude, and Magda a heavy rucksack. "Pierre staggered, he was so sleepy and frightened." By seven the four were at Place Pigalle, where they waited anxiously for the promised truck. The Place—Paris' amusement center near Montmartre and "a nice and gay place in the happy days"—had acquired "a desolate aspect. Groups of French soldiers came along, some on foot, some on bicycles; their uniforms were torn and they looked exhausted. One of them collapsed and lay on his knees crying like a child. His comrades boxed at his ears to make him rise and walk. They told him to not lose his nerves...they would escape if he could run. He rose and staggered away." From the soldiers' conversation Magda realized that Hitler's victory-giddy forces had encircled the city. Then, "suddenly we heard a woman's voice screaming. We saw her under the gate of a house crying for help. She was in labor pains and there was no vehicle to take her to a hospital." Finally two police officers helped her walk to the next Metro station, but "after a few steps she collapsed and refused to walk." The officers took her to the next café and with their help "a few minutes later the child was born."

Magda, Catherine and the young boys waited outside the café "in great tension and forgot all the war and were even happy that everything was all right with her." Noticing that an hour had passed and the truck had not arrived, Magda decided "there was no sense to wait any longer" and the abandoned would-be travelers began heading for home. "As we were starting I saw a group of soldiers in a strange uniform. One of them made signs for us to go out of the way." It took her several seconds until Magda realized that "these were no French soldiers." She stared at them and then understood: "All was finished, the Germans were here."

The humiliating collapse of France had endless repercussions for the Shostals—for Walter stranded in the desert as well as for Magda trapped in Paris: both were unsure how to proceed. For Walter, perhaps, the choices were clearer given that in the terms of armistice which Marshal Petain had signed with the Germans, the French had to reduce their military presence in North Africa and the Legion had to release recruits like Walter—inductees who had been half-hearted soldiers at best. The ex-soldiers were free to leave, but "where to? To France? The country was in chaos. Let these ex-soldiers go to Morocco and Algeria with no place to go and no money to live on? That seemed a sure road to brigandry and civilian disorder."

In this vacuum the French colonial regime in North Africa toyed with the formation of *campagnies de travailleurs*, civilian units intended for use in mining coal or finally building the long-planned railroad across the Sahara. In such a confused situation only a few of the men would succeed in returning to France. Walter found that "it took a good deal of persistence, luck and finally cheating to be among them. It really seemed stupid to go there, so why was I so eager to return to Nazi-dominated Europe? I wanted to be with my family." His decision turned out not to be so stupid after all, however, as ultimately most of the ones who stayed slipped back into the ranks of the inducted. After the Allies landed in North Africa such castaways became part of the Eighth Army, which Walter reported "fought its way against stubborn German resistance up the Italian peninsula" and "not many of my friends were to reach France."

The France which Walter found upon his return to Europe was defeated, divided and demoralized. The so-called *zone occupée* of the North and *zone libre* of the South fell respectively under the administration of the Nazis and the Vichy government. Despite connections between the two regimes, officially no communication "whatsoever" existed between the two zones: no travel, no mail, no telephone and "the only formal messages which could reach across the dividing line were preprinted Red Cross cards—one-liners where you could check off one of five messages. And then, there were messages smuggled through the underground; this way I learned that my family was still in Paris, but hoped to leave soon and join me in Marseille."

Knowing he again would have to provide a roof over his family's heads, Walter immediately began a "desperate search for that elusive apartment or whatever," even if that seemed "impossible, as Marseille's population had almost doubled" with the arrival of first so many central-European and then North of France refugees. Eventually he found a place for his family, "a small summer home on the outskirts of the city—*Villa Santuzza*, at Chateau Gombert, on tram line #5. His find, however, came at a steep price: "The rent was exorbitant; it took most of the money I had. There was no heat, no gas—but there was water and electricity, if it worked. There was a small garden where we might be able to grow things...it seemed like heaven." Fine, but without his family even heaven would have seemed empty.

In Paris, Magda had her own worries: namely, how to escape the Nazis—who had arrived in June 1940, six months before she received word of Walter's whereabouts. Once she learned that he was in Marseille, though, it meant only one thing: she would *have* to find a way to join him.

Shortly after Walter's letter arrived before New Year's Day of 1941, Magda met a female smuggler who agreed to take her and Pierre to the South. She would not take twelve-month-old Claude with them, however, for as even Magda acknowledged, "it would be too dangerous and difficult because we had to walk miles and miles in the night through forests." Forced to make one of the most agonizing of decisions, she agreed to leave the infant with a friend in the hope that the Red Cross would bring him to Marseille a few weeks later. This deal with the devil meant that at least most of the family would be reunited, but Magda deemed it "the hardest decision I ever had to make in all my life."

Besides her baby, Magda also had to leave behind most of her family's belongings. Once all the preparations had been made, she was ready to meet the woman on the appointed Sunday evening at the train station. "We waited and waited until the train was gone and the woman didn't come. I was crying" she remembered, "and so was Pierre. It was late and we had only half an hour until the curfew." As the occupying administration allowed no one to be in the streets after 11 o'clock they hastened on the Metro to the woman's apartment: "I had to know what happened to her." She learned from the building superintendent that the woman had been arrested two hours earlier by the Gestapo. Magda assumed that the woman had her address with her, "so I couldn't go back to my apartment, where the Gestapo...would find me. [The two found] a little room in the next hotel, an awful dirty place with a patron who looked like a criminal. I could not sleep and I cried. It was a terrible disappointment."

For a week Magda found shelter with a friend where she could stay while seeking an alternative means to Marseille. All the while, though, she was "desperate," thinking "my husband was anxious because he was expecting us." In her desperation she finally took a bus to Bordeaux, as "somebody told me about a little town on the frontier where the bus drivers helped people to go on the other side. But" she conceded, "it was all very vague."

Leaving Paris in a severe snowstorm, Magda and Pierre arrived in Bordeaux early the next day and went to the station cafeteria to buy some coffee—"or what they called coffee." Sitting in the cafeteria was a drunken German soldier sipping champagne at seven in the morning: "He offered everybody a glass and I didn't dare to refuse because he was drunken and I was afraid of having trouble with him. [At least] Pierre didn't understand German [for he] would certainly have answered in German and that would have been bad."

The trap Magda feared did not materialize and she began a conversation with a man who inquired what she was doing there. She told him the truth, "knowing I could trust a Frenchman in things like that." "My poor lady!" he responded, "It is impossible to go through here. It was possible a few weeks ago, but since then so many people have been arrested by the Germans and in the night they make patrols with dogs along the frontier and everybody is shot on sight." When he saw Magda's tears and "hopeless face," though, he tried to console her. "I will try to help you" he promised: "don't despair."

Then Magda was in for a "terrible surprise," for there were German soldiers in the passageway inspecting the papers of every traveler. "I could not show my papers" she knew, as "it would have shown them that I was an

Austrian and inhabitant of Paris." At the last moment her "new friend" gave her his name and address so that she could supply them to the inspector. But then, she had a "bright idea." Later, with the idea's success, Magda could "understand how it is possible in moments of great danger to find a solution which you never would be able to find in normal life." She recounted: "Pierre always was afraid of German soldiers and so I told him: 'Pierre, run away, you see the German soldier, he will put us in a prison, if he can seize us.' And Pierre ran...and I after him, calling his name. The German believed that I was a poor mother running after her naughty boy and he let me run through the passageway with a smile, perhaps remembering his own naughty boys. He didn't even look at my papers. I was through the passageway and the first round was won, but the most difficult was always before us."

Outside the station "Monsieur B." was waiting for Magda and Pierre: "He gave me his arm and so we went down to the town. In Paris the streets were always crowded with German soldiers but I never before saw so many in one place as here. I was afraid and I understood that it would not have been possible to ask the bus drivers to help me. Every step was observed by the Germans and especially people who approached the bus going to the unoccupied zone had to pass a lane of inspecting soldiers. But, talking to Monsieur B. like a just-arrived friend, we moved safely in the streets without troubles."

Monsieur B. helped Magda and Pierre find lodging with a "nice elderly woman who had a hotel with a few rooms." By now it was February, cold and foggy: "You can't stay in the streets with your poor little boy" the woman told Magda, who took that as a signal that she understood the situation and "was willing to help." At noon, for example, as the two runaways "had dinner with her and a lot of German soldiers," the woman introduced Magda as her cousin and "nobody...asked a question. It was a funny situation" Magda recalled, as the Germans "had not the slightest notion that I understood every word of their conversation. They tried even to speak to me in French and it was hard for me not to laugh. Their conversation was not very interesting. I noticed it very often when I heard German soldiers talk together, they never said anything personal. I don't think they trusted each other."

After lunch Monsieur B. visited Magda and Pierre in their room. "I have thought it over" he told her. "There is only one man here who can help you...Monsieur Dasse, the electrician. He hates the Germans [and] is a Gaullist...I am sure he will do something for you."

Magda went to the man and shared her story with him. She thought he was "a very nice man," but at first he hesitated. "You know very well" he told her, "that I risk my position and I promised my wife never to [smuggle people across the border] again." His wife—the village midwife—saw Pierre, though, and said to her husband: "Do it for the little boy, so he can see his father again." Still unconvinced, the man told Magda to return to the hotel and stay there for the rest of the day; he needed time to consider such a move. Besides, it was Sunday and he couldn't do anything until Monday morning.

In this state of uncertainty, to Magda "the day seemed very long." Before going to bed in the evening the proprietress warned her that because the Germans always came at seven o'clock to inspect the papers of "every stranger," she and Pierre best had leave the hotel early in the morning. That night Magda could not sleep and at six they were "in the streets. It was dark and cold...[we] did not dare go to Monsieur Dasse so early and so...found an open gate where we stayed for two hours in a terrible cold always in fear of the German patrols which we could hear in the streets. Pierre cried, he felt so cold and I tried to keep him quiet. Those two hours seemed to me longer than two years. Finally it was eight and we went to Monsieur Dasse. His wife gave us tea and milk and so we came back to life."

In her absence the clever electrician had devised a plan where Magda would pose as a dressmaker friend of his and thus pass through the border using the special permit which allowed locals to report for work across the newly created "frontier." The catch? The Madame was 48. Thirty-five-year-old Magda fretted because "her picture was not at all like me but with a little retouching we tried to make me look old enough...It was easy" she quipped, as "I was so tired and looked so grieved." Donning glasses and a shawl instead of her customary hat, she memorized the woman's birthdate and birthplace, and "all the data about her husband and children. And so, I was Madame Guerin. I never saw her in my life, but I never will forget her kindness. [She tried to leave a present for her] but Monsieur Dasse didn't accept it neither for her nor for himself or his wife. It was all pure goodness."

When we all found my disguise very satisfactory, Monsieur Dasse asked for all my papers and money and all the little things in my handbag like a compact and a lipstick, things a country dressmaker certainly never carries with her and he hid everything in the rim of his wheel." Instructing Magda to tell the German inspectors that she was going to a fitting for a dress for a customer, he started the car and left the village. On the way, he told her "all depends on the German officer. Some are nice, but all is a question of luck."

As they approached the border Magda "could feel the palpitation of my heart." "I think we are lucky" the Monsieur whispered: "The only Austrian officer we have here is on duty. He is nice and easy. He is not" he added caustically, "at all like the Germans." Just then the car stopped before the border control: "On the right there was the officer and on the left of the car several soldiers who asked for our permits. And once more, Pierre helped a great deal. The officer began to speak to him and to caress his hair because Pierre looked at him anxiously. I tried to intervene and told Pierre not to be afraid because the officer was a nice man. [So situated, Magda] looked always in the other direction and the inspecting soldier could not see my face.

They looked in the car and in my handbag, [but then] several other cars arrived which diverted their attention from us. The officer gave the signal, the barrier was lifted and we went through. When I heard the barrier fall down behind us I began to cry and sob." Monsieur Dasse smiled at her—the thirtieth person he had helped across the border: "Cry as much as you can, it will do you a lot of good. You are not the first one I saw crying in this situation" he comforted her.

Magda was still crying "when the French barrier rose for our car and I saw for the first time in eight months French uniforms and the Tricolor. They opened the door and helped me out," she recalled, saying "they understood everything after looking at me: 'Don't cry any more Madame, now you are in France, safe. Forget the *Boches.*'"

Magda likely could forget the *Boches*, but Walter could not forget her and the boys. In crowded Marseille he spent "endless hours" observing the train station where he expected them to arrive, but did not dare get "too close, as there were too many police around, checking on people and asking for papers. Anybody who was not French or who spoke with an accent was likely to be taken along. And once 'inside,' only Heaven knew when you would see daylight again."

Somehow Walter had informed Magda that he would be waiting for her upon her arrival at the station, but she and Pierre simply did not appear. As it had gotten late the discouraged Walter "headed home on #5, the last tram to run that evening." He noted heavy heartedly: "It happened to be my birthday, 25 February 1941."

Magda felt equally disappointed on this rainy day, as she had expected to rendezvous with her husband—but, "there was no Daddy at the station." As he had given her the address of the cottage he had rented for them, she decided to avoid the expense of a hotel or a taxi and set out by tram for Chateau Gombert: "We had to run to catch the last tram leaving at nine o'clock and we just got in as it was leaving. And there I saw a very well-known silhouette a few seats before us. [Noting that] it was very funny for me to meet my husband in a street car after a separation of more than a year, I crawled forward and covering his eyes with my hands I asked: 'Who is it?' You can imagine his surprise." The jubilant Magda asked Pierre "if he could recognize the gentleman. But even knowing that we took the trip to join Daddy," she marveled, "he did not recognize him."

For his part, Walter explained to her that he had been at the station every day till the previous one. Then he had lost hope of seeing his family ever again, thinking that the Germans had arrested them.

Magda said "there began a very happy time for us three," one "spoiled only by Claudie's absence."[19] The Shostals eventually solved that problem, too, as they were able to arrange for a former neighbor—who later went to Auschwitz, where her mother perished and she received a tattoo which forever would remind her of that nightmare—to bring the baby to a certain point on the border and pass him across a fence. As with virtually all other refugees of the time, they also had to surmount an amazing, discouraging array of hurdles before they could secure passage to America—where they subsequently found a haven among Quakers in Iowa and could recover from their seemingly endless drama.

Once she reached safe, quiet Scattergood, Magda composed a 25-page account of her version of the family's travails. She concluded her story by writing of the ambivalence she felt regarding their fate: "I am well aware that all that happened to me was not the worst because there was a happy end: we are all together and safe in this country. But a great deal of our life and energy, even of our health, remains there and we can't be as happy as we have reason to be, thinking of our friends who live there under terrible conditions. Sometimes I feel ashamed that we escaped."

1.) Scattergood's guests came from much of Nazi-occupied Europe. Most consisted of Germans (86) and Austrians (67). Eight Poles also found their way to West Branch, however, as did seven French nationals [their ethnicity not confirmed as French]. Czechs and Russians each totaled six, Hungarians five. Four Luxembourgers and a Latvian completed the list. Also, in age the guests ranged from six months to 60 and by occupation they ranged from butcher to banker. As AFSC's Julia Branson explained in a form letter to Friends Meetings in North America in late 1938 or 1939, "Most of the people [with whom we are working] are from the professional group, among them numerous physicians, teachers, lawyers, social workers and former government officials. Recently there have been quite a few business men and persons employed in business, ranging from clerks to executives in large concerns. There are practically no farmers or farm hands among this group, very few skilled artisans and no unskilled labor." Out of a total of 185 persons, 68 consisted of couples. Sixteen of those 34 couples had among them 23 children. Three additional children came with single parents. The rest of the refugee population consisted of 47 single men over 30, 26 single men under 30 and 15 single women. Of the last group, most seem to have been over 30; perhaps a sign of etiquette at the time which discouraged inquiring about a woman's age, most their ages are not known.
2.) Sources disagree on the spelling of her name, using both "Baeck" and "Beck."
3.) Upon request, the names have been changed. All material in this section comes from an interview with "Ilse" conducted by four former hostel staff, who interviewed Ilse in her home in autumn 1994 and later asked me to withhold the contents of the tape for fear of political recriminations. In biographical notes which he wrote in my biographical files on 30 October 1994, Robert Berquist noted: "The [Stahls] had to have a special bill approved by Congress in order to get permanent visas due to one-time Communist Party membership, from which they had been expelled." After some 55 years in America, Ilse still spoke English with a broad German accent; her lingual mistakes and idiosyncracies have been left intact.
4.) The move to Iowa was not the Stahl's first, but rather at the time their seemingly *only* choice. Soon after arriving in America, Friends showed them pictures of Scattergood and Ilse responded: "I didn't want to go; I didn't want to go... This gray-haired lady took my hand and said, 'That's the best you can [do]'. 'I don't want to go to the camp they showed! Let me sit here! Dump me in the water!' and things like this. Total hysterical—I mean, I was just *finished* with *everything*. If you would know how we came on the boat, you would not wonder. We were over two weeks on the boat... [Ernst] didn't feel too good, but he wanted to calm me down: I was out of my senses. I didn't want food...and everybody could see—I was 82 pounds weight: that was much too little for me... But I was absolutely dormant. Finally, 'Okay, okay, okay'... They gave us four [or] five days, then we would go and we had the choice of going by bus or train and...we talked to our friends who were already living in New York a few months. They said, 'Oh, that's elegant...wonderful—that's like a pleasure trip'. We chose the bus because we thought it would be more elegant. We did not know [that it would take] two days and three nights on the bus. My knees were swollen and the buses were *so tiring* on the seats. [Lillian Pemberton retrieved] us at the station in Iowa and giggled all the time—but then I giggled, too. I saw the cornfields—the corn was so high! And I had begun by this time saying [Ilse's voice cracks] 'Like home, like home'. She gave us *such* a relief through her presence, coming and picking us up. Never had anybody picked us up—only the policemen [had]. She made us feel so easy and I looked

91

out and we drove on in this station wagon—all wood; an auto all wood: we never had autos! And she said 'How do you like America?' and I said [Ilse laughs], 'Like home, like home' [Ilse laughs again]. I never in my life had seen corn, corn, corn. I said all time, 'Like home, like home'—the two words I knew well; I wanted to say 'It feels like home,' but I couldn't say it. I said 'Like home, like home.'"

5.) Boris could run halfway around the world, but the world he left in Berlin would follow him—as suggested in the 29 March 1940 entry in *The Book of Scattergood*, the hostel's communal log: "Helmut [Ostrowski-Wilk] arrives and wants to speak only English. In persuit [sic] of this aim he talks the whole evening with Boris, who was in Berlin his neighbor during two years and whose acquaintance he happened to make at Scattergood."

6.) Originally called the American Jewish Joint Distribution Committee, the "Joint" came into existence in 1914 as in the course of World War I American Jews sought to respond to the hunger and destitution of their Eastern European counterparts. Comparable to AFSC, JDC found its program changed by the events taking place first in Hitler-ruled Germany, then in Nazi-occupied Europe. Namely, JDC attempted to help find means of escape—i.e., provide affidavits of support and reform U.S. State Department policy in admitting applicants—for Jews who fled and consequently means of self-support once they reached the U.S.

7.) After Germany invaded the Soviet Union Boris' family was exchanged for Soviet-held German civilians and sent via Turkey to Siberia, where the wife and oldest son lost their feet and the daughter lost her toes to frostbite, then all but the daughter lost their lives to hunger and cold. Following the war, Tamara rejoined her father in Portland, Oregon.

Boris remained a solitary, dejected figure for the rest of his life. John and Ruth Kaltenbach visited him in Portland in 1956. Ruth later wrote: "We found [Boris] in a nursing home...unable to speak, but his eyes showed his joy in seeing John again."

8.) Her time there left a deep impression on Marie, as evident in the letter of 23 March 1943 which she wrote to Martha Balderston upon learning of Scattergood's imminent closing: "I am very often thinking of Scattergood and all friendship and love I received there. I will never forget this part in my life... The time I lived in Scattergood gave me strength for my soul, the best gift I could have gotten."

9.) Even under the care of her son-in-law Emil Kirschmann, however, Marie longed to return to her *Heimat*—which she did four years after the Nazis' capitulation. She moved to Düsseldorf and worked to revive the well-respected *Arbeiterwohlfahrt*, which she had founded in 1919 and following the Second World War served as honorary chair until her death in Bonn in 1956. At the time of her return to Germany in 1949 the Berlin *Stadtparlament* officially welcomed her to the divided former German capital. In her reply of thanks Marie proclaimed "it is a miracle, that despite Hitler and everything else which has befallen us, here today there is still—or, again—so much joy and love among people." In Germany, Marie eventually worked with Marianne Welter, a returned social worker and fellow former "Scattergoodian."

10.) Alfred's fellow internee Lion Feuchtwanger described psychological conditions of everyday life in a French detention camp, not just physical ones. For him, "the most difficult thing to bear in the camp was that one never could be alone with himself, that always—day and night, with every act, while eating and sleeping and going to the toilet—hundreds of people were around you—chattering, laughing, screaming, sighing, crying, gorging, slurping, snoring, farting, stinking, sweating, bathing people. Yes, every act took place in the largest public and of course no one felt the slightest shame in front of the other."

11.) Grete's mother, Hedwig Katz Kaufmann, perished in Theresienstadt in 1943.

12.) According to a line in the *Nachruf* written after Friedel's death in 1994, at the time of the Third Reich "authorities recommended Frieda that she should divorce Sigmund, but she responded: 'You always say that German women should remain faithful to their husbands.'"

13.) Robert Balderston was no stranger to relief work in Germany: he had volunteered after the first world war as part of the Quaker-run *Kinderspeisung* program and after Hitler seized power to try to help victims of Nazism flee the Third Reich. He also was in Antwerp in June 1939 when ill-fated refugees on the *Saint Louis* returned from closed New-World ports.

14.) After Sigmund's departure his oldest sister, Erna, was arrested in the Black Forest city of Freiburg-im-Breisgau, deported to the Gurs concentration camp in southern France and later sent to a death camp in "the East," where she perished. Similarly his father, Salomon, also of Freiburg, met an "unnatural end in Poland"; word of his fate came via a phoney death certificate sent to Sigmund's wife Friedel—along with a bill for the "ensuing costs!"

15.) Walter was not alone in avoiding the U.S. as a refuge. Playwright Carl Zuckmayer once admitted, "we did not think about America [upon fleeing occupied Austria in 1938]... No, we said like obstinate children. One flight is enough. We're Europeans and we'll stay in Europe. What would we do in a country where people pour ketchup on beef and where our greatest linguistic achievement would be to say in English: 'I am not able to express myself?'"

16.) Later Magda and the boys remained in their apartment during air raids, as, "indeed, nothing happened"; they "even became a little accustomed to the sirens, which we never could hear without shuddering. I heard the sirens again in New York" she later would recall, referring to ambulances or fire trucks, "but it wasn't the same, they didn't get through your nerves and were not half as loud as in Paris." Despite that, "Pierre always screamed when he heard them" and "even Claudie showed signs of excitement."

17.) Adolf Hitler was not the only German whose dream was to act important in Paris. Walter wrote that after the occupation, "from time to time came simple soldiers on furlough...who looked for friendship and services...The Germans descended like locusts on Paris and picked the shelves clean of wares they had not seen for years...[Magda would never forget] a certain Herr von P. who in his arrogant way declared, 'No, he would not buy any suits; he would rather buy them in London.'"

18.) Magda was not the only refugee mother trying to save her children from the on-coming Germans. As Edith Lichtenstein Morgan later recounted, her mother Elizabeth "always had nasty things to say about the refugee committees [in Europe as they] didn't help a lot. We had a number of bad experiences with them, which is one of the reasons why even in this country we steered away [from them] as much as possible; the Quakers didn't have those characteristics. For example, when we were in Paris and the German army was coming down in June [1940], my mother went to try to see if she could get us passage or get out of there somehow [when] my mother, my brother and I were mouse-trapped in Paris: she went to the refugee committee to try to get money and transportation and some kind of help and found that they had closed the office down, taken all the funds and departed for Southern France, so we had to get out on our own. That meant going out on foot and heading south and hoping we could stay ahead of the German army. We were usually not very far ahead—ten or 15 miles ahead, and *walking*! We walked south: it was maybe around 200 miles from Paris to Limoges, and then the armistice was signed when we got to Limoges, so we stopped there."

19.) Although between them Walter and Magda had survived military service, being shot at by German planes, Gestapo checkpoints, lack of food and no housing, they found being stranded in Marseille the most challenging of all. Not only was Claude not with them, but the family recognized the crowded city to be a tentative safe haven at best, so planned to escape to America. Walter knew, however, that Marseille's U.S. consulate was "besieged by thousands of people [and they] stood in line for hours and days, only to get inside the building, where a small staff was overwhelmed by the desperate crowds"—so he did not even attempt to go there to get an application form, "it was so completely hopeless. Then, the miracle happened... A letter came from the American consulate. They had received a cable that Washington had granted me an emergency visum as an endangered person...but only for the emergency, and that it was for me alone. Would I take it? My answer was that I could not possibly leave my family behind. The man smiled, as he was also empowered to change this into immigration visas for the whole family. Would I take that? Would I!!!" Even "miracles," however, can present problems. For starters, upon the visa's issuance every name listed on it had to be present in person—but baby Claude remained in Paris and no one could foretell when the Red Cross might deliver him. In addition, it was impossible to postpone "that vital appointment" to accept the visa and it might take months to secure second one. So, Walter and Magda "borrowed" a baby—"or rather, we rented it. Its mother was a refugee, too. The rental fee was Magda's horde of knitting wool, one of the many things which had disappeared from the shelves and was worth its weight in gold. For the visa, we all had to pass physicals given by an American physician. The man marvelled how well-developed our son was. No wonder, given that the rental baby was three months older than the original. And so it happened, that our son entered the United States in fraud; I hope there exists a statute of limitation for such misdeeds. [At any rate] we walked out, visa in hand and ready to return the borrowed baby."

SUCH JOY

*"The ten children who have been here have
been such joy, we miss them as they leave."*
~ **Martha Balderston**

For the adult guests who managed to escape Nazi-occupied Europe and reach
Scattergood, the next steps in reconstructing their lives were relatively clear:
they had to become reasonably fluent in the native language of their new
homeland, learn some of the fundamentals of American history and culture,
make connections and find a new job, if not launch a new career. In other
words, regardless of their own personal confusion or suffering, as self-
interested individuals of legal age, as professionals and breadwinners, they
simply had no choice but to cope with the conditions placed upon them by
the very circumstance of their displacement.[1]

For the children among the guests, however, the task ahead of them was
not so clear. For one thing they were no longer Europeans, but also not yet
Americans. For another they were not autonomous and would continue to be
dependent upon the skills and decisions—as well as raw luck—of their parents. Unlike that of their fully Old World-socialized parents, though, the future which awaited the children remained wide open.

Arriving at Scattergood, refugee children were cast into an open-ended
ambiguity in which each somehow had to carve out her or his own niche.
This was no easy task, given the lack of meaningful role models and the fact
that most of the adults around them understandably were preoccupied with
other pressing worries. Naturally parents cared greatly about what would
become of their offspring: after a certain point, however, uncontrollable or
unforeseeable forces outside the artificially safe sanctuary of Scattergood
would have much more say about the destinies of their young than the
strongest of hopes for their welfare ever could. The West Branch public
schools, for example, would prove to be an effective if *de facto* center for the

Americanization of its newest charges.

Despite appearances that the hostel's organizers were not fully clear about how to respond to the special needs of guests who were not of legal age and despite the difficult *attaché* status of its youngest members, the children, too, eventually became an integral part of Scattergood Hostel's comprehensive program. Partially by providing much-needed distraction from the emotional fallout inherent in the traumatic experiences which their seniors had encountered head-on in the *Heimat*, they helped the hostel fulfill its mission of offering refugees a place where they could rebuild shattered lives.

As already stated, the first guests to appear at Scattergood consisted of five men; thereafter additional numbers of single men formed the ranks of the newcomers until the Ladewigs came in mid-June 1939 and the Deutsch family appeared a month later. Local Quakers and the hostel staff celebrated the arrival of each new "guest," but the presence of the red-haired Deutsch children changed the feel of the place in ways which the addition of more adults could not. Upon their arrival the keeper of *The Book of Scattergood* wrote: "Our first family...arrived in the afternoon. We shall enjoy having the children around to liven things up." From the records available, however, it seems that although the staff and other guests at Scattergood initially may have welcomed having children on hand in theory, in practice they weren't certain what to do with them. Later remarks concerning the children which were written in the community's usually lively log were without exception completely factual. On the occasion of the children's first day at the West Branch public school, for instance, an unofficial hostel historian merely wrote "Michael and Hannah [sic] start to school," while the subsequent issuance of grades warranted the utterly colorless comment "Hannah and Michael brought home their first report cards from school". The last time the freckled nine-year-old boy and his little six-year-old sister were mentioned in the context of having lived at Scattergood, though, at least a modest mention of appreciation for their having been at the hostel was made. Martha Balderston—then serving in an "advisory role"—wrote in the *Scattergood Monthly News Bulletin*: "With [the recent exodus of guests] we have lost the two children, Hanna and Michael, who brightened the life of the Hostel and supplied the youthful spirits and interest we so need."[2]

The adults' needs aside, Scattergood represented a major watermark in the lives of its youngest guests. Little Hanna Deutsch, for one, had suffered a disorienting loss—that of her home, her native environment and a culture which till then she had perceived as her innate own.[3] Scattergood Hostel would symbolize a turning point between a biography she once had and one which she had yet to assume. In writing about her experiences decades later as part of a master's thesis in humanistic and clinical psychology, she recorded free-style images reflecting scars left by being uprooted at such a vulnerable age: "Throughout my life, when caught in inner conflict I have often been immobilized. In one case, I cannot even remember the resolution. Perhaps this was my parents' conflict which I made my own. It was the conflict between leaving our loved home—people, beautiful countryside and city, the known—or risking death at the hands of the Nazis. I have many memories before and after our departure, but none of packing or leaving. In this case I did not even acknowledge the alternatives, inner pulls; I just 'checked out.'"[4]

The changes and traumas which rocked Hanna left considerable wakes. She attended the local West Branch elementary school with the other refugee children, yet did not thrive there because of her vague struggle to integrate an upsetting, lost past with a difficult-to-comprehend present. As an adult she remembered that "somehow, being an immigrant, that messed up school for me a lot. Because there...I felt shy and had an awful time reading. We took the school bus...and I often didn't want to get up. I also remember once missing the school bus and walking to school. Reading continued to be a problem for me, as [did] writing. Even though I managed [as an adult] to get a master's degree, it's been a struggle always and I spent so many sleepless nights writing; I would not want to tell...how many nights I stayed up all night doing it [but still earned] a master's degree in psychology...when I was 53 years old."

Of course the psychological gauntlet of cultural adjustment did not end upon leaving Scattergood Hostel. Once the refugees reached their next homes and settled into new lives, children especially struggled to integrate the worlds and lives they had known in Europe with those they found themselves enveloped in as "new Americans. Like countless other first-generation Americans, Hanna felt ambivalence regarding her parents and her own cultural identity—as she went on to explain in the same narrative: "Later, in junior high years [in Des Moines, Iowa], I was torn between love and respect for my parents and wanting them to be different. I treasured long walks home from downtown with my father; hearing the Saturday afternoon opera while he gardened; his Viennese, Tyrolean, Jewish, Czech, and Polish jokes, all told in different dialects; his stories of mountain climbs; and long recitations in German of passages from Homer, Wilhelm Busch, or his own poems. I loved my mother's warmth, interest and laughter, her way with people; her Viennese cooking; and the clothes she sewed for me, though I felt beholden. But I was torn. I wanted them without their accents, their self-effacing ways, their protectiveness toward me, and I wanted the lifestyle of the 'popular kids.' On the one hand, I was filled with deep embarrassment and resentment at how our home was different from other homes, and my parents different from other parents and, on the other hand, I defended and protected them from others and from my own censure. Often it felt like I was cut in two, and I wore embarrassment and self-rejection."

As Hanna's recounted early internal struggles attest, children have difficulty *not* perceiving subtleties in their surroundings. To what degree, then, were children at Scattergood a mixed blessing? On one hand they might have provided the adults around them with lively distraction, but on the other they also may have reminded them of painful memories or truths which their elders rather would have forgotten. How might this dynamic have complicated the role of young people at the hostel?

It seems that with time the childrens' relationship to Scattergood Hostel did become clearer, more animated and integral to the budding life of the community. By the Rosenzweigs' arrival on the scene on 7 September 1940, for example, the ground broken by the lively little Deutsches had become fertile soil in which young people could re-orient themselves and begin the transition from the life they had known to a life they barely could imagine. Author Louise Benckenstein Griffiths asked adolescent Irmgard Rosenzweig to record some of her impressions of the hostel for inclusion in her book *Brothertown*, a "course for junior high school groups on the theme...*Living Together in Today's World*." The girl's thoughtful comments appeared in a chapter entitled "Fatherland to Brotherland." In her piece the gentle-eyed, black-haired girl first explained how her family had felt forced to leave Germany, but since her parents feared it would take "quite a while" until they might arrange their own departure, in spring 1939 they shipped 13-year-old Irmgard to England and her brother Ernst, then 17, to a boarding school in Wales. After almost a year and a half of separation, Irmgard joined her relieved parents in America in July 1940, but as war had erupted in the interim Ernst had been interned and was thus unable to leave Britain.

Irmgard went on to describe life at the Scattergood Hostel, touting it as "a real example of cooperative life," where the Quakers "do their best to make us refugees as happy as possible." She said that residents shared "everything we have, the work and the pleasure, and therefore" she held, "we can live a very nice life." She mentioned, for example, that they divided the dishwashing and laundry, cooking and cleaning duties, which "makes lots of fun." Irmgard also told her young readers about the surrounding farmland and that Scattergood once had been a school. The important aspect of community life at the hostel did not escape her. She noted: "On birthdays we have a little party, and then people think back to what happened to them in the last few years and are glad to live a cooperative life in Scattergood." She continued: "On Christmas many old 'Scattergoodians' came back and we were happy together with them. They said...when they saw all the old faces

97

again: 'We are glad to see all members of our family back and to be at home again. We are sure we all shall enjoy Scattergood like in the olden days.'"

At that early age, this future social worker and therapist possessed a keen sensibility for deeper emotional truths, commenting then that "all people in our community are glad to be here. When they leave Scattergood they are sad, because it is like a second home for them. Many do not have their family here [but despite that] they nearly forget all their sorrows, because they all live in a peaceful and happy way." For herself, Irmgard felt "very happy to pass this time in Scattergood. A good fortune brought me in early years to this country of freedom." She took care to add: "I am grateful that after this way through the hostel I can try to do my best to become a good American."

Four decades later Irmgard would see her family's stay in the Iowa Heartland slightly differently. For one thing she admitted that as a girl, she had not "heard much about the Middlewest and was somewhat scared that it might mean meeting wild animals."[5] In that same essay in which she reflected on AFSC's impact on her life, she asserted that "attending meetings every morning at the Meeting House, getting used to the Saturday-night supper of baked beans and Boston Brown Bread, picking corn and meeting people from all walks of life were enlightening experiences." In regard to the professional as well as personal course her life later would take, she felt that "Scattergood opened up opportunities for me and my family which allowed us many growth experiences. It...also allowed me to give to others what was given to me"—perhaps a reference to her endowment of a scholarship for students attending Eureka College. A Disciples of Christ-sponsored institution, the school offered the Rosenzweigs the chance to resettle in the Illinois town of the same name, as well as a tuition-free, post-secondary education for Irmgard.[6] Or perhaps Irmgard was making a reference to the Holocaust section of the college's library, which she decided to fund after fellow-Eureka-graduate and U.S. President Ronald Reagan chose to visit Bitburg cemetery despite controversy over German military personnel buried there.

By the end of the Rosenzweigs' five-month sojourn at the Scattergood Hostel their temporary home had come to mean much to them. "Saying fairwell [sic] to all at Scattergood was painful" Irmgard would explain later, as "we had had such a wonderful time with staff and other residents." Apparently the fondness was mutual, for upon the family's departure on Valentine's Day 1941 someone composed a song to memorialize the event:

Die Rosenzweigen

The Rosenzweigs are on their way
To Illinois from Ioway.
Eureka says they cannot wait
So now they're leaving this fine state.

98

CHORUS:
Good luck to you and happiness
And may the future hold success.
And don't forget (as if you could!)
The past few months at Scattergood.

Our Louis studied keeping books—
He burned the light till break of day.
The tutor met him with blank looks;
"He's teaching me," we heard her say.

Grete's fame spreads far and wide
For the talents she can't hide.
She helped to make our Christmas nice
With decorations low in price.

Parallelogram, isosceles,
Trapezoid and pyramid—
And other problems such as these
Queer things Irmgard is lost amid.

We wish them all the very best;
We know they'll more than pass the test.
And always we'll remember how
We liked this Vater, Tochter und Frau.

Though it gives us so much pain
To have to say auf wiedersehen
We're glad they're on their own fine way
To a good start in the U.S.A.

In our hearts your names are starred
Grete, Louis and Irmgard,
You'll always be on our minds
Won't you be our Valentines?

Like the Rosenzweigs, the Seligmanns (by then the Seamans)[7] also left Germany splintered as a family: Sigmund preceded Friedel and the two children to America by more than a year and a half, to Iowa by almost a year.[8] He had found a job at a nursery in Shenandoah, yet his pitiful pay and other less-than-favorable conditions made the possibility of the rest of the family's staying at Scattergood a while seem preferable to other options. Indeed it was at West Branch that the family enjoyed their long-awaited reunion after such a distressing separation. On the night of Friedel, Helmut and Ilse's scheduled arrival on Wednesday, 17 September 1941, Lynn Zimmerman and guest Fritz Schorsch waited at the station in Iowa City for the "Rocket" to appear—which it did, but an hour late. The excited immigrants didn't seem any worse for the extra wear, however, for Fritz and fellow guest Kathryn Werth reported in the next issue of the community's newsletter that "in spite of this delay we were glad to receive [this] lovely addition to our family." It must have been more wearing, however, to wait until Saturday, when Sigmund first could leave his post at the nursery and welcome his family to their new homeland. What a joyous weekend in West Branch it must have been!

Eight-year-old, blond-braided Ilse later would not recall "all that much" about the four months that she, her brother Helmut and their mother Friedel spent at the hostel. She would remember very well, however, her time at West Branch's school. Both her parents arrived in America speaking English and Ilse had received English instruction in Heidelberg in preparation for their emigration, but she still had to have some English lessons at Scattergood before she could attend the local school. Once that requirement was sufficiently met, dimple-faced Ilse waited with the other hostel children "for the yellow school bus at the end of the road, which" she later remarked, "was certainly a new experience for my brother and me."

Ilse "liked" the school, even though she had to begin the first grade over. A problem more serious than at what level she could begin scholastic training at the school consisted—strangely—of how the others there would address her. The teacher was "unable" to pronounce her name or, as Ilse speculated as an adult, "thought it was too German during war time" and demanded that the little foreign girl spell it "Elsie." Ilse recounted later: "This troubled my mother. Not only was Elsie not my name, but Elsie the Cow was a prominent Borden advertisement. So Mother and I changed my first name to Elizabeth, after my Aunt Elisabeth." Similarly, the teacher thought the thoroughly Teutonic name "Helmut" would be more palatable to American ears and tongues as "Harry," but the 12-year-old boy "simply refused." Once all those involved had settled on permanent names for the two new pupils, their careers took a turn for the better and Ilse found the teachers and other children at the school to be "friendly and helpful.[9] If there was feeling against refugee children" she once reflected, "I was certainly unaware of it."[10]

Perhaps predictably, given what an extremely important role children play in each other's personal internal constellations, the West Branch school left indelible impressions on other Scattergood Hostel children besides Ilse. Eleven-year-old, sparkling-eyed Edith Lichtenstein also found American school life interesting—so much so that she wrote an essay entitled

"Thoughts on School Life in America" for inclusion in the *Scattergood Monthly News Bulletin*, the staff-and-guest-written newsletter which was mailed to Iowa as well as East-coast Quakers, staff members' families, friends of the guests and others interested in life at the hostel. A native of Limburg, Germany, Edith confided: "When I first came to the United States, I laughed much about the children with red nails or lipstick, but I got used to it. I was, like any other child would be, a little lazy, and was glad that we didn't have any lessons to write and learn at home."

Edith formed the impression that "all children, little or big, called their mothers by telephone, and I thought that was wonderful." She changed focus, saying "I usually love to go to school, but I didn't know enough English at the beginning to go in a higher grade...although I was ahead of all the children in arithmetic," she added, "in France we study harder than here." It was social and cultural differences more than academic ones, however, which commanded the precocious girl's attention most and in her text she complained "I don't like this habit of calling two children 'boy friend' and 'girl friend' as soon as they play together. This wouldn't happen if boys were separated from girls like in Europe, because they learn other types of work than girls do. But after all" she conceded, "I liked school very much and we can't compare it with other schools, each school having its own advantages."

Like the other children, Edith spent her time not only in West Branch's school, but also in the fields surrounding Scattergood. She later recalled:

I have a recollection of going out into the field and catching a field mouse and getting bitten... When they cut the hay or the wheat, [mice] were running around in the field there and I wanted to hold one: they were so cute—small and brownish. I was holding it in my hand and it bit my finger and I didn't want to tell anybody. So, I let it go. We spent a lot of time out in the open out in the fields, which was a new experience for me, because we were brought up in the cities... Even when we lived in Paris my mother had always taken us for walks wherever there were woods... I can remember going to pick lilies and violets in the spring, so she tried to get us out in the open but in the city it's much more difficult. So this was nice. Also, we were away from all the adults; we kids used to go out there in the fields together and hang out out there while the grownups did whatever they did. The farm and all the open space was fascinating.

Perhaps it was daring Edith[11] who suggested how the children at the hostel might respond to a letter from unknown pupils in Downers Grove, Illinois, in late spring 1942, which read:

To the children of Scattergood Hostel:

The children of the fifth group in the Avery Coonley School want to make you children a little present of part of the money we made writing and selling our School Journal. The other part we used to buy a flag for the Defense Center.

We heard of you through Mrs. Stein, our group teacher. Do with the money what you want, get something that will give you joy in this time of war. We hope that you will be happy in our country. Very best wishes we send to you.

Varrell Williams
For the Fifth Group

The Scattergood Hostel children replied:

Dear Children:

We were very delighted when we heard that you were so kind to us. We decided that with the five dollars we would buy something that will be here after us for other children. We are going to buy a tent and water wings to learn to swim.

Your teacher, Vita Stein, was here once for a few days, so we know her. We are very much obliged to you for the $5.00, and especially because we know your teacher.

Many thanks again from,
Edith Lichtenstein—11 years
Frank Keller—12 years
Louis Lichtenstein—9 years
Annette Keller—2 years

The young refugee children at the hostel who attended West Branch's elementary school enjoyed close contact with their would-be fellow Americans in the playground and classroom—as the older Scattergood young people who attended the local high school similarly did. Like Edith, 16-year-old Günther Krauthamer—apparently not as resistant to teachers' pressures as Helmut Seaman, given that he submitted to suggestions to assume the name "George"[12]—also recorded his "First Impressions of an American High School" for use in the hostel's newsletter. The bright-faced, fair-haired Berliner was "very much surprised about the much friendlier attitude between pupils and teachers. In Germany, more even than in France, a teacher was always an unapproachable person. [In contrast to the case in Iowa] speaking with teachers, who were in Europe with few exceptions men, made me quite often feel uneasy, and I was afraid to say a word more than was necessary. The higher the rank was, the more we were afraid. [At West Branch's highest institution of learning] I was astonished...over how kindly the other pupils acted towards me. Coming into a new school in Europe, it was very difficult to be considered one of them. The first days they usually treated the new pupil as badly as possible. I was very afraid it would be the same here, and how different it turned out."

In addition to the relationship between individuals and other pupils or their teachers, Günther—or "George," rather—also took notice of the level of academic standards. Reported as having been fluent in German, French, Latin and Flemish as well as English, the basketball-loving tenth grader judged that "schoolwork is certainly more difficult in Europe, and European children take many more subjects than children of the same age in the United States. But by contrast, American children learn many more practical things. Doubtless, I shall like it much better in an American school."

That was in September 1942; perhaps he spoke too soon, for in late October George's glowing impression of American school life would be sharply tested—as he related in the following issue of the little community's common journal:

Friday we had to be initiated! I was very anxious to know what would be done to us. As we don't have this over in Europe I believed everything my classmates told me—and they exaggerated quite a bit. Wednesday two seniors told us what to wear. All boys were to wear a skirt, a sweater, no socks nor stockings, a turban and to carry a foot-long doll. The girls had to wear overalls which must be three times too big and to carry a one gallon milk pail. Besides [this] we had to learn a poem.

There was much laughing when we came to school. Many boys had lipstick, finger-polish and so forth. I think we boys looked so much funnier than the girls did. When the bell rang we went to our classrooms. Despite that I am a sophomore I had to be initiated because it is my first year in any American high school, so I was the only one in my classes who wasn't dressed the right way. They naturally paid more attention to me and to my doll than to the teacher.

Saturday night we had to come back to school. We all went in the assembly and the rest of the initiation began. One freshman after the other had to go up on the stage, where he was asked some silly questions. One of the girls was asked the difference between her and a cheese. The answer was, "A cheese is yellow and I am not." I had

103

to sing like an opera-singer. I hope my tune didn't give them a headache. The tenth grade was very disappointed; they said we were not treated as tough as they were last year. After that we danced and had hot dogs. Now I hope that I'll soon be initiating somebody else.

———————

The older children seemed to have experienced their stay at Scattergood largely in relation to their experiences at the West Branch school, but many of the others were too young to excel in academics or group leadership. Little Pierre Shostal, for example, was so impressed by Scattergood's physical plant that most of his later memories would involve it and not the school.[13]

Unraveling the tangled memories of the lad he had been, Pierre later wrote:

> *What I remember most vividly was what a very different world Scattergood was from the New York City that I had known for a brief time after we left Europe. I remember it very much as a farm...with pigs and sheep making the strongest impressions on me. The sheep grazed in a nearby pasture...and I enjoyed visiting them. They were very quiet and peaceful except when it was time to shear them. There was a lot of noise and activity then! The pigs were big, and very noisy and not at all pleased when identifying clips were clamped onto their ears.*

Pierre's recollection of the Main Building was slightly mistaken, as it was not a "farmhouse"; more accurate, however, was his image of it "as a large, friendly place presided over by the farmers, whose names were Walter and Sarah [sic]. I don't remember very precisely what they looked like, but I think Walter was rather tall and thin. To what extent I confuse Walter and Sarah with the famous farm couple in Grant Wood's American Gothic, I'm not sure, but there must have been some resemblance. I think they were warmer and friendlier than the couple in the picture."

Of the other staff and guests at Scattergood Pierre carried "only dim recollections." He did note: "The person I remember most strongly was Roger Craven, a devout Quaker and conscientious objector. He was tall and thin, and I compared him in my mind to Gary Cooper." Pierre described how he could recall "very clearly Roger speaking slowly and deliberately during meeting at the Meeting House, with the congregation listening carefully and respectfully to what he said." Like so many childhood memories, however, this one was only a partial account of an event which others—namely the adults present—saw differently. Pierre's father, Walter, for example, told in his version of the tale how one Sunday Pierre—then age five—wanted to attend meeting, too: "Permission was given after he had promised to sit still and not utter a sound. This he did. Somebody asked him later how it had gone. His report: 'It was ok. Everybody was good and kept quiet... But Roger! He started to talk and would not finish. He was really bad.'"[14]

Besides his two-year-old brother Claude, Pierre would retain memories of only one other child at the hostel, André Braun—son of the trigger-happy Pole who left France so bitterly disillusioned with the French. "I don't think I liked Andrew very well" Pierre recalled vaguely, adding "I was certainly jealous that he had a scooter and I didn't." Perhaps "Andrew's" quite prominent place in his foggy Scattergood memory can be attributed to the fact that Pierre at one point stole the coveted scooter "and was punished for this." The reprimand Pierre received must have been severe, for—in contrast—the significant event of his sixth-birthday party in January 1943 evoked the faint impression that "quite a few of my classmates came to...Scattergood," without mention of names, faces or even genders.

In any event, the future State Department career diplomat found his family's eight-month stay at Scattergood quite formative:[15] "For me, the time [there] was a real introduction to life in what later became known as Middle America"—a place far removed from future assignments in corners of the world as far-flung and diverse as Kigali, Rwanda and Hamburg, Germany.

As Pierre's reminiscences intimate, for the youngest of the refugees who had landed there life at Scattergood indeed did consist of more than simply attending the village school; the hostel itself provided the children with various pastimes, distractions and—often inadvertently—training for their future incarnations as Americans. And as suggested earlier, over time the role of children in the daily life of the hostel's emerging community became more exactly defined, as well as more expressly valued. By spring 1941 then-director Martha Balderston could write on the front page of the *Bulletin* that "the 10 children who have been here [over the two years since the hostel opened] have been such a joy, we miss them as they leave." She added proudly: "Those who have attended the West Branch school have made splendid records there"—no small feat, considering that in aggregate the little scholars had been jerked around much of the Western world, having attended classes, for example, in England, France, Cuba and New York.

Now, however, the children had reached the quiet, windswept Iowa prairies. To entertain themselves in such an isolated setting they whiled away hours doing what children do naturally—they played.[16] Someone presented Michael Deutsch with a cowboy costume, for example, of which he enjoyed making use.[17] Five-year-old Ruth Weisz—in contrast—formed a club of girls from her school class and invited them to Scattergood several times—despite

Martha Balderston's doubts that "Ruth is not a little too domineering to hold her position of leadership in that group for long," even if "the association with the children in West Branch is good both for West Branch and Scattergood." At Christmastime 1941 Helmut Seaman (age 12) and Louis Lichtenstein (9) built toy boats in the hostel's woodworking shop in the Main Building's ground floor. To mark Mother's Day the following May, along with Frank Keller (12) and Louis' sister Edith, the two boys formed the Scattergood Junior Theatre and performed magical tricks, sang French as well as German songs and closed the performance with the last verse of *America*. Other amusements included playing baseball and football, erecting Indian tepees in the pasture, rollerskating, digging in the hostel's sandbox and swinging from the towering maples in Scattergood's expansive frontyard, sailing boats they "manufactured in the workshop" on the lily pond (or as they called it, "Scattergood Lake") and, of course, dallying with the hostel's assorted pets[18]—which at various times consisted of dogs, cats, a pony, hamsters and a bird. Such tamed creatures came to serve a truly therapeutic if inadvertent role in the rehabilitation of the refugees—both for the uprooted youngsters and their nerve-racked elders.

Presumably, if they were well-behaved the children also could join the adults' recreational activities, which—as long-term visitor Gertrude King of Philadelphia observed—the war-weary exiles kept subdued. She reported that "they do not want anything strenuous and enjoy talking, reading, playing games such as Chinese checkers, croquet or listening to the radio." The children usually also were included in the numerous community celebrations and freetime activities such as scavenger hunts, hayrides, swimming outings, dances, formal teas, birthday as well as farewell parties,[19] readings by Scattergoodians or addresses by guest speakers. They also enjoyed films, sing-alongs, amateur theatrical performances, taffy-pulls or popcorn sessions, and gatherings at Easter, the Fourth of July, Thanksgiving and Christmas.

Perhaps the community's most significant and emotionally charged celebration was that of Christmas—despite the large number of Jews among the guests. That tradition-bound holiday was a time when a majority of the hostel's "alumni" returned to pay a visit to their adopted home and also when all the adult refugees surely were aware of banishment from their respective homelands—with its attendant heartache. Especially at such times children were bittersweet bonds with a painful past, welcome distractions from an uncertain present and valued promises for a happier future.[20] In each year's record of Christmas at the hostel careful note was taken of the children's reactions to this holiday. In 1939—for instance—the Deutsch children constructed colorful paper chains for the tree, as well as a star-shaped coaster for the table decoration and got "nearly every second gift, so they could not get through opening the pretty wrapped gifts." In 1940 Saint Nikolaus seemed "to be a little late," as he came on Christmas Eve and not on the 6th of December as in Europe, but in any event he did appear—"in a long brown coat and shawl, heavily loaded with a large pack," and at first "this well-known friend of the children did not care about anything but the boxes bearing the names of little Bertel [Weiler] and Doris [Arntal]: shouting their names, he handed them over gift after gift, toys and garments that at last surrounded the two little girlies." Christmas 1941 found the hostel children disguised as angels or dwarfs in their role of helping Santa Claus "distribute his wonderful gifts, each of which bore an appropriate poem," and prompted them to write a letter of "many, many greetings" to the 11 children who had preceded them at Scattergood. By 1942—the last Christmas to be celebrated at the hostel—the four children present "could hardly be held back any longer when at last the Scattergood bell rang, calling the entire family for the celebration of Christmas Eve. We assembled in the living room" guest Klaus Asher of Berlin remembered, "and sang together the songs for this night of love...and while some sang *Silent Night, Holy Night*, others sang *Stille Nacht, Heilige Nacht*. Then, the Christmas Story from the Gospel of Saint Luke was read in English and in German taking many of our thoughts back into the past and over the sea." With telling understatement Asher added: "It was a little bit of luck that three very insisting little gentlemen...and one very excited little girl...kept us from getting sentimental."

Regardless of how effective an emotional cushion they proved to be, the children of Scattergood were not at the hostel as mere appendages of displaced adults; although older individuals stole most of the stage most of the time, the hostel existed at least in theory as much for the benefit of the youngsters as for their elders. Certainly the lingering legacy of their sojourn at Scattergood had profound effects on most of the 23 children between the ages of ten months and sixteen years who found a Friendly refuge among the Iowa cornfields. Remarkably, besides two known exceptions, most of them later went on to become social workers, counselors, teachers or other people-oriented professionals. Perhaps their early experiences of being helped in time of need predisposed these children to become adults with finely tuned sensitivities to the needs of others.

While still a guest, one of them—referred to only as "an eleven year old child"—wrote a poem reflecting her or his impression of those peculiar folks who made this influential experience at the Scattergood Hostel possible:

The Quakers

The Quakers are good and helpful to one, in every way.
No cross or evil words we ever hear them say,

Remember the time the negroes were slaved
And the Quakers did their best to have them saved?
They helped the persecuted across the land
Against the slavers, the Quakers were able to defend,
The helpless and the homeless that were in need
And don't we today see and read
How the Quakers help us persecuted Jews?
They don't just say, "How dreadful the news"!
That Hitler is in Germany
And is ruling the people in tyranny
But help as much as they can, and wouldn't it be fine
To have less sorrow in the world all the time.
And the Quakers are doing their best
To have the world in peace and rest.
So let's try to cooperate and help the best we can
Because the Quakers are truly good to man.

1.) Adults were not the only refugees who came under the scrutiny of the hostel staff. Its desire to insure that children were armed—rather, "shoed"—with the means to compete on the social scene led it to champion funds for outfitting them per local norms. In September 1940, just as the West Branch school had resumed classes, director Martha Balderston petitioned AFSC to maintain the $2-per-week allowance which children received beyond the costs of room and board—the same sum budgeted for adults. She argued that "for children under school age the amount [given as an allowance] could be cut if the clothing could be taken care of in some way. For children in school we do not approve of a cut [as proposed by AFSC and agencies which financed the stay of refugees at its hostel]. The ability to do what the others do helps a lot in their adjustment and Americanization. Besides that they must meet charges on books, note-books and gym shoes etc., etc."

2.) Scattergood clearly left an indelible, mostly positive impression on both Deutsch children, who returned as pupils when it reverted to a boarding school. They both attended notable Quaker colleges—Michael studied at Haverford and both at Earlham. Michael later became a psychologist and counselor, Hanna first an elementary school teacher in West Branch and later a counselor for at-risk young people in Detroit. Both have maintained life-long connections to Friends and, as stated elsewhere, Hanna (like Emil) married a Quaker.

3.) As an adult, Hanna reflected on the process of her adaptation: "I think one the most difficult adjustments for me somehow was leaving my home... It seems like the after-effect mostly was turning out to be a very shy, retiring, unsure person. When we got to Scattergood, somehow that was the first place that seemed like home—partly be-cause it was green and where we lived in Vienna [was] also green. Later, after I [visited] Vienna in 1983 and came back to visit Scattergood again and I turned around to look at the landscape on the way back from the farm, I realized that the topography of the land was the same as I saw from my backyard in Vienna... I think the hostel was the first place I felt secure and like I had a community again."

4.) Expectably, Hanna's memories of that time remain fragmented, as she explained: "I remember [after the *An-schluß*] waking up at night and having somebody pounding on the door and saying 'You better get out of here!'—'*Ihr müßt weg gehen!*' And, actually, my father [talked] about Nazis in our neighborhood taking care of us by doing that—that people would do that, that Nazis would 'take care' of their local Jews by telling them to get out of there. I don't know if that was true in other places, but we went to another part of the city before we could leave. And my uncle—my mother's oldest brother—had to scrub the streets. We were among the last people to get out of there—it was September or October of '38. I don't know, but that was pretty close to when people couldn't make it out, so [Hanna's voice trails off] And I can't remember leaving: I can remember lots of stuff before we left and I can remember England after that, but I cannot remember leaving. I don't know *what* happened in there. Someone told me that some children were given sleeping pills or something so that they couldn't make noise: I don't know if that happened or not... I just know that my doll got taken away from me [by a Nazi] and one of my aunts [lost an heirloom] necklace made from a chain from grandmother's big long chain that she wore... But everybody got out; nobody got left behind."

5.) In New York, Irmgard "was sure we were going to where the lions and elephants were; I had no idea about 'Iowa'—people convinced me that it was safe, but.... We went on a bus and going from New York to Iowa on a bus was an experience; I was sick...at every other stop"

6.) Irmgard received the scholarship because of academic excellence she exhibited at the Eureka high school, where as a senior she was elected vice-president of her class and won a Daughters of the American Revolution award.

7.) As why Sigmund changed the family's surname, his daughter said he "changed [it] first thing: someone told him, 'If you're not Jewish, don't have a Jewish name.'" She also noted: "I do recall asking once why Seaman, and was told that Father thought of Freeman, being now a free man—but he had handkerchiefs, shirts, cufflinks and other items that were monogrammed with his initials, SS—thus Seaman. I suppose it's true; it seems logical."

8.) Irmgard, Ilse and Helmut were not the only children separated from one or both of their parents before reaching America: 11-year-old Werner Selig of Würzburg, Germany, for example, spent a year and a half in England before being able to rejoin his parents Ernst and Lucy at Scattergood on 27 May 1940. A middle-aged single parent, Wilhelm Feist spent most of his time at the hostel searching via post and phone for his nine-year-old daughter, Martina, who was thought missing in Belgium but whom he later located.

9.) After a stint in the airforce Helmut later attended Iowa State College and became an architect, while Ilse/Elizabeth became a teacher, then a tutor for learning-disabled children.

10.) Despite Ilse's impressions, *some* neighborhood children remained less than "friendly." According to a visiting *Des Moines Tribune* reporter, "a class of war refugees lay on blankets in the shade of a big maple tree at Scattergood hostel [with] their attention...on John Kaltenbach, 24, youthful Pennsylvania-Dutch Yale graduate and hostel director who was giving a lecture—in English—on the Declaration of Independence. Fifty yards away, on the road, a bright yellow school bus roared by, raising a cloud of dust. The heads of school children stuck out of all the bus windows toward Scattergood. They were yelling wildly. 'Hi, yi! German spies. Hi, yi! German spies!' The reporter jerked his head quickly toward the road—then back to the solemn-faced group of refugees. The expressions on their faces did not change. And Kaltenbach, without a change of expression, continued his lecture."

11.) Edith seemed to have a knack for directive leadership, given that as an adult she worked as a Kindergarten-12 teacher before building a career in educational administration and later sitting on the Worcester, Massachusetts, school board. Fellow Scattergood child Doris Arntal also took to teaching. After graduating from the U of I in speech and drama, she taught for a year in Denver, then earned an M.A. in theater production—specializing in children's theater. She later worked a Denver educational television station, then moved to the Bay Area.

12.) At least in Gunther's case the name change seems to have been made willingly, perhaps out of admiration of or loyalty to an esteemed teacher at Scattergood. Margaret "Peg" Hannum Stevens later said that "I found his name one which would be very unfamiliar to most Americans and called him 'George'—and the name stuck. He was 15, tall, slender and blond, a serious boy, easy to work with (I was his tutor, as well as [his father Michael's]). I recall one day when I was rather tired and planned to rest after lunch, that Michael asked to begin his lesson early. [His wife] Ellen, a good-looking even-tempered woman, admonished him, *'Die Peggy hat keine Pause gehabt'*. (I was grateful, but shortened my rest because [Michael's] eagerness to learn pleased me.) Did G. want to smoke because his father was a heavy smoker? E. told him: 'Yes, you may smoke one cigarette if you smoke it to the very end'. Whether he did so or not I don't recall, but he never, apparently, smoked again."

13.) With one exception: Pierre never forgot a painful incident of having been teased "quite a lot" when he appeared at the school in snowpants although the other children came in blue jeans ("known as dungarees then") and "made it clear that only sissies wore snow pants."

14.) Roger Craven—according to Walter "well over six feet tall and one of the gentlest and most loveable people I have known"—did not impress only Pierre. Walter recounted: "Our Claudie was at mealtime still sitting in his high chair, where Roger liked to feed him and Claudie liked the procedure. Roger remained a friend for many years." Pierre was not the only lad at Scattergood to remark on the quality of messages given in meeting. Once Peg Hannum took Pierre's brother Claude and his arch enemy André Braun with her to meeting. Israel Larson, "an elderly Norwegian-American Quaker...rose to deliver a message. He spoke at considerable length, but his speaking was nearly incomprehensible because of his heavy accent and (I presume) an ill-fitting set of false teeth. Finally after 15-20 minutes a fit of coughing choked off the remainder of his message, and he withdrew to the corridor which ran/runs alongside the meeting room. For some time we could hear him walking up and down, the coughs fading gradually. The meeting room was utterly still. Andrew leaned close to me, and in a faint little voice said, 'When man was, much noise.' Quiet a comment on a Friend's message, with overtones of which he wasn't aware. I learned later [that] Israel's sons had been trying for a long time to persuade their father to give up speaking in Meeting."

15.) Regarding the impact Scattergood Hostel had on his development, Pierre identified later in life—shortly before his retirement—ways in which that early experience fostered in him "a sensibility toward people being responsible for each other. The fact that people at the hostel took in others who they had no connection with at all, is a kind of a standard or a kind example that I'd like to try to emulate or at least be worthy of—especially now that my working life, my career is coming to an end. I'd like to continue, in a sense, to be in public service. I'm very happy and proud of the professional life I've had, but the idea of public service and service to others is something that I find very appealing and that I want to continue... Only as I've gotten older and looked back [have I thought] about why I became the person I've become. What were the influences? Certainly some of the people who we met there and we remembered —like [Scattergood Hostel staff] Peggy Hannum and Roger Craven—are very fine examples of human beings at their best. I know that having been through [the hostel] experience, it certainly did have an impact on the way I've led my life and the things that I've done. I think there was a strong connection between that and going into diplomacy and spending in fact a great part of my time working on European affairs. To me it's been a particular satisfaction to work on German affairs—in a sense as a kind, also, of reconciliation."

At a point that he was taking stock in general, Pierre also considered the hostel's impact on the rest of his family and concluded that his parents "came away with a great respect for Quakers and the Quaker tradition, and I think with a great degree of...a sense of responsibility for others." As a family, the time he, his younger brother and parents spent at Scattergood Hostel became "part of our personal history and I think it's part of [the wider] modern history. I know it wasn't perfect and I know there were problems, but it was still an example of one of the finer sides of the American character, of what America means to me, which has been a country of openness and tolerance and readiness to give shelter to others."

16.) According to a draft of an anonymous, undated article entitled "Children at Scattergood," one observer noted that the hostel's children "enjoy the same kinds of games that American boys and girls do—basketball or football, or dolls and painting books. They read very much the same variety of books that American children the same age read. They enjoy the school plays, sports and Boy and Girl Scout troops." As the line between "play" and "work" could not be firmly drawn, the same writer went on to say that "at the Hostel the entire household shares the daily work and the little folks feel very proud when they are given special duties on the schedule, like setting tables or helping keep the living room in order. One boy who is fond of machinery did the mangling himself when assigned work in the laundry... One little girl came to Scattergood just as the baby chicks were hatching in the spring and received four as her own special possession. She also cared for two kittens and could never decide which she liked best—her chickens, the kittens, or to ride on the horse."

17.) He was not the only child at the hostel to discover the joys of Wild West dress-up. In November 1940 the "What's Going on at Scattergood?" weekly column printed in the *West Branch Times* reported: "Our littlest members of the family, Doris [Arntal] and Bertel [Weiler], have discovered a grand old American game, 'Playing Indian,' and now run around decked out in feather and head-dresses. So when you come out to visit, be prepared to surrender your scalp at the flash of a young lady's dimple! Or perhaps by that time they'll be playing pioneers, and you'll be invited to be the all important horse and help them ford a river."

18.) Scattergood's were not ordinary pets—as Martha Balderston reported to Mary Rogers in January 1940: "Giles [Zimmerman] brought back a 'refugee from Des Moines,' a Scottie named MacTavish. He is learning to play soccer, catching the soccer ball on his nose and bouncing it back with real soccer technique. With the Scattergood cat playing ping-pong and the Zimmerman dog playing soccer, we are developing quite a variety of animal athletes!"

19.) To make their guests feel important and worthwhile, staff made efforts to observe *each* birthday. According to a "What's Going on at Scattergood?" column in July 1941 the hostel held a one-year birthday party for little Krystine Salmon, but "as she has not yet reached the age of cakes her birthday candle appeared as the centerpiece of a plate of red jello."

20.) At the time of her family's stay at Scattergood Hostel a child of three, Nicole Hackel later described this dynamic from a child's pre-rational perspective: "I felt both doted on and ignored [by the adults]. When important things were happening, it didn't really matter what I was thinking or feeling because the urgency of what had to be dealt with was so strong. On the other hand, when adults had a tension I felt—in a wordless way—that I was going to give them hope, because the role of kids was to give grown-ups hope that there was something that could still come out of all of this."

BROAD TOLERANCES; FIRM CONVICTIONS

"Whoever takes the job, must above all things be fond of living with and working with people...a person of broad tolerances and firm convictions...of untiring enthusiasms and deep religious convictions."

~ Reed Cary

Eleven-year-old poets who have been saved from ugly, dehumanizing persecution and likely death might indulge in exaggerated hero worship, but one fact is certainly clear: no Quakers, no Scattergood Hostel. The hostel's enthusiastic, versatile staff provided the vision as well as grunt work vital to the program's success. Were it not for them, the guests could not have found the "place of peace in a world of war, a haven amidst a world of hatred" which they so desperately needed.

The number of staff grew from a handful at the hostel's beginning to—at times—up to 15. While refugees enjoyed Scattergood's restorative atmosphere *on average* for three to four months, staff members tended to stay at the hostel for either short stints (particularly in the summer) or for a stretch of a year or more. Except for thirteen individuals, the staff consisted of young and mostly—but not exclusively—Quaker volunteers.[1] AFSC paid only core staff—and that at subsistence levels, with more than a few of the "volunteers" even paying for their bread and bed!

Their 300-year-old "Peace Testimony" may have motivated them as a group, but what led staff as individuals to volunteer time, energy and love on behalf of complete strangers—people with strange-sounding names, peculiar customs and often rather radical worldviews, who were mostly of an ethnic-religious heritage despised by large numbers of Western peoples? Once these volunteers arrived at the hostel and began working so intensely with those they had come to help, how did being members of the Scattergood community affect them? How did the experience affect their attitudes toward the oppressed and their sensitivity to suffering, their shifting interests in social issues as reflecting their own *Weltanschauungen* and still-forming value sys-

111

tems, their future career choices and the course of the rest of their lives?

The case of Sara Pemberton provides a typical example of what sort of person volunteered to help out at the Scattergood Hostel. Born to Zimri and Hannah Hinshaw of Galena, Kansas, in 1887, Sara had attended Olney Friends boarding school in Barnesville, Ohio, and Westtown School in suburban Philadelphia. She later became a teacher and accepted a staff position at Scattergood School, where she met Verlin Pemberton (a pupil there) and married him in 1914. It was partially the birth of their four children—Lillian, Beulah, Ernest and Alice—which motivated Sara to help found Young Friends in the early 1930s. She thought such a group was important as at that time Iowa Yearly Meeting Conservative Friends met in October—after the autumn harvest. Such a schedule, however, meant that the Yearly Meeting's young members could not attend because of conflicting school obligations. Therefore they began meeting in August at the Clear Lake Methodist Camp—but on a shoestring of a budget. Many of those present helped pay for their participation by bringing garden produce, with the Pemberton contingent bringing so many tomatoes that Lillian later would remember "some days we ate tomatoes for breakfast, lunch and dinner." Along with endless helpings of red "love apples," Young Friends enjoyed visits from leaders of other yearly meetings, "work camp" projects, guest speakers and endless discussions. All this was punctuated by periodic dips in the nearby water and bound together with hearty camaraderie.

Once Young Friends had committed themselves to pursuing their "leading"[2] to found a program which might benefit the growing flood of refugees from Nazi-occupied Europe, modest and mild-mannered[3] Sara committed herself to guiding gently their youthful idealism until it could be converted into practical reality. She received no monetary compensation for the endless hours she devoted to contact making, letter writing, problem solving and—finally—guest greeting. This busy farmwife—and at various times also a Farm Bureau supporter, the "clerk" of and a First Day School teacher at the West Branch Monthly Meeting, a member of AFSC's executive board, a chair of the Federated Women's Club of Cedar County and a local community 4-H leader—became the most integral non-resident "staff" at Scattergood Hostel. She undertook that role as an expression of her conviction to speak to "that of god in every one." Her daughter Lillian labeled this motive simply as "a concern and love for people."[4]

The eager and endlessly helpful Pembertons played a fundamental role in making the Young Friends' vision of a project at Scattergood possible. It was obvious from the beginning, however, that a paid staff would have to be chosen to carry on the work of early volunteers—some of whom consisted of

112

University of Iowa co-eds who came to Scattergood in temporary work crews to clear and clean, or of Iowa Quaker housewives who scared up old sheets and extra silverware for use in the hostel. Friends from Des Moines came to help make the minute plans necessary in executing such a massive undertaking, and other, non-affiliated individuals who believed in the vision behind the founding of the hostel also assisted in some way that they could.

Almost from the start and with Sara Pemberton's prompting, AFSC courted the Scattergood property's caretakers, the Stanleys, asking that they remain and continue in the capacity they had filled since the year before the school had closed. In a formal arrangement, the hostel administrators agreed to pay them $40 per month in return for oversight of the garden, yard, furnace, water system, laundry and fieldwork. The hostel would provide them space for their horse "Lucy" and two cows, plus seeds for garden planting, but Walter and Sara would have to keep their car "at their own expense." A trickier point, however, involved their accommodation as they resided in the Boys' Dorm—a fairly commodious space sorely needed as housing for refugees and staff. In a desperate attempt to solve the stubborn problem of lack of space, Mary Rogers had the odd idea of housing unwitting staff in the gymnasium or "a tent for the summer" or trailers. Both one-time Scattergood School pupils, the Stanleys finally found refuge of their own in the former manual-training building (the one-time one-room schoolhouse moved onto the property decades earlier to expand Scattergood's facilities) "until other suitable living accommodations [could] be arranged." This promise never materialized, but to no apparent distress of the cheerful caretakers.

Walter and Sara Stanley proved to be ideal *ersatz* parents for the little flock of castaway souls who washed up onto Scattergood's safe shores. Already in their 60s, they emitted a quiet, reassuring calm to which most of the guests not to mention the task-taxed staff happily resonated; they seemed to embody the peaceable, noble ideal of meditative living and universal goodness to which Friends had always aspired. Remarkably, in document after document guests and staff alike recorded—without exception—positive, appreciative images of this simple Quaker couple. And, somewhat humorously, many referred to the uncanny closeness with which Walter and Sara resembled a classic American icon. Perhaps Walter Shostal said it best: "I cannot speak of Walter and Sarah [sic] Stanley without thinking of that Grant Wood painting 'American Gothic.' It was not so much a physical similarity between the Stanleys and the couple on the painting, it was the mood, the spirit of it. Both stood for me like symbols of an American past that was going, if it was not already gone: a rural, stern, god-fearing, righteous and limited-in-its-outlook but loving and good America."

Besides caretakers, Scattergood Hostel would need a director. Although

AFSC planned to utilize the idealistic energies of young volunteers to execute most duties, it sought an older, experienced figure to administer the day-to-day life of its refugee center. To fill that salaried position it turned to Albert and Anne Martin. Albert and his attractive, dignified-looking wife had just returned from Germany, where for two years the couple had worked at the *Quäkerbüro* in Berlin. A former professor of German at Brown University in Providence, Rhode Island, Albert had served Friends well in his role as their representative in the Nazi capital. Meanwhile Anne had proved to be a helpful assistant in the Quakers' efforts to assist in finding *konfessionslose* Jews passage out of Hitler's Third Reich. Despite what AFSC or Iowa Quakers might have hoped, however, it seems that short, stocky, balding Albert tentatively planned to be at the hostel only through the summer. In any case, given his standing commitments to present talks around the country about his experiences in the "New Germany" and his desire to interview at various academic institutions for a professorship, the Martins would be unable to arrive at Scattergood until May—she first, he later.

As soon as Anne arrived with their two boys early in that month she set about helping with the endless details inherent in preparing the hostel for its as-soon-as-feasible opening, as well as massaging public relations so as to procure an as-flexible-as-possible popular opinion regarding the placement of refugees in the heart of Middle America. The first assignment required elbow grease, the second a resilient voice box. Anne's many efforts even caught the AFSC's attention in faraway Philadelphia. Mary Rogers marveled at Anne's efforts, commenting that "we are much impressed by your list of speeches made and I don't see how you can do all that you are doing—work with paint brush and hoe and scrubbing brush during the day and making speeches in the evening." AFSC was much less impressed, however, with Anne's dispersal of the rather bare-bones budget with which the hostel had to fund its operations. In the same letter Rogers complained "we do not quite understand the accounting except that we think that your bills are probably running far ahead of the original estimate." As it turned out, though, AFSC's piqued feeling over Anne's use of monies allocated for the Iowa branch of its refugee program would pale in comparison with the massive headache it would get over her husband's reign of error at the hostel.

Scholarly, authoritative Albert appeared at Scattergood the day before Mary Rogers penned her letter of 26 May 1939. Soon after he arrived the previously relaxed, amiable mood at the hostel shifted. According to a letter sent by 22-year-old Bob Burgess (AFSC's Student Peace Service field secretary, a frequent visitor to the hostel and later the beau of staff member Ruth Carter) to Clarence Pickett: "during the first few weeks of the project, under the direction of John Kaltenbach, everyone coöperated nicely and thought of the Hostel as an experiment in community living. However, since the arrival

114

of Albert Martin the atmosphere of the project has changed a lot. I have a great deal of respect for Albert and the things he has done ever since my undergraduate days at Brown University, but I can't help feeling that he was a rather unfortunate choice for the position that he is now filling. He has tried to rule Scattergood with an iron hand, and in doing so seems to have destroyed most of the cooperative spirit that existed previously. Rules and regulations, while they are certainly necessary, should come from the group and not be imposed upon them by 'the boss.'"

The frank young man's impressions aside, within a fortnight of Albert's appearance the previously amiable guests fairly bristled with contention; their willingness to swallow hollow assurances that instruction soon would begin suddenly disappeared. They seemed unsure that without prodding the unpopular professor would deliver those aspects of an effective rehabilitation and integration program which they really needed. The hostel's "Meeting for Business" minutes of 16 June, for example, suggest that the less-than-satisfied refugees had grown impatient with unfulfilled promises of instruction and job-placement searches, for they appointed the thorough, respect-commanding Kurt Schaefer to represent the refugees' sentiment on three points. For one thing they felt that "placement work should be started now," with a committee being selected for the purpose of reviewing the backgrounds and qualifications of guests seeking employment, as well as to establish contact with potential future employers. Second, they suggested forming a committee "to plan study and recreation" and that "English classes start immediately," with "opportunity [being] given for the discussion of social, economical and cultural problems of this country." Third, they wanted the administration to consider allowing former guests to return to the hostel in the case that "someone is unable to continue on a job inspite of [sic] his [or her] best efforts."

In any event Albert decided to accept a professorship of German and a position as head of the department at McMaster University in Hamilton, Ontario—according to him, "just the sort of position which Anne and I had hoped for." He wrote Clarence Pickett regarding this development on 3 July and hinted that he and his family would stay at Scattergood till mid-August. The problem was, the Martins no longer were welcome at the hostel.

At about the same time that Albert was writing Clarence Pickett, Sara Pemberton wrote AFSC's Reed Cary—in uncharacteristically blunt words—pleading for help. "We are hoping that Anne Martin and her boys can take a vacation while Albert Martin is away on his speaking tour. Poor woman, I believe she is working on nerves, and trying so hard to manage that she fails to let any little detail escape her. Result—all are on nerves [sic] edge." She went on to say that 17-year-old son Joe[5] "hates the place" —adding "of course, his position is a sad one. He and his mother both long for the things they could have and do if in a home of their own. Joe is a very intelligent young man with the energy of 180 lbs. back of him." However, "at present [he] fits into no place...He is not a German refugee neither is he a volunteer worker. Therefore what he does or says is no concern of anyone else on the grounds except his parents."

In her unusually long, four-page, hand-written missive of concern, Sara went on to mention the deteriorating opinion of outsiders regarding the hostel, noting with alarm that:

> Strangers have been taken aside and told that the whole project is a failure and it is impossible to do anything with the Germans. We are sorry that things have turned out this way but it seems too sad for the hostel to be a failure now, when it has other prospects of a real success. [Underscoring this assertion, she added that] before George Laurie left he remarked that he was surprised at himself because he had liked it so well here and appreciated what it had done for him. It is so different from another place he had lived. [The speech the quiet Hamburger gave at his farewell party] carried [the] thought that he had grown into the Scattergood spirit.

At a later point Sara reassured Reed: "I think of Scattergood as thy small child, and I am here trying to see that she, or he, does not get too badly hurt." It seems, however, that the thoughtful farmwife was not alone in her protectiveness of the fledgling hostel, for even as she was writing him, Reed was writing desperate letters to Iowa trying to contain the damage spilling out of Scattergood's recent explosion of ill will. In a letter to Sara which had as its first sentence "Please consider this letter extremely confidential," he stated in unmistakable terms that "it would appear highly desirable that we remove Albert from contact with Scattergood. The problem is how soon. If the situation will not be too serious the shift could come most easily...If, however, the success of the enterprise is likely to be jeopardized by having him there for five or six weeks, we had better face eventualities and in one manner or another withdraw him from the picture." While in a letter to John Kaltenbach written the same day Reed noted "I think you know how sincerely we all regret the personality difficulty which has arisen at this rather crucial time," he closed his letter to Sara by remarking "I sincerely regret now not having gone into this whole problem with thee when I was at Scattergood. I then had hoped that the storm had been a passing one concerning which the less said the better."[6]

Before the thunder claps caused by the storm at Scattergood were heard, there remained the untidy detail of showing the man out. On 11 July Clarence Pickett wrote to Albert Martin with typical Quaker tact to suggest that "the course of affairs at Scattergood has not followed the pattern pictured at the beginning." Recapping the anticipated upheaval expected due to Albert's planned August departure for Canada, Clarence went on to say: "Considering all the facts in the case, we have decided that rather than have the hostel led further along the line of one set of adjustments to be followed by another set of adjustments only a short time later, we should put the new line-up in charge as quickly as possible." Admitting that "they are probably not equal to the task of building up all of the necessary services for Scattergood," AFSC's executive secretary claimed "we are confident that the remaining members of the staff are competent to maintain temporarily the orderly conduct of affairs, and we feel certain, therefore, that it would be for the best good of all concerned that you leave before coming further involved in the life of Scattergood."

Besides straining to move gently, Quakers also are known for the lengths to which they will go to find reasons to express gratitude—again, so as to honor "that of god" in even the most difficult of souls. Predictably, then, the day after the Martins' much-awaited exit Reed sent his boss in Quakertown a communique in which he said: "There is one feature [of this whole affair] that I deeply regret, and I would be glad if it might be remedied." Referring to Clarence's letter notifying Albert Martin of AFSC's wish that he leave earlier than planned the scene which had erupted at Scattergood, Reed noted that it "did not contain any word of appreciation of their work here." He himself had drafted the letter to which Clarence later lent his weighty name. After Albert's dismissal, though, Reed felt "particularly deeply this neglect, for the facts are that [the Martins] cared very deeply for the project, worked extremely hard, and gave unstintingly of their best, and to take no official recognition of these facts" he charged, "was a grave injustice." To support his claim that the couple had indeed contributed to the hostel's development, he pointed out that "Anne was here from the first and shares with John the credit for much of the excellent spirit which prevails.[7] Albert, of course, came much later and saw various points in the work where improvement might be made, and the difficulties which ensued were in large measure brought about by the attempt to change too rapidly, rather than because the goals were not desirable."

Although very much a Friendly politician, Reed also was a man of genuine integrity. Thus he tried his best to show the Martins due respect to the very end and was on hand as a crowd of reporters gathered at the hostel to record the departing director's last hours at Scattergood. Keenly aware of public appearances, he also knew that the staff's general dislike of Albert Martin was keeping many of its members "occupied" and at a safe distance from the impending send-off. He set off, then, to flush out at least some of the hiding young volunteers. He found Lillian Pemberton talking with Kurt

Schaefer in the gym. As Lillian later would recall, however, she was to learn "a very important lesson [on that occasion] which has stayed with me to this day. The Martins were packed up ready to leave in the station wagon. [She and Kurt] were ignoring the scene...when Reed Cary came by and told us that we needed to join the farewell as the Martins were human beings and as human being to human being we could do the human act of saying good-bye. That's the spirit of what he said" the future peace activist remembered decades later, adding "I'll not forget the message."

When Albert Martin originally notified AFSC of his decision to resign as director of Scattergood Hostel, he concluded his letter with a bit of barbed advice concerning the search for his replacement: "We should like to suggest that you select someone for Scattergood who is young, without a family and in good health, to devote their whole lives to this job." He noted that in his opinion "there is no possibility of family life here." Little did he realize, but he already had made the acquaintance of his young, childless, physically robust successor—and intimately so.

As early as the day following the Martins' leave-taking, Reed Cary thought out loud to Clarence Pickett about the effectiveness of a project such as at Scattergood: "From what I observe here, I am very sure that the hostel method of resettlement of those who for one reason or another have to shift is thoroughly sound, providing there is adequate leadership. This proviso is a most important one and I find myself wondering whether the requirements are not impossibly stiff. I can see clearly what is needed here and when I look at the people who might be drafted for the work there is quite a gap between the two. On one hand, the director should have the qualities that come with chronological age, and at the same time be young enough to be sufficiently flexible to adapt himself to and understand the reactions and problems of those differing greatly in age and mental condition." Reed went on to say that "an unbelievable amount of initiative in a wide variety of directions must also be on tap at all times. Then there must be a deep understanding of human nature to attain just the right balance between pressure for accomplishment of objectives and freedom for individual personality manifestations. If the balance between these two is lost, friction and dissension on the one hand is sure, and on the other slovenliness and a failure to progress toward the necessary goals will ensue. Whoever takes the job, must above all things be fond of living with and working with people...a person of broad tolerances and firm convictions...of untiring enthusiasms and deep religious convictions. This is an oppressive list of specifications. To the degree which the director departs from these specifications, the hostel system is likely to fall down." Luckily for the hostel, such a leader was to emerge from the ranks of its own staff. On the day after the controversial academician from Providence left

Scattergood, Reed sang praises to Clarence Pickett regarding John Kaltenbach—whom he described as a "tower of strength." He held that "if only [John] had the psychological advantage of having people know that he was forty or fifty years old instead of only twenty-three, he would be absolutely ideal as director of the hostel." As it turned out the young Friend would prove to be that anyway, despite his "chronological age."[8]

Initially John officially served as "acting director"—under the public premise that AFSC would seek a replacement for its first appointment to the post. In reality, however, he simply continued the role he had played at Scattergood since first pulling into the driveway in mid-April of '39 with a carload of excited foreigners. As he had done before Albert Martin had arrived, John again could parent the crucial early phases of Scattergood Hostel's infancy—albeit now without the upsetting influence of a heavy-handed intellectual some three decades his senior.

Despite his young age, John satisfied the very "oppressive list of specifications" which Reed had outlined for AFSC's head. He seemed to have an astonishing understanding of Scattergood Hostel's function as a rehabilitation center for refugees as well as the difficulties they faced as newly arrived immigrants in America. And, a spiritually grounded sensibility backed his clarity of vision. That is not to say he was a saint, however, for sources have indicated—"off the record"—that the tall, strikingly handsome and athletic youth often played the part of the hostel's Romeo. It had been he, after all, who single-handedly coaxed cars full of co-eds from the university in Iowa City to trek out to the abandoned school to sort and scrub. One former staff member claimed his amorous advances toward Clarence Pickett's daughter Rachel—a hostel summer volunteer—prompted the well-known Philadelphia Quaker to yank his little girl back to the East Coast.

Regardless of any romantic urges, though, the future farmer, father of a large family, author and later Director of Development at Wesleyan University possessed amazing insights which made him a natural leader—and fully aware of the task in front of him. In a tract it sponsored, AFSC explained that Scattergood Hostel's function "is complicated, like most human service. It is, first of all, a shelter for body and mind, a brief haven from the bewildering difficulties and insecurities of life in a new land. In the second place, it is a school whose curriculum will contain organized lessons in English, American History, Government, and Institutions, but also informal lessons in American social etiquette, American cooking and marketing, American business and farming—even American professions." John saw such an approach, however, as partially unrealistic. He wrote Reed Cary that:

I have so far been going on the policy that the workshop is a better teaching place than the classroom, particularly on problems of human

119

*rehabilitation and personality adjustment. I have observed a tendency
among us to do what may be "too much" for our "hostages."[49] I suspect
that many of them expect to start at the top of the pile, to transfer to
this country and take up at the same place they left off over there.
Whether we would like this to be or not, John Q. American has different ideas, and a number of refugees are in for a prolonged bump. If we
can bump them first and do it gently, we may be doing them a greater
service than we would by treating them with kid gloves and exposing
them to a course of ten lectures on American civics. They will not be
kid-gloved by the general populace, and they will have to get most of
their civics and history from books anyway. I think the experience of
Friends in work camps will be most valuable here [in conjunction
with] a work project with a directly connected course of study.*

Besides with the main office's rose-lensed images of professional placements after as-brief-as-possible stays at Scattergood, John differed with his
fellow Easterners' naive scenario of shipping freshly landed Jews to a
promised New Canaan on the Iowa prairies. Fritz Treuer in particular arrived at West Branch expecting to establish himself as a self-supporting
truck farmer—*a la* Zionist dreams of "making the desert bloom." John explained: "It appears to me that this is about the worst possible place to hope
to establish anyone without capital. The average capital investment in farms
here must run from $20,000 to $100,000. Land sells for about $95 per acre
and is hard to buy in less than 80 acre lots. It is extremely difficult for the
small and intensive kind of agriculture that refugees look for to find any start
here. And what is worse, there is a very limited market for truck, eggs, etc.
Every man has his own patch and coop."

The goal of settling refugees from the Third Reich in Iowa as farmers *a
la* the *kibbutzim* model was illusionary at best. With characteristic humor
melded with directness, John set about disabusing his Philadelphia-based
bosses of their delusions soon after arriving at West Branch. On 7 June 1939
he wrote to Reed Cary: "I feel rather as if I had not been seeing the field for
the corn stalks... The only way I out that I can see for those who are thinking
of us as an opening into mid-west agriculture [such as Fritz Treuer] would
be a cooperative farming venture which would have to be financed practically in toto by some outside group. It would be extremely difficult to get any
local capital into such a venture. This would call for a whole set of revised
aims for those whom we hope to settle in rural districts. In the meantime we
ought not to send anybody out here with the hope of getting more than a
hired hand's status in agriculture." Referring to his fondness of "the community experiment idea," John went on to suggest another solution to "this agricultural problem" and "present farmer-hopefuls":

My stay in North Carolina makes me remember the plan we worked out there as it could possibly fit the situations of men like Fritz. That effort is a small one, but I feel that it will be one of the most valuable for us in this particular phase of the refugee problem, particularly because the South needs new blood more than the Plains, and because the land situation is such there that small agriculture with limited capital investment is more feasible than here [Therefore] I am concerned that the N.C. project be followed more closely...

There is much more here [in Iowa] for the people who are interested in small industry... People spend there [sic] spare nickels for fertilizer in Iowa. Roadhouses and shops belong to the East. I think we must concentrate on industrial development for this region if we are going to make the kind of creative contribution we hope for. This ought to be in mind in picking Scattergoodians.

If there are a number of refugees who are looking to agriculture, and there may be more than we think among the Jews who have been affected by the New Palestine movement, they should be sent to the South, unless someone has in mind a large scale project. I understand that most of this type [of] refugee is going to Australia, and I suppose most of the cases we will handle will be those of commercial and professional types. We have recognized this latter point, but I wonder if we are taking the best path for adapting professional people to their future in America.

John's musings to Reed expose weaknesses in the initial concept of Scattergood Hostel's mission, not to mention realistic potentials. For starters, the Philadelphia office shipped disabled refugee Fritz Treuer to Iowa apparently before *any* AFSC staff had confirmed the wisdom of such a move—and thus John's detailed rejection of such plans. Next, one must wonder if the 23-year-old tactician merely acted diplomatically in his letter to the head office in suggesting an alternative to what he saw as an impossible fantasy for the Iowa program, or if he genuinely pondered spawning an experiment in Dixie. If the latter, he was acting naively, too, for the Ku-Klux-Klan—long a vocal, deadly presence in the South—and local authorities would have had something to say about Northerners shipping scores of Jews past the Mason-Dixon line. Were he really being so unreflective, then he was guilty of the same poorly thought-through visions his older counterparts sitting in isolated East Coast offices nursed.

Another weak link in the chain of arguments for agricultural refugee colonies in Iowa consisted of the lack of capital, to which John referred. The fact was, from start to finish Scattergood Hostel existed on a slim budget, usually teetering on the edge of insolvency. The kind of project hinted at by individuals like Reed Cary—far exceeding the scope and cost of the program at Scattergood—would have required unavailable supplies of necessary capital, thus insuring its failure. Fortunately, such plans were dropped early and instead of attempting to propagate *kibbutzim* in America's Heartland, Quakers focused on the more pressing business at hand—rehabilitating, integrating and assimilating their refugee guests.

It would be a much more esoteric point than professional training or the impracticality of establishing *kibbutzim* on the prairie, however, which would raise John's ire—namely, what to call the very people Scattergood Hostel wished to help: "I think we ought to call a spade a spade. Part of the kidding we are doing is in the use of the word 'guest' in place of 'refugee.' I have turned completely around from what I thought about this when we talked about it in the east [for] the refugees do not hesitate to call themselves refugees, and every time any of us use the word 'guest,' it is with an effort that has not grown natural with use. It always sounds as if there were some pampering being done."

Whether or not they were being "pampered," the "guests" certainly did impress John with their fortitude. He marveled once that "to know these people is to wonder at their ability to rise above such seemingly overwhelming difficulties and to go on living with such courage and hope and freedom from bitterness. Nowhere is it more clearly demonstrated that 'only the destructible can be destroyed.'"

John's ability to shift focus from the minute or mundane to the subtle or sacred had very much to do with his own internal complexity—the cheerleader and the casanova, the smart mouth and the sage. Surely a great deal of his personal motivation for devoting fourteen and a half months to the cause of reviving the defeated arose from a vivid spiritual life. Perhaps one of the best-recorded signs of his inner strength survive in the form of informal journal entries. As he had done with the beginning entries of *The Book of Scattergood*, John also wrote the closing ones. Exactly one year after arriving at the soon-to-open hostel with an odd-matched group of ill-prepared urbanites in the middle of the so-perceived "sticks," he marked that special anniversary by doing something most ordinary. He simply sat down and wrote from the heart:[10]

When I left Scattergood on Monday I had a nice long list of events to record here, but on my return I could not find them. Perhaps it is better. They were about clear days and rainy days, about friends and about quarrels, about visiting sociologists, people who sleep in the afternoon, cats, dogs, Philadelphia people, and spring plowing.

Perhaps it is better they were lost. Some of them might have hurt people, some might have been only false rumor that came to my ears. All of it was on a background of blasting radio that booms continuously through the house, WAR, WAR, WAR—England, Germany, Norway, Roumania, France, Allies, submarines, bombings, eternally braking the peace and quiet of our home and setling already frazyled nerves on edge.

It has been a kind of nightmare—the press of affairs, the pain written on faces, the loss of friends, the sorrows and sins of men written large and sharply engraved in sensitive minds and loving hearts—this the last of fifty-two weeks that round out Scattergoods first year.

But one night of this week when I came late and tired to my room I found a letter lying there—and it kept a light burning—in these words—...Christianity is still existing. We may fulfill in becoming active, somehow, the requirements of the ten Commandments......and do something good, everybody in his circle. I know every day's life is mercy and grace. I love the reflection of sunlight in the eyes of human beings. Oh—may this life of mine be God-centered forever.

There are faithful ones among us whose love continues, working, bring cheer into any room they enter. Suffering has made them forgiving rather than bitter. They are the holy fellowship of saints. They tell their love in washing pans and scrubbing floors and hours of trying tutoring and being tutored. Their love is boundless and their spirits are kept fresh in loving.

Everyone has given and received of this blessing at some time here. Man keeps alive the capacity for love. It is never driven from him. It makes life precious, and death a time for increase of love.

This book ends with several blank pages. There are some not with us who may come back and read some day, who will be far enough away to discover in these pages a thread of life which bears a precious burden, a way of life which knows joy and sorrow on the same road! Let them write that we have been blessed and that our hearts are grateful. They will not find among men any key to this curious document. Let them write that our failures have been in places where we have not loved enough, and our joys where our faith has been whole and clean and our love endlessly forgiving, and let them ascribe the glory of loving lives to the mercy of God.

John Kaltenbach had been on hand on the day Erhard Winter arrived at the hostel along with Anne Martin and her sons, and soon won the respect of the lad from Lüneburg—even if Erhard wasn't having the best time. Despite difficulties with the milieu there, Erhard's days at Scattergood weren't completely filled with disdain. He developed a strong affection at least for the physical place and later praised its "pristine simplicity and beauty sitting in a huge cornfield." Also, although he harbored decidedly critical feelings toward his fellow guests, Erhard grew quite fond of other staff members besides the hostel's *de facto* director and soon became "special friends" with Camilla Hewson. She was a lively and gifted 16-year-old Quaker girl who had finished a semester early at Des Moines' Roosevelt High School, so offered 14 months of her life before college for use at the hostel. As Camilla later would admit, she "was one of a group of young people...who pitched in with more enthusiasm than expertise" at the fledgling hostel—which she characterized by asserting "it would be hard to imagine a setting more removed from the horrors of Nazi persecution or the crowded refugee settlements in New York City." She later would comment gratefully that "the 14 months I spent [there] were eye-opening, mind-expanding, and enriching in ways I never could have anticipated"—with Scattergood Hostel proving to be 'the best place to round out young years.'"[11]

In terms of her maturation and coming to understand people better, the future social worker, counselor, wife, mother and grandmother explained: "At the time, I took things at face value, and more personally, rather than analytically or objectively... It surely helped me grow up fast, and taught me a lot about human nature. [Also] knowing the refugees and sensing their histories even in a general way convinced me of the resilience of the human spirit. One had to admire their willingness to start new lives with almost nothing, and for the most part with good spirit. They gave so much in return for what they received, though often their gifts were intangible... I am eternally grateful that I was given the chance to be part of the SH staff and treated as an equal by those older and wiser than I."

Camilla did enjoy a special status—technically being a member of the staff yet having less authority than others because of her age. Apparently the staff seldom pulled rank on her, however, for she felt that "while I suspect, looking back, that older staff often kept a discreet eye on me '*in loco parentis*', I never felt patronized or supervised." In later describing her role there Camilla emphasized that "I don't mean to suggest that my role was the most important, but I WAS on the team and gave no one any cause for concern—as far as I know."[12]

Still, Camilla's youth predictably predisposed her to forming a "fond, but platonic" bond with her peer and fellow teen—the strong-willed Herr Winter. Because she was not an adult and because he naturally liked her, Erhard allowed himself to become attached to Camilla—although with a condition, namely that he could play the mature one. Nonetheless the two developed a close relationship, "arguing philosophy, politics, or anything under the sun." Erhard also happily played devil's advocate, according to Camilla "to provoke me—and make me think."

In later dissecting their relationship Camilla realized that "while I was fascinated by him, [Erhard] treated me with a distancing toleration. We enjoyed each other's company and I respected his reserve, and let him teach me German, sometimes up in the big maple by the main building. He was moody and often arrogant, and as I realize now was in emotional pain." Still, as an impressionable teen she "agonized over his absences and the times when he seemed to ignore me," yet "delighted in the simple activities we shared." Camilla later conceded that their's was an adolescent relationship in which they "spent many hours together, and never so much as held hands, but shared our thoughts freely, and learned from each other."

That summer, weekends usually found floods of volunteer work crews, reporters, visiting local and out-of-state Quakers or curiosity seekers washing across the shores of the young community's common life: Erhard and Camilla—among others—would disappear sometimes to the flat roof of the Main Building to "spy on and escape them." Over time, Erhard entrusted Camilla with the gruesome, tragic story of his father's murder, of how his family and he had fled first into Berlin's nameless masses and then abroad, and of his plan to make his way to Paraguay to join a Bruderhof community. In the end—given Erhard's limited financial resources and emotional stamina necessary to chase such a dream successfully—a community in the decidedly less exotic setting of South Dakota had to suffice.

Recapped in shortest form, it seems that in spring and summer 1939 two teens crossed paths on the Iowa prairies and helped each other find a bit of friendship and life experience. Certainly, their time spent at Scattergood was like none either had ever known and, at least for Camilla, the hostel experience would be one which she could designate "one of the most formative of my life." Already as a first-year college student she realized that her time as a hostel volunteer had touched her in a very important way. As an Earlham College English assignment in 1940-41, Camilla wrote an "Autobiography" in which she said "a conception of religion, a smattering of German, a few ideas about farm life—these were not all that I learned at Scattergood, and although I am aware that I probably cannot yet realize all that it has meant to me, I believe it has done much to make me the person I am today. Granting the effect of home atmosphere...I must say that Scattergood also has influenced me profoundly."

In re-examining her rich sojourn at Scattergood Hostel more than 50 years later, Camilla would list some of the most memorable impressions of her stay at the hostel. She recounted that there was:

So much to remember...
...the awful hush as we gathered to hear the radio tell of Hitler's

125

invasion of Poland.

... the way some people couldn't talk for long without glancing over their shoulders, out of long habit of caution.

... how Ewald [Peissel], who had been in a concentration camp, wolfed his food when he first arrived.

... the times when Sunday visitors, some sympathetic, some just curious gawkers, swarmed over the place...

... the warm hospitality of West Branch Quakers, which helped balance the hostility of some Iowans toward "those Germans."

... the occasional Pall Mall cigarette smoked to assert my "adulthood" (but thankfully I never got "hooked").

... trekking to Iowa City to see "Gone with the Wind."

... someone speaking in Meeting for Worship in German, the words strange but the spirit familiar.

... Walter and Sara Stanley, beloved Quaker caretakers inherited from the school days, whose gentle ways helped heal our guests' wounded spirits.

... the respect I gained for the strengths of ordinary people, who could lose everything, yet have the courage to build new lives in a new land.

...my 17th birthday party, just before I left to prepare for college, and how I cried as I left the Hostel for the last time.

Camilla was the youngest but not the only Quaker girl to bump into the wider world while still treading upon Iowa soil.[13] While an English major at the liberal Grinnell College some hundred kilometers west of West Branch, in the summer of 1941 Amy Clampitt volunteered as Scattergood Hostel staff. A daughter of a Quaker farmer near New Providence, Iowa, who was active on the Scattergood Committee and spent time there as the leader of a work-camp, Amy later moved to New York City. There she initially pursued graduate studies in English at Columbia University but then dropped out and worked as a secretary and writer in Oxford University Press' textbook department. She next worked as a National Audubon Society reference librarian and as a free-lance editor—according to one biographer "earning a reputation for her ability to fix up difficult manuscripts." Amy wrote novels, none of which were published, but eventually earned sudden acclaim as a poet eleven years before her death from cancer, beginning with the publication of *The Kingfisher*, which "drew many rave reviews."[14]

Already at Scattergood, however, the gifted writer practiced her beloved craft of writing—in the form of an essay which appeared two-thirds of the way through her three-month sojourn at the hostel. The sensitive, quiet young woman titled the work "Impressions of a Summer Volunteer":

> *Very shortly I shall be saying goodbye to Scattergood, after two months here as a summer volunteer. And these months have proved so varied and eventful that I scarcely know what has impressed me most; but it is perhaps this very element of surprise and spontaneity which for me characterize the place. There have been dull moments, of course; and when the thermometer reaches a hundred in the shade it is sometimes difficult to recognize excitement even when it appears. And there has been routine, because after all Scattergood does have a schedule—though struggling with lunch preparation in the midst of the mountains of pots and pans which I always managed to accumulate, or splashing around with the laundry crew, was something of an adventure, schedule or no. But Scattergood is a place where routine is not the first consideration. I have been amazed at the smoothness with which plans suddenly evolved are put into effect, and delighted with the large part which the purely impromptu has played—the evenings of singing on the lawn, the practical jokes, the conversations which made of tutoring something more than the giving of lessons. In an article in the last news bulletin Margot [Weiss] mentioned that some of the most memorable people she had known had been among those at Scattergood. I feel the same way. For an American there is of course a certain superficial glamor surrounding those whose backgrounds are so different from his own, but the really unforgettable qualities go deeper than that; and at Scattergood, where there exist a freedom and informality which are really democratic, there is an opportunity to know these people well. This above all has made my summer at Scattergood one which I shall not forget.*

Indeed, Amy would never forget her stay at Scattergood, nor the people she met there. The lasting impact of her experience remains, however, circumstantial, for it did not appear directly in her later poems. According to her brother—who read all of her published poems—"there are suggestive hints from her life and work there that summer...was somehow important. The other side of Amy's spirited affirmation of life—expressed in her summer's work at Scattergood in 1941, and in later years in great numbers of her poems—was a profound opposition to war and violence and killing (and all kinds of injustice); her Quaker roots went deep on this issue. She first began thinking of herself as a poet, according to her own account, during a protest of the Vietnam War outside the White House in Washington, D.C. in 1971. One of her poems in *The Kingfisher*, 'The Dahlia Gardens,' was inspired by the self-immolation of a [32-year-old] Quaker, Norman Morrison, in front of the Pentagon in 1965 as his protest against the Vietnam War."[15]

Another of Amy Clampitt's poems, "The Burning Child,"[16] makes vivid reference to (among other things) the Holocaust, an episode in human history made more personal through the stories of persecution and flight of guests whom she encountered at Scattergood Hostel:

> *The people herded from the cattle cars*
> *first into barracks, then to killing chambers,*
> *stripped of clothes, of names, of chattels—all those*
> *of whom there would remain so few particulars:*
> *I think of them, I think of how your mother's*
> *people made the journey, and of how unlike*
> *my own forebearers...not one*
> *outlived the trip whose terminus was burning.*

Lillian and Beulah Pemberton—neighbors from just down the road from the Scattergood Hostel and two of Verlin and Sara's three daughters—also discovered a bit of the globe at their own doorstep. Both became involved in running the place and both were touched for the rest of their lives by the intense display of humanity which they were to find there.

Early on, before the first working guests ever arrived, AFSC sought the services of individuals less removed than its own paid staff ever could be from the swift developments taking place at the once-empty boarding school. Perhaps it was her mother Sara who gently nudged Beulah into action, but in any event the Pemberton's second daughter agreed to lend her name to the Scattergood Committee's list of designated officers—despite having been a full-time State University of Iowa student of commerce. The dark-haired, attractive young woman's duties included keeping account of the hostel's modest yet growing budget and issuing periodic financial reports to AFSC as well as the Scattergood Committee regarding the project's financial health. A future mother of an adopted son, as a volunteer at the hostel Beulah learned much about flexibility for later she shifted posts, from having been treasurer to becoming a stand-in substitute for her sister Lillian as dietitian.

Short, black-haired Lillian had completed a bachelor's degree in home economics at the university in Iowa City in spring 1938 and had spent a year as a dietetic intern at the Ancker Hospital in Saint Paul, Minnesota, before joining the Scattergood staff as the hostel's dietitian[17] in June 1939. As she later recounted, Lillian's diverse position involved "planning meals, buying food, working with the kitchen crew [consisting of] guests taking turns [and] helping them learn English as related to food." Little did Lillian suspect but her job description would include public-relations stunts as well.

From the moment that West Branch Friends announced their intentions to bring refugees into the area some rather loud members of the surrounding community expressed opposition and happily fed the already buzzing local rumor mill. Over the four years of the hostel's operation all sorts and forms of imaginable as well as utterly preposterous charges, tidbits of gossip, unfounded tales of sinister plots and proof of pure paranoia would pass back and forth like summer heat lightning across the nearby telephone lines, between pews at the rise of Sunday service, over the drugstore counter, in front of the scales at the farmers' cooperative elevator and behind closed parlor doors. To counter this irritating, potentially dangerous hearsay and tittle-tattle, the Scattergood staff concocted the delicious idea of combating slander with—of all things—*Apfelstrudel.*[18]

As head of the busy hostel kitchen, Lillian helped organize the visit of local women's groups—with flash-happy photographers and reporters near at hand. These smalltown ladies were treated to a demonstration of proper Viennese *Strudel* making by none other than Claire Hohenadl-Patek, a former food-and-fashion editor for the demoted Austrian capital's largest newspaper and a future confectioner at New York's chic Helene Rubenstein Kitchens. The sturdy yet grand-looking *alte Dame* patiently demonstrated and explained—in a thick Teutonic accent—the painstaking procedure of stretching the thinly rolled dough over a big floured- and sheet-covered table, followed by sprinkling finely chopped nuts, raisins and slices of crispy apple over two-thirds of the dough before rolling the whole thing up and baking it. The results of such effort, Lillian testified, were "spectacular and delicious." After the *Strudel* was ready the calculating staff conveniently offered their note-taking guests refreshments and a tour of the place. Their wooing of local gossip mongers and respectable citizens alike seems to have been successful, though a scientifically proven connection between taste buds and prejudice remains elusive.

When not fighting fear and hate with pastry, Lillian had the demanding assignment of keeping anywhere from 45 to over a hundred tummies full and content (depending upon whether visiting guests were joining the usual "guests" for a meal).[19] Still, she managed to carve time out of her heavy, unending work routine for some semblance of a personal life—including embarking on the road to matrimony.

In December 1939 two University of Iowa friends distracted the active George Willoughby from his political science doctoral studies long enough to take him on a blind dinner-and-theater date with Lillian and later hauled him out to West Branch—supposedly to introduce him to AFSC's refugee program over dinner. Whatever the hostel's dietitian served on that cold wintry day, it must have been pretty hot, for by June Lillian had abdicated her culinary throne in favor of her sister-in-waiting successor and on 19 July 1940 she and George were married on the Pembertons' front lawn, with Scattergood's staff and guests present.

Perhaps not surprisingly, given the physical and emotional closeness with which staff and guests at Scattergood lived, the brief courtship and wedding of the hostel's dietitian were destined to become a community event from the very start. Some individuals knew of Lillian's amorous activities early in the New Year but kept her secret until she took the opportunity to openly declare the impending union during a sewing party in the area, at which some female hostelites were present.[20] Apparently a guest then proceeded to pass the news to the wider Scattergood family with the publication of the following quip in the folksy *Scattergood Monthly News Bulletin* (the cartoon below the announcement accompanied it and has been attributed to Camilla):

It seems that even at Scattergood cupid is on the job. Anyhow Lillian would tell you so if you were to take the trouble to awaken her from her "Liebestraum" to ask.

While we all (or most of us at least) thought that she was being a good little dietitian and minding her peas and carrote [sic] she had another interest, too, as time has shown. This gradually evidenced itself in the person of Mr. George Willoughby a Ph.D. student of political science at the University in Iowa City.

It has been announced that 'wedding bells will ring out,' as the saying goes, on July 19th at the Pemberton home. We are quite thrilled with the glimpses we get of preparations and planning. Scattergood ladies were present at the sewing (announcement) party which made the glad news public, and are proud to have contributed their blocks to a quilt for the happy couple. (Incidentally, isn't LILLIAN WILLOUGHBY a rather lovely and liquid sounding name? Don't know where she could have found a better one!)

****

"LIEBESTRAUM"

Having already thrown a wedding shower for the couple beforehand, immediately afterward the vows the members of the hostel community bid Lillian and George a temporary *adieu* as they took off with their matchmaking friends on an extensive trip to Mexico City via Texas in a customized clunker. Lillian later recounted that "George sold his old Ford roadster and bought a roomy, old, eight-cylinder Hupmobile" to use on their less-than-private yet nevertheless "delightful" honeymoon.

When the newlyweds returned on 1 September 1940, George—who had been born in Wyoming but spent most of his childhood in Panama[21]—moved into the hostel but soon found living at Scattergood, full-time studying and managing the university's cooperative dorms concurrently to be "too much." So, he took leave of his graduate fellowship and devoted himself to life at the hostel—and how! Besides offering lectures on American politics or history and, of course, tutorials in English, George conducted a series of workshops in public speaking; they were intended to help people feel more at ease in their adopted language and in front of others, with each person giving a one-minute presentation on a topic about which they knew something. With Lillian formulating the hostel's food program in the Main Building's ground floor kitchen and George arousing political awareness and activism upstairs, the couple remained an integral part of life at Scattergood until their departure for Iowa City and beyond in July 1941—not realizing that "beyond" would someday include stints in many places. While engaged in nursing, teaching, non-violence training, championing women's issues, campaigning for civil rights, advocating the release of political prisoners, conducting relief work or other projects, the deeply committed pair would act as social-change agents in numerous U.S. states, as well as in Poland, Japan, Southeast Asia and India, Africa, Latin America and other places far removed from their first shared home at Scattergood.

George and Lillian were not the only couple to serve at the hostel. Not coincidentally—given the first guests' complaint about the lax job-placement efforts and AFSC's sobering realization that it had to get serious about that part of its offer to the refugees it had lured to the quiet Midwest—the dynamic pair of Giles and Lynn Zimmerman arrived at Scattergood Hostel just a month after Albert and Anne Martin left. The 25-year-old Giles had been assigned the rather difficult task of securing positions for the hostel's charges, taking into consideration their previous professional experiences and the late-Depression job market—which until the United States entered World War II in December 1941 remained discouragingly "competitive." His wife—a year younger and born as "Ethelyn"—was to serve as office manager. Although he had not been hired for the job, the childless couple's black Scottie terrier "Mr. MacTavish" was to play the role of hostel clown.[22]

As a boy, Trenton-born Giles had attended George School—a prestigious Quaker boarding school in suburban Philadelphia—before going to Wittenberg College and the University of Pennsylvania. Lynn, on the other hand, was very much a Midwestern girl and had left her native Kalamazoo to attend Antioch College in Michigan's neighbor state to the south, Ohio. There she had worked as a campus switchboard operator to help finance her studies; thinking the call was a prank, she hung up on Franklin Delano Roosevelt once when the nation's chief executive called to offer Antioch's president Arthur Morgan the position of director of the Tennessee Valley Authority.

While lanky, curly-black-haired Giles—according to Dresden native and guest Hans Peters—"looked just like Lil' Abner," his Catholic-reared, fine-featured wife seemed to the young Camilla to be a "fairly worldly lady" who dressed "wildly," smoked and was "popular with everyone." Staying for a year and a half, the Zimmermans came to work at the hostel as a natural reflection of their commitment to human service with an intercultural twist—which made possible the life of voluntary material poverty which they had chosen to lead. Their daughter Sally Weiss later reported that "they loved Scattergood Hostel." Certainly, their lively personalities mixed well with the crowd they found there. Jovial Giles made a devoted, reassuring job-placement jockey and Lynn's serious determination became legendary—with her daughter swearing that Lynn nonchalantly continued teaching during a tornado while part of a dislodged roof blew past the classroom window.

Giles later would have to serve the war effort as a conscientious objector, acting as director of the Philadelphia State Hospital's Civilian Public Service Unit. From 1943 to 1944—while still on leave from a ten-year stint as an AFSC fieldworker—he worked as chief of the Employment Division of the War Relocation Authority's Colorado Relocation Center, a Japanese-American internment camp at Poston, Arizona. Following the war he assumed first a secretarial, then the director's position at International House—a facility for foreign students in Philadelphia—which he filled for the rest of his life.

And Lynn? The couple divorced in the mid-1950s and she moved to Arizona, where the by-then "convinced" woman remained active in Quaker as well as other peace and human-service projects for the rest of her life.

Another "convinced" Quaker couple, Earle and Marjorie Edwards, also were led to Scattergood. Both natives of New York, Earle had been born a Baptist and Marjorie a Methodist, but participation in various AFSC work camps and peace-education programs while in college interested the amiable, upbeat pair in exploring further involvement with Friends. Specifically, an American Association for Adult Education study grant provided them eight months of "getting acquainted" with residential adult-training institutions in England, Scotland and Wales in early 1939. The experiences they harvested there whetted their desire to continue such work in the United States.

132

Back stateside they sought a suitable program where the duo could apply the ideas they had brought back with them from Britain. As soon as they discovered "the simplicity which characterized AFSC volunteer projects [and that] whatever practical experience one may have had were very relevant to the refugee hostel situation," Earle and Marjorie applied to serve in AFSC's growing refugee program.[23] "As it turned out" they later explained, "our temperament and experience were quite suited to the Hostel program so we were delighted when we were assigned to West Branch."

When the Edwardses arrived at West Branch in late September 1939 they found the guests "understandably preoccupied with their own personal situations." As they soon came to realize, "adjusting to a new country and to close cooperative living probably crowded out some of the larger issues"—such as national and international social, political or historical developments. The guests clearly had much to deal with, yet "all things considered, residents behaved in a more normal fashion than one might have anticipated"—which did not mean, however, that there weren't subtle tensions and, at times, not-so-subtle conflicts; "normal" doesn't assume uninterrupted harmony.

"An anti-Semitic remark made by a high-strung Roman Catholic was shocking but highly unusual" the Edwardses claimed. Beyond religious belief, however, political persuasion also led to periodic discord. They mentioned, for example, "political refugees upon whom some other refugees looked askance."[24] In considering this point, they acknowledged that "political controversies or conflicts might have been reflected in German conversations carried on when we weren't around." The Edwardses noted once that according to one German political refugee, "the Austrians, who tended to be more liberal in their political outlook, were more congenial than most Germans."

Indeed, regional differences within the Teutonic realm created very real variations in how the German-speaking population of the hostel appeared to the young Americans. "Perhaps the most prominent conflicts were those involving North Germans who prized efficiency and orderliness,[25] whereas Austrians, especially Viennese, were much more easy-going"—a contrast which "tended to show up in relation to tasks involving day to day responsibilities affecting the community."

Differences of ideology and affiliation aside, the refugees at Scattergood had to live together as personalities—with all attendant needs, wishes, habits and quirks. "Although one might easily conclude that any unusual or difficult behavior on the part of any Hostel resident was a result of experiences related to the political situation" the Edwardses said, "some problems undoubtedly were precipitated by the group living arrangements, including sharing rooms with other refugees." Moreover, being operated on a cooperative basis the hostel depended on each adult present doing his or her share of

133

necessary tasks such as gardening, food preparation and preservation, general housekeeping or the physical maintenance of buildings and grounds. Still, "some people were entirely unprepared for such work, especially the men. Even using simple tools was a new experience for some highly intellectual men. Many of the women [on the other hand] had been housekeepers [in the non-professional sense] and were able to adjust to working as part of a team, whether in the kitchen, the laundry or on the cleaning crew."

Earle and Marjorie—whose assignment superseded mere English lessons to include the responsibility of organizing household as well as outdoor projects—did encounter some difficulties in executing their duties: "Most of the residents had been accustomed to employing someone to provide the day to day services needed in one's own home. Since those services are as important in a cooperative community, everyone was expected to assume some responsibility for them. In what even in those days was something of a do-it-yourself society, taking part in this aspect of community living was in a sense an important part of the educational program. For some residents this was quite stressful and the reluctance of a resident to do his or her part sometimes became a community issue. It was not surprising that individuals who had been through exceedingly trying times on occasion found living in such close quarters difficult."

To deal with issues such as individuals shirking their chores, staff and residents met weekly to discuss plans, experiences and—in the Edwardses' words—"occasionally problems." They thought, however, that "relations between residents and staff were remarkably good," a state helped in no small part by the ample opportunities to focus on more than only problems: "Impromptu parties celebrating the departure of residents for employment and more elaborate social events featuring holiday themes were an important part of the community life as well as the education program. [In addition] residents contributed significantly but informally to aspects of the program through suggestions made in the weekly meetings or at other times in conversations with staff. Bureaucratic influences were minimal."[26]

Naturally, Scattergood Hostel didn't exist as a closed system or as an organism separate from the environment around it. The Edwardses were quite aware of this and noticed the "special treatment" which outsiders showed the foreigners in their midst—both positive and negative. "Though Iowa Quakers frowned on smoking," for instance, "they accepted smoking by refugees, whereas they would have been intolerant of smoking by the staff." Of course, Iowa as well as East Coast Quakers had invested much emotional and tangible capital in the hostel, so they granted their "guests" polite behavioral license which otherwise would have been grounds for confrontation —including the consumption of alcohol, cardplaying, dancing, the wearing of make-up or "excessive" jewelry and other signs of "worldliness." Still, as the enthusiastic Edwardses freely acknowledged, "the Hostel would not have been so successful had it not enjoyed the support of local Friends."

As for Scattergood's connection with non-Quakers, they claimed that "public relations problems with the larger community were infrequent and not serious." As proof of interest in and goodwill toward the refugees on the part of the locals, Earle and Marjorie related: "There were opportunities to speak at Rotary Clubs or churches and it was not difficult to find persons [among the refugees] interested in such contacts with the outside world." Also, specific townspeople in West Branch made significant contributions to the hostel's relationship with the wider world; they noted that "the Mayor of West Branch [William Anderson] could not have been more helpful."

Unfortunately, potential employers did not extend the same warm welcome that open-minded community leaders did: "In at least one case there was reluctance to hire a well-qualified Austrian engineer for a position in a firm with government defense contracts, but after many months he was hired by a heating and air conditioning firm."

As far as their own professional fate following their departure from Scattergood in mid-April 1941, Earle and Marjorie would be guided for the rest of their lives by the values strengthened during their 19 months among the dispossessed of Nazi-occupied Europe: "Intensive exposure to the range of adjustment problems hostel residents experienced resulted in our interest in securing professional social work training." Thus the couple eventually moved from West Branch to the Windy City, where Earle enrolled in the University of Chicago's School of Social Service Administration and Marjorie became a mother. Deeply committed to the people they had encountered at Scattergood, while still in the Midwest they often sponsored gatherings of hostel alumni in their home or at the Chicago Friends meetinghouse. Later, their solid bond to Quakerism led the Edwardses back to the East Coast, where they established a home in Swarthmore, Pennsylvania. Forty-two years after the hostel's dissolution, they sponsored a last reunion for the remaining Scattergood family—so durable were the impressions and the importance of what had taken place under the wide-open Iowa sky.

Scattergood would prove to be an important station on life's journey for numerous guests and staff—particularly those in need of the healing effects of being part of a stable, supportive community. Although it certainly possessed its share of shortcomings, the hostel often was able to provide many of those who sojourned there a sense of belonging, well-being and sometimes even life-long direction. Due to their experiences in that Friendly environment some individuals later were led to on-going engagement with Quakers, some married guests or staff whom they met at Scattergood and some undertook helping professions as future careers. For some, two if not all three of these categories would apply. One could say, for example, that Robert Berquist stumbled across Scattergood by "accident," became a Quaker by convincement and subsequently undertook the training necessary to become a teacher through closely calculated design. Originally he intended on visiting Scattergood for two weeks—but ended up staying a lifetime.

Of course, like most stories, this one is not quite so simple. By the time the 26-year-old native of Mankato, Minnesota, had arrived at the hostel he already had embarked on a personal quest which would lead to decades of service. Presbyterian-born, the serious young bachelor had attended the Chicago Theological Seminary for a year before abandoning the world of dissecting the sacred for one of shuffling insurance forms. From 1936 to 1940 the bespectacled office worker managed claims for Ministers Life and Casualty Union in the Protestant stronghold of Minneapolis, Minnesota. He explained: "Though I was with congenial associates there...I became increasingly dissatisfied with the work, especially as I was a conscientious objector to military service and expected to be drafted under the Selective Service Act. It seemed to me that my sincerity in making a claim for C.O. status would be questioned, in view of the conventional business position I held."

In early 1940, Robert met several volunteers of AFSC's Student Peace Service who made a deep impression on him. Then, in July of that year, he happened across an article in the *Christian Century* which would change the course of his entire life. In it author Marcus Bach—a professor at the State University of Iowa's School of Religion in Iowa City—described the year-old Scattergood Hostel near West Branch, Iowa. Calling it "America's first camp for refugees," Bach praised the project and its work. Claiming that there refugees could "find the strong, unselfish hand of welcome," he so impressed the devout young believer that out of a desire to practice his faith Robert promptly wrote AFSC and inquired if he might spend his two-week vacation in August as a volunteer at the hostel. Not surprisingly, the staff only too happily accepted his offer—as he marveled, "although I wasn't a Friend."

By nature task-oriented, Robert quickly jumped into the swirl of work and activities at the hostel, as he found that "the demands on the staff, made up mostly of young people recently out of college, were great." His own assignments involved individual as well as small-group tutoring in English, evening educational programs on U.S. history and culture, and leadership of what was called "men's work"—which upon his arrival consisted of digging new ditches for the hostel's malfunctioning septic system.

As Robert openly acknowledged, his involvement in Hostel life was "a bit less than total" because he soon enrolled in education courses at the university in order to meet requirements for a secondary teacher's certificate. On most of the trips to Iowa City," however, Robert "took one or more passengers from the Hostel, and these two parts of my life were closely interrelated." During the half-hour jaunt from Scattergood to the university campus Robert took advantage of the opportunity to become acquainted with various members of the hostel community: "I came to have deep respect for many of the European guests and developed close friendships with some of them as well as with staff members."

Following a fortnight of tasting the sweetness of a shared life in the name of the greater good of helping outcasts from Europe, Robert returned to the Twin Cities. He found, however, that the security and financial compensation of stamping requests for insurance payments all day could not compare with the ever-changing, stimulating parade of people he had encountered at Scattergood. After considering the implications of such an action, Robert wrote to West Branch and asked to return as full-time staff. Upon receiving a positive response he gave notice at his comfortable place of employ and after a short time packed his bags for Iowa, arriving 30 September 1940.

Robert's autobiographical account of his stay at Scattergood written some five decades after the event consists largely of facts. His journal entries from the time, however, reveal a searching, sincere young man trying to find his way in a world of war, violence and mass murder on a scale seldom seen in saner ages. In response to a letter from a friend which spoke of "deep thought and study on community"—for example—he wrote: "it impressed me anew with the urgency that we, who call ourselves pacifists and think we see a glimmer of a better way, actually undertake to live differently in a way that makes possible the actual expression in living of the professions which are so easy to make." Arising out of a commitment to practice what he and like-minded peers preached, he approached the Edwardses and "mentioned...the importance of those of us at Scattergood who are deeply concerned...to come together regularly for discussions and meditation in this realm."

Robert's effort to schematize his and his associates' convictions led to a meeting of area conscientious objectors at the hostel at which they discussed "some of the questions in the special questionnaire for C.O.s" and coached each other on strategy. "It was the general feeling" Robert reported of this meeting, "that answers [given to the local draft board] should be as concise as possible, and definite in nature, rather than vague, and attempting to justify our course in a way that would seem to give the impression that we regard ourselves superior to those who differ with us." If such sincere idealism seems self-indulgent, it is important to remember that for Robert and the others, their practiced pacifism literally was a matter of life and death—especially given the times in which they found themselves.

This newcomer to Quakerism was a modern-day seeker—not unlike the restless George Fox—and reacted like many zealous converts: he strove to apply his new-found beliefs to every area of life. Even the merry, at-times-frivolous holiday of Christmas, then, needed to be interpreted anew through a lens of complete earnestness until it, too—as Robert wrote in his journal—"emphasized again the importance of simple and consecrated living—in every situation of life." The world was breathing down Robert's neck, he knew it and he sought answers—fast! The experiential and committed lifestyle typical of Friends proved to be a most comforting backdrop with which to act against the raging madness which seemed to have broken lose of all control by the end of the dire '30s.

All the young staff members at the hostel—especially the male ones—had to grapple with the very real gravity of the times. Not everyone grappled as intensely and soberly as Robert, though. And it showed. Staff as well as guests lovingly teased him for his constant note-taking, eagerness to accept responsibility and characteristic single-mindedness. His departure from the hostel upon receiving a summons to alternative service at the Civilian Public Service Camp in Merom, Indiana, for example, provided one outlet for such non-malicious ribbing. Fellow staff Esther Smith wrote a humorous narrative to be presented with sound effects as Giles Zimmerman pantomimed being "Bob" during the farewell party given in Robert's honor on 31 October 1941.[27] The piece testifies that at Scattergood Hostel individuals—quirks and all—could become integral parts of a dynamic whole. At the same time, though, despite his bent for orderliness Robert fit in well and complemented a staff which sometimes lacked adequate discipline or perseverance.

More than anything else, for the previously "dissatisfied" Robert his sojourn at Scattergood seemed so significant because of the relationships he formed there. Though enjoying camaraderie with American co-workers, he especially relished the hours spent talking with the guests—apparently, the more intense, the better. Whether analyzing Nazism with Irwin Blumenkranz or exploring Christian socialism and community with Otto Bauer or sharing Paul Frölich's sadness at being separated from his family on that former Reichstag member's birthday, Robert savored the earnest exchange of experiences and ideas. Even a theme as non-philosophical as the development of motion pictures—which he visited with Joe Mauthner—gave Robert a depth and meaning in human contact for which the chummy yet at-times-superficial Midwest is not known and for which he had hungered.

Several of Robert's relationships with guests grew to be close and lasting.[28] In a letter to director Martha Balderston after leaving Scattergood for Long Island in which he reflected on the relationships he had known at the hostel, Paul Frölich exclaimed: "Scattergood people! You know, dear Martha, how I felt happy in this quiet community. Indeed, the time I spent with them was the happiest since the two years in wartime-France with all their mischief and misery. The best of all was to find new friends there, men and women to whom, since the first hour, I felt myself like a brother." He went on to say: "I hope I will offend nobody when I say that he who stands nearest to my heart is Bob. I fell [sic] the deepest admiration for his *Lebens-anschauung*—though I may differ with him in some ideas—of which he never spoke but which speaks out of his attitude, of his earnestness, his zeal and consciousness of duty. I should like to tell him only that life is not only duty and that in looking for more joy of life he would strengthen his power to work."

A Leipzig native who later ended up in the New York suburb of Kew Gardens in Queens, Froelich wasn't the only guest to grow fond of the thoughtful young man he had met at Scattergood. Later, as he was in the Civilian Public Service, Kaethe Aschkenes visited Robert while he convalesced at a Whittier, California, hospital—she having found a job at the Los Angeles Sanatorium in nearby Duarte, awaiting emigration to Israel. Still later, after Robert had married and become a teacher at the re-opened Scattergood School, he and his family stopped several times at the Hammond, Indiana, home of former guest Franz Nathusius, a member of the *Bekennende Kirche* in Berlin. During those stopovers Robert found "jovial" Franz to be "very talkative in poor English....always smoking a cigar and...a poor pianist"; these characteristics, however, didn't matter: the connection did. Robert liked this man—and that was enough.

It did not take long after leaving his post at the Scattergood Hostel for Robert to value what he had found there. Already in fall 1941 he wrote a piece for the *Iowa Peace News* about the hostel in which he said that "several months in the rural atmosphere of Scattergood can bring about an almost unbelievable change." Whom did he have in mind as he wrote that? Was that true only for the refugees inside its walls? Or what about his comment that "former members look back on the Hostel as their American Home in a very real sense?" Robert went on to say that "more important than the material assistance it has been able to render some 200 individuals is its work in developing understanding and friendliness toward the refugees on the part of many persons from Iowa and neighboring states [Minnesota, for example?]—who have come in contact with the hostel." In concluding the article, which he subtitled "What Can I Do?", he advised: "Trying to put oneself in the place of a refugee and helping others to do likewise is the greatest contribution anyone can make toward the working out of this human problem."

Perhaps Robert had succeeded a little too well indeed in identifying with the refugees, for when he left he suffered a great loss. Even before he left for AFSC's alternative-service project at Camp Merom, Robert complained in his journal that upon receiving word of his assignment: "my first reaction was one of reluctance to leave the work at Scattergood, which seemed to me of greater importance to other people than the CPS experience would be." He did concede that the notice "came as a climax to a deeply stimulating and satisfying time at Scattergood. I felt more than ever a close affinity for the

139

Friends and a desire to be part of their fellowship."

Visiting his parents in Mankato to bid a "sad farewell, not knowing when I might get home again," Robert returned to Iowa. There he left his car in Des Moines and signed its title over to guest Rolf Arntal, a young Jewish businessperson from Hamburg who recently had gotten a job with the Henry Field Seed and Nursery Company in Shenandoah, Iowa. He then set out for southern Indiana. He was at the camp less than 24 hours when he confided in his trusty journal that already that first day his "feeling was distinctly one of being lost, which explains my desire to be busily occupied [painting window sashes]. The change from Scattergood where my responsibilities were clearly marked out, to CPS, where I was still an added appendage, was a bit too great."

As soon as he could arrange it, Robert took leave of his busywork at the camp and trekked "home"—not to Mankato, but to Scattergood. The journal entries from his three-day road trip read like a classic homecoming tale:

February 13, 1942
We got off for Iowa at 5 o'clock (P.M.), our party including [fellow CPS campers] Vern Devore, provider of the transportation in the form of his 1930 Model A, Sam Stellrecht, Millard Mills, Vail Deale, and me. We stopped at Bloomington [Indiana] about 11, where Vail paid a brief visit to his girl friend.

Feb. 14
Arrived in Muscatine about 5:30, and stayed with Sam Stellrecht (at his parental home) for breakfast and a couple hours rest. He then took me over to Scattergood in a beautiful snow storm. It was his first visit, so we made the rounds on arriving there. The first person I saw was Josephine Copithorne, who came out to see who had driven in. She told Bob Cory about the company, and then in quick succession I met Kaethe Aschkenes, Victor [Popper] and Julius [Lichtenstein], and in the other building Anny [Harvey] & Lisl [Harvey], Lisa [Lausen], Martha [Balderston] and Peggy [Hannum]. I had a nice talk with Verlin [Pemberton] as he was pouring the milk, and greeted Elsie [Kepes] and Elisabeth Lichtenstein in the kitchen. After lunch with the Stanleys, Kate, Lisa and Martha, I helped tack paper on the porch screen doors, and then joined in snow shovelling. Before dinner I had a long chat with Martha, looking through her Scattergood pictures, and then a short visit with Paul [Singer] and [Paul's bride] Elsie in their room, where Paul was in bed due to injuries resulting from a fall. After supper I called Mrs. Guthrie. Before the Valentine party, I fulfilled a request by talking briefly concerning the CPS program. The party was lots of fun, including the exchange of Valentines. During the course of it, I

worked in a little visiting with Walter & Sara, and Kaethe, and read a letter she had received from Paul Fröhlich [sic]. Before bed I had a nice walk with Bob Cory in the freshly-fallen snow. We discussed the W.B. peace group and contact with the community.
Feb. 15

About 9:30 started out with Walter, Sara and Martha for West Liberty. There I got a ride with a driver of a gas truck directly to Muscatine and reached Sammy's about 11:45. After a brief repast we went to Millard's and his folks took us to Newport, where we met Vern. Our trip was uneventful until about 4, when we had the first of three flats. We stopped at Bloomington again and had coffee and cake at the home of Vail's girl friend. Due to the tire trouble, necessitating patching a tube in the rain, we didn't get back to camp until 3 a.m.

The 24 hours at Scattergood seemed like a dream come true. Without any question it was the most wonderful experience since coming to camp, and in many ways the happiest day ever spent at Scattergood. The refugee friends still there were so genuinely glad to see me, and seeing again Martha, Walter & Sara, and Bob C. was an inspiration to me. I realized more than ever how much all of them mean to me. I derived something which brought me back to Merom with a greater sense of significance in living, and a deeper gratitude for the privilege of having been associated with Scattergood and the Friends.

Whether or not he knew it, Robert's association with Scattergood and Friends was just beginning. After six months in a CPS work project in coordination with the U.S. Soil Conservation Service, he was transferred to a camp near Coleville, California, where he worked with the U.S. Forest Service before moving on to four different camps and projects—such as one where he served as a camp counselor for refugee children during a furlough from CPS. Following his discharge from CPS in late 1945, Robert moved to Philadelphia to work with AFSC for nearly a year, during which time he made contact with former hostelites living in southeastern Pennsylvania and western New Jersey. He also briefly visited the recently established Powell House, an information center for refugees in New York City headed by Martha Balderston and Par Danforth—respectively Scattergood Hostel's former director and second job-placement officer. Amidst his usual busyness Robert also found time to court and marry Sara Way, who at the time was a nurse at Westtown School. Having learned from Sara and Verlin Pemberton about the planned reopening of Scattergood as a school, Robert and his bride went to Iowa in 1946 to teach and nurse, respectively—positions they held until their retirement in 1979, after 33 years of very close "association with Scattergood and Friends."

Working as a Scattergood Hostel volunteer had, of course, various effects on various people: some found outlets for altruism, some were confronted with others' negative reactions to difficult personality traits, some discovered a world bigger than the Iowa prairies, some became politicized, some found mates and the seeds of future careers, some discovered a sense of place and belonging which they so acutely had needed. And, at least some of the volunteers learned something about what it meant to be a refugee in a world which had subjected such unfortunates to unspeakable wickedness and anguish, which had slammed closed too many doors and which promised a future devoid of familiarity or security.

One of the volunteers who seemed to have learned this last lesson well was Margaret Hannum. Peg—as she also was known—had been born into an Episcopalian family in Windber, Pennsylvania, the daughter of a civil engineer and a nurse. After graduating from Goucher College in Baltimore and teaching high-school French and English for three years in Maryland, small-built, chestnut-haired Peg lived in Paris from 1937 to 1938; she returned to Europe in summer 1939 for eight weeks.[29] An English major, in the summer of 1941 she nonetheless went to work at AFSC's Sky Island refugee center in Upstate New York's Hudson River Valley—partly as an assistant to the dietitian. There she developed a sensitivity to refugees' lot. When she learned of the Scattergood Hostel she decided to continue as a volunteer. At Scattergood, though, much more than just her culinary skills or expertise in English was utilized.

Peg made numerous friendships with hostel guests, including the Shostal family, with whom she stayed in contact for more than five decades. Walter would remember her fondly as an English tutor who gave a class in phonetics "where attendance was fairly obligatory. I am in no position to judge how generally successful Peggy's efforts were [but] it is possible that under her guidance I eventually learned to produce a sound which had some similarity to the Anglo-Saxon 'w.' The effort to do so must have been considerable, since presently when speaking German I often come up with the same sound, for which my loving wife strongly criticizes me." Walter admitted, though, that "in spite of Peggy's efforts, I have never learned to produce an English-sounding 'r'. After more than a half-century in America" he groused, "new acquaintances will still ask me 'Where do you come from?' I am resigned" he shrugged, noting "you can't win them all."

In her role as kitchen wizard, phonetics coach, eager co-worker, would-be friend and integral community member, Peg became familiar with the plight of many of the individuals she endeavored to assist. It was this intimate knowledge of the sorry plight of such people which led her to compose

"Our 'Enemy Aliens'"—a moving, in-depth article about refugees—for publication in the spring 1942 edition of the *Goucher College Quarterly*, excerpts of which follow:

The present world conflict has as one of its concomitants a movement which has attracted relatively little attention from the general public, engaged in following closely the course of events political and military. It is one, however, whose effects upon America's social, industrial, and cultural life are being felt even now, and will be felt increasingly in the next few decades. I speak of that immigration of Europeans to our shores which began in 1933, and which has continued at an increasingly rapid rate since 1938. It is not necessary to analyze here the differences which distinguish the present movement from others in our history...Americans who learn to know the refugee realize that America is just as truly a haven for the homeless and oppressed as ever it was to our ancestors whose religious convictions led them to the New World, or to those who came in the succeeding centuries, fleeing from material hardship and spiritual servitude. The thoughtful person will readily imagine in what respects the present-day refugee differs from his predecessor of only twenty years ago: he comes, on the whole, from a higher social stratum, and from the corresponding cultural level; the average age is higher, and the chances of employment therefore proportionately fewer; and he comes into a highly industrialized society which offers much less opportunity of earning a living to the foreign business or professional man or artist, than it does to the worker or artisan.

What are the problems which the refugee faces upon his arrival in America? They are of two sorts, personal and professional, with the solution of which his age and previous training have a great deal to do. Among the former we must consider these: the refugee must first of all accustom himself to the accelerated tempo of living which characterizes our large cities and even our small towns. He must overcome, in many instances, a very definite language handicap; and only those who have been thrown upon their own resources in a foreign country know to what embarrassment, discouragement, and sense of loneliness the unfamiliarity with the language of that country can give rise. He arrives, perhaps, with his health seriously impaired by his experiences in concentration camp; or his confidence and self-respect almost destroyed by the infliction upon him of indignities such as we happier Americans cannot very well imagine. He must accustom himself to his altered social status; to doing without the pleasures and luxuries which he formerly took for granted, and to accepting money for his support

143

from a relief agency until he finds the means of supporting himself and of repaying that moral obligation.

To all these difficulties, add the refugee's incertitude as to the fate of those he left behind him; a wife and children, perhaps, who must wait until the father has earned or borrowed their passage money; elderly parents who were unwilling to risk the long voyage and the uncertainty awaiting them at its conclusion; a sister, a brother, in concentration camp, or in internment camp, or—worse still—not heard of for eight months or a year.

Even granting that the refugee was fortunate enough to have been able to keep his family together during the turmoil of the last three years, and to bring them with him to America, it may be that his exit from Europe was a hurried one, that he has only a visitor's visa or a "visa de danger" as a political refugee; in that case, the uncertainties as to his status add to his depression; he can no longer, if he is a German national, enter Canada in order to re-enter the U.S. with a permanent visa; Cuba and Mexico are likewise closed to him; he may obtain a work permit, but the process is long and complicated. Fortunately, the State Department and the Department of Justice have been willing to consider his case with leniency, and he does not face deportation. Even a work permit does not solve the problem, though, for many industries, such as defense, are obliged to exclude him; and a round of those in which he formerly made his living often gives discouraging results: no chance for employment.

With all that to face, what wonder that even when the refugee has secured his personal liberty by coming to America, he cannot at once begin the business of living and working like an American?

The problem for refugee children is somewhat different, the future for them is brighter than for their parents. The plasticity of their youth makes them readier and more able to adapt themselves to changed conditions; and though at first they suffer at being different from their schoolmates, they soon lose the distinguishing marks which may make them objects of dislike to some of their new associates, retaining only those which seem to gain the admiration of their comrades, and which give them a pleasing sense of superiority to offset the initial unhappiness. Many of them will keep the heritage of their mother tongue; and many also will take more seriously the business of living and of preparing for the future because in their childhood they have known fear, hunger, homelessness, and a broken family.

Such are the chances for refugee children—excellent, on the whole, for American colleges and universities are generous with aid and scholarships to worthy students. But what of those who come with their *training already completed, and with few or many years of business or professional life behind them?*

How aware is America of these people and their children? They need our encouragement, material but also—and chiefly—moral. We must let them know that we understand why they are here, appreciate what they have passed through, believe in their reasons for coming. Americans are helping these new refugees to some extent. But this help must be increased and continued if we are to prove our belief in the democratic way of life by helping these people to become good Americans.

Note: Cornell end Estelle Simms Hewson had served with an AFSC child-feeding program in Russia in 1921-22 before returning to Indiana, where Estelle gave birth to Camilia and Cornell worked for the employee-owned Columbia Conserve Company (CCC), which pioneered in "industrial democracy." The family moved to Iowa's capital city in 1932. There the Hewsons became involved in the Friends Church and AFSC's regional office in Des Moines, as well as in other social-activist efforts. Estelle attended the January 1939 gathering at West Branch at which Iowa Quakers committed themselves to sponsoring Scattergood Hostel's creation and Cornell often stopped by during early phases of its development; Camilia later wrote that "it was only because of their involvement that I was aware of SH and chose to volunteer there." That involvement led to life-long contact with numerous guests and staff. Erhard Winter said Cornell was "one of the 'originals' or founders of SH. I liked him immensely, he was ever up-beat, a great anecdotalist, and had that most American of all professions, 'traveling salesman.'" Camilia noted that Estelle "was one of the Des Moines Friends women who shopped for furnishings for the hostel, often negotiating with store owners special 'deals' on price, or even donations. She helped furnish the living rooms [at SH], in particular...with concern for an attractive and homelike 'ambience'. I don't think Cornell was on the [Iowa Yearly Meeting committee] that advised after things got underway, but he seems to have been an unofficial 'mentor' to John [Kaltenbach] in particular, and also to Giles [Zimmerman]—perhaps because at times an 'older and wiser' head was needed by the young staff. Because he traveled thru the week for a wholesale grocery cooperative...he was frequently in the area, and would stop for a night—I think he did this even after I was at Earlham. In Des Moines, the Hewson home was a sort of SH 'annex', where a number of refugees stayed for brief visits at times of special stress or need. Sometimes they were job hunting, sometimes, like Lotte Liebman, escaping stress at SH. When Helmut [Ostrowski] Wilk got a job in DM [first with Lifetone Studios, then with Drake University as an accountant] he lived with my folks for more then a year—and also [a close friendship] developed between Estelle and Regina Deutsch over many years. Mother once told me she was comfortable to let R. give her special gifts of food, etc. because it was good for people who were so much on the receiving end of help to be able to reciprocate—a lesson I've never forgotten. My parents' involvement at SH was just one aspect of the dedication to AFSC throughout their lives, as a few years later they helped start a hostel for Japanese-Americans in Des Moines (AFSC) and had several of the Nisei students at Drake U. living with them. Later they moved to Kansas City, where Cornell ran AFSC's Job Opportunities Program for a 2 year trial period (before the civil rights era), and he spent a year in the Portland, OR AFSC office in 1959-60 as director [after Estelle's death in 1955]." Cornell died in 1975 in Oxford, Ohio, where he had lived with Camilla's family. In her first year at Earlham College Camilla wrote of "the effect of [her] home atmosphere" in influencing her character, saying that she had "parents whose interests were...peace, racial and economic justice, and spiritual freedom."

1.) Those over than 30 consisted of Martha Balderston, John and Josephine Copithorne, Leanore Goodenow, Albert and Anne Martin, and Walter and Sara Stanley. The non-Quakers at Scattergood were Robert Berquist, Joyce De-Line, Peg Hannum, Esther Smith and Lynn Zimmerman—all of whom later either became or maintained lifelong contact with Friends.

2.) "Leadings" are what Quakers call actions which seem divinely inspired. They often are submitted to rather rigorous questioning—sometimes in the setting of a "clearness committee" consisting of several individuals from the community who meet with the inspired person for a process of collective contemplation to ascertain if the leading really is "Spirit-led" or actually is the product of ego-based self-projection.

3.) Sara's hobbies included the utterly domestic talents of quilting, sewing, gardening, knitting, crocheting, leather work and jewelry making. She couldn't have been completely utilitarian-minded, however, as her daughter Lillian later wrote that "at 45 or 50 she slid down a banister in a house"—but "even so she carried herself with dignity."

4.) Sara and Verlin Pemberton were only two of numerous non-staff Quakers who volunteered much time at and invested much emotional capital in Scattergood Hostel. A description of Cornell and Estelle Hewsons' involvement follows at the last end of this chapter.

5.) Camilla Hewson Flintermann later said that Joe Martin was "the only person who ever hassled me" at Scattergood. According to her he was "a pest... in typical US teen male fashion" and "not mourned when he left."

6.) Albert Martin's disruptive legacy as director, however, was not a passing one. Ten days after his departure on 17 July 1939, for instance, John Kaltenbach felt cause to write to Reed Cary: "It seems that the reverberations from our past experience hit harder in some quarters that [sic] I suspected, and harder" he ventured, "than the Pembertons and Stanleys were willing to admit. All of the ground work which we laid at the outset has been plowed up in the interim and we shall have to sow our seed all over again. I look forward to a fall and winter" he bid hopefully, "of rebuilding and realigning the support."

7.) Camilla later held that "folks liked Ann [sic]."

8.) As it had been for Hans and Heid Ladewig, John Kaltenbach's age seemed to be an issue for many—including AFSC's leadership, which ultimately decided it *had* to create at least the appearance of balance in the age of the hostel staff. On 1 July 1940 56-year-old Martha Balderston of Chicago assumed the role of director, which she retained for almost three years.

Both Camilla Hewson Flintermann and Robert Berquist felt strongly that a biography of Martha should be included. Unfortunately, no memoirs or other biographical accounts of this rather important Scattergood Hostel figure surfaced during the research phase—except,for the personal memories of her shared by one former staff member and one guest. Robert wrote of her: "While she wasn't the most efficient person, she had a deep interest in and concern for the people from Europe and she was well-liked by them as well as the staff. She was a very good conversationalist and spent much time talking with people. [I] held her in high esteem.." Walter Shostal said: "I cannot say, however, how strong a leader she was...but in a way she must have been. To my knowledge no friction or conflicts—as they are bound to happen in any segment of society—grew into proportions which became a disturbance. This may have been her doing. There was, though, one little thing that made the female guests snicker behind Martha's back. Day in and day out she wore the same woolen jacket. It had holes in both elbows. Martha did not care; she did not darn those holes, which grew steadily. This seemed strange to these European women, who had been raised with the stricter code of a German *Hausfrau*. Was that the American way?"

9.) At least one refugee agreed with John's assessment: upon receiving word of the hostel's closing, former guest Charles Bukovis (née Karl Bukowitz) wrote to staff members Josephine and John Copithorne "with deep regret [over] the forthcoming conclusion of Scattergood... I felt always Scattergood might be an eternal refuge and that there were still a few persons interested in one's matters and that you only have to apply to them in order to get advice or help. In any case you have done there a magnificent job, sometimes...even a too good one because you pampered us refugees too much and considered us persons worth of more help and consideration than average people. In fact we refugees having escaped the murderous atmosphere of Europe are just plain people to be envied since we are living in the most wonderful country of the world and this one who does not get along here or at least tries hard as he can is just a good for nothing."

10.) In the spirit of the piece's raw honesty, all mistakes remain in this reprinting of the author's original work.

11.) John Kaltenbach wrote these words as an inscription in a copy of Howard Brinton's *Divine-Human Society* which he presented to Camilla, for whom he thought it had been true.

12.) Camilla did indeed carry out her duties—and more. Records indicate that she went well beyond the daily tasks which were assigned her, volunteering her time and youthful zest for projects which enhanced the community even if they didn't fall under the category of "necessary." On 22 May 1939—for example—someone quipped in *The Book of Scattergood* that "Camilla...is going to raise the humidity of the bathroom by painting a phoney mural of fish. The talented young artist also painted a small mural in the kitchen of a plate, assorted utensils and tableware dancing around a box of soap flakes—as can be seen in the picture of Annie Harvey and Louis Lichtenstein washing dishes in winter 1941-42.

13.) Not only Quaker girls encountered new horizons at Scattergood. In summer 1940 teenager David Hughes of Madison, Wisconsin, bicycled approximately 450 kilometers round trip to reach the hostel, where he volunteered several weeks. His father, a professor at the University of Wisconsin, wanted David to "have the experience" and paid $100 for his son's keep. According to Camilla "he was a delightful kid, whom I took under my wing, as did Fred Lister—I was his 'mom' and Fred was his 'dad'. He pitched in and worked with the rest of us... His easy acceptance into the group was in keeping with the feeling of 'family' we strove to achieve." Besides "some lessons in German" David received the thanks of those in charge, one of whom reported "the 14 year old boy mentioned last meeting... has proved very helpful." Friends in Madison obviously supported Scattergood's mission, for in mid-December 1939 Scattergood "received thousands of books from [them], some 1939 publications, some classics—in all, by far the best books coming to the hostel."

14.) Phil Clampitt wrote: "Amy had published four more volumes of poetry between 1983 and 1994, which further enhanced her reputation as a major American poet. The last of these was *A Silence Opens* inspired in part by the writings of George Fox: '...also I saw the infinite love of God, and I had great openings' (from *The Journal of George Fox*): the final poem, 'A Silence', borrows those very words as it ends. A review of this book applauds 'the wholeheartedness that...went into the writing', and Amy's 'generosity of spirit', and else-where refers to 'perceptions that can only be called religious'. Amy had something of all these qualities as a young woman volunteer at Scattergood Hostel. They matured and deepened as she grew older, and stayed with her throughout her life. The Scattergood experience—though it was relatively brief and relatively early—only enhanced that process."

15.) Amy once wrote: "But about becoming a poet...well, the word 'poet' I didn't want to use right away. The first time I used it was when, in 1971, I went to Washington with a bunch of people in a bus, and we gathered outside the White House and we wore these Vietnamese hats and banners across the chests that had words in Vietnamese. It was called the Daily Death Toll. They were still bombing North Vietnam, they were killing several hundred people a day, and nothing was in the papers about it anymore. So we went out there, and there were these signs, 'Teacher', 'Student', 'Farmer', 'Poet'...and I took the one that said 'Poet.'"

16.) Amy dedicated the poem "For Hal"—Harold Korn, a Jew and Amy's self-described "best friend" for the last twenty-six years of her life. Just a few months before her death in 1994 —at the age of 74—the two married, both knowing that Amy did not have much longer to live.

17.) AFSC paid Lillian $45 a month, plus room and board. Apparently Lillian's duties also included looking for cheap appliances, given that in September 1939 "Walter and Sara [Stanley] took Camilla [Hewson], Ruth [Carter] and Lillian to a sale of household goods (an auction). Lillian returned triumphant with a wooden potato masher." Peg Hannum served as dietitian from 1941 to 1942 and "was paid only $40 a month, plus room and board!"

18.) Other responses to local bad will towards the guests were not always as tasty as *Apfelstrudel*, but were often as clever. Hans Peters remembered the time that "there was a rumor [of] a huge refugee colony at Scattergood, taking jobs away from U.S. citizens. Giles Zimmerman loaded up several cars with not more than 30 refugees, including children, and presented us at the [local office of the state] employment service in Iowa City and we received our Social Security cards. Rumors and gossip were killed."

19.) Hostel food-program records show that from April to December 1939 the Scattergood kitchen served 16,935 meals at an average cost of nine cents per meal per person, or $1.90 per person per week. From August to December alone 614 of those meals were for visitors to the hostel. In 1940 the kitchen served 38,780 meals—1,619 of which went to "transient guests."

20.) On 31 May 1940 someone noted in *The Book of Scattergood* that "George Willoughby has been a good friend of the hostel, but the women learned that there is one reason more important than all the rest for his frequent trips to see us. He seems to have been just as satisfied with our Lillian as we have been, for news of their engagement was broken at a Pemberton afternoon sewing party. We are happy about everything temporary."

21.) An unapologizing non-conformist and amiable radical from the start, George once admitted: "I must have been a bit of a trouble" as a child—for example, playing with black and Hispanic Panamanian children "in violation of the local social norms" and his parents' own rules. Having been chased down the street for several blocks by a teacher once, he ran away at 17 and came to Iowa, where he lived with the family of one of his teachers—no doubt, not the one who'd pursued him through the streets of Balboa—finished his studies and became a Quaker.

22.) The popular pet's antics, however, were not always funny. "During the afternoon [of 27.II.40] MacTavish killed a young skunks [sic] and brought it into the main building—very proud of his accomplishment! Giles [Zimmerman] burried [sic] the carcacs [sic] and then he and John [Kaltenbach] washed the dog. By supper time the house and dorm were sufficiently aired for guests." The following day the *Des Moines Register*—which coincidentally had a reporter on hand at the time of the smelly affair—carried news of the skunk episode under the headline

"Mr. MacTavish an Exile from Refugee Hostel."

23.) In response to queries connected with the writing of this history of the Scattergood Hostel, Earle and Marjorie were most helpful in sharing their memories and insights *as a couple*—and even signed each letter of correspondence as "Marjorie and Earle Edwards." It seems that already as AFSC volunteers they worked very much in tandem, so much so that Camilla Hewson Flintermann once exclaimed, "I always think of them together!" She added, "They were a young married couple—tall, blond, delightful [and] filled several roles on staff." Given this decades-long collaboration, not to mention their stubborn resistance to speaking in first person in letters and during interviews, their comments shall be presented here as a unit.

24.) Some 55 years later, "Ilse Stahl" said in an interview: "I don't know if I should blow it out, but we were communists. At almost the same time in this country [that we arrived], there was a *big* uprising against the communists and all kind of government rules made against the communists, *not* to come into the country. So, when we came, finally, after big [efforts including a special vote in Congress to grant the Stahls entry]...we told [the other refugees from the first that we were communists]—contrary from the beliefs of most people that communists never say the truth, we... [Ilse's voice fades out] If we had not told the truth, we'd have saved us plenty of trouble—but we couldn't have. We didn't want to and we did not... We said to each other...'From now on, no more [Ilse laughs] different names and different dates and different whats: we will end up in the insane hospital'. Because, for different names and different papers and different places, we did not know our wedding day! Everything was falling out, but we didn't know what we wanted to say... You know, if we had said 'socialists', that might have been better. [The communists were said to be] people who were the bloodiest, rottenest people: 'they lie, they kill, they lie, they steal, they do...' and still today, you find these notions [about communists]. If ever we made a statement, we had to repeat it so often. Also, to the Quakers. And we *keenly* realized that 'They don't trust us...'"

25.) Martha Balderston noticed these tendencies, too, and commented: "The German mind does not 'adjust to reality' as quickly as the American and we have discovered that we must give ample warning of any change of plan, even unexpected tickets to the concerts."

26.) As a twosome the Edwardses penned an article about the hostel's common life which appeared in the 21.III.1940 edition of *The Friend* and is included in Appendix III.

27.) For a copy of the text refer to Appendix IV.

28.) Of course staff-refugee friendships didn't benefit only the former—as suggested by Ernst Malamerson, who was befriended by Giles and Lynn Zimmerman: "I got along with them perhaps because I was more flexible than most of the others—being young and single and also having changed cultures before." Whatever the reasons for the affinity, the relationship facilitated Ernst's recovery: "Giles was an excellent, perhaps the *most* capable of the staff members... His wife [Lynn], for whom I had great affection at the time, was extremely important for me psychologically and she gave me what I needed (it was not planned, it just happened): some sort of affection, association or whatever, which I very much needed at the time. These two staff members for me were the universe."

29.) Peg later wrote that besides ending up in France again, she went "first to England, then Norway [and] Germany [where she] only passed through—didn't want to spend any money in Hitler's empire." In the Third Reich, however, she was "accosted at the overnight hotel by a mannish *Hitlerfrau* who insisted I attend a meeting of *Hitlerfrauen*—needless to say, I did not." She also could recall "especially a man on the train who spoke fair English and who kept asking, 'But what about Poland?'" Peg's involvement with AFSC refugee programs grew out of her personal concern for those effected by the war in Europe: "A French friend visiting the U.S. in the late summer '39 came to us in Sept. We had the radio on hourly. When Britain and France declared war on Germany after the joint German-Russian invasion of Poland, Paul said, 'I must go home'. After the invasions of Norway in April '40, and France a few months later, I wrote the AFSC...begging to be sent abroad to do something—anything—useful in Norway or France—or wherever... AFSC was sending no one at that point, especially not a non-Quaker stranger. So I went instead for 8 weeks to an AFSC work-camp in New Hampshire, met two refugees there among the 20 or so college and post-college work-campers. The next summers—'41 through '44 or '45—I was on the staff at AFSC's vacation hostel for refugees in Nyack, N.Y... I gave English lessons—as did all the staff, plus planning excursions and hostel events—and was assistant to the dietitian. For that reason, I was offered the same post at S.H. in the fall."

SPIRIT OF THE COMMUNITY

*"Perhaps you must wander around the earth; you have lost all
things which are beloved and valuable for you; you are alone
and homeless in the world. All that is not the worst poverty
when your heart is able to receive the spirit of the community."*

~ Otto Bauer

"Scattergood" has been the name of a Philadelphia chemist, a Quaker boarding school and a refugee center. With the last two usages it also has become
the name of a place—a windy, open spot in Iowa where people and worlds
meet, interact, enrich each other and then resume their individual journeys
in various directions, with various destinations. In its incarnation as a hostel
for uprooted Europeans, it consisted of a fluid constellation of single young
adults, married couples, children, infants and the elderly; its only constant
was an ever-changing mix of nationalities, anchored by a core group of
American volunteers. Both guests and staff, then, formed a community
which very soon after the founding of Scattergood Hostel assumed a character of its own, independent of the particular personalities of those who happened to reside within its protective walls at any given time. This community
came to represent decency and continuity for souls who had not known either
for far too long. As intended by its sponsors, one could gain "membership"
in that community very easily—by daring to care in a world where cynicism
and egoism had plenty of disciples. The pervasive sense of belonging felt, if
not by all,[1] by most of its members provided the stability for which many
hungered and assisted the refugees' rehabilitation as more fully functioning
members of a larger society. As best seen in their own words, the rich sense
of community found at Scattergood served as glue and gluten in the lives of
those it touched—those there from the New World as well as the Old.

On the whole, the "evidence" to substantiate such a seemingly subjective
claim must remain circumstantial, as few hostelites left reflections dealing
directly with the theme of community. Of those who did, Otto Bauer had very
personal, not just political, reasons for doing so. The middle-aged Catholic

149

"Religious Socialist" had fled Vienna in 1938 with his wife Rosa and their four children due to a faith inseparable from public life. Upon reaching the hostel the Bauers knew scarcely any English, yet it didn't take long before the handsome father of four children (who boarded at East Coast schools while their parents spent five months in Iowa before going to Cuba in order to apply for permanent U.S. visas) began writing poetry and religious prose in a new tongue. Perhaps the wide, open prairies were a conducive landscape for such yeasty contemplation. In any event he produced numerous works, in some of which he reflected on the meaning of "community" in general, but undoubtedly as seen through the lens of the one he found at Scattergood:

Life of Community

I.

The community is a very hard task.
Yes, it is a task and not a present,
falling from heaven.
This task is as hard as life itself, and
it has no end throughout life.
The simpletons like to decree: Today
we are living in the community. But the
community does not listen to command.
The wise people have good will for
common life, and nothing else. And see, the
community is coming into existence.

II.

If you have the will to live in a community
you must be joined by a common
matter. This common matter should be
greater than your particular interests.
As the sunshine awakes the flowers that
they grow up to it, so the service for a
common matter brings forth the common life.
You and he and I—we are nothing but
isolated stones lying side by side.
You and he and I, and for us a work for
all, that it is which makes even stones alive.
"Where two or three are united by my
name, there I am among them, and I am the
way, the truth and the life."
And the life!

III.

Life becomes poor without community.
Your life, too!
You may be hungry and cold; this is not
the worst calamity. It is worse to have a
heart which is not able to beat for a common
life. This heart is sick unto death.
The desert is not so waste that there
would not be remnants of the life of the community.
A heart, can it be poorer than the desert?

IV.

Perhaps you must wander around the
earth; you have lost all things which are
beloved and valuable for you; you are
alone and homeless in the world.
All that is not the worst poverty when
you [sic] heart is able to receive the spirit of
the community.
It will help to find a new home for you
because you will not pass by the helpful
hands which are giving from the abundance
of the community.
Without a heart like this, you would not
see the thousand helpful hands and you would
not be able to receive the sacrament of love
and community.

·V.

Community will be lived day by day.
Community is not to be purchased, not
to be enforced. The hypocrite and the
flatterer remain strangers to the community forever.
Neither money nor goods nor knowledge
secure a place in the community.
Nobody and nothing is able to make members
of a community except this: You must
enter into it with all your hearts and
must give yourselves for the community.
This is the foundation of every community.

151

VI.

Open wide your heart to those who are
coming through the small gate into your community.
Remain in love and goodness to those who
like to use broad stairs.
Refresh everyone who is standing at the
gate of the community and give him from
the wealth of its life.
But never forget the brother who sits
at the common table and hungers after your good news.

VII.

Many a man [or woman][2] *is deluded by himself.*
He thinks the community will come into
being if he makes many words about it.
But in this way grow only empty stalks without fruit.
This man, when he grasps for the fruit
in the hour of his misery, will have empty
stalks in his hands.

VIII.

The love of the community heals what
is sick and develops what is healthy and good.
**

Loneliness gives new strength of mind,
and life in the community multiplies it.
You are blessed pentifully [sic] when you
know both: loneliness and community.

IX.

To those will be added the leadership
of community who are servants of all with pure heart.
**

And this is the most important experience of common life:
To give is more blessed than to receive!
No one is so poor that he could not
give his mite to the common life.

Otto Bauer was joined in his ponderings on the common life by a fellow Scattergood Hostel guest, Richard Schuber of Vienna.[3] Accompanied by his wife Angela and their 14-year-old son Erich, the former newspaper editor and publisher showed keen interest in the life of the Scattergood community—for example traveling with AFSC's Reed Cary to an Iowa Friends Service Committee Meeting in Oskaloosa and duly filing a report of it for public perusal, and offering a presentation on German propaganda at the hostel one evening as part of its education program. Camilla Hewson Flintermann later remembered him as a "blustering, big man...uncomfortable with his 'fall from Grace'"; his demoted professional status, however, did not keep Richard from engaging in the hostel's shared life during the 11 and a half months that he lived there before finding a publishing job in Elgin, Illinois. In February 1940 he wrote an essay he titled "SCATTERGOOD on the anniversary of its spiritual crystallization." In it, he wrote about his new, temporary home—but from a slightly critical point of view, which also was an exercise in community given that to have been positive and complimentary would have been easy, whereas to share honestly was riskier. He explained:

Much has already been written about Scattergood, and still more said. Many enthusiastic superlatives have been applied to this lonely house in middle western [sic] America.

Have not refugees in giving an account of this hostel perhaps dipped their brushes too deeply into the brightest sky-blue of their imagination, in the effort to discharge their debt? Is there not a possibility that Quakers have been dazzled by the light that the creation of their own work has reflected? Have not guests rendered back the opalescent sector of a fleeting and therefore not profound impression?

There are permanent asylums, and those installed ad noc [sic] for refugees, more or less the whole globe round about since the migration of expelled ones has set in such as history has never known. This migration has for the first time made vivid to many the course of history, and has brought them to see how Ahasuerus' brethren, having begun to migrate in the land of Egypt and going through the millenniums, have distributed themselves over the whole world. Is Scattergood more than such an asylum?

As I write these lines, the hard, grim winter lies outside, storming and roaring without hindrance from the Arctic into the country. It seems as though the world would remain under eternal snow. Well sheltered from battering sorrows in the hard struggle for the daily bread, multiplied by the mercilessness of the extremities of an unaccustomed climate, does perhaps the cozy warmness of Scattergood threaten to induce me also to a dithyrambic gratitude? To a gratitude for the exemption from being forced to tremble forth into the next days somewhere in New York. Exploring yet more deeply, I reject the thought of these securities as not decisive and relevant, as precious as they incon-

153

testably are. Precious as food and shelter if one has none, precious as the consciousness of being protected against the possibility of lying on the street one fine morning after a lost job. For nobody is hard-heartedly left here to shift for himself [or herself] and be therewith surrendered to an uncertain fate. All is devised in affectionate friend-ship: our nursing by which our first steps are led into English; the op-portunity to spend our time with people and things after a day's work which has been done under no pressure and coercion; the restless care taken for our settling, trying to find work and earnings for us. This is very much indeed, but it is not all.

People from the north and south of Central Europe are here to-gether. All stages of life are represented: younger and older single women and men, married couples, families whose children are daily fetched by the school bus to the modern and excellent school in neigh-boring West Branch. Coming from the most varied professions, it is now required that they take leave of real and hypothetic [sic] values. Only for a few can Scattergood become a refuge, this is implied in the limitation of its capacity and equipment.

With anguish of heart we will keep in mind our brethren still there where once our home was. With deep grief in our soul we will remem-ber all those whose graves stand as milestones at the edge of the thorny path where uncounted thousands of people were forced to go. With silent affection we will think of the bitter distress which lies buried un-der the already stale and trite-sounding word "refugee."

To all these Scattergood is consecrated—a symbol for all the faith here altruistically going on—to recall to life, to erect again, to give steadiness anew—a symbol of love that never and nowhere dies, for all the dust-laden, pursuing their way. And thus arose, built by Quakers and excogitated by men whose forefathers [or -mothers] themselves experienced the affliction of being persecuted, and today already the memorial of the unknown refugee: Scattergood.

It is no abode of retraining in the conventional sense. It is a retrain-ing, a transformation, of souls. Restless ones become peaceable, imper-fect ones enriched, heavy-laden and burdened ones free men [and women], asocial ones contributing. An invisible clockwork is running, into which each little wheel can finally be built in. Quietly and imper-ceptibly a good spirit lives and moves in Scattergood, and everybody becomes woven in. Those being unwilling, incredulous, skeptical, be-come collaborators, believers, affirmers. Nobody is here important, even if someone or other, legitimately or not, holds himself [or herself] so. For egocentrics there is here as little room as for adulators and tale bearers. All are in like manner important and insignificant. In liberty

154

a disciplined idea of community shapes itself. An ideal experiment, daily tested with devotion for more ameliorations and refinements by all being responsible or making themselves responsible for this work, becomes fulfillment. A new human being is born, ripe and apt to step out into this big country as out of a hatching oven which has transformed people and retained the dross, gently and softly, without their perceiving and often without their will. People have been remodeled in a few months. Not by making handicraftsmen of intellectuals, but by leaving everyone what he was, have they been made good for a sowing which will come up and has to come up. In the retort of this Quaker island, kindly warmed by the fire of charity, injured souls recover. The ovary cell of coming valuable American generations is disclosed.

Mayflower of refugees! Also in that boat carrying the first hundred and two men to America, sat the liberty and happiness of millions which sprouted after them out of the humus of this enormous country.

This is Scattergood and its ultimate meaning.

While men might indulge in verbose intellectualizing and the clever construction of grand abstractions, perhaps women tend to speak more of the personally familiar. Although she didn't address head-on the oft-vague, value-ridden theme of "community" as a concept in itself, fair-haired, sturdy-faced Lucy Selig of Würzburg, Germany, did allude to Scattergood's rich shared life in a talk she delivered while living at the hostel for nine months. The wife of a wine merchant, a mother of two children—of whom one joined his parents at Scattergood after a 1-1/2-year-long separation—and a social worker, 40-something Lucy later transcribed her talk into essay form. Excerpts illustrate in minutiae how at least one guest saw practical, everyday traces of the philosophical constructs her male counterparts extolled.

It is not easy to talk about Scattergood because Scattergood means a certain spirit, a certain sphere, a certain attitude. Scattergood Hostel...is based on community life... There is no sharp distinction between the American staff and the Refugees; all share in the tasks of lectures, household and fields. The group of Refugees [is] now stripped of all money, possessions and occupations, and exiled from their countries because they hold liberal ideas—what you call American ideas—or because they are Jewish. Now these different kinds of people are living together, united by the same past fate and the same aim, to become real Americans and to find a productive work in this country.

All work at the hostel is done by members of the community. Women mostly do housework and kitchen work; men are occupied in the fields and in the workshop. In the very beginning of the Hostel it was difficult

155

to train Germans, that is to train city people to work in the fields. Because until now the Refugees were using their heads too much and their hands too little. They tried to live with only their brain functioning. But at Scattergood a curious thing happened to most of them: they feel a deep satisfaction during their work time; they lose all thoughts of worry and sorrows and you may imagine what that means in our special situation. The housework is mostly done in the forenoon. In the afternoon we have classes in American history and Government and in English and we have spare time to study. The evenings we spend in different ways. Sometimes we are sitting together in the living room, singing American and German songs, sometimes we walk and talk together.

The Scattergood landscape in the evening is one of the most beautiful things I have ever experienced. The stars come out, pale at first, then brightening to silver. And we look up at the stars——remembering what was and is going on in European countries while we walk and talk here—and we feel deeply grateful. But we realize too that these stars are the eternal stars which always and everywhere have looked down in beauty on man's [or woman's] effort to act civilized. And Scattergood means a work of high civilization and humanity. It is not only that the Americans with whom we live stand behind us and give us back the confidence in life and human beings that we have lost by the experiences of the last years in Germany; it is also that we get a new sense of life if we only are willing to understand their way of living.

The Americans we are living with are mostly Quakers, those persons who love humanity less and humans more. It is so easy to profess one's love for humanity but it is so difficult to love the unhappy ones that constitute humanity, in our case the Refugees... I only want to mention two members of the Hostel staff, Walter and Sara Stanley, that wonderful couple always working, always helping. They are generals in the army of spiritual forces. Once I asked Walter about the Quaker [cemetery] and he told me, "Our gravestones are very simple. We spend money for the living and not for the dead. It is of more importance to take care of the living." And I think this kind of active sympathy for all human beings is the secret of the Quakers and—last but not least—of Scattergood Hostel.

While only one of the handful of guests to leave in-depth narratives about communal life at the hostel was a woman and saw it from a more "feminine" perspective, more than one guest attributed maternal qualities to Scattergood in the process of personifying the place. Sara Pemberton may have told Reed Cary that she saw the hostel as his "child," but guests were inclined to pin motherly labels to their descriptions. After all the upset, heartbreak and loss

West Branch's Main Street, looking east; spring 1939

Scattergood's Main Building in summer 1939

Hickory Grove Meetinghouse after meeting, with Ruth Carter (third from left), Günther Meyer (fifth from left), Ludwig and Käthe Unterholzer, Kurt Schaefer, Leo Jolles, Walter Stanley and John Kaltenbach; autumn 1939

Arrival of the first "guests," with Verlin Pemberton (walking toward the camera), Fritz Treuer (behind the hatted woman), Walter Stanely (in front of wheel, wearing cap), Kurt Rosegg (next to Walter), John Kaltenbach (with foot on bumper), Kurt Schaefer (on the extreme right) and the "Conestoga" (to the right, background); 15 April 1939

The first arrivals: (left to right) Kurt Rosegg, Kurt Schaefer, Karel Gam, John Kaltenbach and Fritz Treuer; 15 April 1939

Martha Balderston; 1 January 1941

Walter and Sara Stanley; February 1939

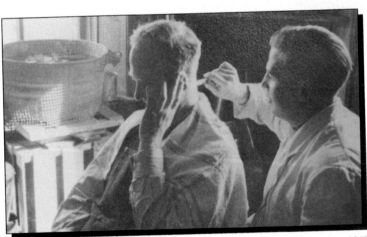

Lillian Pemberton weighing Frank Schloss; summer 1939

Mildred Holmes in Scattergood Hostel's office; early 1940

John Kaltenbach cutting Otto Joachim's hair; 1940

In-class scene, with Otto Joachim (left), Gus Bardach, Ruth Carter, Ted Tuerkel, Heinrich "O-Henry-5¢" and Anna Schoental, and Boris Jaffe; spring 1940

Margaret "Peg" Hannum helping Günther "George" Krauthamer practice English pronunciation; autumn 1942

Sonia Braun, Arnold Friedman and Ernst Turk using the Scattergood library; late 1942

Anna Harvey and Julius Lichtenstein in the Scattergood kitchen; winter 1941-42

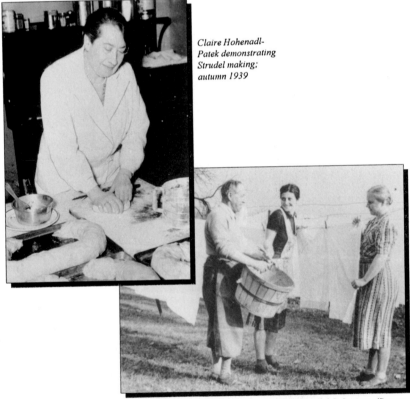

Claire Hohenadl-Patek demonstrating Strudel making; autumn 1939

Paul Singer, Marianne Welter and Friedel Seligmann/Seaman hanging laundry; autumn 1941

Fritz Treuer harrowing the Scattergood fields; spring 1939

Ernst and Lucy Selig and Ruth Carter planting tomatoes; spring 1940

Werner Selig (left), Gus Weiler and Louis Croy; summer 1940

Leo Jolles checking the
sweetcorn; late summer 1939

Friedrich Lichtman
"harvesting" tomatoes;
August 1940

Husking sweetcorn, with Günther Meyer behind Gerry Schroeder in hat
(foreground), Frank Schloss (center), with visitor Bob Tesdell of Des Moines to
Frank's right and Ruth Carter to his left, Lynn Zimmerman on chair (left) and
the two Deutsch children, Michael and Hanna; late summer 1939

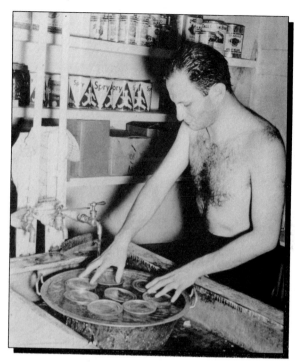

Kurt Rosegg cooling off canned corn, and trying to keep himself cool in the process; late summer 1939

Erhard Winter sun-drying sweetcorn on the roof of the Main Building, with the Hickory Grove Meetinghouse in the background; later summer 1939

Alfred Adler (left) and John Copithorne working in Scattergood's shop; winter 1941-42

Otto Joachim (left), Karl Violin and Rudi Schreck repairing screens on the Main Building; 24 April 1940

(Left to right) Annette Keller, Louis and Edith Lichtenstein, and unidentified girl; summer 1942

The Deutsches—Regina (left), Michael, Emil and Hanna; summer 1939

Michael (on bell platform) and Hanna Deutsch; summer 1939

Doris Arntal (left), Karl Violin and Bertl Weiler; winter 1940-41

*Doris Arntal
(left) and
Bertl Weiler;
Christmas 1940*

*Martha Balderston (left) and Giles Zimmerman at opposite ends of the sofa and
Anna Schoental between them, with Angela Schuber (left) and Herta Schroeder facing
the camera and Werner Selig in front of the piano; Christmas 1940*

Kurt Salinger (left) and Gerry Schroeder on "Lucy", the Stanleys' horse; summer 1939

A picnic with Becky Elliott, Lillian Pemberton, Ruth Feigel, Michael and Regina Deutsch, Esther Smith, Elsie Kepes, Anna Schoental, Elinor Jones, Doris Arntal and Jane Elliott in the front and Lora Larson, Emil Deutsch, Paul Singer, Giles Zimmerman and Max Schiffman in the back; summer 1941

A theatrical performance with Karl "Othello" Liebman, Mildred "Desdemona" Holmes, Director Ruth Carter, Camilla "Eilia" Hewson and Hans "Iago" Peters; 9 February 1940

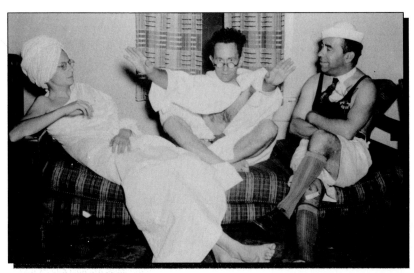

A skit with Gerry Schroeder (left), Willi Leitersdorfer and Karl Violin; early summer 1940

(Left to right) Friedrich Lichtman, Frank Keller, Hans Popper, Helmuth Ostrowski, Lucy and Ernst Selig, Hans Schimmerling, Ted Tuerkel and Karl Violin standing and John Kaltenbach, Mildred Holmes, visitor Bob Burgess, Ruth Carter and Martha Balderston sitting; 1 June 1940

Hostel members in Dining Room

they had experienced in Europe and during the passage to America—often via second, third or fourth countries—some of the refugees saw their present, albeit transient, home as a place of safety, comfort and encouragement for eventual entry into the foreign culture of their adopted homeland.

Upon the occasion of Scattergood Hostel's third birthday, for example, the Rosenzweig family—now settled in Illinois—wrote a poem as a vehicle to express their sentiment towards the institution which effectively had served as a bridge between their former lives in *Europa* and their new ones in Eureka:

> *Dear Friends,*
> *We thank you so much for the*
> *kind invitation*
> *For Scattergood Hostel's third birth-*
> *day celebration.*
> *It cannot be possible that we join*
> *you this day,*
> *Because we are really too far*
> *from you away.*
> *We think of the Hostel like children of*
> *a mother,*
> *Who had with her babies much*
> *trouble and bother.*
> *As soon as the children are able to*
> *walk*
> *And in their mother's language*
> *to talk*
> *And to make their living in the*
> *right and best way*
> *No longer in mother's home they*
> *can stay.*
>
> *Though we cannot come home like*
> *we should like to do,*
> *Our thoughts and our feelings are*
> *still living with you.*
> *We never forget, but we keep in*
> *our mind*
> *The help and the kindness which*
> *you let us find,*
> *And we hope and we wish that*
> *good spirit and mood*

At the time of that much-celebrated third anniversary, numerous past and present hostelites contributed to a fund with which to buy something useful to present as a tangible sign of the refugees' appreciation. The selected person(s) gave the gift of assorted kitchen utensils to Martha Balderston on behalf of the hostel "alumni," along with the following poem written on construction paper with crayons:

> *Strange to say, that only three years old is Scattergood,*
> *yet breeds hundreds of children every year*
> *and gathers all in her protecting motherhood,*
> *Our mothers birthday full gratitude we cheer.*
> *For cooking many wholesome dishes,*
> *please, take these things with our hearty wishes.*

Just as children project feelings of security and love onto their parents, so do they their fears of inadequacy and reproach. Even after the Scheider family of Prague had left Scattergood following a three-month stay, wife Rosl (known affectionately as "Mimi" and later as "Mary") very much cared what her Scattergood "mother" thought of her. She wrote to Martha Balderston on 12 January 1941, about one month after her lawyer husband Georg(e) took a job as a ski instructor at a resort near Frostburg, Maryland, and moved Mimi and their 10-year-old son Wolfgang (later "Walter") out East. In a four-page, single-spaced missive, Mimi reported the joys as well as frustrations of being once again a "family" of three and not 40, as at the hostel. At the end of the letter the 30-something teacher of Spanish admitted that "we are at home at Scattergood even when we have left it. I often think we behaved very badly there. When George left...he excused himself that he had often done what he himself had known to be wrong. It seems to me we had to use all our energy to keep up our minds the two years long before we came to Scattergood. And there we had the feelings we could relax and nobody would blame us if we would behave like naughty children, who did not get up in time and did not do what they were supposed to do. We had the feeling of being with a very loving and understanding mother, who spoils her children because she knows that they would soon leave her and have a hard time to go thru. And so we often abused the kindness and felt very guilty for it. But we hope our dear mother has understood however that we learned from her how to do our duty and how to overcome misfortune by helping other people who need some help and encouragement." She continued, although with a shifted motif: "I hope this letter did not become too sentimental for your taste. It had to be said once and I feel I expressed my thoughts in a very poor way. But you will understand me and you will not mind the hundred [sic] of mistakes. If George would get to see the letter he would be sure to throw it away. And then you would not get any news from me for another 4 weeks. So I shall send it away without his knowing about it."

Even if some of the guests did what was "known to be wrong" and behaved "like naughty children," visitors to the hostel rarely left with anything other than the most glowing impressions of the place. Herself a refugee, Vita Stein visited briefly in spring 1942. A future resident of New York's International House and doctoral student, Vita later wrote Martha Balderston to "tell you how very much I enjoyed my short stay at the Hostel. I was impressed very deeply by the fine spirit and the peaceful atmosphere everywhere. It's a unique experience for me to see this living example of the Spirit of fellowship and brotherhood [or sisterhood] and the more I see it the stronger becomes my longing to be allowed to become a member of a group which lives religion as a way of life. I feel it is a great privilege to share this spirit and to learn from the Friends how to live the supreme truth of life. We struggling and persecuted people are sometimes in danger to lose our belief in humanity. An experience like Scattergood helps to regain the belief that 'God created man in His own image.'"

American visitors to Scattergood scarcely saw the hostel any differently than the several refugees who were recorded as having visited it in capacities other than as longer-term "guests." AFSC's Mary Middleton Rogers, for example, made a trip to Iowa to help the hostelites celebrate their beloved home's second birthday in April 1941. Although she had been there numerous times before and in an "official" capacity, Scattergood obviously impressed her anew with its special atmosphere and ripening richness of spirit:

Spring sees the beginnings of many good things and so Scattergood had its beginning in spring... The spirit of helpfulness and understanding, the belief in the right of human beings to be different and to contribute to the common good from that very diversity of belief and of culture were woven into the fabric that is Scattergood. The spirit of dedication of those who started Scattergood has been carried on by many since then and the splendid part of this heritage is that it is a cooperative product. Neither Americans nor Europeans could have created alone this new entity, this Scattergood.

When huge forces seem to be blocking out those things in which we believe so intensely, the value of a small demonstration of another way of life is increased. One candle shining in a lighted room may be passed over, but a candle in a darkened room becomes of great moment. Each of Scattergood's guests and staff brings his [or her] candle of faith in democracy, of belief that a new world of tolerance can be built. If our candle is burning low we can be grateful for this demonstration of the way of light.

Certainly no stranger to Scattergood Hostel, by the time of its second birthday John Kaltenbach had become an "outsider." Offering his best wishes to the current staff and guests upon that anniversary, he bid that "at the end of two years of its present service, it is my hope that some of the permanent aspects of Scattergood are being felt throughout the community which joins in its spiritual dedication. Here the worship and service ideals of the Society of Friends have been given a geographical focus, which, augmented by the contributions of spirit which have come from a suffering Europe, has raised a powerful witness to meet the condition of our time. It will be good if Scattergood can continue its place as a home for troubled souls and a refuge for all in need, at the same time developing the power so many of us have found there as a continued training center for the life of the spirit."

Indeed, such an intangible, nebulous realm as "the life of the spirit" was exactly one which seemed to reign consistently at Scattergood. Guest Hans Peters was "at home"—his words—for a two-day visit as an "alumnus" for the second time in eight months. In a report he wrote about the changes he had seen and the emotions he had experienced during this pilgrimage, Hans quoted an American Friend whom he had heard addressing an audience in Des Moines. This individual had come to the hostel once as a visitor and afterwards advised others considering a glimpse at the community which was flourishing there, that "if you go to Scattergood, someday, to visit the folks there, be open-minded and prepared for the things you cannot see, you cannot touch. I mean the spirit, the atmosphere...." Hans added that "the spirit is still alive, moving on to responsible service among human society, inspiring greater action in this life."

Of course, visitors saw what the refugees and staff wished them to see—or, as often the case, what they themselves wanted to see. This deceptive love affair with the *ideal* of what Scattergood Hostel was *supposed* to be misled and disappointed numerous individuals, for the records include stories like that of the Ladewigs and the Martins, Erhard Winter and others. The hostel still served as "home" for many, however, to the point that the community came to be seen as a familiar "homestead"—a word the Latvian-born photographer Rosa Eliasberg used to encapsulate her image of it. Like a biological family and its traditional place of residence, the people (especially the core staff) and the physical place making up Scattergood came to symbolize stability and support for many refugees even after they left, evoking strong sentiment and nostalgia.

The hostel's former Reichstag member from Leipzig, for example, had much to feel sad about, for he watched helplessly in safe America while his youngest son, brother and a brother-in-law perished in Nazi death camps. According to Robert Berquist, 60-something Paul Frölich was "a wonderful, quiet scholarly gentleman" who was "sensitive to needs of others" and who worried "much about suffering people in Germany." A socialist and avid reader as well as writer, he resided at Scattergood for a brief two months. Once back in New York, however, he often meditated with fondness on his short stay in the Heartland and found emotional refuge from his travails in comforting, pleasant thoughts of the hostel long after he had left it. He wrote to Martha Balderston in October 1941, explaining:

Often, when I am reading and jotting down my notes, my thoughts suddenly begin to wander a thousand miles from here. Then I walk from Pemberton's corner, along the corn field to the meeting house and the pillars with the number "1926" [presented by a graduating class. The Zimmermans' black Scottie terrier] Mr. McTabish [sic] comes philosophically trotting, not knowing if it would be in contradiction to his dignity to welcome too noicily [sic] an old friend. I look at Sarah [Stanley's] flower garden—a little irritated, for I cannot make out in my mind which plants may now stand in flower. The asters, surely. But what may be with the bed of plants which I weeded every day and of which I didn't know, is it a kind of salad or an unknown flower. And then I am in the living-room and I meet all good Scattergood people.

Scattergood people! You know, dear Martha, how I felt happy in this quiet community.

Yes, it was the people who made the difference at Scattergood. Already more than 50 years old, the Main Building had become a bit worn and tired; the barn was simple, the meeting house warped from the buckling of frost and the blistering of summer heat. It was not so much the slightly shabby feeling of the physical plant, then, that made most hostelites develop such an intense loyalty to Scattergood the institution. Rather it was the singular quality of the human interactions and relationships which prevailed there. The unique and tender respect with which the staff treated those whom fate had smiled upon and sent to Scattergood also strongly impressed virtually everyone whose life was touched by the hostel.

Even the kindly, yet often-critical Walter Shostal could not live very long at Scattergood before conceding that something about it set it apart from other human endeavors. In an essay he wrote as an English-class exercise, he said: "Now we are at Scattergood and it is quite different from anything I had expected and everything I had known before. It has nothing to do with charity (what a relief). At least we don't feel it. It is much like vacations. But not quite. It is of course connected with school and learning. This is more accidental. I like Scattergood. I enjoy our life here like I have not enjoyed anything for many years. Why?" His conclusion was:

> There is something much more important about Scattergood. For the first time in my life I have met here people who are good. I don't mean just kind and helpful, qualities already rare enough though I have found them before. But really good in the Biblical sense, living up to a moral postulate, to which I never thought people could. That's not all. This goodness, direct and natural as it is, seems to be distilled through a sieve of tact. There is no aggressiveness, coercion for anybody to fight or submit but simply an atmosphere to breathe. The best and poorest feeling I had up to now experienced was friendship between men. The special kind of friendship that may develop between men under certain difficult conditions, especially common danger and hardship, and which reminds one in many ways of school comradeship. There is no question of dividing the last piece of bread and the last cigarette and maybe even of risking his life for the other. But that has nothing to do with goodness. This tie exists between very definite people excluding the others. That's exactly what goodness does not do, it includes everybody whether he has loveable qualities or not.

Walter's fellow exiled Viennese Jew, Regina Deutsch, also recognized that the unusual atmosphere at Scattergood Hostel had everything to do with the folks behind its creation and continuation. In her mind, "seeing and considering individual human beings, engulfed by problems and suffering by them, seems the secret why the Friends succeed in solving these problems, where others fail more or less."

The red-haired Regina—"who seemed to want to 'mother' the whole world"—would know something about how successful Quakers had been in "considering individual human beings," given that her family remained so closely involved in the life of the hostel even after Emil found work in Des Moines and they moved there. For them Scattergood symbolized a "family" which replaced the loved ones they had left in Austria. As with "real" families, it punctuated their lives in various ways and claimed a large space in their psychological landscape. Twelve-year-old Michael spent two weeks at the hostel in the summer of 1942, for example, while his mother and sister visited Chicago. Also, when Regina's 7-year-old niece Ruth Feigel[4] managed to make her way alone to America, Regina was sure to bring the "skinny, shy child...who looked unwell" to Scattergood—to the Deutsch Family "homestead" in the New World. As noted elsewhere, when she herself needed to convalesce from thyroid surgery, it was to Scattergood that Regina came in spring 1941 to recover. Again and again, then, like birds leaving a nest, not only the Deutsches but numerous guests are recorded as having returned to Scattergood for either later visits or longer stays—only to leave once more, possibly to return again.

For her part, Martha Balderston felt ambivalent about the ultimate departure of every guest who ever set foot inside the hostel's door. On one hand the staff hoped to help the refugees among them build new biographies in their new homeland. At the same time, in the process of training them in English conjunctives and American customs, in growing sweet corn and baking apple pie, the strangers the staff encountered at Scattergood often became friends. Martha wrote: "It is with mixed feelings that we celebrate each departure, glad for the new opportunity to get established in America, and genuinely regretful that we are losing from the Hostel friends of whom we have grown very fond."

On the occasion of Scattergood's first anniversary, acting director John Kaltenbach noted the central role that friendships played at the hostel. In the April 1940 edition of the *Scattergood Monthly News Bulletin* he reflected that "on the fifteenth day of this month Scattergood rounded out the first year of its Hostel life. On that day of 1939, five men arrived to begin a new venture, to open a new frontier of social pioneering. In the days between we have found new friends and opened new areas of life for all who have been able to take part in the activity of Scattergood. We have found joys and sorrow along the same road. We have found out that simple friendship and the everyday acquaintance of human beings is the best way to avoid wars and most of the pain that the world knows."

At the risk of borrowing a cliché, it seems John was alluding to "the human family," an image which in the aftermath of World War II would be plagiarized from the pamphlets of its left-leaning, pre-war advocates and find widespread press in the heady years of the founding of the United Nations and popular movements championing a "global village." This post-war harvest of goodwill had its planting in fertile soil like that of Scattergood: in miniature, various nationalities lived, learned, worked, struggled together there and grew intertwined as only "family" could be. This metaphor didn't escape hostelites who, even as they inadvertently embarked on this experiment in living, realized that something very special was emerging in the common space between them as individuals.

Twenty-one-year-old Peter Siedel (later "Seadle") of Berlin joined in the chorus of those who sang praises of this unique "family" born of love mated with social action. A student and would-be actor, the sandy-haired, fine-faced youth didn't miss a chance to roam Middle America as placement-director Giles Zimmerman made one of his frequent rounds of the Midwest to follow up on guests already placed and to ferret out positions for those still awaiting one. A speaker of German, French, Italian, Spanish, Portuguese and English, Peter used his considerable talent in the last to convey to readers of the *Scattergood Monthly News Bulletin* some of what he saw during his tour:

> *Our family is perhaps the largest family in the country. It is scattered all over America. Its members have different interests, different professions, different points of view and they come from different countries, but they all have the same home: Scattergood. I don't think it is too much if I call it home, because home is the place where we feel we are free and can relax, and it also is a place that will always be alive in our memories as a refuge where we can turn in times of trouble and desperation. This is the impression I received when I went out with Giles to visit the different "children" of the family recently.*

A true family shares hard times along with the good. And among those displaced, dispirited refugees, for a very long time there had been plenty of hard times and not nearly enough good. Just because they were now safely out of Hitler's reach didn't mean they did not suffer indescribably over the fates of friends and family in their former homelands. Entries in *The Book of Scattergood*—that common log of a shared life—chronicle how the hostelites, refugees and staff together, faced the gathering clouds of catastrophe over Europe in late summer 1939. Already on 24 August the normally cheery pages of the group's journal housed the entry: "European crisis over Poland dominates our thoughts." What until then had been an utterly apolitical document then became very concerned with events beyond America's shores: "Meeting and program were in Mtg. House [tonight, 28 August]. John [Kaltenbach] and K. Rosegg were the main speakers. And, even after all that there were still seven who kept on till 2 A.M. discussing war, peace, methods of life, etc., in the kitchen, fortified by lemonade." On the following day "a concern was expressed as to the attitude of the Hostel in case of war. We deferred any decision until such time as we might know all legal requirements and determine our own individual course of action. This is a matter of personal conviction, but does affect the group as a whole. Hot discussions on the evils of the capitalistic system etc. etc."

Two days passed with *The Book* digesting only the usual fare of reports on canned corn and croquet games, departures, "picnic supper at quarries and singing far into the night." On the third day of a tense week, the last sentence of that day's entry consisted of the terse appraisal, "Europe is in a bad way." By the next morning the die had been cast, creating "a day we will long remember. Beginning of hostilities between Germany and Poland. Our sympathy and grief for our overseas brothers [and sisters] is boundless—but America must not fight! We can only hope and pray for Peace."

The following day's entry contained only four sentences, the last half of which noted: "All remains quiet on the Scattergood front. Many went to see *The Wizard of Oz*." On 3 September, however, right away: "France and England declare war." Evidently once America's future allies took aim on the Third Reich, the folks at Scattergood assumed that a new status quo of open warfare would punctuate their days and nights for the foreseeable future and "that was that," for thereafter the next remotely political entry in the hostel family's log appeared on 16 September, when someone recorded that "Giles called from Lincoln, Nebraska, to say he was having a good time and was speaking on the Peace Forum over the radio on Sunday morning." It seemed clear: from then on life at Scattergood would be "business as usual," even if that business was of a most unusual sort—that of rebuilding broken lives.[5]

No matter how meaningful the Scattergood family came to be for those living at the hostel, the refugee members of the community never would forget the beloveds they had left behind in a Europe sinking in the ravenous flames of war. All the pleasant smiles and kind words in the world could not erase the ugly things the refugees had experienced in their native countries or in lands where they falsely assumed they had found safety. To claim a precious chance at survival, however, they had to adopt and adjust to life in a new, oft puzzling and sometimes distasteful culture. This was not easy—but requisite. Perhaps above all else, Scattergood provided its guests a lifeline in the form of an *ersatz* family and then a bridge from the consuming fires of despair which they had known to an island of hope which would save them. For this single act the refugees would never forget the Quakers.

Marianne Welter was one of the guests who struggled with the inner tension inherent in—on one hand—peering over her shoulder at the fragments of what had been a complete and fulfilling life, but on the other looking forward to a new one. The 34-year-old, Essen-born social worker had fled Berlin in 1933 with the Nazis' accession to power. In the company of her special friend Nora Hackel and Nora's mother Hedwig ("Omi"), she fled to France—where Nora later gave birth to daughter Nicole. The foursome then landed in Gurs concentration camp after the Germans defeated the Paris government; only through blessed luck were they able to secure a way out of France and to the United States. During the half year that they stayed at Scattergood the slender, black-haired Marianne attempted to put into words some of the swirling images which raged in her conflicted mind:

165

You see, when we had to leave country and people on the other side, we did leave them as a very part of them. Even though one tried to exclude us from all that was happening, we did take part in all those happenings and problems—in people's conditions of living—in their despair and their hope. When we arrived here, we remained rooted over there. Thus it was and is a part of our conviction that frontiers between people do not have any meaning, at least not for ourselves, we actually felt completely forlorn and isolated. All was horribly strange; everything was so different from all we had seen and heard and thought before. There was a large and deep gap, which seemed unbridgeable. So we came to Scattergood—being still on the other side of that gap. It was by Scattergood's kind and good and still ways that a first bridge could be built. A very human, a very natural process—and yet you hardly may guess what it meant to us, how important and precious this experience was! How good it was! On that first small fundament, it was possible to come closer to this country's specific character, to listen to this new rhythm and become interested in its problems. We may have very different ways, where to go—very different places and fields in which to work, according to our different capacities, beliefs and convictions; but you must know, this, I would like to say, first meeting with friends will never be forgotten.

1.) One guest who did not perceive a community at the hostel was Ernst Malamerson, who maintained that "the refugees themselves, on the whole, disliked each other considerably. I must say that did not find myself particularly interested in any of them and I think they had a sort of...well, let me put it this way: to begin with, [they were] psychologically anti-America. If you had asked them they certainly would have said they were grateful, pleased and so on. And they were; that was also true. But they felt—as a reaction to the strange and new culture, and to being deprived of whatever positions they had had in the past—a certain superiority... At the same time they also doubted fully their ability to re-establish themselves, so they were all ambiguous. My own feeling of, not really dislike, but lack of interest in these people? They were all older than I was, they were all from a different social strata—middle-class notions and things like that. And I felt, not superior, but that I was from a different social strata. And they? Well, each one felt that the other did not recognize his or her importance in view of their position. On the whole...I think the Quakers tried very hard to form a community as it were but they didn't really succeed in this because [the refugees] were Europeans and to form a new community would be for them psychologically to renounce—to finally renounce totally—their European status. And that was a struggle for them... [Therefore the group of refugees at Scattergood] didn't form a community, although it pretended to, partly to please the staff and partly because, well, there was nothing [else] you could do."

2.) Because such documents' sexist language reflects the time and social attitudes in which they were written, and because inserting [she], [her] or [herself], etc. each time would be cumbersome as well as distracting, I have left the texts mostly intact and noted the omission only in the first instance in a given document—and thereby referred to the too-common mistake of overlooking the needs, experiences or dreams of half of the human race.

3.) Not only a professional journalist, Richard Schuber also practiced hypnotism. In January 1940 the *Des Moines Tribune* ran an article—with a sensational headline "Schuber of Vienna Brought a Hobby; Hypnosis Comes to Scattergood; He Also Practices in Telepathy"—in which a reporter related an interview during which Richard demonstrated his skill on a couple fellow refugees. The bearer of an Austrian license to practice hypnotism since 1919, Richard named Adolf Hitler as "an ideal subject for hypnosis," given that he was "suggestible. The last man who speaks to him is the man who is believed and sympathized with."

4.) As a high schooler Ruth attended the reopened Scattergood School for a year or two, but didn't graduate. As a teen she later committed suicide. Ruth was not the only European to pass through the hostel's doors who took her or his own life. In an interview in autumn 1994 with Earle Edwards, he remembered once reminiscing with a fellow former staff member and discussing a number of one-time guests who later ended their own lives. Upon questioning, however, he could name for sure only one, 30-something Jew Oskar Kovacs first of Vienna and later of Chicago and New York, whom they described as "unstable."

5.) A little more than two years later, the United States' entry into the war changed life at the hostel once again—as reported in the January 1942 issue of the *Scattergood Monthly News Bulletin*: "The declaration of war brought excitement and anxiety here as elsewhere in the United States, and then the family settled down to a philosophical acceptance of the limitations of a state of war. Those who had been through this experience knew what to expect. Restrictions were not new to them. Governmental proclamations were awaited with interest.

"Wild rumors have been flying about—such as the one that the roads leading to Scattergood have had to be patrolled, etc. No! Life is going on much as usual. Members of the family are leaving for new homes and new jobs. We are waiting with keen anticipation newcomers from New York, who will leave there as soon as they receive permission to travel. We have tried in every way to meet the requirements of the Government, and in turn have found the authorities helpful and understanding. The so-called 'enemy aliens' must apply for travel permits to go outside the district in which they live. Iowa City has been interpreted as being within our 'municipality', so we go back and forth as we always have done. Three cameras were surrendered to the Mayor of West Branch, and the one guest-owned radio with a short wave band has had this band disconnected, as the regulations prescribed.

"Scattergood household budget, like others, is feeling the rising cost of food, and other increasing expenses. Peggy Hannum, our dietitian, has been telling us from time to time that this or that item of canned goods can no longer be purchased; paper napkins are costlier and more difficult to get; sugar has been rationed, etc. We are becoming more and more conscious of lights left burning unnecessarily; hot water used more freely than needed, and other like extravagances.

"A member of the family is an expert with old sewing machines, so with his help, the one Mayor Anderson kindly obtained for our use is now in running order, and the pile of finished Red Cross garments is steadily growing. The machine stands by the window in the dining-room and we sew whenever we find the time."

Later, as the U.S.'s role in the war intensified, notices appearing in the *Scattergood Monthly News Bulletin* spoke of the hostel's scrap iron being collected and rubber or gasoline being rationed.

FOR THE BENEFIT OF ALL

*"We enjoy the kind of life we have here which consists
of well organized house work for the benefit of all."*
~ **Sonia Braun**

Of course developing a satisfying sense of a shared life doesn't consist
merely of finding a few new friends or sitting down on a winter's night,
taking pen in hand and scribbling out nice words about noble ideas. Rather,
genuine community arises out of a common daily life which provides the
necessary context for friendships to bud and noble ideas to bloom. In essence,
at Scattergood the journey *was* the destination, for the very act of living together in an American environment prepared guests for the post-hostel lives
on which they pinned their hopes.[1]

Along with organized instruction and semi-organized freetime, work offered the refugees myriad opportunities to learn new skills, adapt to new
customs and values, learn or improve their English and regain some of the
self-confidence which had been shattered in the wake of Nazi persecution
and subsequent flight. In short, the rehabilitation and integration of the Europeans living at Scattergood Hostel happened not during some magical, appointed moment, but during many mundane moments. Daily life afforded a
vehicle with which the guests finally could "arrive" in America—the land of,
if not their dreams, their last hope.

Of what did this daily life consist? What did it look like? Who planned
how it would look and who changed these plans? Moreover, what were some
ways in which it affected those who participated in it and what lasting value
did it have in helping those in need? How did "work" enhance "community?"

Insofar as the Scattergood staff intended to incorporate the necessary
work at the hostel in their efforts to rehabilitate and integrate their guests,
they had to make a daily plan. Within this structure all common activities

168

had to be coordinated and then executed. At least, that was the plan. As the staff quickly learned, holiday observances and seasonal changes threw wrenches into the works without apology. Similarly, the offer of a whistle-stop visit by a renowned figure could instantaneously overturn the most rigorously observed routines. Important English lessons also decimated the ranks of many a work crew. So did the capabilities of the guests; the elderly or disabled simply couldn't be expected to accomplish as much physical work as their younger or more fit counterparts, while other guests lacked manual dexterity or basic technical skills. Also, as time passed during the hostel's four-year existence, the folks in charge as well as the refugees living there had differing attitudes and needs regarding work. Thus the Daily Schedule changed...well, daily.

Sources indicate the reign—no matter how temporary or amended—of at least four distinct daily schedules at Scattergood Hostel, with some sources also mentioning how non-work activities fit into the daily routine. Listed in chronological order, they include plans as described by Camilla Hewson (in use during at least part of her stay spanning May 1939 to July 1940), by education director Ruth Carter (August 1939), by Earle and Marjorie Edwards (August 1940) and by an anonymous source writing in the *Scattergood Monthly News Bulletin* in February 1941.[2] Of the "Typical SH day," Camilla wrote:

Most folks made it down to breakfast, and many went to Meeting, too. Crews then got into the work of the day, and those not working would probably be in a class or a one-on-one tutoring session. After lunch, often a trip to West Branch or Iowa City, and a driving lesson for someone. In summer, the garden took priority, and we had big canning sessions for corn and beans. Dishes were washed, of course by hand, after each meal, tables set, food prepared. People were on cleaning crews, washing and ironing, and often if there were visitors someone would be designated to show them around and answer questions.

After dinner, free time, unless a community meeting for business was scheduled. Group activities (large and small) such as hikes, movies in Iowa City, jigsaw puzzles, singing, and other games were organized spontaneously. Visitors gave talks. Sometimes we put on a play for ourselves. Ruth [Carter] and Mildred [Holmes] sang with an Iowa City chorus. People read, listened to the radio (no TV of course), or just sat around talking. A memorable "snipe hunt" played a good-natured trick on a couple of new arrivals, and a scavenger hunt was enjoyed by all. In summer there were frequent excursions to the Quarries, not far away, for picnics and swims (even at night, on occasion). People were also invited to homes of Friends and neighbors. Little was regimented,

most things were flexible according to individual tastes and needs.
Everyone did something, and most jobs rotated weekly, with a
schedule posted on the bulletin board.

Whereas Camilla wrote her account some 55 years after the fact and spoke of what seemed to her "typical," New England-born Ruth Carter—in contrast—recorded her sense of the exact schedule while Scattergood Hostel still existed. "Days at Scattergood are not all alike," Ruth warned, "so that it is difficult to describe a 'typical' one. However, this general framework will suffice to show the scheme as it was in operation this summer [of 1939]. (Present plans are for a change of intellectual labors to the morning hours, if possible)."

6:30	*Rising Bell*
7:00	*Breakfast*
7:30-7:50	*Meeting, down the walk in the meeting house*
8:00	*Morning duties begin*
	(i.e.: dishes, table setting, laundry on
	Mon. Wed. and Fri., sweeping, cleaning,
	ironing, out-door work—grass mowing,
	picking vegetables, weeding, carpentry,
	painting, etc.) If there is a particular job
	which needs special attention, all but
	the most essential regular duties are
	suspended and all concentrate on the
	business at hand, be it canning, fixing
	up the meeting house, or whatever it
	may be.
12:15	*Lunch*
1:00-2:00	*First tutoring hour*
2:00-3:00	*Second tutoring hour*
	(Each of the volunteer American work-
	ers is given from two to four Germans
	[or individuals of other nationalities]
	for individual work in English, gram-
	mar, and phonetics. At present this is
	arranged so that each German spends
	one hour a day with a "tutor" in this
	intensive study.)
3:00-4:00	*Lecture*
	Mon., Wed., Fri.: American History, by John
	Kaltenbach. Every other Fri.: Government by Lynn

170

Zimmerman. *Tues, Thurs.: Phonetics by Prof.
Snedeker (Iowa U.)*
4:00-5:00   *English Grammar Class (Ruth Carter)*
5:00-6:00   *Third Tutoring hour*
6:15   *Dinner*

<u>Evenings</u> *are free for relaxation, with the following special events:*
    *Monday evening is the weekly Scattergood business meeting which
all attend. It is conducted as much like a Quaker business Meeting[3] as
possible. All are free to discuss any problem which has arisen during
the week, or which seems likely to arise, or discuss any policy, or idea
deemed important by the group.*
    *Friday evening is often set aside for special outside lecturers who
come to the hostel.*
    *Saturday evening there is an opportunity for going to Iowa City, to
the movies or whatever else offers. Saturday afternoon is also a
"holiday" and trips are frequently made to the quarries for swimming,
or to Iowa City for movies, or to any of several possible places.*
    <u>Sundays</u> *follow no set schedule except that the afternoons are di-
vided into 1 1/2 hour "guide periods" which have become necessary
because of the great flow of visitors at this time. So that all the work
won't fall on the most willing, guides are appointed in advance.*
    <u>Outside contacts:</u> *There are many opportunities for hostelites
(both American and German) to accept speaking engagements in various parts of the state, where an active interest in the hostel exists
among many different groups.*

Exactly a year after Ruth filed her report, Earle and Marjorie Edwards
listed the daily schedule as it had been since the previous winter and
spring—complete with changes regarding the number of tutorials per week
and an increased emphasis on manual work:

7:00   *Breakfast*
7:30   *Voluntary period of meditation (worship) in the Meeting
        House on the campus*
8:00   *Household work*
10:00 *Classes*
12:30 *Lunch*
2:00   *Manual work on buildings and grounds*
4:00   *Tutoring*
6:00   *Dinner*
7:30   *Various activities, including weekly business meeting,*

171

lectures by visitors, chorus, literary seminar, etc. During the summer work has been shifted to the second half of the morning to avoid the afternoon heat. Tutoring has tended to replace classes.

Whoever it was at Scattergood who outlined the daily fare of work and play in the hostel's monthly newsletter in early 1941, she or he provided a detailed, humor-laced sample of:

A WEEK AT SCATTERGOOD

Ever spent a week at Scattergood? No? Well, then, come with us through the looking glass and see just what transpires there in the course of an ordinary seven day period. From Monday to the following Sunday residents will be engaged in many ordinary tasks and many extraordinary ones. Some will be doing things completely new to them; some will be right at home in their special fields. But all will be working and sharing in the homemaking for a family of thirty or forty people and all will be trying to make this family organization run as smoothly and comfortably as possible.

At 6:30 A.M. Monday morning the first bell rings. This is supposed to be the signal for rising. Breakfast will be at 7. Not many people get up at 6:30, however, but by the time the second bell sounds at 6:45 some are thinking about it. The breakfast bell at 7 means general commotion in both buildings as people scurry here and there in a frantic effort to arrive in the dining room somewhere around that time. After breakfast comes Meeting in the Meeting House at the end of the lane. Then general clean-up tasks such as dishwashing, floor scrubbing and cleaning of rooms, take place. Also the washing. On these jobs will be people who have never washed or never scrubbed before coming to Scattergood. Positions in banks or offices did not require such exercise. Furthermore, European men are not as accustomed to household work as are American husbands and sons. But we all catch on quickly and soon become pretty expert in the arts of homemaking!

Monday afternoon finds the hostel busy with English work. Individual tuitions are held. Right after lunch a class in Household Mechanics is conducted by the dietitian. An expert in the phonetics field comes out to put some of the hostelites through their paces in this sphere.

After dinner, which occurs at 6, comes Business Meeting. At this time every week the whole group gathers together to discuss common problems and interests. Plans are made for the coming week. The past week is reviewed through the reading aloud of the logbook. Bath tubs, fire buckets, trips to Iowa City, kitchen rules and regulations, even the newspapers and their place in the living room all come in for their share of the hour or so that this meeting occupies. Afterward, the household schedule for the coming week appears on the Bulletin Board.

Tuesday morning finds a new breakfast crew trying to get the toast arranged, unburned, on the several plates, the hot cereal made, the coffee brewed, all in the short time between 6:30 and 7. They are seldom successful in completing it in this half hour the first morning but one is surprised by the proficiency that can be developed during the course of a week. After Meeting the dishes again, and ironing and mangling instead of washing. On this as on any day, men who have no other special responsibility may be doing necessary repair and maintenance work on the building and grounds. In the afternoon will come the first of the two general weekly trips to Iowa City. Therefore it will be quiet around the Hostel for those few hours. In the evening there will be a lecture by one of the staff on American government and politics. These occur twice a week.

Wednesday finds us, after the household work is completed, deep in classes and tuitions. There will be individual work again, a class for beginners, special courses in commercial subjects. The evening will often be taken by a trip to Iowa City for a concert or lecture under the auspices of the University. Many outstanding phases of American cultural life become available to us through this medium.

Thursday morning is like the rest except that special cleaning is added to the regular routine. The garbage pails are scrubbed, woodwork gone over, the dishwashing equipment scoured. Tuitions and classes again in the afternoon and American government lecture in the evening. Or this may be the time that a special lecturer from the University will be scheduled to have dinner with us and speak to us afterward.

Friday finds us washing again. Ironing and mangling for the week are finished if possible. Classes again in the afternoon. The evening is devoted to that exciting feature, the Public Speaking class. A hilarious time is often had by all, but also a profitable one, we hope, as residents discourse for two minutes or more on "Why I like to go to Iowa City" or "My first impressions of Scattergood" or perhaps read some famous English poems. Criticism may be rather severe but the benefit of the speaker is always in mind.

Saturday is the time for special end-of-the-week cleaning. The *laundry rooms are scrubbed thoroughly. Floors are made spotless. Before we know it it is twelve noon and time for dinner. By one-thirty people are spruced up and ready for the second general Iowa City trip for that week. This is the festive time for those who venture forth, the peaceful time for those who remain at home to listen to the Opera or just catch up on letter writing. The evening brings either an unscheduled respite or a party of some kind. Perhaps the festivities will be in honor of a birthday or a departure or perhaps there will be a party just because we like them and like to get together and improvise out of nothing.*

Sunday brings the breakfast bell at 8:30 instead of 7—much to the relief of all. Then comes Meeting or Church in West Branch and dinner at 1. The afternoon will be filled with visitors or perhaps reading, studying and letter writing. Supper comes at 6 and then a quiet evening for some, an evening of meetings and preparation for the next week for others.

So it is that we pass our time at Scattergood. Indeed, as our alumni often say after their departure "One feels rather lost after this busy life in which there is always something going on."

As a present to Scattergood on its third birthday, former office manager Lynn Zimmerman and Esther Smith—a Church of the Brethren volunteer who served on the staff for one year—composed a poem which recounted various aspects of daily life at the hostel. While some allusions had to do with obscure "insider" incidents, it generally offered a thorough, amusing look at *Alltagsleben* at Scattergood:

SCATTERGOOD'S THIRD BIRTHDAY [4]

Our Scattergood saga began they say
Three years ago to this very day.
John Kaltenbach and a crew of four
Drove in Sta-Wag to the Hostel door.
They were welcomed by Walter and Sara of course.
They talked to reporters until they were hoarse.
Friends came in from the neighborhood
And thus began our Scattergood.

With painting and pounding and many repairs,
We fixed up our rooms and built the front stairs.
By Christmastime, as you all know,
There was no more room for the family to grow.

174

Then some got jobs and went away,
Jean [Reynolds] sent us new ones every day.
Farewell parties occurred and occurred,
They're now a tradition, as you have heard.

In our history there were a great number of things,
Time sped on as if it had wings.
There were events too numerous to mention
We list some here for your attention:

Midnight walks to Centerdale.
The postman bringing the morning mail.
Windows broken by summer hail,
Hauling our water pail by pail.
A cat having kittens in someone's bed.
Sunburned shoulders turning red!
Flocks of chickens to be fed.
A happy couple being wed.
Driving lessons going strong,
(Suzy-One—they did her wrong.)
All asleep at the breakfast gong.
Sunday evenings filled with song.
Station wagons upside down.
Semi-weekly trips to town
Residents of great renown,
The faithful Duchess who had no crown.
Cleaning house in an awful hurry
(Philadelphia guests were making
us scurry!)
Budget not balancing—oh what a
worry!
Macky's coat all muddy and burry.
Visitors coming and no clean sheets.
Picking corn where we'd planted
beets.
Birthday parties and special treats.
Screen making, ditch digging—
wonderful feasts!
Learning to pronounce "ah," "oh"
and "ooo."
Eating ice cream with chocolate goo.
"Scattergood boys" in overalls new.

175

Dishes done by a Latin crew.
Business meeting on Monday nights,
One was followed by Northern Lights!
Trips to Amana to see the sights.
Columbus and Milquetoast having
fights!
"Sheeps" and chickens (some indoors)
Necessitating additional chores.
Nights all quiet except for snores.
Sunday visitors coming in scores.
All of our children being so smart.
Finding places in everyone's heart.
Station wagons refusing to start.
All of our birthdays on a chart.

There are other events we all recall
But space prevents us writing them all.
Have lots of fun at your birthday party.
The Alumni send their wishes hearty.

Despite how it might sound, "work" did not consist of endless excuses for socializing or even genuine learning. For some work proved satisfying in its own right, either as an alternative to idle hands—which so easily led to overly busy brains—or as a means to find a sense of meaning and accomplishment. In an unpublished essay she wrote in October 1942, Polish chemist Sonia Braun claimed that:

A day in Scattergood is all made up of enjoyment. I certainly don't mean that we have fun from morning until night—it would become rather ennoyant [sic] after a few days. What I want to say is that we enjoy the kind of life we have here which consists of well organized house work for the benefit of all... If we happen to be tired at the end of the day it is a sound fatigue which makes you sleep fast all the night through... If the refugees like Scat. it is chiefly...because of the moral rest they get here from all the worries they have faced at their arrival in this country... Now as far as the staff members are concerned it is quite different. If they enjoy Scattergood in spite of the fact that they are busy all the day long with housework, office-work, English teaching and so on, they get satisfaction, as I understand it, from doing what they believe they should do. And doing what one considers as his duty is undoubtedly one of the most sublime feelings that a human being can have in his [or her] lifetime.

176

Not only staff had influence over the planning and organization of work at Scattergood Hostel. As noted, during the Monday evening meetings and at other times guests also could suggest tasks or projects which they considered needed attention. Predictably, their proposals reflected not only their cultural values but their own idiosyncratic characters, too. Vienna-born Friedrich "Fred" Pollak—whom the Edwards described as "very German and not-laid-back"—joined in the chorus of voices offering ideas for group undertakings. His, however, was discredited given that he was "not very popular...because of his aloofness and refusal to cooperate." Even the forgiving Robert Berquist noted that Pollak was "very critical of others, who he felt often shirked their work assignments...spoke German much of the time [and was in] a great hurry." Still, the middle-aged Austrian Jew did submit

Suggestions for Springtime work.

I think that the first goal we should aim at is the repair of all doors and windows.

The office-door must be repaired in order to attain a normal shut of the same lest the wall in which it is mounted be ultimately shaken and destroyed.

The door between workshop and hall should likewise be put in shape (no shut now).

The western door of the hall needs repair in order too [sic] keep out flies and, in winter, superfluous cold.

The door of 3 W (room and bathrooms) is likewise needing reshape because it never shuts.

There are at least 2 doors moreover which have not even a lock.

It scarcely needs explanation that all windows of the kitchen, dining room, and pantry must be opened. But at least one of them in the above mentioned rooms.

The same is true for bathroom 2 W (at least upper half of window) as it is an impossible condition there is a bathroom without any ventilation.

All other windows must be put in shape so at least 1 window in every bedroom can be opened in the upper half, as the lower half does not provide the least adequate airing of the room, especially not in summer (in winter neither). Other windows are to be repaired. This is first true for bathroom 3 W.

Putting on screens should be left to those whose heart's desire requires it. People who think that screens are only fly-breeding-apparatusses [sic] (like me) should be left without screens. At least

177

there should be in every bedroom <u>one</u> window without screen so it can
be opened by night and in heavy rain-wheather [sic], when no flies
come, and the room properly aired, as the high-grade lack of fresh air
we had last year <u>is just what breeds flies.</u>[5]
That is twice true for the kitchen and dining-room.
All faucets in the home must be put in shape so they cease making
a noise like a machine-gun.

Not every guest took such a thorough (if not compulsive) view towards shared work. In fact it seemed that more than the work itself, many hostelites took note of *who* was working—specifically, which professionals were rolling up their sleeves and dirtying their hands or which gender lines were being crossed in the process. As Grete Rosenzweig noted, "men in Europe do not take part in household tasks, but the right idea of the Quakers was that husband AND wife should attend to household duties since—to get a new start—both members of the family had to go to work, so men washed, ironed, cooked, washed dishes and cleaned together with the women."

Except for the 15 or so children who would pass through Scattergood's doors, all of the guests took turns between tutorials to make the Hostel run on a minimal budget and with considerable efficiency. Even light household work, however, was foreign territory for these mostly urbane folks. The European men were unaccustomed to lifting a dish towel[6] or folding laundry, while many of their distaff counterparts had enjoyed the help of paid servants in the old country. The loss of a bourgeois lifestyle and social status provided a challenge for both. Staff members reported that men suffered from this *de facto* demotion, as many of them had been wealthy, well-known judges, doctors or other professionals in Europe and their credentials were not automatically transferable nor their advanced ages an incentive for being hired. Then, to come to America and find themselves doing "women's work!"

The rational reason for this forced role-switching did not consist only of the need to get much work done in a short amount of time so as to leave blocks of time free for instruction or group recreation. Even teenage Camilla Hewson realized that "because [most of the men's] lives were on hold, the chores were a way to keep up their self esteem...and [make them] feel they were not completely dependent and helpless." She noted: "there were often a few complaints, but I recall no outright rebellions...because the staff worked along with them, and no one was exempt."[7] Some resistance seemed inevitable, for as the precocious Quaker lass observed, "German males didn't come equipped to know how to hang shirts!" Generally, however, "newcomers for the most part adapted to changed roles with good grace—only a few 'stuffed shirts' tried to pull rank on the basis of their professional backgrounds, etc."

178

Well, *most* of them exhibited reserves of good grace: proud Walter Shostal did not. Years later he would recall that Peg Hannum ignited in him a reaction born of reflexive resistance "when she drafted me to help with some special drastic cleaning of the living room—an activity which I thought senseless and unnecessary. I was full of rage but did not dare to refuse—male chauvinism, I suppose. I was more cooperative when John [Copithorne] drafted me to help him paint our red barn. High up on a tall ladder I felt insecure, but had a feeling of accomplishment when it was finished."

Indeed, for those guests who simply couldn't bear household work, that under the open skies beckoned and offered a welcome escape from floor wax, wash cloth and wringer. Not exactly an agricultural enterprise, Scattergood did possess some of the elements of rural life typical of the North American prairies in the 1930s-'40s. Like their farming neighbors, the folks at Scattergood raised a good share of their own food, both on the hoof and in the garden. City slicker Leo Keller of Vienna took delight in this aspect of life at the hostel—so much so that this middle-aged, unemployed lawyer took pen in hand and drafted a few lines to share the bliss with the wider Scattergood family in the pages of the community's newsletter:

> With the coming of spring Scattergood becomes more rural than ever and takes on more of the aspects of a small farm. In back of the youth hostel [which was a small-scale outreach project] 275 new residents have taken up quarters in a small house with lots of windows. These baby chicks, white ones, brown ones and black ones, are now three weeks old and growing rapidly. They are very comfortable in their little home which is equipped with a central heating plant and electricity. The chicks have only to eat, to play and to sleep. They have no other worries—not yet! Every day several of the Scattergoodians troop down to the chicken house to observe the progress of the baby chicks. But that is not all. Out in Scattergood's picnic meadow 18 sheep now find a comfortable home. There are 9 ewes and 9 lambs. The ewes are to be sheared of their wool soon and the lambs are big enough to be sold. Even though the sheep bleat every morning, they do keep the grass in the meadow trimmed.

Because the hostel's organizers intended from the start that it should be as self-supporting as possible, as time allowed an extensive garden took shape on part of the twelve acres which Scattergood occupied. Per contract, the Stanleys were in charge of the garden—the vegetables of which filled the stomachs of the hostel family, while the flowers graced the place indoors and out. Sara twice included reports about the garden in the *Scattergood Monthly*

News Bulletin—obviously feeling that they had a rightful place there, given that the garden played such an important role in the work life as well as the nutrition of a good portion of the newsletter's readership. She wrote her first essay in June 1941, the second in May 1942:

THE HOME SIDE OF HOSTEL LIFE

The garden has made very satisfactory progress. It seemed fortunate that it had not been planted before the hard hail and rain storm which came Fourth Month 19th, as the ground was packed so hard the seeds could hardly get through. The rhubarb came early and everyone enjoyed the sauce and pie. We are hoping to have a large supply of asparagus by another spring as the plants that were set out last spring are doing well. We have been having an abundance of radishes, lettuce, spinach and beets and will have our first peas in a few days. Other work has been pushed aside for the present so the time could be spent for the many strawberries with which we are favored. They are very nice and of good quality. We have enjoyed them served fresh in many different ways and have made jam, canned and have some in the frozen food locker which will be enjoyed next winter. The surplus juice has also been canned to be used in cold drinks. Many cabbage, tomato, broccoli, cauliflower and some pepper and eggplants have been set out and are doing nicely. Early potatoes are in bloom and the late ones have recently been planted. Many different plantings of sweet corn have been made and more will be planted so there will be a succession for several weeks. So much for the vegetable garden, but of course it would not be complete without some flowers, too. The many gay tulips gave much color for vases and bowls and were very attractive out-of-doors as well. Violets, narcissus and daffodils were followed by pained daisies, columbine, iris, peonies, roses and pinks. Several different kinds of annuals and perennials and also summer flowering bulbs will be enjoyed later.

THE GARDEN IN SPRING

We have found that the garden has been a valuable asset to Scattergood, and will no doubt be more so owing to the advance in prices of most food products [following the United States' recent entry into war]. This season we will endeavour to increase our crops. Five hundred pounds of potatoes were planted early and will soon be large enough for cultivating. Radishes will appear in a few days, and lettuce,

180

spinach and peas are coming along nicely. A little later we will have to reset our own plants for tomatoes, cabbage, cauliflower, broccoli and celery, and will have to plant cucumbers, squashes, melons, pie pumpkins, okra, and a little later a few turnips. Considerable sweet corn has been planted, and more will follow at intervals of two weeks in order that we have a plentiful supply throughout the season, and in addition plenty to put into our freezing unit at the locker. As our past experience has proven, this manner of preservation is preferable to canning, for there is no loss from spoilage. We will also use the freezing method again for beans, peas, strawberries and cherries. The strawberries, which retain their original flavor almost one hundred per cent, we enjoyed at Christmas time and on other occasions up to a few weeks ago. A new bed of three hundred strawberry plants was set out early this spring, and is doing nicely. Already we have had asparagus from the plants which were set out two years ago.

The flowers have not been forgotten. Of course, we have been enjoying the wild flower garden, bloodroot, blue bells, violets, wild geranium, phlox and columbine. The tulips and daffodils are bright and gay. We have also planted many annuals and summer flowering bulbs, which we hope to enjoy later on. A very nice gift of ten lovely varieties of tea roses was received on Scattergood's birthday from a former member of the Hostel family. We are looking forward with pleasure to the time when they will be blooming.[8]

Not all food raised at Scattergood found its way to the dining room table. In spring 1940—in tandem with the Pemberton family, which had been doing so for years—the hostel family committed itself to using some of its prime Iowa loam to grow some 6,300 tomato plants, half of the yield of which the Heinz Company planned to make into ketchup at its cannery in Muscatine, Iowa. The hostel intended to make good use of the other half of the harvest. First, though, the tomatoes had to be planted. A tired Lynn Zimmerman later declared:

I'll never again be indifferent to catsup. [Planting the tomato plants] was the best example of perfect cooperation in work we've ever had. Everyone except Camilla [Hewson], Mildred [Holmes], Martha [Balderston] and Sara [Stanley], who were otherwise engaged, was out there digging, watering, or planting. We had teams and had contests for speed. For example, our team worked this way: Boris [Jaffe] dug the holes, Helmut [Ostrowski-Wilk] carried water to Lucy [Selig] who poured it in the holes, and Ruth [Carter] and I planted the tomatoes.

181

Needless to say, on [the next two days] none of us could sit, stand, walk, or climb stairs without groans of pain as our unused muscles rebelled at this unaccustomed activity. We all got dizzy and had headaches, probably from so much stooping over in the sun, but no one complained and no one quit until the job was finished. We only paused to take occasional pictures, and to drink the iced coffee Sara provided. We were lucky enough to have rain that night, and the plants are now flourishing, even the tired anemic looking ones! Because we were all so utterly exhausted physically, we didn't have the energy to talk over the increasingly tragic news from Europe [regarding the Wehrmacht's *occupation of Paris]. We all trot out before breakfast to admire the progress of our plants.*[9]

Picking the ripened harvest—which weighed in at ten tons and earned the hostel $75—later proved a far-from-effortless project, given the nature of the work and that under a burning summer sun. To avoid the intense afternoon rays the staff and guests shifted the daily schedule and announced in the August *Bulletin*: "We...have inaugurated the system of rising at 5:30 on tomato picking mornings. This speaks for itself as a Hostel innovation!" In September a hostelite noted: "Since the last bulletin, life at Scattergood has been characterized by the following: picking tomatoes (millions of them); packing tomatoes; shipping tomatoes; eating tomatoes...."

Even in the tomato patch, then, the staff and guests of Scattergood Hostel built their community—one long row to hoe at a time.

1.) The role work played in altering refugees' attitudes or abilities to "Americanize" should not be over emphasized—as attested by Ernst van den Haag: "From my own experience, but for all Europeans, [American social] mobility is not necessarily greater, but more accepted [than in Europe]. Nobody [in the U. S.] minds doing any kind of work really, temporarily... The idea of doing manual work [such as a bus boy, dishwasher, vegetable sorter, etc., which Ernst later undertook] was extremely humiliating. It would not have been for a native American; you accept jobs... [For an upper-class person] in Italy, the idea of doing manual work was just inconceivable. But I learned to accept that indirectly—not by lectures or so—at Scattergood because everybody did it, including the staff... I did it when I had to and I stopped feeling humiliated after awhile. Here, too, I think Scattergood helped me come through—but the help was always indirect... Simply the atmosphere...there's some Quaker element in this; the Quakers have a tradition of being accepting and to some extent that helped."

2.) John Kaltenbach also wrote about daily life at Scattergood—characteristically, with spiritual overtones. For excerpts from his report see Appendix V.

3.) Quakers differentiate as little as reasonably possible between the "life of the Spirit" and the affairs of the world. Because of this unprogrammed Friends closely pattern their monthly "meeting for business" after the weekly "meeting for worship": the community gathers at an appointed hour to share a period of silence in which to "center," then the clerk of the meeting ("chair" in other circles) names the issues to be discussed. Often between items Friends observe a few minutes' silence to reflect or refocus. Because Quakers believe "that of god" in everyone must be honored, decisions are made through pure consensus—a process that is slow and can draw out particularly divisive matters for months, maybe years; when the clerk has distilled an acceptable "minute" which captures the "sense of the meeting" (the general consensus), she or he reads it out loud for approval. If an issue finds Friends in sharp disagreement the clerk usually will suggest a period of silent "expectant waiting" in which those present seek clarity and unity. The meeting ends with a few minutes of silence. Business meetings at Scattergood, however, very much reflected the diverse crowd which composed its ranks. As such they were often lively, as attested by the following *Book of Scattergood* entries of summer and fall 1939: "Held a meeting at four P.M. at which everybody said a lot and systems ran from Communist to Facist [sic]. Restricted Democracy adopted." "The meeting broke up because of disharmony of spirit and most of us took a walk." "At 5 o'clock we have meeting in the Meeting-House—with a beautiful sunset, well typifying the genuine temper of our group as we are together on the eve of a new year, ful [sic] of hopes and confidence."

4.).) The following are explanations of unfamiliar terms: "Sta-Wag" was the name given the station wagon in which John Kaltenbach and the first four guests drove to Iowa. Jean Reynolds served as AFSC's Refugee Section officer in charge of selecting "guests" to be sent to Scattergood from the East Coast. Centerdale is a nearby hamlet , at one time said to have been the home of a roadhouse. Duchess was a car and Suzy-One (sometimes spelled "Susie") the 1929 Model A Ford used for driving lessons, damaged in an accident and later replaced by Suzy-Two; "Macky" was a nickname for the Scotty terrier "Mr. MacTavish," whereas Columbus and Milquetoast were beloved Scattergood cats.

An entry on 8 May 1940 in the *Book of Scattergood* describes the allusion to Centerdale: "There were rumors about a night-club at Centerdale and it was necessary to investigate the matter. Mildred [Holmes], Ruth [Carter], Camilla [Hewson], Angela [Schuber], Louis [Croy], [a cat named] Bill, Mac[ky] and Mil-toast arrived marching and singing at the destination, discovering only a very few dark houses and a railroad line. So they decided to march back right away and came home in higly [sic] spirits after having had a very nice walk."

5.) Perhaps Friedrich Pollak should have focused on structural problems in the Main Building which posed a greater threat than becoming fly-breeding grounds. In May 1940 Lynn Zimmerman wrote: "The other day Karl [Liebman] stepped in the wrong spot in the dorm attic and his foot came straight through the plaster and lathes and hung down just outside Martha [Balderston's] door. We all laughed so hard we could hardly extricate him. He didn't think it was especially funny, but you can imagine how his foot, in its not so small working boot, looked waggling through the ceiling."

6.) The men must have attacked the job of dishwashing with more enthusiasm than skill, for in autumn 1939 AFSC Refugee Section staff member Mary Rogers made an appeal for household items for the hostel, noting: "Dish towels, dish rags, scrub rags are greatly needed. With so many men washing dishes and so many heavy dishes to be washed the mortality is high. Really good rags can be used in large quantities. The floors are rather rough and are unpainted which is hard on rags and mops."

7.) At times hostel guests voluntarily undertook projects. According to an Executive Committee report of 29 August 1941, "one of the refugees has built shelves in the library, which make ample space for the books. Another refugee is cataloguing and sorting the books."

8.) The hostel "family" fully enjoyed the greenery the garden and yard yielded. Lynn Zimmerman wrote in May 1940: "Scattergood right now is one of the most beautiful places I've ever seen. The lilacs are out, and the evening air is heavy with their fragrance. The tulips, which Sara Stanley guards with an eagle eye against our picking, are beautiful [and] one big round bed looks exactly like a birthday cake with candles. The bridal wreathe is out now, but the apple blossoms have already done their bit towards beautifying the place, as have the peach and wild crab blooms. Just for fun, Boris [Jaffe] mowed the word Scattergood into the big side lawn, so Helmuth [Ostrowski-Wilk] mowed his entire name behind the Meeting House. Of course, they mowed them right out again the same day, but we all had fun looking at them first."

9.) In late May 1940 Lynn boasted to Mary Rogers: "We all look beautifully tanned and healthy from our work in the sun. So far, John [Kaltenbach] is ahead as far as getting a...tan is concerned, but I'm going out to catch up right now by hoeing. I find that even if the [office] work doesn't get done so early in the morning, I feel much more peaceful and hopeful after I scratch around in the garden an hour or two before I tackle the cash accounts or letters!"

183

To Accelerate Mastery

"In its formal aspects this includes individual and group instruction designed to accelerate mastery of the English language and to present as complete a picture as possible of the varied aspects of the American scene."

~ **George Thorp**

In formulating its daily plans the Scattergood staff vigilantly juggled adequate time for work with ample time for instruction and recreation, as it realized that the reason for the guests' presence did not consist of changing sheets, flipping pancakes, gathering eggs or turning the garden. Writing down new vocabulary, cracking the civics books, mulling over history lectures and opening the door to the driver's seat counted as much as other aspects of life at the hostel. The staff's European charges found themselves in a foreign land with often unfamiliar ways of living and thinking: to make the myriad adaptations necessary to fully functioning in such a culture the refugees *had* to become—in essence—new people, whether or not they wanted to do so. The degree to which they would find satisfying niches in American society would be directly commensurate to the degree to which each was able to release old ways of living which did not fit the modern New World and to tailor their social selves to match a new set of expectations.

What motivations and goals guided the staff in constructing its program of education? What did the teachers as individuals consider important as they tried to instill new ideas or values in the guests? How did the refugees receive efforts to "Americanize" them and what did they think generally of the quality of the instruction offered at the hostel? How effective were efforts to prepare the refugees for post-hostel life?

First, of course, a program had to exist before it could be judged as successful or not. A trained engineer who had taught for 11 years at the Carnegie Institute of Technology in Pittsburgh and at an AFSC program for refugees in Maine before coming to Scattergood, George Thorp became edu-

184

cation director at the hostel in August 1942. In the October-November issue of the *Bulletin* that year he outlined his vision for "The Scattergood Educational Program":

A vital part of Scattergood training is its education program. In its formal aspects this includes individual and group instruction designed to accelerate mastery of the English language and to present as complete a picture as possible of the varied aspects of the American scene. In its less formal approach the program merges largely with the other phases of life at Scattergood. In the process of sharing the work program, the household duties and other essential activities and through daily social intercourse and more pretentious social affairs this side of the program supplements in innumerable ways the more formal part of the educational plan.

Instruction in English is fundamental in importance. Each guest, upon arrival, is assigned to a member of the staff for tuition, in accordance with his [or her] needs. Each person usually receives three hours of individual tutoring a week.

Supplementing this, there are lectures or seminars each week in phonetics and general English, in which principles and practices are discussed with larger groups.

Another side of the formal part of the program consists in the presentation of a variety of facets of the American picture, accomplished through lectures and discussions on every important aspect of American life. The plan in effect is to make a complete round of these subjects once in three or four months, the period usually spent at Scattergood by a guest.

History, from the early settlements to the present, occupies a weekly place in the program and serves as a background against which the other subjects are presented. Those range through such varied fields as labor, government, educational systems, geography, home economics, politics and racial problems.

Speakers or discussion leaders are obtained from various sources. The faculty of the University of Iowa is drawn upon frequently and advantage is taken of the presence of visitors who can make contributions of this sort.

Informally, most important education results come about through daily contacts between Americans and Europeans, guests and staff. Such situations afford continual opportunities for the practice of English and for instruction in American customs and habits. Special festivities such as birthdays, farewells, holidays and sundry celebrations help very greatly toward preparing for life in America.

What did it *mean*—"preparing for life in America?" The following compilation of the "Scattergood Hostel Report of Lectures and Field Trips" for January, February, March and April 1941 provides an idea of what topics in American society and which aspects of its daily life staff thought important to include in the program:

LECTURES ON AMERICAN GOVERNMENT AND PROBLEMS
OF DEMOCRACY
(given twice weekly)

1. *Basic principles of American government.*
2. *Organization and functions of our national government.*
3. *Organization and function of Iowa government.*
4. *County government in action.*
5. *The courts of the State, organization and functions.*
6. *The problem of social welfare in the United States.*
7. *Public health—one aspect of social welfare.*
8. *Health insurance programs in operation to-day.*
9. *What America is doing to improve the public's health.*
10. *The University of Iowa Hospital—a specific example of Iowa's aid to its citizen's health.*
11. *Insuring America against old-age. Problems of aol-age [sic], old-age pensions. (To be continued.)*
12. *Insuring America against old-age. Problems of old-age assistance, etc.*
13. *Government in Business.*
14. *Labor movement in America 1860-1904.*
15. *Labor movement in America 1904 to present. (A.F. of L. and C.I.O.)*
16. *Green and Lewis—two American labor leaders.*
17. *Workers without jobs—unemployment and its problems.*
18. *The problems of conservation in America.*
19. *The problems of conservation in America. (continued)*

Special lectures:
1. *Amana—The first German immigrants to Iowa in search of religious freedom.*
Field trips:
1. *Visit to the University Hospitals.*
2. *Visit to the Amana Colonies.*

ELEMENTARY CLASS IN GOVERNMENT
(given once a week)
1. The many units of American government.
2. The problem of naturalization.
3. The American Constitution and some basic principles of government set forth in it.
4. The Bill of Rights. Can the government do this?
5. Class discussion and questions on the Bill of Rights and things government does.

Objective of the group
1. To learn fundamental concepts of American government historically and pragmatic
2. Improve vocabulary of words and terms relating to government.

Field trips: Two trips to Johnson County Court to see the court in session, empaneling of the jury, trial of the case, etc.

Guest lecturer: Walter Daykin, Professor of Economics American Labor and National Defense.

PUBLIC SPEAKING COURSE (held once a week)
CLASS No. 1 (beginners' class)
The purpose of the class is to give beginners practice in the use of the English language. The mediums used are reading and recitation of poetry, Carl Sandburg's life and poetry, Walt Whitman, newspaper articles, recitation of tongue twisters and short public speeches.

CLASS No. 2 (advanced class)
This is a course in the fundamentals of good public speaking. With the objective in mind to give refugees a chance to think aloud in English. Each member of the class gives a two minute speech on such subjects as: My first impression of Scattergood, An impression of Lincoln, or Why I like to go to Iowa City; a humorous situation.
1. Introductions.
2. Conclusions.
3. Body movements while speaking.

FOODS AND NUTRITION AND HOUSEHOLD ARTS
(are co-ordinated as much as possible with daily meal preparation)
(held twice weekly)
1. General nutrition and health.
2. A study of wheat and cereals.
3. The principles of bread making.

4. *Weights and measures used in American homes.*
5. *Meat and meat cuts.*
6. *Meat and locker plants.*
7. *Meat cookery.*
   private lessons of one hour and a half—three

Lectures:
1. *Home furnishings No. 1—Farm Bureau Lesson.*
2. *Home furnishings No. 2—Farm Bureau Lesson.*
3. *Milk*
4. *Ice Cream*

Field Trips:
1. *Demonstration: How to Make Slip Covers*
2. *Swaners Dairy.*
3. *Piper's Candy Shop.*
4. *Meat Market.*
5. *Locker plant.*
6. *Chick hatchery.*

Laboratory:
1. *Making Ice Cream in the hand freezer and in a mechanical refrigerator*

Household Finance Movies:
1. *Stretching the clothing dollar.*
2. *Meat selection, buying and carving.*
3. *Budget: How to make it work.*

GUEST LECTURES:
1. *Prof. Kurt Lewin. His experiences in adjusting to American life, hoping they might be of help to others.*
2. *Heinrich Bruening—exchancellor*
3. *Professor Creery from the University High School. Secondary education in the United States.*
4. *Miss Goddard American Youth Hostel movies.*

UNIVERSITY SYMPHONY ORCHESTRA AND CHORUS
Easter Concert

At any given time the education and training program's offerings directly reflected the abilities and interests of individual staff members on hand—or, in the case of a dearth of expertise or adequate numbers, members of the University of Iowa faculty were recruited for special guest appearances. A report in the 17 November 1941 issue of the *Bulletin* provided an idea of how particular persons were integrated into specific niches of the teaching roster:

> *The Education Committee has completed plans for its winter program. In spite of the loss of three staff members we are planning to continue the individual lessons which have seemed quite successful. We are doing this with the help of Jean Simpson and David Mitchell of Iowa City, and the individual lessons are supplemented by a very popular class in phonetics offered by Jean Dewey, also of Iowa City. These lessons take place in the afternoons and consist of whatever the pupil needs most. Sometimes it is conversation which proves not only helpful but interesting to both pupil and tutor. Sometimes it is grammar or an emphasis on reading and writing English. A special class in conversation is offered once a week by Mrs. Chester Clark of Iowa City.*
>
> *Besides these lessons Bob Cory has organized a class in American History, meeting three times a week. This must be interesting as the students never find excuses for missing it. The evening program is not completed yet, but on Tuesday evenings Bob Cory lectures on American History; the present series has been about the presidents of the United States. George Willoughby comes on Thursday evenings to continue his lectures on political science, and these lectures are proving to be as popular as ever. On Wednesday evenings we have lectures given by some of the professors from the University. The person who instituted the public speaking class last winter started something which shows every indication of becoming a permanent fixture. John Copithorne has taken over this group, and on Friday evenings we take our turn in speaking on the assigned topic.*

According to the lingually talented Walter Shostal, "language training was the center of the Hostel curriculum. It was a rule of the place that no speech but English was to be used at all times—a rule not strictly enforced, but gently encouraged.[1] At mealtimes we had our assigned places, but the staff rotated their attendance so that there was usually one of them presiding—so to speak—at each table. Therefore, mealtime conversation tended to be in English and kind of sparse. Each staffer also was assigned one or more guests who were his or her special responsibility for language instruction. They met every day for an hour or longer for individual tutoring. Magda and I both had the good fortune to be assigned to John Copithorne. Or should I say, to be adopted by him? I don't know what the procedure was."[2]

Indeed, professional instruction in phonetics proved of great importance at the hostel, given that many guests arrived not speaking English and those who did usually had been weaned on King's Standard; both groups had to learn to navigate through the at-times-unclear pronunciation of their American hosts. On top of that both the British and North American varieties of English included rules and customs which baffled even the cleverest Continentals: "To a German, in whose language vowels have a relatively constant value, the fact that an English 'a' may have six, and an 'o' eight different sounds is very perplexing. Add to this the difficulty of new consonant sounds such as 'w' and 'th,' which do not exist in German at all, and the further difficulty of the English 'r'. Is it any wonder that pronunciation should be one of Scattergood's greatest problems?" The anonymous author of this article on "Phonetic Lessons at Scattergood" which appeared in the 15 March 1942 *Bulletin* went on to say:

> On Tuesday and Thursday, you will find almost every Scattergoodian in the Library studying phonetics under the guidance of Jean Dewey. The first thing to master is distinguishing with the ear and forming with the tongue the 29 vowel sounds. Then come the consonants. Each pupil must know how to find the correct pronunciation of these in the phonetic key in the dictionary. If a visitor should invade the privacy of individual rooms after the class is over, he [or she] would be amused to find Scattergoodians making strange grimaces in front of mirrors in an effort to control stubborn tongues.
>
> Every member of the class has a notebook in which to keep lists of words to illustrate the vowels and consonants, and the advanced class spends most of its time reading aloud articles, stories and poems. Thus phonetics enlarges the vocabulary.
>
> An atmosphere of friendly rivalry is encouraged, for no matter how many times a sound is repeated in class drills, students are bound to make a few mistakes and other pupils are always to make correction. The enthusiasm for this work is so great that unofficial classes are often formed in leisure hours to continue the practice. Everyone feels that progress is being made in adjustment to American life. No wonder that Jean's classes are popular.

The frequent visits and input of phonetics teacher Jean Dewey weren't the only well-received contributions to hostel life by "visitors." Some among the hundreds of people who visited Scattergood during its four years of life even rated as celebrities.[5] Iowa's native-son Grant Wood—then riding a wave of lasting fame for his "American Gothic" and his popularization of everyday images at a time when politicized realism heavily influenced international art trends—dropped in on 9 November 1939 to see what all the excitement at West Branch was about. Also unexpected guests, the Trapp Family Singers made an impromptu appearance at Scattergood on 21 March 1942; some of the hostel family had seen the ten-member ensemble the previous evening at a concert at Iowa's Cornell College in Mount Vernon and invited the exiled Austrians to visit the refugees at Scattergood. An excited Louis Hacke later reported that on that day "lunch was forgotten, the coffee was getting cold, and the whole family gathered in the living-room and the rule to speak only English was out of order during the next two hours. There was a long and hearty conversation between the Scattergoodians and the Trapp Singers in the home language. And then [they] gave a concert especially for us...in their colourful Tyrolean costumes [and] sang English songs, Tyrolean songs and old German songs. They encouraged the Scattergoodians to join their voices with [theirs] and finally everyone was filled with the joy of song. Then the mother of the Family, Baroness von Trapp, gave a speech about the experiences of her family in America. To begin to have confidence she said, is the most important thing to be successful in the new life in America. Beginning may be hard but perseverance will bring success. Finally, having given a last song, the Trapps had to leave us. There was hearty handshaking and with the sound of the Scattergood bell, the two cars of the Trapps went away."

Scattergood Hostel made good use of its continuous flow of visitors—famous or not. An excerpted outline of only one month's fare of roving thespians, guest speakers, sojourning students and similar visitors suggests how the presence of every sort of caller could be of use:

After a big tea party with Mrs Clark, Biff and Jean Dewey, George and Lillian Willoughby, Dave Mitchell, Verlin and Sara Pemberton as our guests on Sunday February the 1st [1942], Eddie Bowman, a neighbor and a student at the State University gave us a dramatic sketch, "Red Riding Hood of the Machine Age," which we and especially our children enjoyed very much.

On Tuesday, February 3rd, Professor Alden McGrew, Chief of the Art Dept. at the University spoke to us on "Modern Art." He demonstrated to us in a fascinating way the evolution of Architecture, Sculpture, Graphic Art and Painting by means of well selected slides. John [and] Josephine [Copithorne], Par [Danforth] and Marianne [Welter] came back after a four day trip to Sheldon and Rowan. Marianne gave two addresses, one at Sheldon and the other one at Paullina. In addition to this they had three blow-outs and two bouts of car trouble.

On Wednesday evening Bob [Cory] and John discussed Social Se-

curity and Insurance before an interested group. They warned us to beware of the "High-pressure" Insurance Salesman.

The following Saturday afternoon the Art Gallery in Iowa City was honored and amused by a visit from our group. In the evening Bob Berquist, who had arrived earlier in the day much to our surprise and delight, told us about life at Camp Merom. The evening closed with a Valentine Party which was thoroughly enjoyed by everyone.

Tuesday evening, John showed moving pictures of the United States and the Rocky Mountains which he had obtained from the State University.

On the occasion of the World's Day of Prayer, Friday, February the 20th, John was one of the speakers at the Community meeting in the Friends Church in West Branch. In the evening Alfred and Martha Adler returned from a week's visit to Rowan, Iowa; they were brought back by two nice, young school teachers from Rowan, Misses Mary Ellen Shanefield and Thelma Whitford, who stayed with us until Saturday afternoon.

Monday, February 23rd, after a short business meeting, we listened to the President's Fireside chat, and followed his explanation on several maps.

On Wednesday the women of Scattergood were the guests of the Alliance of the Unitarian Church in Iowa City. After a splendid luncheon they listened to a lecture about Clara Schumann, the wife of the famous composer.

Professor Hoeltje gave us a very interesting lecture on Thursday, on the beginnings of American Literature. We hope to hear him again in the near future.

At the Public Speaking Class on Friday, Maria Altman gave her maiden speech and spoke about her first job in America.

To round out the month, and to help us to recover from the many activities we had engaged in, we celebrated Lisl Harvey's [seventh] birthday on Saturday February 28th with a grand party.

Maria Altman was only one of dozens of Scattergood Hostel guests who gave speeches about contemporary conditions in war-torn Europe, their escape from the Nazis, life with the Quakers or any number of other topics to church or synagogue congregations, fraternal organizations and women's clubs, youth groups or other interested parties. Sabine Hirsch—a middle-aged chemist from Vienna who came to America as one of the leaders of a children's transport and later became a professor of physics and German at Quaker-founded William Penn College in Oskaloosa, Iowa—found herself, for example, invited to tell her story once she arrived on the prairies in early

1941. Four and a half months into her stay at Scattergood she described how it felt to be in such a position:

During the winter and especially since the weather has taken a turn for the better, numerous requests have come to the Hostel for speakers to appear before various church groups and clubs to tell something about the work at Scattergood and about the European background of our people. When I was asked to write something about my impressions on the various occasions on which I have given speeches, a question came to my mind which many years ago a professor asked me in my teacher's examination: "What can the teacher learn from the behavior of his [or her] pupils during a lecture and from the questions asked afterward?" I have learned a great deal from my pupils, and I am sincere enough to confess that I owe thanks to all the audiences here in Iowa to whom I have spoken. I have never been a public speaker even in my mother language, so imagine my excitement before my first speech in English! But the cheerfulness and the kind interest of the listeners helped me and very soon the ice was broken.

I have the impression that most of the people here in the Middlewest are not acquainted at all with the real circumstances in Europe and therefore they do not know the reason why we refugees have been forced to leave our country. Sometimes, also, I could not rid myself of the feeling that people are suspicious of the aliens, seeing in each of us a spy, and that they are frightened, too, that the refugees might get jobs which could better be given to Americans. Therefore, it is a good idea when those who are better informed about the situation and those who know what really happened ask the Scattergood Hostel to send somebody to give a speech in behalf of this so-important matter.

I am very glad to say that the results of those speeches are quite sufficient. Many of the listeners are now friends of Scattergood. They come to see the Hostel and its residents and often give help to the Quakers in their noble work. Sometimes hospitality is offered to a refugee or a refugee family until they can find a job. The interest in Scattergood and its goal and spirit is growing daily. We hope we have done our best to convince the Americans that we are no danger for this country and that we are happy to be here after all the dark days we have gone through. We do not understand all the arguments against us in this, our adopted land, which has always been a refuge for those who preferred to be homeless than to live in a homeland without regard for justice and human dignity.

The hostel staff's motivation to send its guests on speaking engagements across Iowa included improving their charges' English as well as improving public relations. As a corollary benefit, in the process of traveling to and from the various communities where the refugees spoke, the exiled Europeans learned about aspects of American life and culture which could not be as meaningfully conveyed in the classroom by even the most artful of presenters. On her way to one talk, for instance, Grete Rosenzweig glimpsed a bit of Middle American hospitality. As she later explained:

> The people [who were guests at Scattergood Hostel] who knew some English were sent out to make speeches to different groups in order to interest them in the refugee problem and to stimulate them to offer jobs. These speeches and the trips connected with them will remain unforgettable to me. One winter night a young Quaker drove [husband] Louis and me to a quite distant church somewhere out in the country. Shortly after we changed from the highway to a black top road he said: "This sounds strange!" and before we knew it the car slipped from the ice-covered road into the ditch. Fortunately nobody got hurt, we climbed out of the car and up to the road, but it was impossible to even stand on the ice. Soon after a car happened to come along, and the Quaker stopped it and asked the people if they could take two riders, but there was only room for one more person, so they took me in. In the dark I did not know with whom I was riding and where I was going, but when they heard that I was supposed to be the speaker at the church, they told me that they would let me out at the right place. The car stopped, one man was standing under a tree—no light. Where was I? The man introduced himself as the minister of the church where we were going to meet, but he took me to his landlord's house first and went with the wrecker to get Louis and our driver with the car. After their arrival we had a delicious dinner, but we were so late that the people were all assembled in the church before we were through eating. The minister had someone give his orders over the phone: "Just let them sing a few hymns." Finally we reached the church, my speech about Scattergood and the refugees went over smoothly. Then came the very animated question and answer period. Afterwards Louis asked me if I knew what I did? The question had come up about Apfelstrudel, an Austrian pastry. Since we had Austrians in the group at Scattergood I was able to give a description as I had seen it made, but I did not realize in my excitement that I rolled the altar cloth into Apfelstrudel!

Grete could laugh at herself, but guests had no monopoly on humor. Despite being mostly Quakers (known for stubborn sobriety), the staff more than once proved to have a sense of humor. Former education director Ruth Carter,[4] for one, left Scattergood in June 1940 to take a job at AFSC's headquarters until her planned marriage to Student Peace Service-volunteer and fellow-New Englander Bob Burgess the following September. Perhaps to offer the hostel guests a light-hearted example of how *not* to speak (*vis- a-vis* with many of the mistaken words, verb forms and constructions which the German speakers often used at Scattergood) or maybe just for fun, apparently her fiancé Bob wrote the following, pre-dated letter to the hostel family at West Branch and read it at the bon-voyage party held just before Ruth's departure for the East Coast.

City of Scattergood Love
June 20th 1940

Dear Scattergooooooooodians:

I am sooooooooo sorry! I had the intention to have you told all about Philadelphia much sooner but had not the time.

It was a beauuuuutiful trip. On the way I tried to make any placement work for those left at Scattergood. When I have seen the bus driver I was remembered of the Susie drivers who have now their licenses and no jobs. At the Cleveland rest stop I was sitting on the table by the driver and made him the suggestion that his company make a proposition with Scattergood. He said he would see if he would have time when we will arrive in P-Delphia.

Well, this city is warm—more warm as Iowa. In the first hours I made a walk around the city and found it the same as before. I miss the little porks and of course Mac [the dog] and the kittens, but also all my dear Scattergoodians, so it is not pleasant to make walks here as to Centerdale.

Huh-huh, well, Monday last I have gone to the office. They said me Mary Rogers would be on the tenth floor. I went to her and said her, "Hi-butch" because at Scattergood nobody ever answers if he [or she] gets not that certain greeting. "How do you call me?" she asked, and I remarked that she had seemed puzzling. At that time Clarence Pickett the door opened. "Hi-butch," again I said. "Hi-butch," said Clarence because he at Scattergood was come in past weeks and knows the greeting.

"What's to do," I asked,—but it was soon a useless question. They said, "Give your hat on the table and start immediately." Since that hour work has been overtaking me. And besides the office tasks is the question of their English. I keep calling them, Dumkopf [sic], since

they determine to say after the verb the object with nothing in be-
tween. We have made like Scattergood therefore. And each morning
all say, before 9, the fat, black cat exercises. They seem it to enjoy.

No place is so nice like Scattergood was. But we all must leave
sometimes, no? And anyhow, Scattergood won't be the same without
Mildred [Homes] and Claire [Hohenadl-Patek] and later John
[Kaltenbach] and Lillian [Pemberton].

It was my meaning that I would not work so hard here in the office.
But we are busy all the day and we will have no vacation, I think so. I
keep asking myself, "What is with this place?" And I can only say that
we need more of Iowa's open spaces.

You cannot come to see me, I guess so. But please write often.
With sincerest regards to you all, I remain,

Your most loving,

Ruth

A language reflects the people who use it and as such can be cleverly used to poke fun at the cultural idiosyncrasies and common character quirks to be found in any society. While English could be the source of good-natured bantering at Scattergood Hostel, the subject of history remained another matter. Often a serious lot, the history-minded staff who landed at the hostel soon set about the pressing business of enlightening the masses through the dissemination and interpretation of their favorite stories. Often, they found a receptive audience.

Sixty-three-year-old Hedwig "Omi" Hackel had seen a bit of history herself. A native of the German Baltic port of Königsberg, she had married a Russian and moved to Saint Petersburg, but fled that ill-fated city when the Bolsheviks seized power. She moved to Berlin, where her sister reportedly worked as the first female medical doctor in the Prussian capital. When radicals of another extreme legally won control of Germany, as a non-practicing Jew Hedwig had reason to leave the country. In 1938, then, she accompanied her Russian-born daughter Nora and family friend Marianna Welter to Paris, where she proceeded to break her leg, then contract both malaria and cholera. Thrown onto the open road by the German invasion of France in spring 1940, the little troop landed in Gurs concentration camp before finally making its way to New York in August 1941. In January 1942 they arrived at Scattergood, where Hedwig became an avid fan of the hostel's multi-faceted history program. It so impressed her that she lauded it on the front page of the community's monthly *Bulletin*:

*One of the most important classes in our education program is the his-
tory class under the guidance of Bob Cory.[5] It is held thrice a week, in
summer outside in the garden.*

*We came to Scattergood for studying English language and for liv-
ing the American way. For this reason we want to become acquainted
with the historical development of the United States, beginning with the
discovery of America in the fifteenth century, and the days of the early
explorers. We heard about the Indians, the first inhabitants of the country, the settlements of English, Dutch, French and Spanish peoples
coming over from Europe for reason of religious or political persecution or for making a better living in the new world. Furthermore our
teacher told us about the foundation of the thirteen States, the Revolu-
tionary War, followed by the Declaration of Independence, the Constitution with its amendments, the expansion to the West, and the Civil
War between the North and the South. We had a review of the Reconstruction Period, the Age of Big Business, the Spanish American War,
the foreign influence in politics, leading to the first World War. Having
studied the problems of American democracy, the institutions of local
and federal governments, the Presidents, we finished our class with the
Social Reform Program.*

*To extend our knowledge of American history, we sometimes have
interesting lectures given by professors of the University of Iowa, or
other educational institutions. A few weeks ago the negro problem was
explained to us, and the lecturer found a most attentive audience.*

*It seems to me that all we learned in our history class will be the
best base for our becoming American citizens.*

Hedwig mentioned visiting professors, yet Scattergood didn't have to
look as far as Iowa City's ivory towers for knowledgeable persons willing to
share their skills with the guests, for sometimes individuals living as close as
the nearest village provided an evening's worth of edifying information.[6]
One such presentation consisted of that given by Doctor Mosher, the hostel's
family practitioner. The French-born physician Alfred Adler later described
the first-aid classes at the hostel:

*Scattergood is up-to-date. We do not want to remain behind the
others. Some weeks ago we began a course in First Aid. Dr. Mosher of
West Branch assumed the task of introducing us to the principles of
First Aid. We are learning how to give an immediate temporary treatment in case of accident or sudden illness, before the services of a
physician can be secured.*

Dr. Mosher gave us first a concise outline of the anatomy and phys-

197

*iology of the human body, and then we started training ourselves in
the skill of dressing wounds and applying bandages. We practiced and
proved our deep knowledge in this art in a bandaging race. Then we
learned how to stop bleeding. We took to heart the exhortation that it
is much better to have a live patient with a dirty wound than a dead
patient with a clean wound. When we practiced stopping bleeding, it
happened that a more over-zealous than charitable samaritan failed
to break the patient's neck in trying to compress his carotid. We are
glad to state that both patient and first aider recovered immediately
their health.* Vestigis terrent!*

*I hope that no one of us has to use at Scattergood the matter we
learned in our First Aid course.*

Besides learning how to stop bleeding, the folks at Scattergood Hostel
also learned how to start a letter on its way, as on another evening West
Branch's postmaster Dick Kinsey led staff and guest alike through "the maze
of postal rules and regulations." The well-liked civil servant returned to Scattergood at a later date—but under Federal orders to collect the refugees' radios and cameras once Japan bombed Pearl Harbor and the United States
entered the war in Europe and Asia. Perhaps the affable postmaster lost a bit
of his popularity upon that visit.

Nifty mechanical devices weren't the only things the refugees lost when
America joined in the fighting; they also lost their right of free movement
The regional attorney of the Department of Justice, Tobias Diamond, reminded the Europeans living at the hostel that they were barred from traveling to certain areas and that they must secure permission for long-distance
trips[7]—which was often denied—even in the case, for example, of job interviews for Klaus Asher in Denver and for Ernst Turk in Chicago. This ban on
unmonitored movement had such a disastrous effect on the morale of the
refugees—not to mention their employment prospects—that the hostel staff
invited the U.S. attorney and his wife for dinner in the hope of convincing
this official that the United States had nothing to fear from these would-be
new citizens.[8]

Still, the hobbled movement of the guests greatly compromised what had
been a diverse, much-enjoyed mobile component of the hostel's education
program which had tapped sources near and far. The annual Grinnell Institute of International Relations,[9] for example, was rendered (literally by the
stroke of a pen) out-of-reach for the refugees, who in years past had greatly
enjoyed and contributed to the gathering's geopolitical fare. This state of affairs seemed depressing—until some clever soul had the idea of bringing the
mountain to Mohammed. The former editor of the *Volkszeitung fuer das
Vogtland* in Plauen, Germany, who came to America via France in

September 1941, Ludwig Hacke—later "Louis"—explained:

Since we, the Europeans, were unable to go to Grinnell, we tried to bring the Grinnell Institute of International Relations to Scattergood. It was possible to discuss only some of the problems which were discussed there, and naturally it was the European problems which interested us most. First, on Friday June the 19th [1942], we had a lecture by Bertram Pickard, an English Quaker, who was the director of the Friends Center in Geneva for seventeen years, and who was one of the Grinnell staff. He touched on some of the European problems, which aroused a lively discussion in the audience. Above all, questions were asked about post-war problems and the social situation in England.

Following their return from Grinnell, on Friday June the 26th, the Americans of the Scattergood family presented a panel of the main points of the Institute program. Martha Balderston introduced the discussion, giving us an impression of the atmosphere of the conference; Bob Cory analyzed the differences of opinion in the conference in regard to the role of Russia in the post-war world. The essentials of a democratic way of life and the problems of democratic education in the post-war world were brought back to us by Josephine Copithorne, and the problems of Fascism and the particular problem of India were discussed by John Copithorne. A question period afterwards enabled the audience to inquire more directly about the points in which they were most interested.

A week later, stimulated by the reports of the Grinnell Conference, we had a panel in which only Europeans participated on the topic: "If the United Nations win the war, how shall we bring Germany back into the society of nations?" Marie Juchacz, in her discussion of re-education for democracy, hoped that there would be a long period of time between the armistice and the treaty of peace to build up a new democracy in Germany. [Former judge and a political figure in the city of Limburg who had spent time in two concentration camps,] Julius Lichtenstein pointed out that there would not be a need of removing all laws in Germany, but the democratic control of judges would bring about a sounder justice. Louis Hacke emphasized that the problems of employment and social security can only be solved in the framework of a new social and political order in the world.

The discussion was continued on Saturday, July the 11th, by the same speakers, and in addition by Robert Keller who [as a political dissident had fled Germany in 1933 and came to the U.S. via Czechoslovakia and France, and] mainly analyzed the political problems of peace making, with particular reference to the problems of na-

tional minorities. In the discussion with [sic] followed, some questions
were asked about the influence which the National-Socialistic ideology
had has [sic] on the spirit of the German people, and what its effect
will be in the post-war world.

The Scattergood Institute of International Relations proved so in-
teresting that the problems touched upon in the panels have continued
to be a topic of conversation, and we are expecting to have other dis-
cussions in the near future about other world problems

Interestingly, as early as July 1942—before the Russians turned back the German forces at Stalingrad—some of the guests at Scattergood Hostel were assuming that the Allied forces would win the war and already were spending much emotional energy on scenarios for rehabilitating their abandoned native homelands. Certainly the ties which bound them to the lands of their births ran deep and remained strong, despite the madness which had erupted there and the personal pain they had experienced as rejected former citizens.

No matter that the passionately political former Reichstag member Paul Frölich had left the hostel almost a year earlier: not long after the report on the "Scattergood Institute" appeared he penned an article in response for the *Bulletin*. He titled his essay "Education for Democracy" and wrote:

As everybody I am deeply interested in these burning questions and
perhaps am I allowed to contribute some ideas or the other to the prob-
lems. I know by experience that there are things in which even well-
meaning people are likely to be misled. There is the question of re-
education for democracy. That seems to be a very human measure in
the interest of the German people as well as in the interest of world
peace. But I am convinced that it is a very dangerous one. Has there
ever been a people which had been educated for democracy? I know no
one. Most of the peoples lived in a democratic commonwealth when
there was no education at all, and the Swiss people saved their democ-
racy from those remote times till to-day. It is not true to say that the
Germans were not fit for democracy because of the Prussian spirit. The
Austrians and the Poles lost their democracy, too, and they were not
infected with this spirit. And what about the spirit of the Italians? It
wouldn't be right to say that the Germans, the Austrians, the Poles and
other peoples had not time enough to experience democracy, and it
would be necessary to compensate the lack of experience by education.
Old democratic peoples like the French lost their democracy, and he
[or she] who would think that the only cause of this loss was the inva-
sion would be thoroughly deceived. Besides it should now be generally
accepted that the word[s]: "This cannot happen with us" is disproved

by cruel experiences. Not unfitness for and lack of experience with democracy led the German people to totalitarianism but a complexity of horrible economic and social circumstances, (by the by, the Treaty of Versailles was by no means the most important of these causes!).

The vocation of an educator is a very honorable one. But so much I heard of education for democracy I never heard anything of the pedagogic principles and methods of this education. I have the impression that the champions of the idea have been prevented by their own enthusiasm to meditate on the question. Perhaps it may be easier than I guess to build up a nice and decent educational system for this purpose with the best universities and teachers and books and what else. But in every case, behind this system will stand the political tutelage, and which people will tolerate to be treated as immature? The result of such education will be a coward, treacherous, hateful, revengeful people, anew the victim of the worst nationalism. Certainly, it is an axiom that a people can be educated only by self-government under its own strong responsibility.

The very existence of Paul Frölich's letter constitutes proof that Scattergood's educational efforts were working, for this "outsider" dared to do in America what had been unthinkable already for more than nine and a half years in Nazi Germany: he published an open letter of critical opinion. The fact that he felt secure enough—even as a non-native—to do so showed that at least this refugee was well along on the road to being integrated into American society: he was exercising a fundamental right in a democratic system—the right to one's own opinion, the right to disagree.[10]

Similarly, as seen in the initiative of other Scattergood guests to organize a public forum, the refugees at the hostel were learning—in addition to how to conjugate irregular verbs, judge cuts of beef, wrap a wound or send a telegram—how to act as self-directed, autonomous individuals. No longer under the thumb of a totalitarian state, the refugees were reclaiming control over their own lives. At Scattergood, then, they weren't only discovering new ideas, customs and ways of living, but rediscovering what it meant to have choices and to be able to exercise them freely.

1.) To encourage at-times-resistant refugees to use a new tongue, the hostel staff coined the oft-repeated slogan "Speak English and be proud of it!" Not all guests, however, took to English eagerly. Edith Lichtenstein Morgan later remembered: "My parents didn't resist learning English—although my dad said when he had had to learn English in school, the way they taught it in school was 'If it looks ugly and it sounds ugly, it's probably English'. It's not a musical or beautiful language; neither is German. When you listen to French and you listen to Spanish and so on, [English] has a lot of unpleasant noises in it. But, that didn't keep them from learning it or understanding British literature, Shakespeare and so on. We learned over there [in Germany] the best of what there was in English literature: that didn't mean you couldn't hate the English, 'cuz we did."
2.) John Copithorne—who before coming to Scattergood at the age of 32 with his wife had been director of AFSC's

201

program at Sky Island, New York, and secretary of the Toronto branch of the League of Nations Society—clearly impressed Walter, who said: "As I saw it, he was by far the most influential figure. He was about my age and Canadian by birth, but with an Irish background [and having attended a Quaker boarding school in Ireland as a boy] which he liked to stress at times. So, he preferred to be called 'Shaun', the Irish variant of his name. Possibly in accordance with this heritage, he had a taste for something stronger than the milk provided by our neighbors' holstein cows—hence Sarah's [sic] soft-spoken remarks [for upon discovering an empty whisky bottle, she would sadly shake her head and say gently 'Thee drinketh too much, John, dear']. To me John would complain of the problems he had of disposing of such empty bottles. In those pre-conservation days—when even the word 'environment' had not yet entered the English language—there was no collection of bottles or paper, so he could not drop such bottles into the garbage; the collector might notice and the standing of Scattergood in an empty Quaker community be severely tarnished. He had to take them along on occasional trips to more distant and less straight-laced places.

"John was a dynamic person with a wide-open mind, whose interests often went in the same direction as mine. He also was a tinkerer and fascinated by gadgets, which I was not— therefore, a reason for me to admire him. He had hooked up his alarm clock to his coffee maker so he could have a cup the moment he got out of bed. It was more reason for wonderment when he put a speaker high up in a tree and connected it with the record player in the living room and he made it so we could listen outdoors to a Beethoven symphony and announce the program in a professional-sounding way. John did many very different things with apparent ease. To me Scattergood would not have been the same interesting and positive place without him."

3.) Then again some didn't—yet still found a receptive audience at the hostel. One such visitor consisted of "Lucy Burtt, an English Friend, who has been teaching for several years at Yen Ching University at Peiping, China, stopped at Scattergood on her way back to China after a year's leave, most of which had been spent in England. Her great enthusiasm for her work and her faith in people were an inspiration to all of us. Our pictures of the new China became more vivid and much more real after this visit."

4.) Ruth Carter Burgess is another former staff member about whom information with which to compile a fuller biography didn't surface. As of a research trip to America in autumn 1994 she was still alive, but disabled by Alzheimers (as also was true of Mildred Holmes Hale); Ruth's husband Bob chose not to cooperate with this project. Camilla Hewson Flintermann, though, fondly remembered Ruth as "my beloved roommate [who was] in her 30s, had been a teacher...a wise, funny lady much loved by guests and staff. I think it was she who taught us a crazy parody of 'Othello' she learned at Westtown School, which we acted, with appropriate lyrics to the tune of various well-known songs. It was utter nonsense, but a huge success. She was a great English tutor, and we missed her when she left."

5.) Born in Englewood, New Jersey and graduated in history from Harvard and Yale Universities, Bob Cory taught for four years at the Fountain Valley School for boys in Colorado Springs and at AFSC's Sky Island program before coming to Scattergood, where he was regarded as the hostel's "history professor, English teacher, poet, lecturer, fire chief, trouble department and athletic leader." Bob later founded William Penn House in Washington, D.C.

6.) In-house presentations also occurred outside of the normal hours of instruction and blurred the lines between "education" and "freetime." A middle-aged journalist who died soon after marrying a fellow-guest—Hungarian-born Else Kepes—and moving to New York, the Hamburg native Paul Singer reported: "Twice each week all through the winter and spring we have enjoyed a course of lectures... [The presenter's] vivid and interesting way of speaking and teaching induces all the residents of Scattergood to attend these lectures where they have the opportunity of learning much more about these important phases of American life.

"A very good training in speaking this country's language is given in the Friday public speaking class. The topics of these evenings are varied. Sometimes we hear about adventures, travels and voyages. Sometimes we hear about strange personal experiences in Scattergood or elsewhere. Often the room rings with laughter at the humorous experiences we have shared. Not seldom we have in this way a very interesting and exciting performance. Another agreeable form of learning, really more like playing than studying, is in the so-called 'singing classes' on Sunday evenings. Our long-suffering conductor is Bob Berquist, who will attempt any song that is requested, not only well-known American songs, but even old folk songs from Germany, Austria, or anything else that happens to be in the book. To appreciate what these evenings mean to us, you should attend some of our useful as well as gay meetings in the living room at Scattergood."

7.) Diamond's letter in June 1942 was presumptuous and not particularly friendly, as excerpts show. He said, for example, that "the applications [from Louis Hacke, Marie Juchacz, Robert and Anne-Marie Keller, and Julius Lichtenstein to attend the Grinnell Institute of International Relations]...are hereby denied on the grounds that the matter of attending such institute is not of such importance, either to the applicants or to the welfare of the community, as to burden the Federal Bureau of Investigation with investigations and reports at a time when the said Bureau is overburdened with investigations of reports of National importance in our present emergency. Moreover, the applications for permits to travel, on the part of aliens of enemy nationality, have risen to such numbers that it has become necessary for this office to impress upon such applicants the necessity of reducing their applications to cases of necessity, such as for the purpose of obtaining positions and the earning of a livelihood. We do not believe that it was intended that aliens of enemy nationality should burden both the Federal Bureau of Investigation and the United States Attorney with passing upon applications for travel when nothing but pleasure on the part of the

202

applicant is involved.... These applications are denied, not because of any personal whim of my own, but for the best interests of the country in general in the present emergency."

8.) To the staff's relief, after dinner Diamond fell into congenial conversation in the living room of the Main Building while Martha Balderston his wife took a tour around the place. When the two women returned to the living room Diamond said to his wife "so you've been seeing the place—I've been getting the *spirit* of it and that's more important to me."

9.) That annual conference on global issues had been conceived in the Pembertons' living room in the 1930s and was nurtured to maturity by AFSC.

10.) Although obviously interested in the American political scene, Paul Frölich did not remain in the United States: he returned to Germany in 1950 and died there in spring 1953.

AN ESPECIALLY ELABORATE CELEBRATION

"An especially elaborate celebration marked the double birthdays of year-old Krystyne Salman and our staff member, Bob Berquist."
~ **Anonymous**

At Scattergood, shades of "work," of "education" and of "freetime" could not be so clearly differentiated, as they continually and so easily blended one into the other. Corn shucking and pea shelling, for example, constituted pure "work"—no? If so, then why do the pictures of those sessions show beaming, smiling faces? Surely that wasn't only a photographer's successful posing stunt. And the "educational" excursions to Amana: if they were *only* instructional why did the folks who participated in them have so much fun? Take Michael Deutsch's cowboy dress-up or Doris Arntal and Bertl Weiler's game of "Playing Indian: that had nothing to do with the children's "Americanization," right? Forget it!

The fabric of daily life at the hostel very much consisted of a seamless garment of rehabilitation and integration woven on one and the same warp; distinctions between the various spheres seem arbitrary and subjective, for, as with any globe, such hemispheres were only diverse sides of a whole. One thing for sure, though: the freetime activities which were planned or arose organically between scheduled shifts of work and classroom training provided a context for the refugees not only to rebuild their lives, but to reorient them according to the differing magnetic lines of a new society.

"Cultural excursions" from Scattergood Hostel provided important links between the lives the Europeans had led in the Old World and the ones they were yet to graft onto in the New. As "the Singers"—Paul and his bride "Elsie" née Kepes—wrote in February 1942 in an article for the *Bulletin*:

> *Scattergood is like an island, but not an isolated island, for it is connected with the wide world. The residents have opportunity enough of*

learning the American way of living and working, not only at home, but also outside. The State University of Iowa especially renders us the best occasion for delving into the sources of the American culture.

Just recently we had the chance of seeing some striking examples of the modern development in spreading news over the land, with the most rapidity conceivable. Our first visit...led us to the building of the [Iowa City] newspaper, Press Citizen. This publishing house was erected four years ago, and is the most modern building in the city. A very charming young lady explained to us the complicated mechanisms and work procedures of a modern newspaper. She led us from the high reception lobby through the editorial rooms into a small room, where three automatically working receivers revealed to us the latest news from all the world. We were astonished to find in the next room a whole battery of linotypes. We saw the "permanent waves" of white paper running through the giant rotary printing machine. The afternoon paper, with all its thrilling headlines, had been finished just now.

[At a later date] our good mentor, Bob Cory, led us to another source of the American culture, the radio station W.S.U.I. of Iowa City. When we entered the building, we had the feeling of coming into an old castle, built up of cinder concrete. But this castle was equipped with the most modern machinery. We heard whispering sounds behind closed doors. Beyond large glass panes, we saw a strange pantomime, the silent acting of boys and girls with bewitching gestures. We attended the birth of "The Bad Boy," the real performance of which play we heard later on at Scattergood. In and out of the doors ran many eager students [sic] helpers of the staff. Out of the cells emerged the sounds of dramatic scenes, of serious lectures, as well as music. All these sounds are filtered through intricate control engines, managed by skilled tone-mixers. That was like a television. This combination of a newspaper, a theatre, and a university of the air sends by the invisible wings of the ether news and knowledge. We found a typical cooperation between newspaper and radio, by help of the School of Journalism of the University. The most remarkable of the programs are the daily "Musical Chats," and the interpretations of classical music by Professor Clapp, the head of the Department of Music and the Conductor of the Symphony Orchestra, whose concerts we have often enjoyed at the beautiful Union Hall.

The third cultural expedition...to the new Cornell [College] Theatre at Mount Vernon enabled us to enjoy an interesting performance of "Taming of the Shrew," by well-trained theatre students. We saw the version of Shakespeare's comedy abridged by Garrick, who made of it a funny farce. Therefore we could laugh enough about the somersaults *and jests of clownish servants, but, besides these parterre acrobatics of flexible louts, we had the pleasure of admiring the very graceful concerted acting of the extremely gifted couple [who played Catherine the Shrew and her cunning tamer]. So, in summary, the play, adorned by old English folk tunes, became a thrill for us.*

In contrast to the ultra-modern facilities of Iowa City's newspaper and university radio station, the Amana colonies—which lie some 30 kilometers to the northwest—seemed ancient. Settled in the 1850s by a German-speaking religious sect called the Community of True Inspiration, the group first lived in Upstate New York, but felt unwelcome and transplanted their commune to a 18,000-acre spread on the frontier. By the time of the Great Depression, economic and internal social pressures had forced the folks at Amana to privatize their collective way of life and form a multi-faceted, stock-offering corporation. The spiritual component of the primitive-Christian faith the Amanites practiced remained alive, yet became separate from the worldly administration of the community's daily life: before the "Great Change" the two had been indivisible.

With the excuse of observing George Washington's birthday, the curious Scattergoodians trekked to Amana in February 1940 to glimpse this unique way of life. Hans Peters filed the following report on the experiment in living which the hostel family found there:

> *East Amana is a nice clean little town, located in the rolling farming country of eastern Iowa. We passed roomy houses, mostly brick, probably a little bit too uniformly constructed, but suitably set up and attractive. What about community life there? They live together like a big family. Everybody does everything for the colony. Each member of the village shares in its undertakings.*
>
> *Skilled and well-experienced workers are busy in the Amana Society. In the woolen mill, with all machinery for blankets and other woolen goods, they manufacture fashionable patterns, first quality, and therefore above the average price. The well-equipped Cabinet Shop constructs furniture, handmade and solid, in a clear and impressive style. The Society sells its products all over the United States, mostly eastwards, where the large cities are good customers.*
>
> *The local bakery looks like an old German Backstube, one hundred and fifty years ago. This shop and the meat markets in East Amana and Homestead [two of the seven villages comprising the colony's evenly spaced chain of villages] also are working for the whole settlement on a stock basis. We were guided through all these buildings and factories, and also visited the local stores, displays, and exhibitions.*

This big German settlement is surprisingly isolated from the outer world. They still speak a low German, besides English. Originally settled by farmers and skilled laborers in one place, they lived on an equal community basis for work and life. The generation of grandparents came from Germany. The following generations split off from the original idea and started independent life in the neighborhood, preferring to speak English. However, lessons in German are still compulsory in the Amana schools.

Today we have: "Seven Villages Practising Modified Capitalism." That is the title of the Amana booklet which gives details about history and present-day life and industry in these colonies.

After having lunch in the Homestead Hotel, we drove home... The highways—certainly not the side roads in Amana—were in good condition, the group of Scattergoodians in according good humor.

Summarizing the result of the trip I should say: A high recommendation for the government of the United States that it was and still is possible to realize such an experiment as proved by the Amana Villages. We refugees could attach another remarkable event to our colorful picture about American life, due to the tirelessly busy staff of the Scattergood Hostel.

Not a Jew but married to one,[1] Hans Peters would have found it difficult to stay in Nazi Germany in any case, due to his left-leaning politics. No wonder then, that his report concluded with a brief political commentary. In a similar way Otto Bauer's personality directly colored his report of a similar outing to Amana the following year. His treatise—not at all surprisingly—emphasized the theme of "community":

Our trip to Amana was very interesting for me. I am sorry to say that our stay in Amana was much too short for my wishes. I would like to stay there one or two weeks to talk to the people about their experience in community life. Long ago in Europe, I was very interested in communities which lived in a Christian and communistic spirit...

I learned from the history of all these communities to see this problem—the religious life and the secular life are one in the beginning, but in the course of the next years or decades, the religious life becomes a matter to itself, separated from secular life. In the beginning the divine service of the people was to work together for all, but the evolution tended to take the same end as the general evolution of Christianity. This means that the religious life retires into the churches or into little communities. The divine service is celebrated on Sunday. What the people do in the course of the week is not divine service, but business,

*politics, and so forth. And all of these everyday matters are uncon-
nected with their religious duties. People say, "Religion is a private
matter." I think that this is not so.*[2]

Not all Scattergood Hostel outings, however, consisted of marveling at
technical wonders or gawking at the natives. Cultural events also provided
the focus of some trips beyond the hostel's front gate. Walter Shostal later
recalled: "One Friday evening all of us were invited to a formal candle-light
dinner at the State University of Iowa campus. I had never dined at candle
light before, and I had never tasted mint jelly with roasted lamb. One of us
quipped afterwards regarding the green concoction: 'You don't have to
shiver like that; I won't eat you.' It sounded funny in his colloquial Viennese.
The dinner was followed by a concert performed by the student orchestra. On
the program—among other pieces—were the 'March of the Pilgrims' from
Tannhäuser and the 'Bridal March' from *Lohengrin*, both rather stately
pieces which did not have a great many black notes. A pretty undergraduate
next to me asked her neighbor 'Anyway, who is this guy, Richard Wagner?'
This was 50 years ago and I believe one is now more sophisticated at the
State University of Iowa."

Sometimes while on excursions the refugees themselves provided the focus of attention, as for land-locked Iowans they were exotic curiosities. One
off-premises visit found the guests providing considerable entertainment for
their hosts, as seen in an anonymous account of a spring outing in May 1942:
"Miss Margaret Cheek, who attended the [third] Scattergood birthday party,
was so enchanted by the Russian dances of our children, that she asked them
to give a performance at the party for the International Student Service at the
Presbyterian Church in Iowa City [one] Saturday evening... Our children
showed their artistic talents. Julius Lichtenstein was the announcer, and of
course he confounded the titles of the dances. But nevertheless Edith [and
her brother] Louis [Lichtenstein] and Frank [Keller] got strong applause.
Alfred Adler then told the audience some of his old stories, but they were
new to the people there. We played several games, such as horseshoes, fish
pond and ski-ball, and joined in community singing."

The same author went on to describe a sports event the hostelites visited:

*Some weeks ago, Scattergood was invited by the Y.W.C.A. to attend
a baseball game at Iowa City. Bob [Cory] had already given us several
lessons in basic baseball. The play started. The pitcher threw the ball,
and the batter tried to hit it. It happened that he could hit the ball, and
suddenly all the people yelled in a foreign language, and when I asked
my instructor at my left about this howling, she rolled her eyes and
cried, "A double out, a double out!" I could not get a satisfying an-*

swer, but I was not discouraged. Suddenly the judge stretched his arms and waved in the same manner as sailors who give code signals. I was told that this meant two hits or two balls, but what does a hit or a ball mean? The players run like madmen [or women], and they always preferred to slip [sic] the last two yards before the base on their backs. My instructor was a pretty, fair girl with great blue eyes, and the baseball excited her very much, and when the Iowa team got the only point in the game I missed seeing it. Why? Because my attention was so distracted.

When the game was over we drove to the Iowa City-City Park. We unwrapped our sandwich packages, and refreshed ourselves with the beverages and the ice cream. We sang old and modern songs, but the music lovers preferred to visit the Zoo, or to play with the ducks.

If the Europeans basked in celebrity beyond Scattergood's front gate, the Americans in the hostel family got their share of it at home. Sara Stanley discreetly recorded the birthday of each refugee *and* staff member as that person arrived—and on the appropriate day surprised her or him with a cake and the best wishes of those gathered to present it. Besides being a very important means of letting the European guests know that they once again could receive loving recognition and acknowledgement of their integrity, the celebration of all birthdays provided a good excuse for having a good time—as Camilla Hewson's account of Giles Zimmerman's birthday celebration so colorfully illustrates:

"Flash!! Important news for all inhabitants of Scattergood"

February 11, 1940, saw great hustle and bustle around the Hostel. It had been announced that that day was the birthday of our dear placement director, Giles Zimmerman.

In honor of this profoundly moving occasion, it was decided that all classes should cooperate in preparing a program to commemorate the great strength and courage shown by our hero in surviving twenty-six years in this cruel world.

After dinner on the natal day the fun began. The first class presented a skit, showing the high spots in the career of this well-known figure. This included his shining performance in school, and that memorable day when he purchased that canine wonder, Mr. MacTavish, having refused a squeaky plush cat and an elephant, "yellow and cheap."

One of the high spots of the evening was the imaginary version of an interview between Giles and an employer on behalf of two Scattergoodians, which involved a slight confusion as to the talents of these

209

gentlemen. However an epilog assured us that everything came out all right in the end. We may safely state that our hero was quite overcome by this tribute to his genius, but recovered in time to lend an ear to the Scattergood Speaking Chorus's rendition of an original eulogy, of which he, of course, was the subject.

As a closing gesture, Mr. Z. was presented with an enormous box containing a very small token of our esteem for him in the shape of one of his own pipes. This event was perhaps the most touching, as the man of the hour could hardly restrain his feelings as he beheld this evidence of our great respect and devotion. However, as before, he managed to revive himself sufficiently to partake of sustenance in the form of nut bread and coffee. Altogether it was a successful evening and a program worthy of our beloved Giles.

Sara Stanley was not the only person capable of pulling birthday tricks; the jolly, "renowned song-writer" Karl Veolin of Austria pulled one of his own—in the form of a song which he composed and sang for the modest Sara "with dessert in the living room after dinner" for her birthday in 1940:

The twelfth of December is a day of delight
We are celebrating Sara's birthday tonight.

She is very busy from dawn till dusk
And always she's smiling without any mask.

To prepare a good lunch is her usual job
B'sides that she is working with scrubber and mop.

When sometimes a helper doesn't well understand,
She is not excited and speaks with the hand.

She knows everything about Scattergood
Concerning the ice-box and the cellars of food.

Her Walter is happy with such a good wife
There's never a struggle in their quiet life.

She loves men and women and all children, too
She loves her good husband and the whole kitchen crew.

America and Europe, Christian and Jew
Unite in the song, Happy birthday to you!

The Scattergood staff and guests made liberal use of birthday parties to lighten the mood of the hostel—as well as just have fun. An anonymous writer recounted:

> *An especially elaborate celebration [which] marked the double birthdays of year-old Krystyne Salman and our staff member, Bob Berquist, on July 25 [1941]. An informal tea party was held in the afternoon for Krystine. In the evening the regular public speaking was interrupted by the "mayor of Centerdale" who had a startling resemblance to Paul Singer. His Honor invited all the family to an "evening in Venice" around the fish pool which was illuminated by colored lights and lanterns. Various speeches of an appropriate character were followed by the presentation of four graceful goldfish to Bob, who promptly christened them and placed them in their future home, the pool. Refreshments were followed by the singing of English and German songs until time for bed.*

A family celebrates—or observes, in the case of loss—important rites of passage: births, birthdays, weddings, anniversaries,[3] promotions, departures, deaths.[4] The birth of John and Josephine Copithorne's first child, for example, found the hostel community offering a hearty welcome to "Susan," announcing on the front page of the *Bulletin* that "the Scattergood family has added a new member to its circle... Early visitors report that both mother and child are doing well and that the father has quite recovered. Mary Susan...is a chubby infant who squalls lustily when presented to the gaze of her admiring public. To date she seems to have inherited her daddy's looks but not his disposition."

Before the child-bearing stage of married life, however, prospective parents first had to meet—which they did at Scattergood, and often. Besides Lillian Pemberton and George Willoughby, Ruth Carter and Bob Burgess, Paul Singer and Elsie Kepes, guests Frank Kellner[5] and Wilhelm Feist met future spouses while living at the hostel. Of the last's union ceremony, Marie Juchacz quipped in a summer-1942 edition of the *Bulletin* that "America has its romances and Scattergood also." She went on to explain:

> *William Feist was a member of the Scattergood family in 1940. Scattergood gave him, like many others, the first quiet refuge for the preparation of the new life in America. If Scattergood had visitors, his sensitive feeling of the good atmosphere in the Hostel inspired him for talking with them enthusiastically about the purpose and the results of the small but interesting institution. And it was at such an opportunity when [he] met [the "quite a bit younger"] Jean McIntyre the first time.*

*In the meantime [the middle-aged native Berliner and electrical engi-
neer] got his first job in Moline, Ill., and then he went to Chicago to
live and to work; and they were engaged. And now they wished to get
married and wanted that the wedding ceremony should take place under the same, beautiful old tree, where they saw one another for the
first time.*

*Saturday, August 8th...—the sky is a tender blue, like silk with white
clouds. The large lawn surrounded with borders of blossoming flowers
and large trees is the setting of the ceremony. Clever hands created the
background of the altar, which is adorned with white gladiolus and
candles. The bell rings and calls all Scattergood—a violin sounds—it
accompanies Elizabeth Lichtenstein singing the Song of Ruth. The ceremony is simple by the request of the couple. The minister the Rev.
James Gable of West Branch Methodist Church, is waiting at the altar.
The bridegroom is accompanied by his friend, [former hostel guest]
Helmut O[strowski] Wilk of Des Moines. Martha Balderston is doing
this service for the charming bride. Both bride and bridegroom speak
their vows with a clear voice. The sounds of Johann Sebastian Bach's
Prelude are fading away. Our congratulations came out of our hearts.*[6]

Whether they left Scattergood to pursue romance, a degree in higher education or a first job, each of the 185 refugees who sojourned for however long
at Scattergood eventually left. Their departures marked significant turning
points in each case and as such were duly celebrated—as related by an un-
named source in September 1942:

*Scattergood's family spent much of the past month saying farewell to
members moving on to new fields. On Tuesday evening...the living
room was transformed into a Court of Justice, and the Lichtenstein
family were made defendants in a trial to determine whether or not they
were guilty of base desertion of Scattergood. After the testimony of
witnesses, among them the kitchen, the garden rake, the phonetics class
and the cats, the jury found the family not guilty. Julius, Elizabeth,
Edith and Louis Lichtenstein left for St. Paul [Minnesota]...; they had
spent almost ten months at the Hostel, and we said good-bye to them
with deep regret. [On the next day] Lothar Gidro-Frank went to Iowa
City to prepare for a college entrance examination. [The future medical student then] returned to his home in New York City...and will
probably be back in Iowa City early in January. Saturday
evening...Robert Keller, impersonated by Louis Hacke dressed in
Robert's favorite costume of short blue shorts, white shirt and blue
beret and carrying an enormous dictionary, was interviewed by John*

212

Copithorne, a self-styled representative of a Milwaukee employment agency. After calling numerous references from Scattergood to prove his "ability" in lawnmowing, dishwashing, child care and English speaking, Robert, alias Louis, was given a wonderful position in Milwaukee. Immediately following this employment agency farce, a special news broadcast was heard over the radio; interspersed with items of international news, were news flashes about the exploits of the well-known European newspaper man, Louis Hacke. The next day, Louis and Robert left with Par Danforth for Milwaukee. Robert obtained employment there, and his family will join him soon. Louis worked part-time as a linotype operator in Milwaukee until [mid] September, and then left for New York City, where a position had been found for him. Walter, his son, left Scattergood on the same day, met his father in Chicago, and went on to New York with him. Walter will return to Cherry Lawn School, Darien, Conn. on the 16th of September. The Scattergood Boarding School assembled on August the 29th; all its scholars had clean faces, red hair ribbons, or white collars and red bow ties. The occasion was a farewell presentation to Adda Dilts, a well-loved member of the Boarding School's Faculty. Anne Marie Keller read an address of appreciation; little Monique Shumaker presented Adda with a bouquet of flowers and a wonder collection of dolls, composed largely of kitchen utensils, dried fruits and vegetables. Jack Shumaker went to Chicago on September the 8th for interviews with department store officials. We learned on September the 11th that he had accepted a position in a store in Danville, Ill., and will start work immediately. His family will remain at Scattergood for a short time.

Not only guests but staff members also left Scattergood for one of various reasons—for marriage, further education and employment or, in the case for young men, following Pearl Harbor for military or alternative service. Having played such primary, intimate roles in the lives of the refugees, not to mention in that of the other volunteers, departing staff also received a special send-off. That of two female staff in particular was well-celebrated—and lives on in the results of a photo session in which all staff and guests on hand were included. The surviving account of it relates:

June 1st [1940] was an important day for Scattergood, for it was then that the famous farewell banquet for Mildred Holmes [a native of Wichita, Kansas, and graduate of California's Quaker-founded Whittier College] and Ruth Carter took place. The entertainment committee (and everyone else too) scurried about for days getting everything in order for the occasion, and we still wonder how, with all the activity

213

*our guests of honor could have escaped knowing what was up. Appar-
ently they did, for you never saw two such surprised girls as they were
when, being duly seated at the big horseshoe table, they were crowned
with beautiful floral wreaths.*

*It was a real banquet, with toastmaster, flowers, speakers' table,
and waiters. After the food business had been attended to, each of the
girls was presented with a book of German songs (Schubert for Mildred, Brahms for Ruth) from the refugees. This was, of course, in addition to the main present of a celluloid toy apiece [sic]!*

*Then Bob Burgess, as toastmaster, read the letter printed [in the
previous chapter of this book] which had supposedly been written by
Ruth after two weeks at her new job in the Service Committee offices in
Philadelphia and showed the effect of "Scattergood English" on its
director of education. When the audience had recovered from the
touching missive, John [Kaltenbach] expressed our gratitude to Mildred in the form of the affidavits she knows so well [she having passionately pleaded for readers of the* Scattergood Monthly News Bulletin *to sign such important documents on behalf of refugees still
trapped in Nazi-occupied Europe, then having been strongly repri-
manded by AFSC for her solo action].*

*Our staff photographer, Mr.[Helmut Ostrowski-Wilk originally of
Berlin and later a U.S. army war photographer] recorded the gathering for posterity, but we fear that the results will be a bit discouraging
for posterity. Not that there was anything wrong with the photography,
but YOU try to hold an expression for ten seconds!*

*So it was a wonderful dinner, a good program, and an occasion of
mixed emotions. We can never say goodbye to one of our people without regret, but we wish them all the luck and joy that there is, and hope
that they will remember Scattergood as long and as lovingly as it will
remember them.*

Of course not all events in and memories of Scattergood's shared life
could be happy ones. Just as the joyous occasion of birth visited those at the
hostel, so did the sorrowful one of death. As with those of happiness, staff
and guests also shared moments of grief. Therefore, the then-56-year-old
Martha Balderston needed not be alone in the pain of her spouse's accidental
death during the first months of her stay at the hostel.

Having served Quaker relief efforts in Europe along with her husband,
Philadelphia-born Martha had come to Scattergood Hostel as a volunteer at
the end of October 1939. On 12 April of the following spring she received
word that husband Robert—who "had interest in a number of meat lockers"
in the Midwest—had fallen on concrete steps during a tour of one of his

company's plants in Lima, Ohio, and received fatal head wounds; he died a few days later "due to either mechanical damage to the brain or a blood clot which impaired one of his bodily functions." Martha soon left Scattergood to be with her children, but her "family" at the hostel—members of which knew Robert due to his relief work in Europe and in the U.S.—continued to mourn with Martha and feel concern for her. On the front page of the second issue of the *Bulletin*, John Kaltenbach wrote on behalf of staff and guests:

> *On the fifteenth day of this month Scattergood rounded out the first year of its Hostel life... Ordinarily an anniversary is an occasion for celebration. This anniversary of Scattergood was overshadowed by the loss of a beloved friend... Robert Balderston passed quietly into the realm of eternal peace. His accidental death was shocking to all who knew and loved him, yet all who gathered at the memorial service for him were comforted in the knowledge of a life which had been rich in the fullness of loving service, and many bore testimony to the light he carried into a darkening world. Friends who had worked with him for years, members of interdenominational church groups in which he participated with lively interest, and refugees who found understanding and help along the difficult way, all of them spoke tenderly and gratefully of his life. When the lights of the world seem to be fading away, it is the continued presence of the spirit of love which he possessed which makes life more precious and death a time for increase of love. It is that spirit which keeps the light burning, promising in this world knowledge of God's truth, and in the world to come life everlasting.*

As in life, Scattergood's common biography remained marked not only by milestones either happy or sad, but punctuated as well by celebrations of events which had their roots not within the four walls of the hostel but in the history and values of the wider culture found at the end of the lane. The staff utilized these days of rest, reflection or reverie for vehicles to accustom their eager guests to yet other aspects of life in America. Holidays, then, also became excuses to acculturate the refugees—all under a guise of sharing light-hearted fun.

Even the seemingly colorless anniversary of Lincoln's birth loaned itself to such ulterior aims. In February 1941 it "was observed...by a special luncheon in honor of the occasion. The tables in the dining room were arranged in horseshoe fashion and for decoration Walter Stanley constructed two delightful, table-sized corncob frontier log cabins. George Willoughby read selected stories about Lincoln to [those present] and [the middle-aged Austrian lawyer] Leo Keller recited the Gettysburg Address. Classes and tuitions also devoted some time to commemoration of the day."

Following Washington's birthday—for some obscure reason apparently an excuse every annum for an outing to the popular Amana colonies—the next holiday on the calendar came on 1 April. According to Otto Bauer it was "a day full of lark and laughter," for on April Fool's Day "members of the staff waked everybody with a goodnight song. Dinner was served in the morning, at 10 o'clock started a folk-dance part in the gymnasium, and at 11 o'clock was given a nice 'five o'clock tea.' The work for the men's work program was suspended, but not the lunch. Lunch was served at one o'clock and the dessert came first. In the evening we had a good breakfast."

On Easter Sunday 1940 Scattergood guests and staff "found before our doors Easter eggs, probably a work of Borneo"—the purported hostel ghost which was blamed for all spilled drinks, missing socks, inexplicable nice surprises, etc. After that weekend of bunnies, chicks and chocolate goodies, except for the Fourth of July[7] a lull in the passage of national holidays then set in. Until, that is, Halloween, when "the season of spirits and spooks did not pass at Scattergood with[out] receiving due attention." According to a *Bulletin* article which appeared in the October-November 1942 issue:

> On Saturday evening, October 31, as decreed by the time-honored American custom, masked and costumed figures assembled in the living room and spent the first half-hour in silently re-establishing identities. Even by the time the grand march was over not everyone had succeeded in recognizing the jongleur in red tights and striped hose as Stan Braun, nor the Spanish señorita in lace mantilla and with flirtatious fan as Eva Standing [of Earlham, Iowa]. Her disguise must have been complete indeed to make it possible for someone to mistake her for Roger Craven. The success of the costuming was due in great part to the energy and ingenuity of Ellen Krauthamer, who persuaded unimaginative or refractory persons to be garbed as old apple women, doctors, Iowa farmers or quaint, old-fashioned ladies. Our neighbors, the Coppocks and the Pembertons, came over for the fun. The high point of the entertainment was a new game, called BEEP, introduced by Roger [Craven]. Cookies, doughnuts, Kipferl and cider completed the evening's festivities, and were topped off by a round of singing.[8]

Halloween provided four years' worth of fun at Scattergood, as evident in Karl Veolin's account of that ghoulish fest from two years earlier:

> On the eve of "All Saints Day" there was an enjoyable Hallowe'en Party at Scattergood. The dining room was illuminated by dim red light radiated by hollow pumpkins, showing cut-out faces with candles in-

216

stead of brains. After a short interruption caused by the necessity of dishwashing, all members of our family and some guests gathered in the "Gym" where similar light effects and some other mysterious things were prepared. Within a period of one hour there were ten different problems to solve. Among them: get two watermelons from anywhere, get a thistle and other unknown plants from our garden, bring different advertisements of hybrid seed corn and, as the high-point of the evening, bring a picture of the Empire State Building and figure out the average age of the Presidents of the United States at death. Right after the distribution of these questions there was a rush to the garden, to the library, and to our neighbors. Expeditions equipped with flashlights and other things started out to fulfill these tasks in the shortest possible time. The victorious crew was captained by our dietician but some competitors believed she did too much coaching. Afterwards refreshments were served and some funny games finished this grand evening.

While Halloween consisted of mindless merriment, Thanksgiving—that quintessentially American holiday—gave both guests and staff cause to reflect and count reasons for gratitude. Twenty-nine-year-old Ilse Stahl—who fled Breslau, Germany, with her politically active, socialist husband Ernst—exclaimed "Oh! Loveliest day, if our harvest comes" upon considering this most sacred of secular fests. A skilled painter of wooden objects who later taught at a Catholic school in suburban Philadelphia, Ilse wrote an article about Thanksgiving in which she recited much of what she'd learned in history class, explaining:

When the first pioneers had settled in America and their first corn on the new earth was grown, they were thankful to God. They were thankful to the Indians, who brought their helpful friendship, and from whom they learned to raise corn. In happiness that this land later on could be their homeland, that this earth would give them their living, that their hard work was repaid in such a rich and plentiful harvest, they celebrated their first Thanksgiving.

And now, years and years later, Thanksgiving is celebrated again. Perhaps some of the people lost the right feeling for Thanksgiving. They never sowed corn and wheat; they never have seen it grow up; they never did this hard and irksome work of planting; however, not all feeling for this holiday is spoiled. In this part of America, where the corn grows around and around, where the meadows are covered with cattle and pigs, where the earth is so fertile and splendid, there isn't a need for a special mind.

Just this day, whoever can, comes home to enjoy with his [or her] family a good meal and brings his congratulation to the blissful year.

Of course, Scattergood would stand back of this nice tradition. And so, it kept open house. Some former Scattergoodians came home...and they all again felt at home under this hospitable roof.

The right holiday dinner was served up, with turkey and plenty of other best food. The dining-room decorated with all kinds of fruits from garden and field illuminated with the sunshine outside, gave the holiday its glory.

Some small birds sang their honor song too. Each Scattergoodian face was a reflection of thanks, gladness and new hope. A sound was singing in us all, a home song, a welcome song. That, which was taken away from us all in our former country, that which was pushed down in us, we got back. This we felt.

In Scattergood we found our first and loveliest home. In America we hope to find our new homeland. For this all, we thank you.

While Thanksgiving is a secular holiday, Christmas remains anchored in Christianity—a fact which did not stir a single recorded objection at Scattergood Hostel, where a good portion of the guests were either practicing Jews or agnostics. Kurt Rosegg accompanied the Deutsch family to Iowa City in spring 1939 to attend Yom Kippur services, for example, and the Lichtenstein family [Elizabeth was a converted Bavarian Lutheran] invited interested individuals to join them in their room on the occasion of Hanukkah in December 1941. Despite these signs of religious involvement on the part of some Jews at Scattergood, not once was a guest reported to have excused her- or himself from the Christmas celebrations due to reasons of confession. On the contrary, more former guests made special efforts to return "home" to the hostel during the Holiday Season than at any other time of year.

At any rate, Christmas seems to have been a truly special event at the hostel, one involving much emotional as well as physical investment. Leo Keller painstakingly recounted the many careful arrangements which led to the Christmas-1940 festivities:[9]

The numerous preparations had started with the baking of cookies by day and night, because of the expected return of many family members from their newly established homes. The work of house repairing, cleaning and adorning, musical and dramatic rehearsals, just gave us enough time for procuring presents, the most enjoyable thing this high time has to offer to grown-up people. Scattergood knew how to enlarge this job; everybody in the house drew the name of another for whom he [or she] was to deposit a small gift under the Christmas tree.

By and by our guests arrived in relatively mild weather, married couples and single men from near and far, evidently happy to spend a week of peace and cheerfulness at the place from which they had started after several months' instruction in regard to their struggle for existence. They all lent hands joyfully and on Christmas Eve Scattergood was in readiness for the holiday. It was inaugurated with a Christmas Eve dinner for which the dining room had adopted a very dignified appearance.

The light of fifty candles, so favorable to a mystical frame of mind, set in wooden candelabra on the large G-shaped table, filled the room. Christmas wreaths on little stands and sprigs of evergreen spread over the white table cloths gave forth the fragrance of firs. The dinner prepared under [Lillian Pemberton's] direction was incomparable. After dinner everybody in good humor waited for Santa Claus except for the children...

After that a Chorus directed by [the middle-aged Viennese banker and hobbyist musician] Hans Schimmerling accompanied at the piano by [28-year-old, fellow Viennese banker and also musically inclined] Rudi Schreck sang old English and German Christmas carols—"Stille Nacht, Heilige Nacht," "Lo how a rose e'er Blooming" and "Here We Come a Wassailing." One would like to thank them again for the singing of those airs. St. Nicholas continued then the distribution of presents, this time among the other Scattergoodians from America and Europe and there was nobody who had not a happy feeling not to be forgotten in this hour of general joy. After the Chorus had sung some other solemn carols, an unforgettable Christmas Eve passed. Hellmut [sic] Ostrowski[-Wilk] took a snapshot of the two little girls [Bertl Weiler and Doris Arntal] amidst their treasures under the Christmas tree; it will remind them of this happy Christmas Eve of their early days in their years to come.

Christmas morning found us in the hospitable home of the Pembertons at a delicious breakfast. It was a fine morning hour. In the following days of this Christmas season teas, music, recitations, funny plays[10] and dances followed each other at Scattergood. All amusements were arranged by [now-so-named] Charles Violin, chairman of our Entertainment Committee.

The week fulfilled the wishes which were expressed on the Christmas menu card. "We hope that our living together at Scattergood has helped each of us to feel the spirit of the Christmas season at odd times and in many situations throughout the year. May this holiday be a time of happy reunion and help to make the coming year truly rewarding for all of us.

It didn't take long for an opportunity to "feel the spirit." A week later, the Scattergood community once again lavished much energy on a holiday—this time the advent of a New Year. Guest director of West Branch's Methodist church choir and a player of four instruments, busy Hans Schimmerling laid down his beloved songbook long enough to file a detailed report:

The preparations for New Year's Eve started early in the afternoon of December 31st. Nobody was supposed to enter the living room and people were anxious to know "What is going on in Scattergood?" But everybody had to tame his [or her] curiosity until nine o'clock when the good old Scattergood bell gave the last signal for 1940. How many fairy tales could our good bell narrate if we only paid attention to it and tried to understand its language. But we do not notice that; it is just a signal, familiar to us and the neighboring farmers, the latter of whom briefly say, "They ring it pretty often." But then it was its last chime indicating the close of a year of oscillation between hope and sorrow.

We enter the living room. Was it really our living room or was it a Viennese night club? Cute little tables, each having a little lamp and all kinds of fancy things on them, plus coffee and "Apfelstrudel a la Viennese." The only startling point was that everybody talked English in that Viennese night club. Did we sleep through the conquest of Vienna by the British and did we sit really there, transferred by magic? How nice to be so advanced with our English now. But there was no time for meditation; gaiety broke out and everybody took part in it. One could not tell indeed how the three hours passed but suddenly it became twelve sharp "and darkness was upon the face of the deep." The New Year broke "and there was light." The Viennese men wondered only why they were not supposed to kiss the ladies when it was dark, an old Viennese custom. We wished a successful New Year to everybody and so we do the same to the readers of this item now.

The young people had a hangover the next morning, having danced on their first day in 1941, but the older people looked well for they did not participate in the folly of youth. In the afternoon again we were invited to be in Vienna. [Austrian-born] Zlata Weisz, giving her farewell party, arranged a Viennese coffee house with all the particular aspects of its atmosphere. Coffee with whipped cream, Viennese cakes served at separate tables, again waiters, and beggars with matches [played by Zlata's 12-year-old daughter Ruth] and an invalid begging [Karl Veolin] whose appearance was very natural and convincing. And many a man thought "once on a time," drank his coffee with whipped cream and asked erroneously for a Viennese paper. The Americans, on the other hand, enjoyed very much being in Vienna for awhile—in the "old Vienna," of course, because the present one has no coffee, no whipped cream, no joy at all.[11] Let us hope that our parties, dreamlike as they were, did not only represent a transfiguration of our old beloved Vienna, but depict a future restatement of the famous Viennese comfort.

Coffee, cream, the ingredients for fine cakes: all that cost money, which Scattergood always had too little of for its basic expenses, let alone for such "luxuries."[12] Freetime activities did not have to cost much,[13] however, as attested by Karl Veolin's description of one resourceful exercise, when "the chairman [sic] of the Entertainment Committee announced last Saturday that everybody should meet in the living room equipped with a pencil and a brain. No other advertisement! Not knowing what might happen we all came and had a wonderful time. Sheets of paper with several different kinds of questions were distributed and a time limit of five to ten minutes for solving each of them was given. The last part of this task was to watch carefully the performance of a murder and then questions had to be answered about the weapon used and about the clothing and actions of the murderer and the victim. While the answers were being scored by the Committee we enjoyed coffee and cake in honor of Rosl Weiler's birthday. Late in the evening it was announced that our placement manager had placed first in the competition."

Another low-budget form of entertainment in pre-television Scattergood consisted of in-house or visiting performances—both the dramatic and comic varieties. For the "children" among the hostelites—of whatever age—the guest appearance one "delightful evening [by] Professor Spann of the State University of Iowa with his staff [entertained] us by a masterly puppet show under the title of the famous 'Dr. Faustus.' This brought back many of us happy childhood memories of the time when we listened to our beloved [knavish German marionette figure] Kasperle, who gave his performances in public for little folks." The Europeans weren't the only ones who enjoyed "Dr. Faustus," which Robert Berquist recorded that night in his journal as "excellently done in every respect and appreciated by our guests [from outside the hostel community] invited for the occasion."

Bona fide "adult" theater at Scattergood included numerous skits, gags and dramatizations of familiar scenes, around which other entertainment could be organized. One time, for example, the guests and staff "enjoyed a really exciting performance of 'This is My Scattergood,' a play specially for the occasion, written and directed by our talented Peter Seadle. It showed in an amusing fashion the life in Scattergood. Afterwards the alumni with the nice guests stood around the piano and sang American songs... The good old moon at length broke through the clouds and smiled down a pleasant 'Good

221

Night' on the happy people of Scattergood."

Even a bunch of intellectually inclined Europeans, however, couldn't just sit around all day and night reading, discussing sobering topics or merely forming an audience to be entertained by clever theatrics. When the extremely varied Midwest weather allowed, the hostel family also ventured into the Great Outdoors—and happily so. Not only was being outside pleasant, one hostelite wrote in *The Book of Scattergood*: "Swimming. It's a good thing for our purses that the quarries are free." And on top of that all sorts of recreational activities could be dovetailed around a run to the swimming hole—including canoeing, hunting for mushrooms or wild berries, bird-watching and the like. In a piece entitled "Back to Nature," one guest or staff member related that "picnics are a special joy for Scattergoodians. Cooking hot dogs and hamburgers over an open fire is fun, and the troubles of the kitchen are soon forgotten. The scheduled dishwasher can manipulate his [or her] food with [their] hands with a supreme sense of relaxation. We pick the beautiful wild flowers without worrying about weeds. Yet in going back to nature, we have to reckon with the weather. We inaugurated our picnic season on May the 23rd [in 1942] with a trip to the Quarries, and after supper were just beginning to sing when a heavy storm drove us home. On Decoration Day, when [the Quaker farm couple] Israel and Lora Larson so generously invited us to have a picnic with them at their meadow near the Cedar River, we were so afraid of the dark skies that we had our picnic right on the Scattergood lawn, and then went to the meadow when the skies cleared. We all got wet anyway, for we went swimming both in the river and at the quarries. In an attempt to confuse the weather, we exchanged Wednesday and Thursday, June the 10th and 11th [1942], when we were planning a picnic to Lake McBride. The storm obligingly came on Thursday the 10th, leaving the afternoon of Wednesday the 11th for a fine swim in the lake and a hearty picnic supper in the park."

When the fried drumsticks have all run out, the ice cubes in the pulpy lemonade have melted and summer's favorite drink has grown lukewarm, the bugs have begun to bite and the conversation has begun to run a bit thin, what do nature-lovers do to pass the time? Start playing games! The good folks at Scattergood may not have been typical Yankees, but even they indulged in what is said to be one of the greatest of Great American Pastimes—group sports. And if the following "Sports Flashes" from the *Bulletin's* July 1942 issue are to be believed, they did so with a passion:

> *Scattergood's croquet court is the scene of many battles. Every day the masters of the mallets, old and young, perform new feats of skill.*

*Even in the hottest sun, our professional, "Lou Lou" [Louis] Lichten-
stein can be seen coaching players of lesser talent. The granddaddy of
the court is [the Hungarian-born] Julius Neumann, whose calculated
shots strike terror into the hearts of his opponents; the baby of the
court is Annette Keller, aged two, who plays with great enthusiasm in
spite of her heroic disregard of rules. Croquet has quite eclipsed the
former Scattergood pre-eminent sport, ping-pong, and the ping-pong
table lies idle and disgruntled in the gym.*

*But baseball runs a close second to croquet on the Scattergood ath-
letic program. Although such notables as [AFSC staff member] Elmore
Jackson and [visiting British Friend] Bertram Pickard have been sub-
stitutes on our team, the regulars who are responsible both for the most
hits and the most strike-outs are Lou Lou "Home Run" Lichtenstein,
Frank "Killer" Keller, Gunther "Babe Ruth" Krauthamer and Bob
"Fire Chief" Cory. The health and strength of the members of the team
have flourished, but the vegetables and flowers of Sara's garden have
suffered.*

*A gift of some golf putters started a new sport at Scattergood, clock
golf. On the second day of play, John Copithorne, resplendent in his
Buchanan tartan, set the course record by making a hole-in-one.*

*But not to be forgotten is Scattergood's most popular sport, lawn-
mowing. The art of cutting fancy patterns in the grass is something to
which every man who comes to Scattergood is initiated. Captain Robert
Keller announces that the Scattergoodians are ready to challenge any
team to a contest, providing only that the contest take place on our own
field, where the grass is tougher, hardier, faster-growing and more en-
during than anywhere else.*

Whether or not they were prepared for it, the fiercest competition facing
these mostly happy refugees was yet to come: they who had found respite at
Scattergood Hostel soon enough would discover that in the "Land of the
Free," each woman and man was just as free to fail as to succeed. After weeks
or months of language training, cultural excursions, freetime recreation and
a modest amount of career coaching, the adults among the guests were to be
tested in a most merciless job market—and too often disqualified due to the
foreign-sounding names they'd been given at birth, the accent with which
they spoke English or the house of religion in which they chose to worship.
If they managed to press past those hurdles, they might well bump against
the blinding fear of or resentment towards foreigners—or even, ironically,
their own "over-qualification."

Still, by the time each refugee left, the staff at Scattergood had done its
best to prepare their charges. Using the realms of work, education and free-

time to prepare their guests the very best they could, the Americans who lived, learned and loved alongside Europe's discards at the little hostel on the prairie could but wish them well—and pray for the best.

1.) As was the case for so many refugee families, Hans Peters could secure from the U.S. government a visa only for himself. He arrived "as a single refugee" on 10 December 1938; affidavits and visas for Lotte, his wife of 14 years, and their two sons had to be secured once he had safely escaped the reach of his Nazi stalkers. He later recounted that his family "arrived in fall of 1939. No kiss. She wanted separation, taking the children, for whom she cared most graciously for years... Lotte was for separation. I was for doing things together as a family. Yes, but she would decide when the togetherness would begin. So AFSC staff invited me to join Scattergood. I paid my way from Philadelphia to Iowa City by bus. And I arrived...a 'new' human being. Günter Meier [sic] and some Scattergood staff members picked me up. They were looking for a man mentally broken down. They never found him. The next morning, I introduced myself in overalls and in perfect English. All of the about 30 refugees, including children, were from Germany and Austria. Some doubted that I was a refugee... I am not a Jew. So, I found a few friends, mostly among the staff. Camilla Hewson I called 'My little flower' and kissed her. That is as far as it went, romantically. John Kaltenbach, director, talked about the 'American Dilemma', etc... To me, the staff was never wrong. Scattergood was to me a 'Greenhorn College'... Please understand that if we refugees do not talk about our experiences in Nazi Germany, it is because they are still painful to remember." Despite his perception of others' reactions, someone at the hostel liked him, for on 27 September 1939 that person wrote in *The Book of Scattergood*: "[Hans seems] a newcomer who already seems like an old member of the family. The first morning he appeared in working clothes and a spirit which makes us feel as if he had belonged with us for a long time." Camilla said Hans called her *Sternchen*—"little star."

2.) Each guest really did see her or his visit to the Amana colonies through a very subjective lens. An account of the 1942 trip to Amana reported that "the whirring of the machinery in the furniture factory thrilled our junior mechanics, 'Lulu' [sic] Lichtenstein and Frank Keller. Others enjoyed the delicious smell of the old fashioned hearth oven. Marie Juchacz and Paul Singer, however, found the greatest satisfaction in the Westphalian hams hanging in the smoke room of the meat market. For [former hostelite] Jacob Winkler [now] of Iowa City...the climax came when steaming bowls of sauerkraut were added to the heavily laden dinner table."

3.) On 11 October 1939 someone wrote in *The Book of Scattergood*: "Our lovely Sara and Walter today celebrate their 40th wedding anniversary. At supper Hans [Ladewig] sincerely expresses all our feelings. In the evening there is singing of folk-tunes and a general feeling of contentment."

4.) As is customary in the Midwest, families often host "open houses," receptions to which friends and relatives, neighbors and colleagues are invited due to one or another excuse to socialize—such as a high school graduation, a silver or golden wedding anniversary, Grandmother's 80th birthday and the like. Being a "family," Scattergood was no different and hosted an open house of its own in October 1939, which one of the hostelites described in *The Book of Scattergood*: "Full of guests from two till the end. All ran easily, with the help of a special schedule, cookies and cranberry juice complete with ice from W. Liberty our helper in trouble. W. Branch failed us miserably. Sarah [sic] and Walter [Stanley] as host and hostess have [given] the festival an atmosphere of dignity and love. Gunter [Meyer], the old faithful played the piano. Guests came from near and far. We had a big cafeteria supper in our dining-room. The days now are so beautiful that if we didn't know it was all natural we could hardly believe that it is so beautiful. The maple tree by the bench looks as if it is gilded with fine gold. This may be a symbol of our golden home-coming day." This was in sharp contrast to a proposed open house six months earlier—on the occasion of the hostel's opening. Scattergood Committee member Jay Newlin wrote to Sara Pemberton: "I have about arrived [at the conclusion] that we are not going to have any formal open house day. If I sense the public interest correctly, we set a date for open house and do our best to keep it quiet. The newspapers will get the story, and we can have a crowd anywhere from 500 to 5,000, which would undoubtedly defeat the object of the visit. Our guests would feel like monkeys in a cage in a zoo rather than receiving a substantial welcome from interested friends."

5.) The 30-ish Vienna native met Anne Jacobson while attending the Grinnell Institute of International Relations in 1940. They embarked on international relations of their own and married in February 1942.

6.) Despite a romantic beginning, the marriage ended in divorce.

7.) Perhaps the 1939 observance of that very-American holiday was representative: "Independence Day. Full rest. Peace its [sic] wonderful! In the P.M. a gang invaded Iowa City and took in the fireworks there."

8.) Robert Berquist reported that "music was very important at the Hostel. There was an album of spirituals and other songs sung by Paul Robeson, which was played often. I can see Werner Selig sitting by the record player in the social room of the Main Building listening to music by Robeson and others. Strauss selections were also frequently played, much loved especially by the many Viennese guests." Camilla Hewson Flintermann noted that the "album (78rpm) of Paul Robeson singing 'Ballad for Americans'...was popular—intensely revisionist-patriotic, extolling the values of believing in the TRUE American spirit of freedom and justice for all—but not exactly pacifistic! Yes, there was a phonograph—in the living room—and it was available for all."

9.) For an excerpted version of Earle and Marjorie Edwards' account of Christmas 1939 at Scattergood Hostel written for *The Friend* see Appendix III.

10.) One play was a satirical piece dubbed "The Initiation of Elsie, the New Staff Member," a transcript of which can be found in Appendix VI.

11.) German-occupied Vienna was not the only spot on Earth where cream was used carefully. Whether or not it was in short supply in America at that time, too, Sara Stanley used it sparingly in cooking for Scattergood's ensemble. Thus, Walter Shostal later told a related story: "Sarah [sic] ruled in the kitchen, but she did not do all the work. One or two of the women guests assisted her, sometimes cheating a little behind her back. Occasionally some of Sarah's cake recipes seemed a little austere to her European helpers, accustomed to a richer diet, so they might sneak another two or three eggs into the batter. Or, if some gravy could be improved by a hefty dose of cream, the helper sneaked that in, too. If Sarah noticed, she would merely smile."

12.) One "luxury" which could not be denied the guests—nor staff, for that matter—consisted of the weekly trips to Iowa City, during which hostelites enjoyed any one of numerous offerings: classical music concerts, lectures, a new hair-do, going shopping, sipping a Coke at the soda fountain, buying a big-city newspaper, visiting former guest Herta Schroeder for tea and a chat in her new home, bowling, dancing at the Student Union, etc. One favorite activity was seeing a film—"Gone With the Wind," "The Wizard of Oz," "On Borrowed Time," etc.

13.) One "priceless" pastime consisted of star-gazing, sunset-savoring, storm-watching or in other ways appreciating the prairie skyscape—which existed in inexhaustible quantities. On 11 August 1939, for example, one hostelite wrote in *The Book of Scattergood*: "Those of us who were night owls were rewarded for our vigilance by a panorama of Northern Lights." On 6 October of the same year, "after [an evening excursion to Iowa City for shopping and cinema] the dorm philosophizes on the front lawn by the light of Pegasus and other constellations until 1:30." And on 16 March the following spring a Scattergoodian recorded that "in the evening during dinner-time we witnessed a wonderful sunset. The sky was fire red." A fortnight later, "a beautiful aurora borealis in the evening seduces [eight hostelites with three cats in tow] to take a longer walk." In a similar vein, Walter Shostal later wrote: "I remember one spectacular thunderstorm that I watched at Scattergood. I climbed up to the attic—where one usually did not go—and looked out. It was an awesome sight. Although it was mid-afternoon, it was almost dark and the tremendous plain on the horizon seemed to be afire. Not only were there lightning streaks on all sides, real fireballs were rolling and jumping around on the ground. I had witnessed thunderstorms in the Alps where the thunder had rolled on endlessly from one rock wall to the next and kept on coming back. This storm on the Midwestern plain was the [most] grandiose natural spectacle ever."

A NEW WAY OF LIFE

*"I decided to start in on a new way of life
in the Middle-Western farm region."*
~ **Peter Lustig**

Scattergood witnessed the efforts of three individuals who undertook the responsibility of placing the refugees in professional positions. These men—John Kaltenbach (15 April 1939-1 July 1940), Giles Zimmerman (23 August 1939-January 1942) and Laurence "Par" Danforth (29 November 1941-mid April 1943)—figured into the fate of their charges in decisive ways, as they helped determine to what degree the guests would feel secure, useful and content in their new homeland.[1] The task, however, was formidable. Some of the refugees were already over 50 and thus of limited value to firms wishing to hire long-term employees. Some held European degrees not transferable to the United States without further education—such as degrees in law or medicine. Some lacked practical skills, while others were loath to accept positions outside their fields of interest or "beneath" their training.

A further personal, internal barrier to the refugees starting new careers in the New World often involved the psychological struggle to accept the reality of their over-turned Old World lives. Trained in psychoanalysis, based on his own experience Ernst Malamerson speculated that placing Scattergood guests "was very difficult because they all really wanted to go back to where they had been [professionally, but in America] they had to start much lower than that. [Had it been their own decision] they wouldn't have come; they had to. None of them volunteered—that includes myself. I came to America because Europe, so to speak, was exhausted... To fully psychologically accept [their new status] would be like accepting a demotion; they also probably exaggerated in their own minds the positions they had occupied in Europe, [so the hostel's job-placement personnel] had considerable difficulty..."[2]

On top of the limiting factors arising from within were those imposed from without: first the crippled job market left by the Great Depression's last gasps, then the Federal ban on hiring foreign workers to labor in "sensitive" fields such as armaments[3] and the imposition of travel restrictions upon "aliens of enemy nationality" once the U.S. joined the war. Also, at least until the days of full employment created by general mobilization, there existed a hesitancy on the part of many employers to give "American jobs" to non-citizens. Thus, at least initially, many guests left the hostel for positions which in Europe they never would have considered filling. Despite their best efforts, then, the three men mentioned above often could offer guests only the initial means to survive, but not to thrive.

Concerning speculation on the "success" or "failure" of Scattergood's job-placement program, substantiating any conclusions ultimately must consist largely of circumstantial evidence portrayed as indicative of a whole. Much is known about the staff's post-hostel life, but the majority of guests "disappeared" into the larger U.S. society, leaving their later curricula vitae unrecorded by any sources found in the course of this work. Therefore, the review of some of the refugees' immediate post-hostel professional experiences must suffice in providing a representative idea of how well Scattergood ultimately achieved its goal of integrating its guests into American society.

Not hired for the job, John Kaltenbach became head of job-placement efforts during the first months of the hostel's life by default. Understandably preoccupied by an endless array of other matters,[4] he had little time to devote to finding meaningful, lasting employment for Scattergood's initial guests—and it showed. With one notable exception, the earliest Europeans who set out from the hostel were the unlucky recipients of a series of false-start, dead-end jobs which had little to do with professional careers besides being bridges from occupational obscurity to the hoped-for gainful position which might make all the difference between sinking or swimming in America's sea of free-market competition.

Of the first five men to arrive at the hostel, Kurt Schaefer had the best luck. His fortune consisted of a half-time offer to teach economics and conduct research at the State University of Iowa's College of Commerce—at a salary of $800 per year. The engaged politico also received commissions to write articles for the *Des Moines Register* and to travel a public-speaking circuit which stretched across the Upper Midwest. The topics with which he dealt included "What to do with Germany?"; "U.S. Foreign Policy and Germany"; "Trends in the German Economic System" and "Whither Europe?" A later biographer of Schaefer, William Bunge held that Kurt's "mission was to arouse people to the Nazi menace and he worked at it with ferocity. Scattergood itself was filled with the human wrecks the Nazis deliberately sought

227

to produce. The horrible knowledge of what had been done to his German friends was thus daily refreshed." Claiming that "toward the end of the Great Depression, the [university] had five or six radicals on the staff," Bunge noted that "Smith's Restaurant provided an informal meeting place for these men. Schaefer immediately affiliated." Soft-spoken and ironic, Kurt "was contemptuous of those who were not as intellectual as he, especially of fellow university professors." This blend of political passion and personal arrogance promised to bring him trouble. Which it did.

In 1947, marrying Mary Strub, a young woman from a prominent Iowa City family, Kurt could have expected to lead a cozy academic life in an ivory tower on the banks of the Iowa River. Instead, with the advent of the Cold War, he became persecuted again—this time by the Americans. In the early 1950s, the FBI began "open harassment" of the clique which met at Smith's, primarily through "shadowing" its targets. Due to fear of those associated with the "Red Threat," Kurt's income fell and his "friends" abandoned him. For a while he withdrew from the scholastic scene and fled to a "rest home in Milwaukee [where he perfected] a new strategy and he decided to stop being such an obvious radical politician." He then returned to Iowa City, where he became a faculty member of the university's geography department. Determined to produce some lasting accomplishment,[5] he spent "much time" translating Lösch's *Economics of Location* from the work's original German version into English and—as a fluent reader of Russian—established an open collection of materials pertaining to the Soviet Union. "His course on [Soviet] political geography was taught from the perspective that the politics were incomprehensible without an economic understanding. He remained interested in mathematics and statistics and applied these skills to geography." According to Bunge: "All told, he appeared to have been about ten years ahead of the rest of geography." Because of an interest in recent theories of political geography, he produced an article titled "Exceptionalism in Geography: A Methodological Examination," which later was published by the *Association of American Geographers* in its 1953 *Annals*. Colleagues in the field praised his work as ground-breaking, an "introduction to geography of [the] modern philosophy of science, and an identification of spatial relations as the subject matter of geography."

While Schaefer's scholarly reputation soared, his political popularity didn't. Try as he might he couldn't divorce his personal passions from his professional life and this inability made him suffer. As Bunge explained:

His first forty-two years had been devoted to a way of life that had been destroyed. He had been harried from job to job and country to country until he was isolated from his world and friends. Deeply tired, he had decided to stand and fight where he was, to marry, to turn him-

228

*self seriously to his profession. He transferred his idealism and ener-
gies from his destroyed world to geography and in seven years of intense further effort produced one great work.*

*The publication of [Schaefer's] article...was not without strong op-
position, which further drained his energies.*[6] *With sheer brilliance of
argument his only weapon, [he] fought to be heard. Fire engine sirens
vividly reminded him of Hitler's terrorism. He became distinctly nervous if a person got on and off the bus with him since he had been
followed by the Gestapo and the FBI for months. McCarthyism re-
pulsed and sickened Schaefer in a way that those...who have not seen
Hitler...cannot understand.*

The victim of a heart attack in winter 1952-53, the stressed, emotionally
tortured Kurt Schaefer died of a second one on 6 June 1953. His associate
and close friend Gustav Bergmann—once of the so-called Vienna Circle and
another Hitler-exile who had landed at the University of Iowa—had to complete Kurt's manuscript for publication, meaning that the idealistic radical
from Berlin "was denied even this satisfaction."

Kaltenbach's four remaining "little Daniel Boones" at Scattergood had
less colorful—if less deadly—debuts into the American work world upon
leaving the hostel. Deaf but endearing, Fritz Treuer found an office job at
Antioch College in Yellow Springs, Ohio, where the middle-aged man combined his previous incarnation as a Viennese stationer with amateur gardening by engaging in farm work after office hours. Twenty-six-year-old George
Laury left the hostel in late June 1939 to take a well-paying accounting job
at Des Moines' Major Engineering Company, but apparently didn't stay
there more than two years, as in May 1941 he reportedly held an unspecified
job in Buffalo; as of December 1942 he was living with his mother in New
York and expected to be inducted into the U.S. Army "very soon." Thirty-
year-old Kurt Rosegg first tried a job in August 1939 in Cedar Rapids, but
finding it unsatisfactory returned to Scattergood, only to leave again at the
end of October to work in the repair division of Mastercraft in Des Moines.[7]
By spring 1940 he had moved to Kansas City, where as a "bench worker" he
helped fill the personnel needs of a jewelry manufacturer; he lost that job in
June 1940 "when the factory closed down for the summer." He wrote that he
was unemployed and "in pretty bad financial straights [sic]." The hostel was
unable to suggest to Kurt any new placement ideas and he then disappeared
from Scattergood's records until 1944, when he was listed as having married
a woman named Sylvia. And well-liked, multi-talented Karel Gam? An obscure reference indicates that the 26-year-old, one-time graduate student at
the University of Pennsylvania—where he had been at the time of the

Wehrmacht's occupation of the Sudetenland—left Scattergood "to accept a position in Cedar Rapids," the world's oatmeal-milling capital and home to thousands of Czech immigrants. He later ran into trouble with his resident-alien status and virtually went underground, surfacing later in a storm of identity controversy at a Texas university where he claimed academic background and titles he didn't have.

The easy-come-easy-go Erhard Winter—a *Sonntagskind*, or "charmed child" born on a Sunday—lucked out once again and fell into a future which many refugees would have envied. In late May 1939 a certain Doctor Binns,[8] a professor of sociology at one of Iowa's numerous small church-founded colleges, brought a class to Scattergood Hostel as a field trip. Erhard would never forget that decisive day: "I well remember it... I (we) felt a little bit like animals in a zoo, but...the upshot was that the class decided they must sponsor a refugee to come as a student to [their school]. They returned to [the college' s hometown], persuaded the rest of the campus of the importance and urgency of this matter, took up collections of funds among the students and faculty and I, being the only 'guest' of appropriate age, education, etc. was 'Johnny on the spot,' got a full tuition scholarship and work in the college kitchen to pay for rm & bd. I personally did nothing. I didn't apply... I didn't ask for anything and I didn't sign anything."

Erhard found a "position," too, but by sheer luck. Little did he know, but his college career would open doors—among them one into his own emotional closet. According to him, "Erhard's alternatives were remaining at S.H., returning to [his mother's boarding house] or hitting the road. As he was penniless (as usual) and the 1st 2 choices were unacceptable he opted for [college]. At least he was assured Rm & Bd and no one to tell him what to do. His career at [the college] was less than meteor. The teaching and the profs were for the most part mediocre, uninspired, uninspiring and highly pedestrian and really irrelevant to the burning issues of the time. Only the English professor, Professor Rhode, a charismatic and enigmatic New Englander aroused [Erhard's] enthusiasm and in [the student's] unconscious search for a father figure (to replace the father he had lost so early) he greatly admired and respected [the professor] and joined what had become a kind of 'Rhode' cult among the intelligentsia on campus."

An average student, Erhard studied the requisite subjects of a liberal arts education. Following graduation he was drafted into the army and after the war became an orthopedic surgeon—a profession which he also practiced from 1970 to 1971 as a volunteer at a union-owned Israeli hospital. In his words: "The rest, as they say, is history."

A former government-licensed ski instructor, Frank Schloss of Austria left Scattergood Hostel on the same day as Erhard Winter—but had not nearly as much luck as the *Sonntagskind*. The experiences of the 30-ish trained auto mechanic[9] provide a case in point in John Kaltenbach's inability to find meaningful employment for his charges. Leaving the hostel on 25 July 1939—two days after the arrival of placement director appointee Giles Zimmemmn—Frank first went to work for a farmer as a hay-baling hand, but according to him "that didn't work out too well" and he soon returned to the hostel. By this time over-burdened, John had been relieved of job placement by Giles. By the end of September persuasive Giles had coaxed Friend Howard Hampton of Whittier—a crossroads Quaker settlement a day's horse-and-wagon ride north of the one at West Branch—to pay Frank pocket money plus room and board for working in his auto garage. Realizing the "job" was little more than a pleasant, paying apprenticeship for learning how to work on big American-made cars, Frank moved to Cedar Rapids in February 1940 for a Dodge dealership position which never materialized, forcing him to sell coffee door-to-door for the Great American Tea Company. He trundled the many miles necessary to peddle enough beans to earn a few pennies through August, when he became a live model for the University of Iowa's Art Department. The following January he received an offer from someone whom he had met in Cedar Rapids: the said position involved minding a sporting goods store and giving ski lessons in Flagstaff, Arizona. Frank manned the counter and slopes until being drafted into the U.S. Army's 10th Mountain Division in December 1942, at which point he became a ski instructor for his company. When it left for battle, he became an interpreter at a German prisoner-of-war camp in Hale, Colorado. Marrying in November 1944 a "young lady" he had met at a United Service Organization [USO] dance in Denver, Frank moved with his bride into civilian housing at the camp and they stayed there till he was discharged in October 1945. Still without steady employment six years and one month after having left Scattergood for the last time, Frank returned to Flagstaff where he assumed he could resume his former line of work. But, "not finding the job I was supposed to have open, I was forced to work in Service Stations, here & there, nothing steady, until Jan 1948. I then obtained a job as an Explosive Operator at the Ordnance Dept, near Flagstaff, starting at $.95/hr. I worked my way up thru the next 26 years to the job of Quality Control Inspector, retiring from it in July 1974 & for 2-1/2 years kept on working in a Camera Shop in Flagstaff." Despite the less-than-ideal experience he had in trying to find rewarding work in America, Frank Schloss felt satisfied enough to conclude his account of his ordeal with the bold summary, "This is the story of a Scattergood hostel Guest."

Adults may have been difficult to place, but young people at the hostel still of college age had an easier time finding a foothold in the American job scene. Not all were as luck-prone as Herr Winter, but most who wanted to study found a place. Arriving at West Branch only five days after Frank Schloss did, "fun" Gerry Schroeder of Hamburg received a scholarship to attend Oskaloosa's Quaker-founded William Penn College, while his mother Herta established a boarding house in Iowa City and translated scientific texts to earn extra income; Gerry later served in the army. Budapest native Lothar Gidro-Frank came to Scattergood "primarily to study" for the entrance exams of the State University of Iowa's College of Medicine, which the 26-year-old hoped to enter in fall 1942. Similarly, the "good-natured, friendly" German Jew Irving Blumenkranz took a short-term job in Corning, Iowa, upon leaving Scattergood, with the idea of later finding a way to go to medical school; Corning's Hotel Bacon paid him "full maintenance and $50 per month." Of course other subjects attracted other students, with Donald Hopf of Aachen selling pencils and working in an orchard until Des Moines' Drake University awarded him a scholarship—with which he hoped to become a certified public accountant.[10] Eighteen-year-old Peter Schick of Vienna sojourned at Scattergood twice; he left the first time to work on the Clampitt farm near New Providence for "maintenance and $2.00 pocket money each week," the second time to attend the Western State Teacher's College in Kalamazoo, Michigan—only to have to discontinue his studies when the army called him to be a signal operator at Camp Crowder in Missouri. Berliner Peter Siedel ["Seadle"]—who AFSC's Jean Reynolds called "the perfect refugee"—also studied for a time in Iowa City,[11] then found a "grand job" in Detroit. One of the luckiest in the wave of students who floated out of Scattergood onto other shores, Friedrich Lichtman ["Fritz," later "Fred Lister"] accepted a college fellowship which led him to become a research chemist at Chicago's Institute of Gas Technology.

Having already studied in Italy and France, once in America Ernst Malamerson assumed himself excluded from a university career because he had the impression that one needed to be a citizen, have a command of the language and some money. As it turned out, however, "Scattergood was for me quite important because of Giles [Zimmerman] and others"—as Giles helped him enter the University of Iowa, where he eventually earned a master's degree in economics. While a student he took odd jobs (dishwashing, etc), as well as got a modest scholarship. It was at the suggestion of Kurt Schaefer's friend and colleague, Gustav Bergmann, that Ernst took his mother's maiden name, as the exiled professor was "a little obsessed with Americanization, basically for fear of anti-Semitism... When he learned of my mother's [maiden] name he said 'change to that: it's more American'. I did." Perhaps mirroring the experiences of other student refugees at Scattergood, Ernst explained: "[Scattergood] served an extremely useful function, but [the one] it served was more incidental than planned. For me, for instance, I doubt that I would have ever have—on my own—got in touch with academic life: I was too lost... I had been under considerable stress in Europe and when I came here I suffered from a very mild, prolonged breakdown. I just didn't know what to do with myself: I was totally disoriented. In some way Scattergood helped me to find myself in some sense, then the university... I had some difficulties originally, but in a sense I was launched and I just knew more or less a direction in which I wanted to move in and I had no real difficulties after that. But [this function of Scattergood's] was incidental. I was very friendly both with Giles and particularly Lynn [Zimmerman] and I think that saved me. That helped me and I felt accepted by them. I didn't feel accepted by the community of fellow refugees, but that was really because they didn't accept so much each other..."

Leaving Iowa, Ernst hitch-hiked to New York and became a University of Pennsylvania fellow. After the United States entered World War II he worked for government agencies, including the Office for War Information. He then taught at a university on Long Island before landing a post in economics at New York University. Besides being a trained psychoanalyst, he also engaged in philosophy. His last job was as professor of jurisprudence and public policy at Fordham University's law institute located at New York's Lincoln Center.[12]

One other student, Peter Lustig of Germany, also came to Scattergood wanting higher education. His goal? To become a veterinarian.[13] Two or three days after arriving at the hostel on 25 June 1941, Peter left to find the hands-on knowledge required of a competent animal doctor. He later wrote about this adventure in an essay titled "A New Yorker Goes Rural":

Anybody who has lived in New York for any length of time has probably experienced, at one time or another, the desire to live in the peaceful and unrestricted atmosphere of the countryside. In my particular case this desire was enhanced by a natural love for animals. It was for that reason that I decided to start in on a new way of life in the Middle-Western [sic] farm region.

Since Iowa is one of the great cattle states, I decided to make it my future home state with the view of practicing veterinary medicine there. As a background it was thought advisable that I should have some experience in practical farm work. I was fortunate enough to be apprenticed to Mr. Sam Hegarty of Stanwood, Iowa, who became to me a friend and father rather than an employer. To me as a city dweller farm life was a new experience, but strange as my new surroundings seemed to me at first, the friendly people of Stanwood soon made me feel like an old farmhand. I began to appreciate the problems and the outlook of the farmer. I had an opportunity to do every kind of work which has to be done on a farm, from washing dishes to milking cows. I do not think I shall ever forget the first time that I attempted to milk a cow. It was probably just as tough on the cow as on me that first day in June, but even I finally got the hang of the technique.

How to spend the evenings proved itself to be no problem at all. Anybody, especially someone not used to this type of exercise, is very happy to be able to retire early after having put in a full day's work from 4:30 in the morning till 7:00 at night. Of course some evenings were spent pleasantly and profitably at Farm Bureau meetings designed to give an opportunity to the farmer to discuss his problems with neighbors and experts for the benefit of the community. Occasional visits to Bever Park furnished an interruption of the daily farm routine. Another experience which proved to me to be new and useful was the All Iowa State Fair in Cedar Rapids. I was much impressed by the excellent livestock show and by the newest machinery which the industry provides as a valuable help to the farmer. The daily routine at Mr. Hegarty's farm started with milking cows early in the morning. After a substantial breakfast we then proceeded to do the chores. By that time it was usually about 10:00 and we began the work in the field. Dinner furnished a pleasant interruption. Refreshed by a short siesta we resumed our tasks such as making hay or threshing. As the day drew to its end we experienced the satisfying sensation of having well completed an important day's job.

Now as the summer ends I realize that it takes more than just a two months experience to get even a superficial knowledge of farming. That, like every other trade, is a highly skilled occupation in which it takes years to acquire a thorough knowledge. I shall make it my business to see to it that in coming summers I add more to my knowledge of farming.[14]

Of course every party sees the same event from a different perspective: what did the Hegarty family of Cedar County think of their exotic guest from faraway Europe?[15] Tellingly, almost five and a half decades years later, Sam Hegarty's son Paul recalled only positive, humorous aspects of Peter's visit—appropriately, given that their greenhorn farmhand's surname means "funny" in German. Paul remembered three incidents in particular. One time, for example, Peter tried to "help" Hazel Hegarty wallpaper an upstairs bedroom, but instead stepped in the wallpaper-paste bucket. Another time he declared the oft-broken grain binder to be a relic from before the Civil War. The richest image, though, involved the gooey quagmire that is an Iowa barnyard in spring: Peter once slogged his way across a cow lot, carrying a basket of feed to dump into a bunk, when the muck suddenly sucked his boots off and he walked right out of them.

Having been—like Peter—about 22 at the time, Paul did note that his parents, who liked their guest immensely, said privately that the would-be vet was "very intelligent but had trouble with everyday life." Did these earthbound Iowa farmers—who rented 200 acres of some of the world's richest loam and had to work it from sunup to sundown in blizzard and in drought—mean that he had difficulty grasping simple concepts, or rather that existential burdens seemed to bear on him on a daily basis? If they intended to suggest the latter, perhaps it was no wonder, given the Nazi nightmare in which he had lived in Germany and with which the Hegartys simply could not empathize or perhaps could not believe.

Regardless of the gauntlet Peter had endured in Europe, in America his chances of realizing his dream of becoming a veterinarian were good—which, if he was of Jewish descent,[16] would have been impossible in the Third Reich, where "non-Aryans" ultimately had to abandon *all* professions. After his stint of walking out of workboots, Peter began studies at William Penn College. The following summer he returned to Scattergood for a three-week stay, then enrolled in a veterinary course at Iowa State College in Ames, where he boarded with a Quaker couple, Edward and Minne Allen. Upon being drafted into the army, the hostel staff lost track of this ambitious animal lover.

Students in any country need teachers—even teachers from abroad, men and women with funny accents and "wild" ideas. This being the case, some Scattergood refugees were able to locate teaching positions which provided meaningful employment. Of varying duration and on different levels, teaching assignments tapped previous skills and knowledge for present application. Whether they were showing others how to do the breast stroke or explaining how to calculate the circumference of Mars, the one-time hostel guests were able to act as valued sources of new facts, ideas or experiences.

The first to find a teaching job was the "marvelous pianist and joker whom everybody adored," 30-ish Gunther Meyer of Hamburg. He left for Cedar Falls—home of the Iowa State Teachers College [later, University of Northern Iowa]—where "the community...has taken an interest in him and he is now getting board and room free of charge... He has a few piano pupils, does some accompanying work, gives a few concerts in the neighborhood, and thus earns a little money to take care of his expenses, etc. His situation is not ideal, but at least he is not going into debt, and as soon as he gets more pupils, (probably when school starts again) he will be all right." Within 11 months, however, he had an address with the Allen Company of Marshalltown. By the end of 1942, the former bank worker and concert pianist surfaced in Camp Barkeley near Abilene, Texas; after the war Erhard Winter saw him selling "phonographs" in a New York City shop, the Record Hunter.

Awarded subsistence posts as instructors, the Austrian couple Ludwig and Kaethe Unterholzer—later "Underwood" and both in their 30s—went from West Branch to Versailles, Kentucky, in autumn 1939. There "Lucas" taught music appreciation and piano, "Catherine" gymnastics and swimming at Margaret Hall School in exchange for "maintenance" and $50 per month. Apparently they came to miss the flat openness of the Hawkeye State, for the next summer the "friendly, rather sophisticated pair" left the rolling hills of the Bluegrass State and worked as camp counselors at Camp Foster near Iowa's Lake Okoboji,[17] where they got "maintenance and $50.00 per month, with a nice vacation thrown in free!"

Following the Underwoods, it took nearly a year before the next guest found a teaching job. A Vienna native, Grete Baeck capitalized upon the acting tricks she had learned as an actress in Berlin, for while still at Scattergood she worked part-time as stage manager at the Iowa City High School. In July 1940 the short, gray-haired Grete found a full-time position as the children's drama director at Omaha's Jewish Community House, for which she got $50 per month and free housing. Evidently that less-than-leading role didn't suffice, for by February 1943 she was selling "Ladies' Dresses" in Nebraska's largest city. By that time she also had completed a screenplay about Scattergood Hostel which she christened "Give Us This Day," which Grete said "shows Scattergood and my experience in America. I dedicated it to the Quaker organization." It could not have been easy for this *Grande Dame* of the stage to end up a big-name nanny for would-be child stars in Omaha. As Camilla Hewson Flintermann saw her, Grete was "a bit uppity, not comfortable with her status as 'refugee'"; could she have been any more comfortable stranded in a city with few bright lights, hardly a social page and no stellar directors? What did it mean to end up so far removed from the exciting metropolis of a young Viennese girl's fanciful dreams? How does the heart cope with the loss of such glamorous visions for one's life? Does life end only when the pulse stops?

Others who sought to be engaged in education-related work fared better than luckless Grete. Another Vienna native, Egon "Joe" Mauthner had been manager of the Austrian capital's *Schönophon*, so was no stranger to media when Chicago's Bell and Howell hired him as an editor in its Film Division Department which produced "educational films for nationwide use in schools, clubs, churches, homes." Fred Altman of Breslau also headed for the Windy City, where he worked for the International Correspondence School and his wife Maria—a former Russian dance instructor—found a job in the radiology department of Chicago's Mount Sinai Hospital; the couple later moved to Ottumwa, Iowa, and Maria worked in the Sunny Slope Sanito-

236

rium's lab as an x-ray technician before they moved once more, to Maywood, California. While her husband George led the ultimately unsuccessful life of a ski instructor and then worked in the Inspection Department of the National Jet Company in Cumberland, Maryland, "Mary" Scheider taught Spanish and later took "a responsible position" at Princeton's Educational Testing Service; the two eventually divorced—which one might have anticipated, given that she had felt the need to write letters in secret for fear of raising her husband's ire.

Scattergood guests did not always have to leave Iowa to find teaching posts. Walter Baron of Berlin and Sonia Braun of Warsaw taught at the State University of Iowa. Vienna-born Peter Grunwald (later "Greenwood") completed graduate studies in economics at the University of Nebraska in Lincoln with the help of "an instructorship which [freed] him from tuition and fees and [paid] him a small salary." After leaving Lincoln he taught at Ames' Iowa State College [today, Iowa State University] before joining the army.

But what of "real" teaching jobs—full-salaried, longer-term ones? They existed, too, although it was exactly the short-term ones which oft turned into lasting positions.[18] Forty-seven-year-old Julius Lichtenstein, for example, took his family to Saint Paul, Minnesota, in August 1942 to supervise a dormitory at Boys' Town, a famous chain of private juvenile-correction facilities scattered across Middle America. In the course of the war he later found work training soldiers in the use of his mother tongue at the University of Minnesota, which in turn led to a professorship of German at Saint Paul's Macalester College—a chair which included teaching Italian and French to music students. Once a judge and outspoken *Sozialdemokrat* sympathizer, Julius remained at that Presbyterian-founded institution of learning until 1956 and in the late 1960s he and wife Elizabeth[19] moved to Waltham, Massachusetts, to be near their then-married daughter Edith and to enjoy the cultural resources offered by Brandeis University.

Theodor "Ted" Frankl couldn't decide on an acceptable "Anglo" spelling of his name—at various times also writing it "Frankel," "Fraenkl," "Frank" or "Franck"—but the young man from Vienna did decide to accept a request to teach Spanish and French at Saint Joseph College in Rensselaer, New York. Downriver in Peekskill, Magda Shostal eventually located a position—also teaching languages and also at a church-sponsored school. A third Vienna native, Viktor Popper, left Scattergood to become a piano teacher and music educator—not on the Hudson like his two compatriots, but in Evanston, Illinois. According to Margaret "Peg" Hannum Stevens, the Friends Meeting there "'underwrote' him to some extent."[20] In April 1943 Viktor was able to write of his lot: "I think I may be well satisfied with my success as a piano teacher and music educator here, concerning the results as well as the number of my pupils, which is slowly and steadily increasing. It is nine at present and there may be a few more before the summer. I hope to be in a position to rent a studio in the fall."

A sympathetic sister of education, social work also attracted some of the guests at Scattergood Hostel—not to mention some of the children there when they became adults. Marianne Welter, for example, had collaborated in Berlin with the renowned social *Padagog* Walter Friedlander in a day-care center for unemployed youth; in the United States, she decided to pursue related work. First she underwent undergraduate training at the University of Chicago's School of Social Work Administration—by coincidence during Earle Edwards' last year of graduate studies there—and spent a summer as housemother at the Ridge Farm Preventorium near Deer Park, Illinois.[21] Returning to her studies in fall 1942, Marianne did graduate work at Cleveland's Western Reserve University and worked at a settlement house in the same city, then moved to New York, where she became the first white staff member of a residential Afro-American school. Following the war she returned to Germany with the Unitarian Service Committee as director, first of a hostel for displaced children from various countries,[22] and later of a retraining program for German social workers who had been certified by the Nazi regime. After half a decade she returned to Cleveland to earn a doctorate, then moved to New York to research the degree to which inter-racial or -cultural adoptions succeeded or failed. Thereafter Marianne worked at Long Island's Adelphi University, where she started a program to train undergraduates to become masters of social work after one year.

Hans and Heid Ladewig had not been happy with their placement as social workers at the Kickapoo Friends Mission near McCloud, Oklahoma, but at least they had a more direct transition to that field than did Hans Peters of Dresden and Berlin. Upon leaving Scattergood in late April 1940 he accepted an assignment working for the Des Moines landscape architecture firm of Robinson & Parnham, where he lived upstairs in the concern's "attractive office building on Grand Avenue." Although he had "some years of gardening experience," he worked "with little pay [$25 per month] but my complete needs cared for." In Des Moines he became a valued part of the extensive Hewson "family" and applied for membership in the capital city's Friends meeting. Two years later he married Camilia Hewson's artist friend Doris Holly. After later serving in the U.S. Army in Mississippi and Florida, he attended Wayne State University in Detroit, where he majored in social work. From Michigan the couple moved again within the Midwest—this time to Rockford, Illinois, where for 18 years Hans worked as a counselor in the public high schools until his retirement in 1971. Until the end of his life Hans remained interested and involved in community issues such as conflict resolution and race relations. He and his family lived according to the principles of "voluntary simplicity" and chose to live in a racially mixed, low-income housing cooperative as testimony to their belief in social justice.

One in the seemingly endless series of Austrians to arrive at Scattergood, (John Kaltenbach once sent a cable to AFSC begging them to "STOP SENDING VIENNESE. SEND MONEY INSTEAD."), Martha Schmidl left the hostel "with much regret." Her regret could not have lasted too long, however, as the very fortunate Martha did so to take an "attractive position" in New York, with the assignment of collecting data on social and working conditions of laborers in various countries and preparing a comparative study from the data. Of her post she wrote: "I like this kind of work, I am very much interested in the results, and am happy that I finally achieved it to work in a line that is close to that I was in in Europe."

Like education and social work, medicine consists very much of human service—albeit oft better paid than the other two—and numerous Scattergood guests found work in the domain of healing the body. In June 1942 the Adlers left West Branch for nearby Oakdale to take positions at a state-run sanitorium—Alfred as a resident physician, Martha as a junior nurse. The pair obviously struck a spot deep in the hearts of their fellow hostelites for during the farewell party held in their honor Alfred was dubbed "Master of the Arts of Cantankerous Gadgets and Doctor of the Philosophy of Domestic Boondoggling," Martha the "Master of [the dog] Mackie's Mysterious Meanderings and Doctor of Culinary and Laundry Science." On 18 March 1943 the couple gave birth to a daughter, Susan Dorothy Adley—the Anglicized version of "Adler" which they chose to use—"a bonny baby [who] looks for all the world like her Daddy."

While still at Scattergood, Lucy Selig had worked at the State University Hospital in the Psychopathic Clinic and after she and her family moved to Dayton, Ohio—where Ernst cut meat for the National Food Market—she earned a bachelor's degree at the university there, presumably in a related field. The "very pleasant, quiet" Moscow-native Eugenia Landycheff accepted a laboratory assistant position at Beth-El Hospital in Brooklyn upon leaving the hostel in November 1941, then sometime in 1942 switched to an opening in "Public Health Research of the City of New York"; an older socialist, following the war she had an address at the Home of Holy Comforter in Grand Concourse, New York. The newly married Paul Singer was mentioned as a "helper in private operation rooms" at New York's Mount Sinai Hospital and Rosa Schiffman as "working long hours in her hospital job" in the same city. Grete Rosenzweig, who had "a short training before [coming] to this country," did practical nursing during vacations from her dietetic assistant job at Eureka College in Illinois and helped medical doctors deliver babies; after her retirement she volunteered as a handicrafts instructor in the pediatrics ward of the Yale-New Haven Hospital and attended dressmaking classes.[23] In a medical-related field, upon landing a speech correction spot at Childrens Memorial Hospital, Francis Harvey of Vienna took his wife Anny and 6-year-old daughter Lislotte to Chicago in April 1942. Margot Weiss of Berlin moved to Chicago and Allentown, Pennsylvania—working briefly as a photographer's receptionist—before settling in New York, where she passed an examination which qualified her as a registered masseuse.

Very different from the world of human service, various guests at the hostel gravitated toward that of business. The first one recorded as having left the hostel to follow a commercial line of work, Vienna-born Ewald Peissel tried his hand as an assistant at the Ginsberg family's Credit Jewelry Company in Cedar Rapids.[24] Starting there on 25 April 1940, he lost the job[25] on 6 July and returned to West Branch, where he stayed until 23 September. He then set out to find his fortune in the nearest metropolis, Chicago.

The next refugees to try their hand at business were the Benndorfs, Elly and Oskar from Hamburg;[26] both in their 40s, she did alterations at Blum's Department Store in Chicago, he sales for the United Grocers Association. Also engaged in an Illinois retail firm, middle-aged, former-lawyer Leo Keller moved to Sterling in 1941 to "learn the grocery business"; by April 1943, he switched to working with "a big jewelry firm" in Chicago which had "a defense job for the armed forces and Leo [had begun work with] dyeing and cutting belts and suspenders...in the factory. He [attended] an accounting course in the evening as an essential prerequisite for some future plans." Also in the Land of Lincoln, the Weilers moved to Silvis in fall 1940; Gus cut meat or staffed the sales department of Tri-City-Packing —depending on his employer's needs—while Rosl found unspecified work in nearby Rock Island. Down the road in Danville, Illinois, once French-born "Jack" Shumaker had settled in at the Meis Brothers Department Store[27] he sent for 6-year-old Monique and her mother Mariette, whom the Meis family also hired; the family later moved to White Plains, New York. Berlin native Ernst Turk—a former judge—took a job in January 1943 in the Foreign Department of Kroch's Bookstore in Chicago by day and studied law by night; in 1944 he listed his address as with the Flitcraft family in River Forest, Illinois. A German Catholic from Bielefeld in his late 40s, Otto Dreyer followed the flood of Scattergood guests flowing toward Chicago. In April 1943, he worked "as an accountant [with a] forwarding company" and took an evening course in "Higher Accounting" at the LaSalle Extension University. By then, the "quite reserved...very kind, thoughtful" Otto had married a woman named Annie. In a city apparently full of German-speaking refugees, 60-ish Ernst Feibelman added one more to their number when he left Scattergood for a "position in an insurance company" in Chicago.[28]

Some guests turned to self-employment as a means of self-maintenance. The scale of their enterprises, however, differed. On a micro-level, Rudi Schreck first went to Corning, Iowa, as night clerk at Hotel Bacon, a "small country inn" where he earned $30 salary per month and "about $15.00 per month in tips"; when that did not last he sold Fuller brushes in Iowa City until finding a "position" in the army and marrying some time before 1944. Late in the hostel's existence, Pole Michael Krauthamer took his wife Ellen and their son Gunther ("George") to Duluth, Minnesota, in January 1943 to open a restaurant,[29] which reportedly went "quite well" but evidently didn't catch the imaginations of Northlanders quite enough, for by 1944 the family moved to Kew Gardens in Queens, New York.[30] In America's next largest city, Julius Neuman of Budapest started training in a new profession, watch-making—an art which he practiced first in Chicago, then in Cincinnati. Theodor Tuerkel of Vienna competed with Julius, as he also took up watch-making in the Windy City; unlike Julius, "Ted" rejoined a wife who had been living there. Meanwhile in New York, confection-connoisseur Claire Hohenadl-Patek tried to fill a niche in the market catering to the American sweet tooth: first working in the famous Helene Rubinstein Kitchens of Man-hattan, she then was "a partner in a new business [which made] *Oblaten* and candies." Her new compatriots' teeth must not have been sweet enough, though, because by April 1943—three years after leaving Scattergood—she had swapped apron for hard hat, as the "dumpy and plain" matron from Vienna found herself a foreign-born "Rosie the Riveter" in a machine fac-tory. A few hours away by train, the former German leftist Ernst Stahl opened a modest electrical business in bourgeois Swarthmore—a suburban Quaker stronghold outside Philadelphia—where customers "considered [him] a capable, dependable person to take care of household electrical prob-lems."[31] Stanislav Braun—although a trained statistician and economist—learned the economics of American small business and opened a typewriter repair shop in Minneapolis, Minnesota, while his bio-chemist wife Sonia took a research position in a laboratory. Klaus Asher of Berlin—according to Walter Shostal "intelligent and high strung," as well as wont to dye his hair "a very yellow blond, maybe to look a little more Aryan"—left the hostel to start a phonograph record business in Chicago.

A sweaty cousin of commerce, manufacturing also employed a number of one-time Scattergood Hostel refugees. The first to find such a job was Arthur Drake, who left with wife Ellen[32] in September 1939 for Moline, Illinois, where he worked as a tool engineer and designer for one of the world's largest agricultural machinery producers, John Deere.[33] A year and a month later the next to leave was Vienna Catholic Adolf Beamt—later "Albert Beam"; with wife Karoline ("Lisa"), he moved to Chicago and worked as an engineer—paid at $25 per month—for the Peerless Air Conditioning Company; "sweet...gently reared" Lisa made a home for her family, which soon included baby Stephen.[34] Until the young Vienna native was drafted into the 1st Platoon at Camp Croft in South Carolina, Adolf "Gus" Bardach worked for the Earl Kellogg Construction Company in Des Moines at $3 per day.[35] A trained electrical engineer who by then was in his 50s, Berliner Wilhelm Feist eventually[36] accepted a job in his field with Wheelco Instruments in Rock Island, Illinois. A manufacturer of paper bags in his hometown of Vienna, Richard Guttmann, 56, left Scattergood in February 1940 for Saint Louis, Missouri, to "work with paper boxes"; single, Jewish and according to Camilla Hewson Flintermann "not especially popular—perhaps a bit 'prickly'" [upon his arrival in autumn 1939 she described him as "tall and looks like Kaiser Wilhelm!"], he withdrew from the hostel family following his departure. Although not manning a conveyor belt, 30-something Otto Joachim of Vienna did work at Minneapolis' Motor Power Equipment Company—but as bookkeeper and accountant, at the very handsome rate of $85 per month. Also from the city of waltzes on the Danube, 27-year-old Paul Schwarz sold dry goods at Chicago's Goldblatt Department Store[37] before switching to manufacturing—but in the payroll-personnel department of the J. Greenbaum Tanning Company of Chicago and Milwaukee; a "handsome and gracious young single man," in Europe Paul had been a member of the War Resisters' League for 11 years and at Scattergood he had been sweet on his tutor, Ruth Carter.

"Wilhelm Leitersdorfer"—later Willy Layton[38]—had been "handyman de luxe" at Scattergood, but left that role for a more lucrative position[39] in steel-tool manufacturing in Burlington, Iowa—where wife Hedy went to work as a nurse and later professionally made slip covers. Women were indeed engaged in industry during the war, as 50-ish Günther Tradelius discovered upon getting "a new job, working in a factory with 40 girls, keeping eight machines in order"—as the "very congenial, competent" Hamburg native described his situation, writing from Illinois' metropolis. Having left Scattergood to accept a shared management position at the Iowa-City Jewish community's Hillel House, the older Austrian couple Jakob and Melanie Winkler later also went to Chicago, where the Scully-Jones Company employed Jakob as a draftsperson. His compatriot Karl Polzer landed a hand-and-machine compositor job at a New York printing plant. Similarly, Charles Bukovis (née Karl Bukowitz) secured a position in the Second City "with the finest art printing Company [sic] of America," where he had "a very interesting and responsible office job, pretty fair pay and...a social and business position which I would not change with anything I used to be in the old country."

Franz Nathusius found work in a factory-warehouse in Hammond, Indiana. A former judge and a relative of the Rosenzweigs, Walter Lenzberg worked in the accounting department of a Chicago clothing factory by day; having dazzled the other hostelites with his magic tricks and having indulged his harmonica and piano skills while at Scattergood, once he rejoined the working world Walter took up more serious pastimes—such as attending night courses in accounting at Northwestern University; Walter had been at the hostel alone while his wife Lisl worked at the Ridge Farm Preventorium near Chicago (coincidentally with Nora and Hedwig "Omi" Hackel), but when the two reunited, she found a new job as a clinical secretary in a hospital.

Scattergood Hostel's track record in placing its guests in professional positions contained extreme examples. For every Boris Jaffe or Frank Schloss there was a Martha Schmidl or Louis Croy. Born as Ljubover Koropatnicky, the latter was a young Jewish lawyer[40] from Vienna who fled to America in his late 20s. After leaving the haven provided by Friends, Louis enrolled in law courses at Washburn College in Topeka, Kansas—on a scholarship—and later at the University of Wisconsin in Madison. Upon graduation a law firm in Manitowoc—"the best (earning)...in this part of the state"—hired him. A happy Louis wrote back "home" to Scattergood: "I am very fond of my job, and, as a matter of fact, I never have liked a job better. I am quite successful, and my work is appreciated by the members of the firm. However, I am not yet a member of the Bar, since I am not a citizen."

On the other extreme were cases like that of Lothar and Edith Leiter, who stayed at Scattergood. An older Austrian couple, he had been a doctor in the Old World but could find no professional placement in the New one. They finally went to Sioux City, Iowa, where their son Herbert had some sort of "practice." Of similar age and background, the Winklers and Schiffmans also needed multiple stays at the hostel—two and three, respectively—before they secured lasting living arrangements.

If not for reasons of advanced age, cases of advanced mental disturbance also hindered placement efforts. Leo Jolles—an Austrian Catholic who fell into a fist fight with Emil Deutsch upon making an anti-Semitic remark while digging a ditch—proved to cause a series of problems for the Scattergood staff. Besides the fact that he had "a mad crush" on Mildred Holmes, he was—according to Camilla Hewson Flintermann—"obviously unstable [and] should not have been sent" to the hostel. Small in stature and "with a sort of smarmy 'Uriah Heep' manner," Leo sent a chill down the backs of many a hostelite and drew the attention of even AFSC staff in faraway Philadelphia. Despite that, by 9 February 1940 Leo seemed ready to set off in pursuit of employment: in reality this was to be a foray in which he terrorized other would-be victims with his externalized internal struggles. As *all* departing guests received an official send-off, even "problem child" Leo got his, a "Leo-Festival" where he received "a wonderful Diploma [created by Camilla and] signed by all members of the Scattergood family and then—at Leo's request 'Othello' is performed again by Mildred [Holmes] Camilla [Hewson], Karl [Liebman] & Hans [Peters] and John [Kaltenbach] as orchestra. Needless to say that it was a great success. After the play we have tea and sandwiches in the living room and sing a Farewell-Song to our Leo."

Leo left the hostel to work as a "handy man for an old couple" who ran a hotel in Iowa City but that trial ended in "disaster"—one so severe that it prompted Mary Rogers on 8 March to advise hospitalization for Leo, which the staff rejected as an idea which "wouldn't work at all." He returned to the hostel long enough to be driven by Giles Zimmerman "to Mt. Vernon 'for a visit' till he gets a ticket to go back to New York." A fortnight later Giles escorted Leo to New York and delivered him "safely into the arms of his brother-in-law," but shortly thereafter Leo dropped back into the lives of the folks at Scattergood—unannounced and unwelcome. On 26 March a Camilla filled with fear wrote in her journal:

We have had a few bad moments lately—last night John [Kaltenbach] called a special staff meeting after he got a phone call from a woman in Cedar Rapids who wouldn't give her name. She wanted references for Leo before giving him a job—something is fishy apparently, and neither party got much information, but John asked her to write him, and she agreed to do so. Our friend seems to have kept his threat of returning to Iowa, despite his brother-in-law's assurances that he would not. We called Reed Cary, who advised a lawyer within 48 hours of getting the letter. We have no more legal responsibility for Leo, but practically, he's our baby! Believe me we were nervous when John reported that a man ran into the ditch [on the road north of the hostel's building site] as he passed in the car last night. If it were Leo, his friends the Cs would put him up, and that's just around the corner! Anyhow, we made Mildred put a chair under her doorknob last night. We don't know if Leo is in Cedar Rapids (or here) but if he has gotten this far, there's no telling what he may intend to do further...

Despite the staff members' worst fantasies, Leo did not return to stalk the "lovely blond single [Mildred], gracious and strong." More than five decades later, however, Camilla vividly recalled that he "really worried us for a while" and accused him of "threatening instability"; she did note that "so far as I know, Leo was the only such 'problem guest,' however." Oddly, Leo later wrote "home," reporting in April 1943 that he had gotten a raise—without specifying in what line of work—and that he had gotten married. Thereafter he disappeared.

But what was it like to be a mean in the range of experiences—to be neither charmed with sudden success nor destitute and dependent on family and friends[41] due to financial weakness or mental illness? How was it for the "average" refugee, that woman or man who suffered a series of low-paying, drudgery-filled jobs in order to find an acceptable New-World occupation? The majority of those whose lives were followed through 1944—the publication date of a special *Scattergood News Bulletin* issue at least a year after the hostel's closing—seemed to have had at least two, if not three or more positions since the one they accepted upon leaving the AFSC project at West Branch. The majority of those of whom some record exists following the war years and into the 1950s and '60s, however, settled into a long-term career, which suggests that the newcomers simply needed at least a minimal amount of time before becoming familiar enough with the American occupational world to find their niche in it.

Vienna-born Walter Shostal is a case in point. From a bourgeois family and later successful in business, during his first years of immigration he floundered professionally—understandably. In France he had spoken the local language well and lived close enough to his family in Vienna to carry on in the same line of work which he and his brother had developed. He arrived in the United States, however, with very little English and hardly any commercial contacts. Moreover, he and Magda were only two of thousands of refugees seeking employment in New York—a city awash with refugees. Walter's work-seeking experiences in America, then, perhaps mirror those of others who landed at Scattergood—those "typical" guests who knew neither uncommon good luck nor genuine destitution.

Upon the family's arrival in New York in late fall 1941, they had but $10 in hand—and $1,600 in debt from money Walter's brother Robert had loaned him for the passage from Lisbon: "a large amount of money at the time, when a cup of coffee cost a nickel, and a subway or bus ride a dime." The travelers found housing at a brownstone on Manhattan's Westside called the Congress House, run by the Jewish Congress, the reform wing of New York's Jewish community. Non-practicing Walter later explained that "there were no religious service and no dietary laws observed, but still it was strange and we felt a little like cheating and eager to leave as soon as possible. Congress House was organized on a cooperative basis, with everybody sharing chores, [Magda] helping in the kitchen and me often running errands." While still living at Congress House, Walter had his "first American job...night work at a gas station pretty far out on Long Island. I had to take a subway to the end of the line and then ride a bus. I clearly remember the happy excitement I felt fighting my way through the subway crowd, most of which seemed to travel the opposite direction. After such a long period of forced idleness, I felt happy to be part of productive life again." As he was to find, however, "this first stage of productivity...did not last long, as there was not enough business to warrant keeping the station open at night. The boss instructed me not to resist in case of a hold-up; he carried insurance. The nightly take barely covered my weekly salary of 15 Dollars. No hold-up happened, but one night a customer stopped to have his flat fixed. I had no experience which prepared me for such an emergency, for I had not yet owned a car... I had neither the strength nor the know-how to pry that tire from its rim in order to get to the inner tube. My customer finally had to do the job himself, but he was a nice man; he paid for the job and gave me a tip."

Walter's night job at the gas station did not last, but he soon found another one which enabled the Shostals to move out of Congress House

—just a couple of blocks and around the corner. I was to become a "Super," which was New Yorkese for superintendent of one of the brownstone houses typical for the area; these were modest but genteel buildings—some of which had seen better days—three or four stories high, with one or two apartments to a floor. Payment consisted mainly or exclusively (I am not sure) of free rent; we had one large room on the ground floor. At the time when one owner had occupied the whole house, most likely it had served as the front parlour. There was a cooking stove in one corner. We got rudimentary pieces of furniture, also pots and pans, so we were ready to face American life; I don't remember, were they gifts or did they come from the Salvation Army? [At any rate, Magda] was expected to keep the stairways clean and to collect the garbage from the landings. She did it most conscientiously; the banister glistened with her polish and I thought she was overdoing it. To bring in a little additional cash, she also cleaned for one lady on the top floor. The woman happened to be a singer, a Wagnerian soprano who at the moment was studying the part of Brünhilde in the Walkyrie. She sang it in the original German, but did not know a word of that language; she had no idea what she was singing, so between her cleaning chores Magda provided her with a basic translation of these strange words. Did that bring a little extra cash? It did not.

Very soon the tenants discovered that it was hopeless to look to me as a general handy man to perform minor repairs for a tip. But, my main responsibility was to provide heat and that duty could not be shirked. Every morning and then again every evening I had to stoke the old-fashioned boiler that was to provide heat as well as hot water. Or rather, it should have provided them, but did not do so under my administration—despite my most conscientious efforts. I remember a scene which to an outside observer would have been hilarious. The whole population of the building assembled in the basement surrounding that recalcitrant boiler and offered each his or her own advice as to how to coax it into performing its duty.

While a "Super," I also found an additional job. More likely, [brother] Robert may have found it for me. In Vienna our business had several facets. One was providing news photos. We acted like an office for an organization called "Keystone" and covered not only Austria but everything east of there. It was not much of a market, but we did our best. This European Keystone organization was a Hungarian-owned family business, but had sprung from American roots. These roots still existed in a rather modest way in New York. They occupied half a floor, one block from Grand Central Station. They had a large and well-ordered file of photographs, the result of the production of past years, but little else.

Mrs. Van Loon (everybody called her "Mrs. Van") ran the show. There was also Mr. Sierichs, the boss—a very elderly and dignified gentleman. I never saw him doing anything else but reading the New York Times , which was followed by the Herald Tribune... Mrs. Van treated him with the respect a loving daughter reserves for her dotard father. There was also a Mr. French, who doubled as salesman and occasional photographer who took still-life or other photos which he thought the market would like. And, I completed the staff.

I had to arrive a little before regular office hours, sweep the floor, empty baskets and ash trays, and generally put things into a semblance of order. Once a week people from the building or a cleaning service would come in and do a more thorough job. Generally, I kept my activities of this kind to the absolute minimum and performed them with a feeling of rage and revolt. During the regular hours my duties were mainly those of a delivery boy. Mrs. Van was forever putting photos into envelopes which I had to drop off at offices, almost all within walking distance. A dozen blocks up or down Midtown Manhattan: that's where publishers and editorial offices were located at that time. At rare intervals when there were no errands, I had to return photos which had come back from customers to their rightful places on shelves. After all these duties were performed and if there was any time left (which happened rarely) I could sort out stories from our files which could be offered to Sunday supplements and general-interest magazines. Mr. French did not like to see me thus occupied and usually found some errand for me; he suspected a budding inside-competition.

247

Even if the conditions were not ideal, Walter had some form of employment and this made a decisive difference in his and Magda's outlooks. Still, it was not enough—and they knew it. Somehow they would have to take a blind jump into a future which they could not yet imagine. As Walter saw it:

We were in America. We were safe. We were not hungry. We did not suffer from cold—provided I had stoked that recalcitrant boiler the right way. But, I can't say we were happy. That life in our single room was far from comfortable. Mostly, there were only three of us. My mother—who with Robert lived only a few blocks away—mostly kept Claude with her. The two kids did not get on well. They never played together, but when brought together were constantly rolling on the floor. Whether it was sibling jealousy or brotherly love, it contributed to making life difficult. And foremost, there was the financial squeeze. We only could afford the barest essentials. An additional subway ride was a problem, a 5-cent cup of coffee a rare luxury. And, there was no prospect of any improvement, of a way out of it. Suddenly out of the blue there appeared one. We received an invitation to go for a time to a strange place called Scattergood Hostel in West Branch, in the state of Iowa.

As Walter would discover, Scattergood would open doors but seal no fates. He and Magda would have to do that on their own—one miserable job at a time. Later, he would never forget that "it did not take us long to decide that we would accept the offer to go to the Scattergood Hostel. Our present situation seemed like a dead end and no hope for improvement was in view. When I told Mrs. Van that I was about to quit, she was taken aback. 'Was not that an unwise decision?' What she meant: 'What sane person would in these times of the highest unemployment in American history voluntarily quit a job, modest as it was?' She probably also thought I was most ungrateful, but she was too polite and well-bred to say so." Walter continued, "I do not remember what arrangements we made to leave town. Did we put our belongings, our few pieces of furniture, our pots and pans into storage; did we return all that to the Salvation Army, where they had come from—or, did we simply abandon all that? I do not remember. I do not remember anything about our trip into the unknown, nor about our arrival there on 21 July 1942. All is blocked out and lost."

Caught in the emotional whirlwind of once again tearing up one's roots—however young and tender—the Shostals set off for new ground. Although Walter was not emotionally present and therefore later could not remember the two-day trip, the Shostal family did arrive and soon settled into daily life at Scattergood Hostel. Diving into English lessons, doing group

248

housework, making new friends and sharing a few laughs along the way, they enjoyed their new home. Despite the idyllic setting and the delicious chance to rest their taxed nerves and to regather inner strength, they soon enough were reminded of their eventual return to the world of work—which as they already well knew could be merciless and disillusioning.

The journey to some semblance of an autonomous existence would not be easy. And the difficulties began already while still in "paradise." As Walter explained years later:

> *When we were invited to the Hostel, nothing was specified as to the length of stay or where we would go from there. "You have a good rest and relax. Catch your breath after what you have been through. As to the future, we shall see." The general expectation was that the Hostel would help us to find a job and to be resettled somewhere. At least that was the general idea. It was, however, made clear that it was not desirable to go back to New York; New York was not really America, not a place where we would quickly and completely become truly American, which was the goal that our hosts had in mind and this was also the goal that we had set for ourselves. We refrained from being nostalgic for the past; we were looking to the future; we had children; like most recent arrivals, we had immediately applied for our first papers, the first step to becoming citizens five years later.*
>
> *We were happy at Scattergood. We enjoyed the peaceful surroundings, the friendly people, the relaxed mood. We were, however, also worried and tense about our future. Where would we go from here, and when would we leave? It was a strange situation; the future would not be discussed. It was kept veiled. The Hostel had been operating for a few years; "guests" had arrived and left. What had become of them? They had been settled somewhere and had been placed in jobs. What kind of jobs? It was not discussed. It seemed taboo—a little like sex in our post-Victorian morality. It was not to be discussed. It was the same with our length of stay: there was a mystery about it. The Angel of Death would give you the sign when it was time to go.*
>
> *The role of the Angel was played by Par Danforth. There was indeed something mysterious about his coming and going.[42] He was the man who was out beating the bushes to find jobs for us. He would stay at the Hostel for a few days and then be gone for weeks. It must have been a difficult assignment to find jobs for this motley group of middle-aged recent immigrants, who mostly were well-educated intellectuals. The country was still in the throes of the Great Depression; the armament of America had only begun.*

Still, Walter had to try—with Magda's encouragement and Par's help. It took some effort, though—and much culling through an array of false leads: "One time Par Danforth took me on a job-hunting trip. We went to Chicago. I suppose I had job interviews there which left no trace in my memory. We also traveled to Duluth on a terribly cold day. I had to walk a few blocks along the lake front to meet Par. I could only duck from one doorway to the next to catch my breath; were there always icy storms greeting me at each new station in my life? My interview was at a department store, but I am unsure what the job opening was. It may have been some kind of apprenticeship, which would have included sweeping the floor in the morning. Luckily, the man felt I would not do: the trip and I were a flop." Eventually Walter did find—if not a career—an occupation:

> Finally, Par found a job for me. It was in Davenport, at the eastern end of the state, part of the "Quad City" unit on the Mississippi river. My job was at a middle-sized assembly plant doing work for the government. I had a tiny room in a small house in a quiet neighborhood. Besides me were two more roomers—girls—and upstairs lived the owners. I don't remember meeting them or my paying rent; it seems the Hostel paid for it. I don't remember, either, how I managed breakfast and lunch. I had dinner at the cafeteria downtown on my way home from the plant. It was the only part of the day I enjoyed. The evenings were spent chatting with my neighbors or reading. I don't remember what I was reading, but I hope it was in English.
>
> At the plant I was under the supervision of an elderly German who was to instruct me and make me into a useful member of the work force. His conversation was not to my liking. He explained to me what a great man the Führer was and that "that man in the White House" should listen to him and not to his Jewish friends and make a quick peace: all would be well in America and everybody would have a job again—like in Germany. Otherwise, there were people who knew how to set things right; he hinted darkly that his son belonged to an organization of that kind. I don't know whether he meant the America First movement or the Bund or some other right-wingers. I kept silent.
>
> Most of our work consisted in assembling by hand fairly heavy iron units. It was not demanding work, just a little tedious. The main problem: there was not always enough of it. And, "One should not sit around, visibly idle," my instructor taught me: one of the bosses might notice it and that was no good. I was taught to take some of the assembled units apart and then begin to re-assemble them. We did not know what the destination of our assembled product would be; that it would have some defense purpose was all we knew. It looked somewhat like a

hollow tray. Somebody speculated they could be used as saddles for pack mules. I did not think so; they seemed too heavy to me. There would not be much to spare for a useful load. I knew: I had a certain experience with pack mules...

To come back from romantic Arabia to my dreary life in Davenport: one evening I was arrested by the FBI. One Saturday I was invited for dinner by people whom I had never met [Arthur and Ellen Drake]; I believe he was a former Scattergood guest who had been settled not very far from Davenport. I had to take a bus, then change to another bus. While doing so a strange, tall man told me that I was under arrest. The way I moved, the clothes I wore, my accent had made somebody suspicious, who in turn called the FBI. Remember, this was wartime and the fear of spies was quite real in the countryside. It was a long session with many questions asked, over and over again. It seemed so stupid to me. They only had to call Scattergood, to check my story and establish my identity. I suppose they did, but did not know about Scattergood, so thought it could have been a cover for a den of evil-doers. During all this questioning I got increasingly mad and told my questioners that if they wanted to catch spies and disloyal people, I could give them a good lead. I thought of my mentor at the plant and his son, but the FBI people were not interested. It was way past midnight when I arrived. My hosts were not overjoyed, but friendly enough. They fed me a cold supper and let me sleep on a couch. There was no more transportation back to Davenport that night.

Although he had an income at the factory, Walter did not have a future there. As soon as he could, he consulted his spouse and they made new plans:

Christmas of 1942 came. There was a feeling of tension and expectation around the work place. Most people were given raises. Most people seemed happy, others a bit disappointed. There was nothing additional in my envelope, as the management did not think I was much of an asset to their enterprise.

I went back to Scattergood for a weekend. [Magda] and I had a long talk. We had to make a decision. We were not told that we had to leave Scattergood, but we felt that the time had come. What should we do? That thing in Davenport seemed completely futile. That tiny room of mine could not shelter a family and the wage which I earned could not sustain me, much less the four of us. We did not like the idea, but we could not see another way but back to New York. A few weeks earlier I had written to Time *magazine, applying for an editorial job. I had a rather hazy idea what qualifications were needed for a job as a jour-*

251

nalist. I was hoping that my knowledge of European life and politics were an asset and that my newly-acquired knowledge of English might suffice. I got a polite answer from Time *magazine: if I were to come to New York, I should come by for an interview. I did not have any real hope that this promised much, but I played the optimist when talking to Martha Balderston. Reluctantly she agreed to my wish to go back; Scattergood would pay the fare. Obviously Par Danforth had given up on me as an abject failure.*

Thus, the Shostals went back East. The dispiriting problems they had left there, however, were awaiting their return. As Walter soon learned, there really was no way out but through:

I have no recollection of the trip to New York in the winter of 1942/43. Our first home there was a furnished apartment on West 110th Street, on the edge of Harlem. We paid our rent monthly, but we did not stay there long. My interview at Time *magazine had no result. I answered a number of questions, filled out a long and complicated form and was sent home with the usual "You will hear from us if...." But, I found a job anyway. It was through the supportive ethnic network mentioned earlier—a friend from Paris, a Viennese whom the children called Uncle Eric. We had gone to the* Stade de Colombes *together and been together at the camp at Melais. I found him in Marseille upon my return from the Legion and now we met in New York again.*

He worked as a sales representative at a small button factory which was owned by three brothers, friends of his whom he had known in Paris. They were an interesting family. The oldest was the organizer, the commercial leader. The second was the idea man, the inventor—always tinkering with new ideas, new materials. In the end he invented a new kind of zipper for which he got international patents. That enabled them to close the button place, which brought in only peanuts compared with the royalties which rolled in from those patents. The third brother was a nice young man. Their sister was a singer who had been prominent at the Vienna Opera; now she was star of first magnitude at the Metropolitan Opera.

I was employed as a stock clerk, regulating production and supervising two delivery men. If my memory is correct, my beginning wage was 18 Dollars a week. The possibility was discussed that I might try to work as a sales rep if I could find additional accounts, but the market—the 7th Avenue Garment Center—was already covered by the three sales people; my friend was one of them and they watched carefully that nobody would trespass onto their territory. The sales rep had

252

to show his new collection to a designer, who might select a few samples for some of his new creations, and a few weeks later they were shown to the buyers of department and retail stores. If a creation found no buyers, that was the end of it. If that piece was a success, the sales rep had to work out the price for mass production and made sure the orders did not go to a competitor who could copy the original and offer it for less money. It was a tough game, the garment business.

Once more or less securely employed, Walter could focus energies on finding a more ideal place for his family to live. His new sense of confidence in an ever-better future—a hunger-awakening first taste of that elusive American Dream—made a significant difference, as Walter

did have a job and we [thus could move] to our first real home in New York—in 1943. It was in Kew Gardens, in the borough of Queens, a 25-minute subway ride from Midtown Manhattan. It was a relief to arrive there after a day of work, to breath the slightly cleaner and cooler air, and to see the green of trees and small gardens. We had two small rooms and a sit-in kitchen where we would have our meals and could see the sky and—at a distance—even a few tennis courts. It seemed like heaven. I remember telling a friend, "If I can only raise my income to make 50 Dollars a week, I would even be able to afford a car." That friend with more experience seemed a trifle skeptical.

We began to put roots down in Kew Gardens. We met friendly neighbors, joined the PTA and joined the local Reformed Church—not out of spiritual need, but because we wanted the kids to attend Sunday school. Also, its minister was the Scout master of the troop that the church sponsored and we thought Pierre should be a Cub Scout.

As the family settled into American life in the "inner suburbs," Walter's professional fortunes continued to improve—steadily if sluggishly:

My brother Robert had a difficult time with his business venture; more than once it seemed hopeless and the few pieces of jewelry that my mother had salvaged from the Austrian shipwreck were pandered to the pawnbroker. By unbelievable stubbornness and some luck, Robert was able each time to redeem them. Today they are safely in my bank safe, not as objects of great value—which they are surely not—but as remembrances of a difficult past.

Slowly—very slowly—Robert's business prospects improved and we could envision the possibility that the agency might support two families in a modest lifestyle. In a way Robert and I made a good team. He supplied the creative instinct, the feeling for commercial possibilities, and I contributed the steady effort and clearer vision to reach those goals.

Since we could not take great risks—our financial resources being so minimal—we had to move slowly, but my bosses at the button place were cooperative. I split my working day: in the morning I worked for them, in the afternoon I moved to my brother's office. When we saw the slow but encouraging improvement due to my efforts, I made the break and bid farewell to those buttons.

Once it seemed unmistakably clear that the Shostals were thoroughly along the road to becoming members of the American middle class, Walter and Magda and sons jumped once more—this time, upriver:

About three years later we decided that it was time to move again. It was mainly because of our children. Kew Gardens was surely an improvement over Manhattan regarding healthy surroundings, but we felt the kids should spend their summers outdoors—away from city pavements—and that we could not afford. Also, [Magda] and I—while city-bred—had an intense desire for open skies and green vistas. We felt we should move to the suburbs. The problem was, we still had very little money. We soon found out that the closer suburbs where commuting was easy were beyond our means, so I had to be willing to accept a longer commute. And, we had to find a place which we could get for little cash and a high mortgage. We found such a place in northern Westchester County, near the city of Peekskill.

It was a tiny house, with kitchen and two small rooms downstairs and a somewhat-finished attic upstairs. It sat on a one-third-acre plot, shaded by two huge elm trees and bordered on one side by the traditional stone wall which had its origin in the first clearing of the land generations ago. It was part of a small community, built around a tiny pond which we called a "lake" and which was good for swimming in the summer and skating in the winter.

And the best part of it was that its owner had served in the army and there was a G.I. mortgage on the house almost to its full value. It was ideal—the one place that we could afford. We were happy and lived there for over 15 years, the longest I have ever lived in one place—except for my childhood home in Vienna. It was the life of the average suburbanite. For me it was a long commuting trip: three hours every day, five times a week, door to door—if all was well. It could be longer if there were any problems on the railroad. There was camaraderie among fellow commuters, one chatted and kept seats; there was a bridge game if one wanted. It had its special rules, with seniority strictly observed. The weekends were spent with gardening and generally working around the house. With very few exceptions, I did not take any vacations but added in summer Fridays to my weekend—a schedule at least partially prompted by financial considerations. It was an orderly, quiet and happy life.

Indeed, an "orderly, quiet and happy life": that ideal has propelled more Americans through their days than any other binding national promise, goal or characteristic of life in the New World. And most likely, many of the guests at Scattergood Hostel sought to achieve exactly that—to capture a bit of the vague albeit much-touted "American Dream" in their transitions to becoming new Americans. Insofar as they were able to survive the jump into free-fall capitalism and come out standing on their feet, the refugees who had briefly found a bit of peace on the Iowa prairies later were able to realize—somewhere in the multi-colored vastness that is the incomparable "United States"—their own corner of the Dream. It had a price, though, and most of them made down payments on it whether or not they consciously chose to. Simply to agree to live in America—and not all did, as the stories of Marie Juchacz, Fritz Schorsch, Kaethe Aschkenes, Robert Keller, Günther Krauthamer and others attest—meant to accept new social rules and living conditions. Staying put and sinking roots in America, then, meant consenting to becoming a new person.

1.) The victim of a simple medical operation gone wrong, Giles Zimmerman died on 29 April 1994, just as I began research into Scattergood Hostel's history; Par Danforth died a few months later in San Francisco: both men took to their graves knowledge of the fates of most of those who had passed through their office—stories which largely went unrecorded in any source I discovered and therefore are "lost." I deeply regret than no one had been led to preserve the Scattergood story earlier—if only by half a year.

Giles and Par, however, were not the only former hostelites to die during the course of this research. Others included Amy Clampitt (10.IX.94), Hans Peters (15.I.95) and Esther Smith Meyerding (19.II.95).

2.) Ernst also claimed that "all the Europeans that I had met basically went back to the positions they had occupied in Europe—unless they were too old. Those who were young had found a self image and lived up to that self image. Myself...when I had been in Europe my parents had been reasonably well to do and so I had always expected [to be well to do, too]. I lost the financial backing [upon coming to America], but somehow I arranged to have pretty much the career I would have had in Europe and I think that happened to most [refugees]... In my opinion, what drives you is self image... That—somehow subconsciously—is a strong force. This was true of most of the Scattergood inhabitants, except that most of them were too advanced in age to really fully adjust."

3.) One exception to this strictly enforced government decree seems to have been that of German-born Max Schiffman (age 52). A Jewish storekeeper, he left Scattergood with his wife Rosa (50), a nurse, and moved via Des Moines to New York, where in September 1942 the *Scattergood Monthly News Bulletin* reported Max as "employed in defense work and...very happy."

4.) Just nine days after John's arrival at West Branch, Sara Pemberton explained to Reed Cary that "of course John Kaltenbach has the real work to do. I called him two in one because there were to have been two Americans, but decided later it should have been even more than '2 in 1'. He is host to our many visitors, manager of the working crew [consisting of the first five refugees to arrive at Scattergood, as well as scores of volunteers—including State University of Iowa co-eds John charmed into helping with cleaning], advisor for our [Iowa Scattergood] committee work, errand boy, his own secretary, contact man with outside groups etc., but seems very capable of managing." Among others, another role he played was that of driving instructor, as entries in *The Book of Scattergood* attest: "J.E.K. and [Anne H. Martin] slipped off to give A.H.M. her first driving lesson. J.E.K.'s comment 'Boy we sure

255

came around that corner' or such." Next day: "A.H.M. drove thru West Branch. She often wonders how to stop. Her worst habit is having one foot on the gas and one on the break [sic]. [Son] Joe keeps hoping she'll give up." While risking his life to offer driving lessons, John also risked the lives of others—those in need of a haircut. *The Book of Scattergood* recorded on 18 January 1940 that "a costless haircut from John costs Ewald [Peissel] a small piece of his ear. Perhaps Ewald did not say clearly that he wished only a haircut." And, finally, John's assumed job description apparently included acting the part—in competition with the Zimmermans' terrier—of hostel clown. The same entry listed above continues: "At night John produced electricity by scuffling his soles on the carpet and then approaching with outstretched finger a person thus electrifying him calling forth volley's [sic] of laughter and so John whires [sic] like a butterfly from one to another sliding over the carpet."

5.) According to Bunge, "On a university form, after the entry 'Achievements' [the dejected man] had written 'Scarcely any.'"

6.) Bunge testified that "Schaefer was deeply involved in his article. When he gave a copy of his final draft to Professor Harold McCarty, who was chairman of the department, he was trembling and said, 'This is my reason for existence in geography.'"

7.) Evidently John Kaltenbach's heart-to-heart talk with the tongue-wagging goldsmith from Vienna had effect, as by the time of Kurt Rosegg's second departure from Scattergood his reformed social skills won the favor of at least some of the other hostelites. On the day he left someone wrote in *The Book of Scattergood* that "the last of the 'old guard' has left us, with bag, baggage and ruck-sack. He is going [to a job] which may turn out to be permanent. We wish him luck, however it develops. We shall miss his apt mockery, spicy comments, and suggestions about this, that and everything. In fact, as Regina [Deutsch] says, he will be missed 'from the kitchen to the 3rd floor.' Kurt was our epicurean, our concocter of novel remedies, our coffee-house waiter extraordinary. With his going the 'amusing committee' has lost another wheel, and Regina wonders who will now worry about educating the children and giving proper advice to the parents?"

8.) All names have been changed per "Erhard's" request.

9.) Like Frank Schloss, 22-year-old Thomas Koessler of Vienna also aimed at using his auto-mechanic training and worked as such in Cedar Rapids until being drafted. Camilla Hewson Flintermann found him to be "young and single and pleasant," but "not outstanding."

10.) As happens with even the most intelligent of students, 21-year-old Donald Hopf exhibited incredible naiveté. A concert violinist and a Jew whose father Ludwig had lost a mathematics professorship at Aachen Universität, he lacked the sophistication to see through Nazi facades of legitimacy and failed to see what their reign would mean for him or millions of other so-called non-Aryans in the Third Reich. Interviewed by the *Des Moines Register* in September 1939, he offered what later must have seemed to him most embarrassing political opinions, excerpts of which include: "No, I do not hate Hitler... I think Hitler is all right for Germany, but he should not be permitted to go beyond his lines. It probably is the WISH of refugees from Germany that the German people do not agree with Hitler. I believe, however, that at least 70 per cent, young and old, are patriotic and support him. I do not think they favor war, but they support him. I have no personal feeling against Hitler or his government. And I hope that, if someone does shoot him, it will not be a Jew. The Jews should stay out of it."

11.) Lynn Zimmerman commented on Peter's success while he was a student at the State University of Iowa: "Peter is covering himself with glory in the dramatics department at SUI, and has been given the leading role in a pacifist propaganda play to be given on Nov. 3 [1940]. He will be a German soldier...just what he left Germany to escape. It's a small world."

12.) At the time of this writing a Heritage Foundation Distinguished Scholar, Ernst had a career behind him of teaching, writing and public speaking. Books he had authored include: *Passion and Social Constraint, The Jewish Mystique, Punishing Criminals, Capitalism: Sources of Hostility, The Death Penalty, Smashing Liberal Icons* and *The U.N.: In or Out?*

13.) In 1937 at age 16, Peter went with his parents from Berlin to Italy, where after a year-long hotel management course he worked as a night clerk. In 1939 he secured an affidavit to migrate to the U.S., but his father and stepmother did not fare as well: they were aboard the ill-fated *SS St. Louis* and "when last heard from were in Amsterdam." According to a report written by Par Danforth in June 1943, "all his life [Peter] was interested in becoming a physician. His father, a pharmacist, had instilled this interest in him. Shortly after [arriving in the U.S.] he realized that it would be a very difficult career for him to pursue, particularly without funds. He was so interested in the medical profession, however, that he decided to study something closely related, that is veterinary medicine."

14.) Peter concluded his essay with a note of thanks to the sponsors of his agrarian sojourn: "An account of how I spent my summer would be incomplete without mention of the swell time which I had during my vacation at Scattergood Hostel [and that without its] assistance I would not have been able to carry out my plans. My memories of Scattergood will always remain...among the best times I had."

15.) The Hegartys were not the only Iowa farm folk exposed to the wider world through the eyes of European guests. From the end of July 1939 to mid-April 1940 the Pembertons hosted Scattergood-sponsored Kurt Salinger of Austria, who left their farm for "a regular job on a large farm in Indiana." An unsigned report of 22.VII.40 described his new workplace as "a regular farm in Goshen, Indiana, where he is receiving $25.00 per month and maintenance to start. [Kurt] writes that he is very happy there, and likes the young man who is his new 'boss'. The 'boss' likes Kurt, too, so the arrangement is most satisfactory." Presumably he worked in that predominantly Mennonite community until called to military service; listed in the *Bulletin*'s December 1942 as "in the services," in 1944 he was reported as injured in the war.

Kurt—"self-effacing and pleasant"—would be most remembered not for turning hay but a quick quip. Camilla Hewson Flintermann later remembered: "He had just arrived [at the hostel when] there was a power outage, and several of both guests and staff, both sexes, hung out on [the] living room floor, circling a kerosene lamp. Kurt walked in on the scene and looked puzzled [and] later told someone he was amazed 'because in Germany you would only see something like that in a brothel!' He was not the first or last guest to be set back on his [or her] heels by the easy friendliness and intimacy of us Americans!"

16.) Not all Scattergood guests were Jews—the Bauers, the Stahls and Hans Peters being cases in point. Of 185 individuals, only 86 are *known* to have been practicing, converted (à la *Madames* Seligmann/Seaman and Lichtenstein) or ethnic Jews. In some instances—for example with "typically Jewish" names like Salmon or Weisz—some degree of "non-Aryan" ancestry might be assumed. When I asked former staff during interviews about the religious backgrounds of their guests, I had the distinct feeling that most of them resisted "naming names"; when I pressed, a common reaction consisted of "we didn't pay attention to who was Jewish and who was not." Therefore, providing an exact summary of the composition of religious or political backgrounds of exiles at Scattergood remains, unfortunately, impossible.

17.) The short-term, relatively informal setting of camp counseling attracted others—including Hans Schimmerling, who spent summer 1941 as a counselor at the University of Michigan's Fresh Air Camp. Sponsored by the Church of the Brethren while at the hostel, Hans was very much on his own after he left Scattergood. By April 1943 he had moved to Kalamazoo, Michigan, and he worked for the Lumbermen's Credit and Warehouse Company, where, he said, "the job is interesting, pays fairly well, and seems to be permanent." Rather uncharacteristic of men of his generation and cultural background, he admitted openly on the pages of the *Bulletin* that "I feel very lonesome having no wife, no children, and very few friends. *Au Revoir* and Good Luck."

18.) Like that of others described in previous chapters, the professional fate of full-time college-professor Sabine Hirsch will not be repeated here, as all known information about her life after leaving Scattergood Hostel is presented elsewhere (see chapter 10).

19.) Having lived in political exile in France for eight years as of March 1933, once settled in the Twin Cities Elizabeth became active in the Women's International League for Peace and Freedom. Peg Stevens became a friend of the Lichtensteins and "when in '59, 3M transferred my [Munich-born, one-time-refugee husband Ed] to the St. Paul sector, we visited the L's several times. They were living in an apartment...across from a private golf course... I recall Julius' comment regarding discrimination when I remarked on the pleasant view from their windows: 'Yes, but we could never go for a stroll in those grounds.'"

20.) Peg and Viktor became good friends while at Scattergood and corresponded until shortly before his death. Besides offering her camaraderie, Peg later said Viktor "taught me a great deal about music. SH had a piano and one day when I had played something for him (I was a complete amateur) his comment was, 'You know, you are a relatively good sight-reader. But then, I've known better.' Typical of Viktor—his frankness was completely disarming, because he was so utterly sincere." She did note: "How open he was with the other staff members I do not know. I have the impression that he talked little about his experiences in Vienna after the *Anschluss*. But I still recall with shudders of horror some of the details he told me of his treatment at the hands of his Nazi persecutors."

21.) Nora Hackel was already working in the same capacity in a house there containing 28 children and her mother Hedwig was serving as a cook; in her spare time, "Omi" also did embroidery work while looking after little Nicole, who was 4 years old by then.

22.) Nicole Hackel later related the following story: "In that setting, the German staff members were the bottom of the bottom: they were *really* getting it after the war, so that...even the rations [was affected]: the Americans would get the biggest rations, then the refugee staff members would get [theirs] and then the Germans would get the least... [Marianne] sort of led a mini-revolution...and as director she said 'Everyone's going to get equal rations'... She said it caused a lot of consternation. On the one hand, because she came with the Unitarian Service Committee, she was aware of the power she had as an American Unitarian to lay that down, but the fact that she was born a German and spoke German—it was so unsettling to everybody... particularly the other European staff members... She [also] had this incredible story of Christmas Eve where the dinning room was really tense...and people really weren't quite talking to each other, although they had made all these decorations and everything... The people sat in their own nationality groups and one group started singing. She has a wonderful voice and she started encouraging it and gradually it evolved into this evening where everybody did what they did at Christmas: the Germans did their's and [so on]." Marianne had experience running children's homes: after she and Nora Hackel fled Berlin—both "militant" SPD members and the latter a Jew—they established a home for refugee children in Paris.

23.) Upon leaving Scattergood 55-year-old Louis Rosenzweig took "college classes for a short time," requalified as an accountant and began work for an auditing firm in Peoria, Illinois—being "on the road sometimes five days a week." As he had done in Germany, Louis assisted members of the Jewish community with legal matters—but this time often in filing claims of restitution from the German government. He retired in 1956 and the Rosenzweigs moved to New Haven, Connecticut, to be near their children, both of whom settled in Yale University's hometown.

257

24.) This company still existed as of summer 1996—with the name Ginsberg Jewelers—as did nearby Smulekoff's, a furniture store which hired Austrian Philip Weiss in April 1940, in a placement made by the organization which had sponsored his stay at Scattergood, Jewish Charities of Cedar Rapids. In December 1942 the *Bulletin* listed Philip as "in the services."

25.) The reason for Ewald's dismissal has become lost with the passage of time. One possible explanation could have been the rather-common disdain for epileptics; a "rather upset" Lillian Pemberton found Ewald in the Scattergood library one day during a seizure. Like Kurt Rosegg, Ewald reportedly also "wolfed his food" upon arriving at Scattergood, a legacy of his stay in a concentration camp before fleeing occupied Austria.

26.) Camilla Hewson Flintermann remembered Elly as "slim, middle-aged, with a slightly diffident manner. Not one to put herself forward or create a disturbance"—in contrast to Oskar, whom she described as "the more forceful of the couple." Walter Shostal suspected "Elly" to be the Anglicized "Helene."

27.) A department store—the mail-order kind—also provided Vienna-born Jean Werth a means to support his wife Kaethe; he worked for Sears, Roebuck and Company in Milwaukee as of December 1941, but by 1944 had an address in Kew Gardens, New York.

28.) A former business person in Europe, in America Rolf Arntal found employment at someone else's business; he worked for the Henry Fields Seed and Nursery Company in Shenandoah, Iowa, for more than 30 years. He then retired and moved to California to be near daughter Doris. When Tekla died in 1977, he married a woman whom he had known in his youth and spent part of the year in Germany, part in the U.S.

29.) Perhaps reflecting Michael's Jewish heritage [according to Peg Stevens, Ellen was a non-Jew], the *Bulletin* noted: "The restaurant is closed from Saturday after lunch until breakfast time on Monday, so [the Krauthamers] have a nice weekend in which to rest."

30.) In New York Michael and Ellen gave birth to a daughter, Charlotte, for whom they asked Peg Hannum Stevens to act as godmother—who by then was teaching at a girls' school in Brooklyn and had the "fear I didn't earn that honor." As for their previous child, "George married a black woman, and...they couldn't find a place to live [in pre-Civil Rights America] except in an apartment over a garage. They subsequently moved to France, where the K's had lived before immigrating to the U.S."

31.) Robert Berquist described Ilse as "an artist with much skill in decorating objects made of wood [who] taught art in a Catholic school in Swarthmore." When I interviewed 89-year-old Ilse in summer 1996, she presented me "Hinze der Kater," a stuffed tom cat she had *gebastelt* in the 1970s out of old socks, stray buttons and various other materials.

32.) Reportedly Ellen had the humorous experience of being stranded enroute from Iowa City to the hostel when one of the Hostel's tired cars again malfunctioned in August 1939. Upon arriving at Scattergood one of the Quakers asked "Ellen, how did thee get back from West Branch?" She replied "A man—oh, I didn't hitch-pick him. He hitch-picked *me*!"

33.) Robert Berquist noted: "The Drakes loved Scattergood and for many years came to visit the Berquists at the school on a summer Sunday afternoon... They were very out-going, genuinely friendly people."

34.) Although once cited as "difficult to place," after Albert found a job he must have excelled, for ten years after his death the Society of Automotive Engineers and American Society of Mechanical Engineers dedicated a Standard for Involute Splines "in his memory."

The couple provided a good laugh while still at Scattergood, for the night they arrived at the hostel, Albert—not yet aware of what kind of place to which they had really come—left his shoes in the hallway outside the bedroom door for "someone" to clean, in the best European-hotel tradition. After Albert died, "blond, delightful" Lisa—who at Scattergood was known to mow the lawn wearing a *Dirndl*—visited Austria several times.

35.) A July-1940 placement report noted that Gus began his stint there on 29.IV.40, but "the work was seasonal, and the job ended after six weeks. He then went to Cleveland and tried to find work. When his money ran out he returned to Scattergood on July 16, 1940."

36.) The professional position in Rock Island surfaced for Wilhelm only after he tried a provisional job in Hinsdale, Illinois, with a "Mrs. Swoboda" as "a sort of estate supervisor." As a Placement Report of 22.VII.40 explained: "Since engineering placements for aliens are almost impossible to make since the government ruling regarding government contracts (every firm seems to expect a government war contract, so are unwilling to hire aliens when they would only have to fire them to accept contracts), William Feist asked that he be placed as a chauffeur etc. in order to save his money to bring his little daughter to America as soon as we can help him find her in Belgium. He has become extremely nervous (very understandably what with his great worry about his little girl) and it seemed best to place him in this job. He's very happy about the prospects. Giles Zimmerman has seen his new living quarters and reports that they are very attractive, radio, shower etc. He will be paid maintenance and $35.00 per month. He is especially pleased by the prospect of being able to ride as much as he wishes, and at having a car at his disposal."

37.) The following entry in a Placement Report of 22.VII.40 explained that Paul "is to be shifted to various departments to learn merchandising. At present he is selling shoes for $22.50 per week, and doing very well. The officers of the company have taken a keen personal interest in his progress and welfare, and are very pleased with him."

38.) A friend of the Beam[t]s before coming to Scattergood, Wilhelm impressed the other hostelites in the group's

258

efforts to erect a darkroom in the basement, where he built an enlarger "out of nothing at all, and exhibited his first photos, which were a great success." A "small man probably in his early 40s [and] liked by all," with the help of staff "Willy" secured affidavits of support for his parents, Heinrich and Helene.

39.) The "job" of repair genius was, of course, a non-paying one, so "lucrative" could only be applied as in comparison with work done gratis. In fact according to a Placement Report of 22.VII.40, apparently Lynn Zimmerman (who signed the following report, written in the exact same style and format) wrote that at his new job Wilhelm was "paid 40¢ per hour. He is supposed to work 42 hours per week, but so far it has always been a lot more. He is being moved around from department to department to learn all phases of the work."

40.) Although not working as a lawyer, Martin Kobylinski—a 50-something former lawyer in Berlin—left Scattergood for a bookkeeping job in Iowa City, but two years later was reported as working as a "legal editor of a well-known monthly edition of new laws...together with a number of lawyers in Chicago."

41.) Or strangers, for that matter. The Placement Report compiled on 22 July 1940 described the "adoption" of two hostel couples by community groups in Iowa and Minnesota:

Henry and Anny Schoenthal

Henry and Anny Schoenthal leave Scattergood tomorrow...for Red Oak, Iowa. A committee made up of members of five churches, of which a Philo D. Clark is chairman, have taken the Schoenthal's [sic] on as a resettlement project. They have found and furnished living quarters for them, have money to support them for six month [sic] if necessary, and have a smaller committee to find work for them. They seem to have the whole town (a small but prosperous community) back of the project, and since the Schoenthal's are so very adaptable, we are sure this arrangement will work out well. The Schoenthal's English, particularly Anny's, is greatly improved, so this is no longer a handicap in their ultimate placement.

Karl and Lotte Liebman

A committee which has been formed in Minneapolis, Minn., made up of W.I.L. members, Friends, and other church groups, has taken over financial responsibility for the Liebmans, and are endeavoring to find work for Karl.

42.) Walter was not the only guest to find Par a curious case. Even 11-year-old Edith Lichtenstein noticed that "nobody ever knew anything about [Par Danforth's] life. He would disappear for long periods on end, then suddenly he would reappear. None of us really knew what he did or where he went. At times there rumors around that he worked for the government or did some kind of nobody-knows. He was sort of a mysterious figure that wandered in and out of our lives. He kept in touch; he would call from a lot of different places, he'd ask how they were; he'd come, he'd bring presents; he remembered birthdays. He was basically a family friend—always. He was a mentally private person: you never knew where he was or what he was doing; you never saw him with anybody else—he was a loner, but seemed totally dedicated to doing his work."

THE MELTING POT

"And how did our family do with regard to the melting pot?"
~ **Walter Shostal**

Once Scattergood's guests had polished their English skills, sharpened their sense of American social studies, refreshed their souls and secured promises of professional positions, they were ready in earnest to settle into America. Often, though, they would find their new country a bit daunting. A wonderful yet sometimes also wretched collection of contradictions, harsh extremes, more ethnicities than one could name, unimaginable potential and disillusioning disappointments awaited them beyond the hostel's front gate: it was, however, their new home. And as such they had to get to know and try to understand it; neither would be easy.

Ironically one of the refugees' biggest obstacles to understanding the United States lay inside their own heads, as many had come with a host of stereotypes which would have to be overcome if they ever hoped to be at peace with their new home—not to mention themselves in it.[1] These impressions or preferences formed long before the exiles ever set sail from Europe largely had one of two effects: the person possessing them either blindly hated America or blindly loved America. Both extremes were only different manifestations of the same failure to see an entire culture in all its diversity and complexity—not as it was *supposed* to be, but as it really *was*. Usually such reactions mirrored the person's own projected need to create external foci of shame or hope.

Perhaps Adolf Hitler best summarized the dominant image too many Germans—if not other Europeans—had of the young land across the Atlantic in the first third of the 20th century: "What is America," the prince of projections once protested, "but millionaires, beauty queens, stupid records and Hollywood...?" Certainly, popular mass culture exported from the New

260

World to the Old only institutionalized clichés of a land populated by Colorado cowboys and Chicago gangsters, Detroit motor moguls and Broadway show girls. Feeling superior to this cacophony of characters, Europeans oft derided the Land of Dreams—or, conversely, flipped from attitudes of disdain to idol worship. For uprooted individuals such as Scattergood Hostel's guests, victims of the latter *needed* to be able to find something worthwhile in this land which from the other side of the water they had used as joke material or as an example of how *not* to run a society but now called "home."

The sharp-tongued, critical Erhard Winter—not surprisingly—belonged to the first group. His repeated attempts to stowaway back to Europe spoke strongly of his initial rejection of America as an acceptable place to sink roots. Writing—tellingly, in third-person—55 years after leaving Scattergood Hostel, he admitted that for the first couple of years of his stay in the U.S. he struggled with love-hate feelings toward the country that offered him safe haven from Hitler's henchmen: "Erhard's feelings that 'America was a great place to visit but he wouldn't want to live there,' i.e. his sense of his unfitness for America, and America's unfitness for him, persisted; and indeed has persisted to this day [of writing in 1994]... [At the age of 17 he] decided that America didn't need him and he didn't need it; and that there really wasn't a useful place for him in this polyglot, vulgar, money-mad, pleasure-seeking, amoral & hedonistic society that was in the process moreover of racial mongrelization; a society that lacked cultural standards & principles and whose cities...were ugly, utilitarian, and dirty, dull rectangular squares without interest or grace or charm. And so he felt was the rest of American life, such as he had seen and experienced. And even the best of Americans were like overgrown children, full of a sense of silly optimism but lacking a sense of history, culture, [unreadable]... America, the historical dumping ground of Europe's (and the world's) 2nd sons, misfits, psychopaths, con-men [sic], swindlers, criminals and other loosers [sic]."[2] Although he wrote the above narrative five and a half decades after his arrival at the hostel, one might hope that Erhard Winter was describing his feelings toward America as seen through the eyes of a fate-battered, raging young man and not as a U.S. citizen of some half a century. If not, Erhard represents one of the most extreme cases of a Scattergood Hostel guest unsuccessfully integrated.

A devoted father and later convinced Friend, Emil Deutsch represented the other camp indicated above—that of those who sought to "rehabilitate" their own image of America, consciously making it possible to live in the country of their former strong disregard. If one considers that many of Emil's one-time compatriots had lined Vienna's streets and wildly greeted Adolf

Hitler's entry into annexed Austria, and that many of them had stood by and watched approvingly as Nazi sympathizers forced his own brother-in-law to his knees to scrub the sidewalks with toothbrushes, one can understand his desire to find a less-repulsive home. Exactly because Europe had turned so obscene, America needed to become so virtuous—at least in his wide eyes.[3]

A year and four months after leaving Scattergood to begin a new life in Des Moines, Emil published a three-and-a-half-page essay in two issues of the hostel's *Bulletin* in which he went to great lengths to cast his adopted land in a brighter light. He felt a clear need to defend America and the Americans—but from whom, internal or external critics? Excerpts from his treatise show the complex arguments he put forward in an attempt to reconcile "The Refugee and American Life":

> *The American way of life and Americans are pretty different from what the newcomers to this country have experienced before. At the same time they are different from what [Europeans] have learned or heard about America.*
>
> *"America is a young country" was one of the slogans in Central Europe. "Without traditions." Most Central Europeans felt pretty adult, cultured, and superior to those people whom they believed uneducated, childish, and without judgment in questions of taste. Nothing is more awkward than this superficial statement. Did anyone of those who promulgated it think how old the living traditions of Europe...are? That most of the Central European traditions which are not dead in books are younger than 150 years? That the Central European attitude toward life—though based upon the dark and barbaric Middle Ages—is post-Napoleonic? That all the European "isms" including Communism, are based upon Hegel's ways of thinking? Did they ever realize that the great tradition of modern German literature, the classic period of Lessing and Goethe is based upon the same ideas—the enlightenment brought forward by the English thinker, John Locke, as the Western European and American civilization? That those eternal and everlasting ideas of human rights and human decency are the very content of the Declaration of Independence and the American Constitution? That they are the living common good of everybody in this country? And that...the oldest common cultural value of humanity, the Bible, is living tradition in this country, not a dead letter as [in Europe]?*
>
> *Yes, America and the Americans are young in their mind. But they are not childish as highbrow Europeans deem, but child-like. As to children every new country, new book, new person they get acquainted with is an "experience" to them. They are willing to learn, and never believe themselves too old for it. What some European cultural thinkers*

believed to be the very essence of a creative genius: not to lose and forget his own childhood and child-like attitude, here amazingly we find it in a whole people. Like children they live more in the present than in the past and in the future. They enjoy life and its small pleasures. They worry less than we used to. They do what they can at present. And like children they know about the importance of gaiety and smiling. They are kind and helpful, willing to give everybody his chance. But everybody has to make use of it himself.

The Americans impressed Emil. He found them to be "a democratic people. They are free. It is natural for them to be so. It is in their political history. They are tolerant, tolerant to an extent that is amazing for us. There is one God in this country. Only the ways of worshipping him are different. Everybody appreciates and considers the other fellow's belief and conscience. No other country but the United States and England considers the rights of conscientious objectors. But not only the general attitude toward life and our fellow men is absolutely different from Central Europe. Manners, behaviors are so, too, to a considerable degree. Here we are approaching the main question touching us as refugees. The Americans are able and willing to learn, to change, to adapt themselves to every new situation and necessity. The inability of others to do so appears to them as unwillingness. Being young in their minds up to their very old ages, they find it hard to understand that people of forty or fifty or even younger ones should not be able to do so. It must look hostile to them, ungrateful, inconceivable."

Grateful to have survived Nazi persecution and for the chance to live in America, Emil took care not to offend his new neighbors—and to convince his fellow refugees to do the same. "Let us free ourselves" he pleaded,

from the prejudiced belief that Central Europe surpasses America by far in all realms of art. The University and the libraries of Iowa City offer to the residents possibilities that very few refugees could find elsewhere. Look at Grant Wood's paintings, read [Iowa writer] Paul Engle's poems or Hemingway's novels. I wonder how much of the European opinion of superiority will last after such an experience. Even if you should think of culture in the quite too narrow meaning of art and literature you will find that America is able to hold its own in this respect, also.

Appreciation does not mean that we have to look at everything in America through rose-colored glasses. There is a lot to improve still. But the hard task of adapting ourselves to the conditions in which we are would be harder for us, perhaps impossible to handle, if we stress too much the features which do not satisfy us or even the Americans.

263

There is so much to appreciate and to affirm. Let us take an affirmative attitude toward our new surroundings and our new neighbors. For our own sake we have to emphasize in our minds the possibilities of life and happiness which are offered to us in this free and tolerant country. We have to learn to look at things from the American point of view. We must try to forget looking at things from the European angle any time. Our experience might help us and others to see institutions and facts from a new angle and to bring more light and more knowledge into life later on.

It cannot be stressed enough how important it is for newcomers to this country to learn to look at life from the American point of view. Even the most democratic and advanced one in Central Europe was influenced still by the general medieval attitude denying to man his inalienable rights. Fortunately for us, we have forgotten already to some extent most of the horrible things we went through. On the other hand we remember too much the secure and nice positions, the experience in our occupations, the contacts we had over there. We have to start anew. Let us try to find the right mental attitude for this start.

Above all, Emil seemed to have understood the significance of his fate—the good fortune of being offered a chance to build a new life out of the rubble of a ruined, violated one. He reminded his readers:

We are the unhappy victims of Nazism. Many Americans are descendants of victims of oppression who found refuge in this free and tolerant country. So they realize our situation and our needs. Nobody here has called for us. It is the chance we are offered, and which we have to assume and make the best of. Let us forget what we were over there before that nightmare came. It is gone. Let us try to be American in the sense of experiencing the new situation. Let us be thankful that we are able to live in this free country, safe, unoppressed, appreciated. Let us appreciate ourselves her institutions, her ways of thinking and living. And let us prove ourselves worthy of the help which is extended to us. Let us try to become Americans.

Emil Deutsch's piece—spurred by his valued, on-going connections to Scattergood—involved the reflections of a man who had been in his adopted country for less than five years. But what about refugees' impressions of America after decades of personal contact? What about later understandings of early experiences of adapting to life in America? Some 55 years after having arrived for the first of two stays at Scattergood Hostel, Ernst Malamerson van den Haag tried to recapture initial attitudes about America and Americans—as well as some of the finer aspects of trying to adapt *despite* those first impressions:

> *[Upon first arriving] I was under the impression [of being] doubly superior, first as a Marxist—I felt I didn't really have to learn economics because I already knew better than my teachers... And second, I felt...fairly educated and I thought that Americans were ignorant ... At the same time, I didn't know where I belonged... I had no friends and no ability to make friends on my own intellectual or educational level. I didn't know anyone. And furthermore, I felt deeply humiliated because my English was very bad, of course. I can still remember how annoyed I was that I couldn't follow a joke. I not only couldn't tell a joke...but I couldn't understand a joke and had to pretend that I had understood it. Simple conversation was very difficult. On the whole, I think I did feel superior, because we learned that. When I wrote to my parents in Italy that I might end up in America, I remember my mother broke down, crying "But you can't even drive a nail into the wall"— which was quite true, probably. But [laughing] "There must be other things I could do." I really didn't believe in myself. My idea of America was sort of Wild West... Again, this is where Scattergood helped me a great deal—not in any direct fashion at all, but incidentally. I didn't see how I could ever be more than a bus boy or something like that... I think that experience occurred with many people. I was totally penniless and arrived with less than $15. I think the normal reaction—which also was mine—is when you feel you are not going to be accepted, you're not getting anywhere, you reject in turn. And that's exactly what I did, psychologically. As time went on, this changed.*

Unable permanently to maintain a psychological barrier around himself or to avoid practical considerations, the sharp-minded young man experienced "a great shock—as...my parents were well to do. In France I made a haphazard living for two years, but I thought it was a temporary matter. Here for the first time...I was confronted with 'How will I eat tomorrow'. I was unaccustomed; I'd never been hungry—but the idea that you didn't have a bank account or a family or something to fall back on was totally strange. It is not strange in America, [where] people do feel they are on their own. And they manage. But I had never had to manage and I suspect that was true for most Europeans."

Scattergood Hostel played a pivotal role in Ernst's process of personal recovery and eventual integration into American society—as seems to have been true for other guests, too: "The major thing was being [at the hostel] and slowly becoming aware of the American life and becoming ready to adjust.

For most people, that's not easy... On the whole [adjusting to America] meant giving up the insistence on trying to pretend that you're still in Europe. That's what most of us did, in fact, because we came—in retrospect, of course—from a marvelous paradise compared to what [refugees] had here at least in the beginning and most of them were very tempted to give up [and] reject the 'inferior' American lifestyle... I think at Scattergood they met a very friendly...accepting, tolerant and even a warm environment—the type that helped them. What Iowa gave to them was a sense of acceptance and a sense of hope which they needed—and that was very important and they were grateful for this."

Explaining that his earlier arrogance later gave way to increased emotional honesty and adaptation, Ernst added: "Now I feel quite to the contrary, that much of American scholarly activity, etc., is quite superior to what we have in Europe. There's also been much change: when I arrived it was difficult to get a good cup of coffee. There were, of course, very, very high-priced good restaurants, but they were few and you didn't get good food anywhere, certainly not in Iowa. But across the country, things have greatly changed. You can get a good cup of coffee—as good as in Italy—around the corner, practically. You get a good meal almost anywhere; it'll cost you in gourmet places, but the whole style has changed—and considerably—since the Second World War. In a sense I am tempted to say that America has become somewhat Europeanized; again this may go too far, but in many ways that has been the case. When I arrived it was really a totally different world."

It's one thing for America to have changed—perhaps, to have become more "Europeanized"—but what of Ernst's personal experience: to what degree does he feel "Americanized?" After more than half a century in the New World, he had developed definite feelings regarding his relationship with America: "I wouldn't want to live anywhere [else]. I go to Europe once a year most years and I have new friends there...I love it, but as for living there, my friends are here and I feel American—particularly when I'm in Europe. [Laughing] Once I'm here I feel in some respects European—but in New York there's lots of people like that... I wouldn't want to live in Europe now; I could manage, probably, but I feel too old to make new friends—and I like it here... I don't find any objections to American life; all the objections I used to have when I first came were really pretexts. When you are not fully accepted you find reasons for not fully accepting those who reject you—it is a subconscious, psychological process, but it's self-defense. Once you've dropped that you have no more reason to defend yourself..."

The feeling of personal strength and security which allows one to drop earlier defenses does not mean, however, that one returns to being the person one was before the crisis which provoked such extreme response. After the fact, one has changed—never to be the same. Once he'd finally felt adjusted to "the strange and new culture," Ernst realized that he had gained an entirely new sense of "home" and personal identity—even if mixed ones. He explained: "I guess in many senses my allegiances have become quite American—not anti-European by any means, but I feel as an American. The word 'Americanized' is ambivalent—it means so many different things. Politically I feel certainly assimilated; culturally, yes I do feel in many ways, but in some ways probably not. Psychologically I feel quite American, but I feel as an American in the same way as I would feel as a German or an Italian. There are many parts of Italian life I wouldn't like a bit, and there would be many activities and so on that I would dislike—and so would be true in Germany or of course in America."

In contrast to the impressions of a refugee about her or his cultural-adjustment process and the degree to which she or he became "Americanized," after long, productive lives on New-World soil how do other one-time refugees evaluate how well they blended into the alleged "melting pot?" To what degree did they realize a personal version of the famed American Dream? And, what had America come to mean to them on a visceral level—despite having been born elsewhere, with all attendant attachments to a very different *Heimat*?

At age 86 Walter Shostal took pen in hand and assessed how well he and his children had adjusted to American society as former refugees. Aptly titling his memoirs *American Beginnings*, in summer 1994 he wrote about the fates of himself and his two sons, who also were at Scattergood:

> And how did our family do with regard to the melting pot? Let's take stock. Many years ago Pierre told me that at a certain time in his youth he had been uncertain whether he should be an American or a European. He had married a French girl with a great deal of charm and few other qualities. As he progressed in life his doubts vanished and he became accustomed to officially represent the United States [as a member of the foreign service]. His second wife in a very happy marriage is British-born... After many years of foreign assignments they are definitely settled in the States... They are definitely in the mainstream.
>
> There was never any doubt about Claude's being American. When in the military, he spent three years in Germany, travelled in Europe and saw its sights, but escaped without deeper emotional dents. He still roots for the home team and opens his newspaper at the sports page. His main interests include [New York] city and state politics as well as the environment and ecology. He is married to a girl from the Texas

Panhandle with nothing but American—even a bit of the native kind—in her. I suppose it was tabletalk heard in his childhood which kindled his love for the mountains; [Magda] and I spoke of the Austrian Alps, where we had hiked and climbed in our youth. Claude's interest goes to the more exotic variety, from the Himalayas to the Andes and beyond, but Manhattan is home to him. He would not want to live anywhere else.

How do I stack up in terms of the melting pot? Had I been asked that question a quarter of a century ago, I may have deserved a grade "A"—possibly an "A-," because of my persistent accent. I spoke only English, thought in English, read only English—with occasionally a little French in between—and [after Magda's death in June 1965] dated a nice woman with Mayflower credentials in her genealogy. We might eventually have married, even though I proclaimed loudly I would never marry again. All this changed when I met most romantically another woman [named Ilse] on a cruise to the Greek Islands [in the 1970s]...

As I acknowledged, the melting pot may not rate me any longer with an "A," but I hope I am still good for a "B+." When we arrive at JFK after seven months spent [every summer at the couple's lakeside cottage in Austria's Salzkammergut region] and a friendly customs inspector greets us with a "Welcome home, folks," we have a very, very good feeling. Yes, we are coming home...

1.) According to AFSC Refugee Section staff member John Rich, "to the immigrant in New York, Iowa or Indiana [the site of another AFSC refugee hostel] sound as remote and forbidding as Siberia. The map of the United States, in their minds, is a strange distortion with New York City occupying the whole eastern seaboard, Chicago a few miles inland, a vast uninhabited desert to the west. Then Hollywood and the Pacific Ocean."

2.) Erhard openly acknowledged the riddle of his unhappiness with America, "despite the fact that over the years he earned and received degrees and diplomas and certificates and fellowships in 'Learned Societies', and awards and credentials sufficient to paper one wall of his library. Another Horatio Alger story? Well, no & yes. He was not a 'joiner.' In those organizations, clubs, profess[ional] societies he was obliged to join he was never elected to positions of leadership. In all his life, he never stayed or lived in one place longer than 10 [years] until the move [to the town of his residence as of 1994]."

3.) This is the opinion of the author and of Emil's son-in-law, Phil (brother of one-time Scattergood volunteer staff Amy Clampitt). Upon reading this essay, Phil said: "That didn't sound like the Emil Deutsch that I knew—the one who wrote those glowing things about America: I just never saw him that way. I think he was maybe trying to wish, to see America in the best light that he could and hope that it was true; then he found out that it wasn't."

WHITE STILL NIGHTS

"No one who ever lived there close to the cornfields, the white still nights, the beauty of the moonlight, the silence of the meetinghouse, close to the eternity of nature and the love of Quakerism, will ever get rid of this atmosphere."
~ **Lucy Selig**

Unlike most Hollywood movies of the time, the Scattergood story did not end with a soaring, uplifting crescendo but more a disjointed, disillusioning crash. While its four-year existence embodied "acts of kindness or selflessness on a significant scale," the controversy unleashed by proposals for the hostel's use following the last European refugees' departures epitomized malice, bigotry and reactionary fear. Paradoxically, although Scattergood Hostel had been founded to counter the most deadly effects of racism, it was tolerated by its neighbors as long as those being helped were "white" Europeans; the idea of helping "yellow" Asian-descended Americans seemed simply unacceptable to enough West Branch townspeople to block a new project. Perhaps now—more than half a century later—we who examine the Scattergood experience for shreds of inspiration and wisdom might learn from what happened there then—and thus armed try to prevent such dynamics from dictating events today.

As with its creation, the demise of Scattergood Hostel was in response to events in Europe. Initially the flow of refugees fleeing Nazi-occupied territories had been a flood—one which overwhelmed the capacity of private as well as government efforts to respond to the desperate need of those unwelcome by the Nazi-German regime. Once World War II had started, however, previous routes of escape such as Prague and Paris closed, necessitating alternative ones such as Marseilles and Lisbon. When those corridors to safety also closed the flood became a trickle. At the beginning of Scattergood Hostel's existence applicants had to be rejected by the score; by 1942, though, AFSC workers in the Northeast had to scramble to find even a minimum number of guests at any given time. Letters between West Branch and Philadelphia fretted over the implications of falling numbers of refugees reaching the United States and, in turn, Scattergood's future. In the first week of 1943, then, the inevitable came, requiring Mary Rogers to tell Martha Balderston: "I think I have never wanted less to write a letter than I do this one, but I feel the time has come when I must lay the facts before the staff and the executive committee at Scattergood... With the greatest regret [AFSC has] reached the conclusion that it is not possible to find enough refugees who are prepared to go to Scattergood to warrant our keeping the hostel open beyond this winter." She went on to explain that AFSC had "exhausted every possibility of referral... We find three, four, or five hopeful prospects, only to have them slip away from us. With the shortage of manpower [sic] which is particularly evident in the east, the Americans in the lower-paid jobs are securing better-paid appointments: refugees are able to step into these less well-paid positions. The majority of them are now able to find work, and their need for money is so great that they are unable to think of one, two or three months of additional unemployment, even though this is a period of preparation. If the hostel were located a few miles from New York and people could go for three weeks, or even four weeks, I think we probably could keep the hostel full—though I am not too sure of this... [In addition we] have been told by the refugee agencies who have cooperated with us by sending refugees to Scattergood that they will be unable to send additional people. It is not a question of finances but of a changed situation."

A bitter irony was that a surprisingly successful fund-raising campaign the previous Thanksgiving had put Scattergood on firm financial footing for the first time in its existence. Now, less than six weeks later, the considerable contributions would not be needed. Mary remarked: "It seems particularly cruel that this complete blocking should come just at a time when we see some means of financial support through the campaign... The declaration of war was our first bad hurdle, and the second was the breaking off of relations with France: this was the final blow to any hope we might have of recruiting new guests. These reasons...are conditions beyond our control and are hard facts that we have to accept."

In the same letter Mary considered alternative uses for the Scattergood site. An initial idea included establishing a convalescent care facility. In the same breath, however, she argued against such usage, given that "so many people who need this type of rest cure are also in need of the services of a psychiatrist; and obtaining adequate care of this type is beyond our means. In addition, it would be extremely difficult to secure medical and psychiatric care in the present shortage of people trained in [those] lines." A more plausible scenario involved re-opening the hostel as a relocation center for Japanese-Americans who had been forcibly removed from their West Coast homes soon after the bombing of Pearl Harbor. As she noted, "there are many well qualified farmers in the relocation camps," so Iowa would be an obvious place to resettle some of the so-called Nisei.[1] Although AFSC had received indication from the government that it would support such a program, Mary realized that the proposition likely would receive some opposition. She thought out loud: "If the farm labor condition becomes still more acute, it is quite probable that the attitude of Iowa farmers may change toward the Japanese. One factor in this situation would be a [U.S. military] defeat in the Pacific, or the publication of long casualty lists. The economic situation might overcome even these hazards if the need for farm help is sufficiently acute and if the public can be educated to the fact that these are American citizens who should be judged on their character, not on their color or race."

Regardless of any possible future uses of the Scattergood site, the fact remained that its use as a hostel had to be dealt with and concluded. AFSC's staff in Philadelphia refrained from setting a date for the closure of the hostel, wishing instead to coordinate this with the on-site staff. It did decide, however, that it was "important that the news about the closing of Scattergood should not be spread among the guests nor in the community until our program is fairly clearly outlined and until some preparation work has been done with key people in Iowa." Also, "the members of the advisory committee [in Philadelphia] expressed great regret that Scattergood would have to be closed, and appreciation for all that has been accomplished for our refugee friends. Those...who have known the members of the [West Branch] staff personally feel even more keenly our sense of gratitude and admiration for the spirit which made the hostel so warm and loving an influence in the lives of the refugees and in the community."

In response to AFSC's notice of the cessation of operations at the hostel, Martha Balderston summoned a meeting of the Iowa Scattergood executive committee and explained "We have seen this situation coming because of the rapid falling off of the number of guests but there seemed nothing to do but carry on until it was clear we could go no further."

The subsequent committee meeting opened with long-time hostel-supporter Jay Newlin "expressing satisfaction with the results accomplished by the Hostel. [Furthermore, the committee felt the project] has had a very definite influence for good as far as Iowa Friends are concerned, as well as the public in the mid-west [sic]." Despite Mary Rogers' musings over using Scattergood as a Nisei relocation center and support for that idea expressed by committee member Roy Clampitt, fellow committee member Charles Thomas felt "there might be a great need for a Friends School to be again established there." The idea of a relocation center prevailed, however, and the committee "spent considerable time discussing this question, with the conclusion that there is much to be considered."[2]

271

Indeed, in Martha Balderston's report on the committee meeting she referred to the complicated nature of the proposal to offer Nisei a new if but temporary home on the prairies. She also mentioned the suggestion that "perhaps we might invite a limited number of American-Japanese citizens to come to Scattergood for a brief stay, to get the reaction of everybody in Iowa. Again, it was suggested that Scattergood might be used as a sort of a residence for these people before and between jobs, or...it might be used as a residence for people who had temporary jobs, or day labor jobs within the immediate neighborhood. Those members [of the executive committee] who operate farms seemed to be of the opinion that in rush seasons 15 or 20 men would be very useful. It was their opinion also that it would be much easier for these men to get jobs on Iowa farms if they had a week or two of experience as day laborers."

In addition to the question of likely use of Nisei labor, Martha discussed possible reaction to such a project in the local community. She noted that West Branch's mayor William Anderson and churches "were sympathetic for such use for the [Scattergood] buildings and grounds. There is some reason to believe that the neighborhood is a little opposed to anything that might lead to permanent residence within the neighborhood. Not officially, but as a feeler, one member of the [hostel] staff talked to the FBI representative in Iowa City. He said you people certainly like to tackle the hot spots and then went on...to say that as far as he knew, speaking as a local representative, there would be no opposition from the FBI."

Perhaps the federal government's local watchdog had no qualms about the idea of introducing individuals of Asian-descent into the area, but Martha sharply underestimated the potential for opposition to it from local citizens. In the meantime, however, as long as Iowa Quakers discussed the matter among themselves the proposal seemed feasible. On 8 February "about fifty Friends" from various local meetings in Iowa met at the Des Moines Friends Church to consider Scattergood's future. The views expressed there indicated the degree to which group-think inhibited Friends' abilities to discern realistically the response their proposed project might evoke.[3]

Those at hand had much to do with the outcome of the conference, given that Quaker leaders were there, as well as unwavering AFSC supporters. Martha Balderston, Mary Rogers and Homer Morris attended the gathering, as did another dozen or so individuals present four years earlier to discuss the opening of the hostel—all of whom had personal interest in seeing the hostel continue in some form. Martha set the tone of the meeting early on, expressing "a wish that more people over the state could have shared in the pleasure of the work there for the last four years. [She went on to say] there is a wide spread interest in Scattergood not only in Iowa but all over the middle west.[4] Her consern [sic] is that we find something to hold that interest and carry on from here." Mary Rogers also spoke from the heart: "What we have proved at Scattergood strikes at the very foundation of our belief, that we can be different and live together comfortably. We want to keep that spirit alive." For his part, Homer Morris was

> reminded of the events of four years [earlier: how] at that time a difficult and unpopular thing was undertaken by a small but willing group. This is another situation concerning which we have a testimony to make, but we should "proceed as the way opens." One of the customs of the A.F.S.C. is to determine which is the right thing to do and then do it. The events [at Pearl Harbor] on Dec. 7th [1941] affect the problems of one group and created another. It isn't a Japanese problem [but] a Japanese Am. problem. It effects [sic] all of us. What of our Bill of Rights? "No person shall be deprived of right, liberty, or property without due process of law." Here is a precedent; first time in history (created by war) and done without protest. So that it isn't just a Japanese problem but a Japanese American problem. It is the policy of the [War Relocation Authority] to relocate the Japanese Am. as quickly as possible, especially during the war. They feel that a fundamental injustice has been done and it should be remedied as soon as possible. It will take a little time to get these people out of camp. They need hostels as places to live during the time they are getting jobs. The W.R.A. already has a number of men doing this replacement work. The A.F.S.C. is ready to take this work to Scattergood if Iowa so wishes. Should Iowa Friends feel this is their problem then West Branch Friends should be united as to whether it is a thing they want to do.

As Quakers customarily observe moments of silence between business items or opinions expressed on a specific matter, probably after some reflection on what had been said, Errol Elliott went on to remind his fellow Quakers that "when all Friends work together they are stronger. We sometimes feel that those in some other place are better able to undertake the unpopular thing than we are in our own neighborhood." Following comments from Scattergood's job placement director Par Danforth, Reverend Bishop of Des Moines' Drake University and a few more Iowa Friends, those attending the gathering agreed to pursue the transformation of Scattergood from a hostel into a relocation center. The meeting closed with someone present noting "the value that has come out of Scattergood to date cannot be over-estimated and emphasized. Through a religious conviction we have made the state of Iowa conscious that something humanitarian can be done. Now is the time to make the state of Iowa know that we can do something about [the] Japanese Am. problem."

Good-feeling idealism and even well-intended, spiritually led inspiration to undertake social action still can lead to fruitless ends. This swell-sounding conference resulted in just that. The last item it dealt with authorized Mary Rogers and Homer Morris to hold "an education program" at West Branch to "survey response from the wider public." What they found didn't resemble the generous-spirited altruism manifest among Iowa Quakers.

Before holding the public forum, Martha Balderston drafted a letter which announced the closing of the hostel[5] and hinted at a new use for the site—adding that "No decisions that can be announced have been made..." A decision, however, had to be made—and soon.

On 11 February a public meeting attended by 103 persons took place in West Branch's high school. After Homer Morris and Martha Balderston "very ably" placed before the meeting the suggestion that Scattergood Hostel be used as a placement center for Americans of Japanese descent, two brothers—"T.A." and Robert Moore—

> spoke out against the proposal, saying that in their opinion it would not be acceptable to the community. They were sure that "our boys" would not approve of the plan to bring Japanese people into the community when they were away fighting the battle of Liberty. This was echoed by A.F. Anderson, brother of the Mayor, who said that he would be embarrassed if he had to write to his boys—who were in the services—telling them that the project was going ahead. A few questions were asked and satisfactorily answered. Then [local Quakers] Lena Edgerton, Irma Guthrie and Laura Larsen [sic] spoke briefly in favor of the project. After some aimless rebuttals, [Mayor Anderson] moved that "The Community Club of West Branch suggest to the A.F.S.C. that a decision on this project be deferred." This motion was put to the meeting and was passed because nobody voted against it. Many of those present did not vote at all.[6]

While the needed decision had been deferred, it was not forgotten. In the meantime Scattergood and AFSC staff corresponded prolifically on behalf of securing the future of their hoped-for project. In a letter outlining conditions he thought requisite for a Nisei relocation center at Scattergood to succeed, John Copithorne tried to protect the project from would-be detractors. He instructed the Philadelphia office: "If you have occasion to telegraph us about this matter...please have your wires sent via Postal Telegraph. The local Western [Union] operator is an old gossip in pants, and privacy is a word he does not know. After the news is out it's [sic] OK to use Western U, but not until then please."

274

The next meeting to discuss the matter was called spontaneously on 24 February. As John Copithorne explained it the following day in a letter to Homer Morris, "Apparently there was a long bull session in WB yesterday afternoon and it was decided to hold a meeting last night. The general call went out over the rural phones at 6 o'clock and about 175 or 200 were present." What transpired at the meeting said much about the people of West Branch, their true feelings towards Quakers as well as the Scattergood staff and their brittle sense of patriotism. That being so, John Copithorne's account of the meeting warrants quoting at length:

> [War Relocation Authority staff member Donald] Sabin did a very fine job of presenting the problem. He started off with a brief historical background beginning with Admiral Perry's visit to Japan. Then he stated that this was a broad problem much bigger than any single community and that it had implications from here to Toyko [sic] and back. He said that it had a very positive effect on the Japanese propaganda beamed at China and India, and on the treatment of Americans interned or kept as prisoners of war in Japan. Then he mentioned the 10,000 Japanese-Americans who were released to help with the sugar beet harvest last summer and told of the good work they had done and the reception they had received. He stated that these 1st and 2nd generation Americans were almost too American in their efforts to prove themselves different from their parents.
>
> In the discussion period: D.E. Edwards—the leading well driller in this area—stated that in his opinion, and as a result of his travels around eastern Iowa and western Illinois, the labor shortage was 80% talk. He felt that when the war was over and his "boys" returned to WB they would find that all the available work had been pre-empted by "Cheap Labor." He kept reiterating "Cheap Labor" even in the face of Sabin's statement that the J-A's did not fall into this category. Sabin said that the real question was not so much how the farmers were getting along now, but, how much more could they produce if they had additional help. Then Tom Moore rose and suggested that the Japanese be allowed to join the Army. He went on at great length, and in the course of his discourse satated [sic] that "Morris made a statement which I would certainly call disloyal and almost traitourous [sic]" (Asked afterwards what he was referring to, he said that Morris called the order to evacuate J-A's from the West Coast very similar to the Nuremburg [sic] order.) He went on in a highly personal manner to say that many people in the community, and "we all know to whom I am referring" are not interested in fighting in the war... "Some of us, and I am one of them, are buying War Bonds to the limit of our ability while

275

these people do not do anything to help the war effort." When he sat down [local Friend] Everett Morris said "The people Mr. Moore is speaking about are much more interested in preventing wars than they are in fighting them when other people start them..."

Then Mrs. H.L. Moorehead—wife of the local Manager of the Wilder Grain Co.—spoke up and said that her son was going to be inducted [soon] and that he "would feel like a dope going out to fight for Democracy when it was not being practised here at home."

After that Mr. Sabin closed the meeting and thanked the people for coming out. He said he would report the meeting to the WRA in Washington.

In closing his report, John added "I spent this afternoon—as I have done every afternoon this week—helping with the rationing in the Town Hall of WB, and my impression is that most of the enlightened people in the community would be glad to see the project gone ahead with but they want the decision to be the government's."

John may have considered the opinion of "enlightened people" to be in support of the relocation center, but obviously not everyone in West Branch fit in that category. As he later learned, the Moore brothers "put the Legion up to the idea of a petition to Congress and to getting Sabin down here." The two felt so intensely about the issue and generated so much emotion about it that the entire community got sucked into a tense showdown between the bellicose brothers and the pacifist Quakers. Martha Balderston wrote to an on-the-road Par Danforth with an update: "Things have been pretty hot in W.B. and John [Copithorne] had a nasty run-in with Lewie Ellyson who accused John of insulting Tom Moore by calling him a 'die-hard.' John went over to Tom's office and apologized before the group. Tom apparently bore no ill feeling, anymore than John would 'if I called you a crusader,' 'Which I am' acknowledged John, and they parted on good terms."

The controversy surrounding Scattergood rippled beyond West Branch. The *Des Moines Register*, for instance, printed "some very pointed editorials and...interesting letters." One from Penn-College president Errol Elliott and another from a man named Fitch from the Iowa Vegetable Growers' Association were "both very good in their analysis of the situation." Another "interesting letter was printed from a prisoner at the state penitentiary [in which] he said that he had lost the privileges of a citizen for four years and hoped that such rights would not be taken away from citizens entitled to enjoy them—a very beautiful plea for tolerance and understanding.[7] John [also] received one 'crank' letter from a woman pastor in Des Moines who thinks we should help the Chinese as being more worthy of help."

Despite the most moving of pleas against doing so, Friends decided to close the hostel and chose 15 March 1943 as the last day of operation—exactly one month shy of four years after John Kaltenbach and his assorted collection of "Little Daniel Boones" pulled into Scattergood's driveway in their "modern-day Conestoga." Regarding the decision not to offer the hostel to the Nisei, the Scattergood staff drafted a press release which, uncharacteristic of Quaker practice, contained thinly veiled barbs for those with whom they disagreed:

> Following a conference in Washington [on 3 March 1943] between representatives of the War Relocation Authority and the American Friends Service Committee announcement was made that for the present plans for using Scattergood as a relocation hostel for persons of Japanese ancestry to assist the W.R.A. in its relocation program would be postponed. Officials of the W.R.A. and the A.F.S.C. expressed regret over this decision but stated that it is the policy to establish relocation hostels only in those communities where cooperation can be readily secured. As a result of this decision the farmers in the West Branch area will not have as accessible a supply of Japanese-American labor as the hostel would have provided.

Although the results of a couple of months' planning, proposing and pleading were disappointing, at least the controversy was over and Friends as well as the few remaining guests—who numbered one more than the seven staff on hand upon the hostel's closing—could face the most certain future they had known since the New Year.

Until the last day of operation, though, the staff remained on duty and had many obligations to fulfill before they could leave for new lives of their own. Even on the last day,[8] however, Martha Balderston found time to write a final letter to Mary Rogers in her official role as director. In it she explained: "It goes without saying that the work here has been very interesting and has brought many rich rewards for all of us, not the least being the acquaintance with thee and others of the Refugee Section... If there is any work I can do for the AFSC where you feel that my experience and training would be useful I would like to consider it. I shall have to do something and I would rather work among Friends than in any other line."

Having offered a personal note, Martha then turned her attention to an assessment of the hostel itself. She recounted:

> The scene changed so quickly for several weeks we could hardly keep up with ourselves—one day we thought we would keep the hostel open, the next we felt it would be wiser to close, then a new editorial or report

277

would send our hopes soaring again. In some ways it has been a relief to have the question settled definitely—for the present at least. No, I do not feel that we are being bluffed. After the first meeting I thought so, but time has called forth so many opinions that now it seems to me that in the long run the situation will be much stronger than if there had not been so much open discussion.

The opposition were so rabid that they overreached themselves, and showed that their objection was emotional and shallow. The Des Moines Register has been openly and loyally in favor of the project and even after it was laid down they have run articles of general educational value about the J-As. The other papers have been favorable, too, for the most part; the editor we know [who] did not approve the project received a rather raw deal from the [Associated Press News Service]. He doesn't hold this against us and has kept quiet with no open opposition, which is very decent of him...

...the Register editors had been trying to figure out a way to get the thinking public to write to the "What Readers Think" dept., rather than those persons who write to see their names in print. They have been very much pleased with the response this J-A situation has brought out... Of course there have been some crack-pots but the supporters of the J-As are objective and analytical and understanding. John [Copithorne] has received ten or a dozen requests for farm help. One woman wrote asking if we could send her someone and added, "I do not [care] what the neighbors would think about Japanese in the neighborhood." One man who lives about a hundred miles away was in the neighborhood and stopped in to talk the matter over with John [as a] personal follow-up to his letter of inquiry. So, it seems to me, that people thru-out the state have stopped and analyzed their feelings in the matter. While there is still, and will continue to be, much sincere opposition to J-As in Iowa and especially in one's immediate community, nevertheless people are thinking about their reasons for supporting and opposing the introduction of citizens from the relocation centers.

Around here the protest was in good degree a personal grudge against the Quakers in general—another reason for not forcing the issue of a hostel right now. How far this was true is a difference of opinion but there seems to be a fair support for the rumor. The opposition was quite amazed—professedly—that Friends should suggest anything that would split the community, in fact they had a good deal to say on this point. The Press stated that the American Legion had led the opposition. Then there was dissension within the ranks!!! The leaders of the opposition were members of the Legion but no meeting was called to take official action and many members of the Auxiliary approved [of] *the hostel at Scattergood and resented being classed with the other side!*[9]

If losing the hostel at West Branch makes people thru-out the state more tolerant and understanding, then it has been no loss in the long run.

On the other hand many folks around here did not realize that giving up the J-As meant no hostel at all and have been very kind in expressing their regret that we are leaving. Many of them are entirely sincere in saying they will miss us—they are the ones we shall miss, too.

Not only some Scattergood neighbors would miss the hostel. So would those who had found refuge there. Sending word of Scattergood's closure both in the form of a mass-mailed letter and in the joint February-March 1943 issues of the *Scattergood Monthly News Bulletin*, the on-site staff gave notice that the hostel soon would be no more. Immediately telegrams, letters, post- and greeting-cards from Iowa Friends, former staff and a few local supporters—but most of all from former guests[10]—arrived at the hostel, prompting Martha Balderston to excerpt and submit some of them to AFSC as evidence of the project's success. The communiqués Martha made public consisted of various reactions ranging from disbelief to deep gratitude. Of the former, Lucy Selig exhibited the shock and denial common to those experiencing great loss: "I cannot think of the Hostel becoming closed; it seems as if a solid ground [were] giving way under my feet, as if we would lose something like home for the second time. Scattergood became a part of my life and an important one and I do feel that it became a spiritual and uniting center for all of us. No one whoever lived there close to the cornfields, the white still nights, the beauty of the moonlight, the silence of the meetinghouse—close to the eternity of nature and the love of Quakerism will ever get rid of this atmosphere. Sometimes I long for one of those moments there that are gone more than for all that the days to come hold in their close-shut hands..." Similarly, Martha and Alfred Adler felt "deeply concerned about the news that Scattergood cannot continue to function as a Hostel for European refugees. We are touched so much the more because we cannot believe that Scattergood has outlived its usefulness. We know too well what Scattergood meant and means for us, what Scattergood gave and gives us. We came to Scattergood nearly broken in health and spirit after the hardship of the last years in Europe. It was at Scattergood where we had the opportunity to recover from the distress we had to go through. We found there friends eager to help us in our difficulties. They showed us American way of life and taught us to speak English. With help and kindness we found ourselves again and became again self-confident. So we realize what we owe to Scattergood."

279

Egon Mauthner, too, regretted that Friends' "wonderful work has now found its end. But I feel with you how satisfying it must have been to have helped so many, many people in their first steps in this country... The Quaker idea will give you more and more work in these times which need so much toleration and mutual understanding. I myself shall never forget what you Friends did for a stranger."

An unnamed individual wished to deny Scattergood's end, holding its essential spirit as inextinguishable: "You are right to hate to say farewell, [but] it is no reason too to say this word—why?—Scattergood isn't gone, Scattergood isn't dead, no, Scattergood exists, now as before... Scattergood surrounded by peace and freedom. Scattergood exists as the sun too, they belong always together and no one can divide them. The spirit of Scattergood exists—the spirit of Scattergood is not a merchandise, you cannot buy it, it cannot be sold, too—but you can have it, if so, then you get it forever."

Instead of subsiding, Rose Eliasberg thought that the need for centers like Scattergood would increase once the war ended: "For all those enslaved, imprisoned or in concentration camps for the time being, many, many centers with the spirit of Scattergood will be a necessity when the peace is won. These refugees, like all those who went through Scattergood, will appreciate the peaceful atmosphere, the cordiality and the good will to remedy and readjust those persons who have suffered persecution, starvation and torture. May Scattergood soon be reopened!"

Like Rose, Louis Croy remembered Europe, too, but from a different perspective, for he thought of what had happened to him in the Old World and the person he had been upon leaving there: "Looking back to my first year in this country I realize the decisive and beneficial rôle of Scattergood in my new life here. I got shelter and friends in the time of my greatest stress, I learned the ways of this country when I was a complete stranger, and a way for my future was paved which proved successful, in spite of my pessimism in the beginning. But Scattergood did more than this. I escaped the European nightmare with very little confidence in humanity. Scattergood taught me that I was wrong. The generosity and unselfishness of Americans at Scattergood was one of the most valuable experiences I ever had."

"Scattergood" evoked different images for different people whose lives it had touched. Some saw the meetinghouse as an apt symbol for the community of souls which had gathered there. Martin Kobylinski maintained that "the symbol of love and humanity, of helpful kindness and friendship, of mutual understanding is this little, simple Meetinghouse, which united all these different people in silence and worship. These meetings have bound us together more than many words. When we left Scattergood we had got a deep love for America thanks to that wonderful work done by the Quakers. We had found friends and had learned what that means: Society of American

Friends. So I am happy...to say you that my connection with Scattergood and the American Friends is not bound to building and time, [but] it will last forever." Newly married, Gertrude Hesse Liepe also spoke of the meeting-house, but in the form of a wish of well-being for the remaining staff:

> *Your letter...distresses us not a little. But we hope another feeling is prevailing, that you and your staff have completed a great task. We are very anxious to know what your further plans will be, personally and for the hostel. There may come back one day new tasks for it; the Meet-inghouse, we hope and think, will remain a precious meeting-place, saved by what was done during these years... When your divisions are done you will have a fire in the little stove and you will sit there, not alone. All who ever were there with you will be there—you will feel it.*

The overriding image the refugees held of Scattergood, however, was—as Karl and Lotte Liebman described it—being "our home, the place you could go to for a rest, maybe the only place where you would be always welcome and where there would be always somebody who would have under-standing for your troubles, difficulties and grief. I wish this feeling can re-main until the day when Scattergood starts again to be a refuge for people who will need a place from which they can start all over."

Calling it "a monument a friendship in many many hearts," Rudolf Schreck characterized Scattergood very well, saying:

> *Scattergood has given so much to everyone of us who went there to find a place of security in a strange, bewildering new world—as America was to many of us—a place of human understanding, help, advice. A place of peace in a world of war, a haven amidst a world of hatred.*

1.) "Nisei" is a commonly used term for Japanese-descended Americans.

2.) One executive-committee member—Wilson Emmons of What Cheer, Iowa—planned, but ultimately was un-able, to attend the meeting. Instead he wrote a detailed letter (24.I.43) to Martha Balderston in which he shared reflections on the hostel's closing:

"Thy letter [announcing the hostel's closure] came as a real surprise as we had not realized the immediate necessity of discontinuing Scattergood as a refugee hostel. We knew of course that such a time would come some-time but had not expected it so soon. [Regarding the proposed relocation center] I do not hear any opposition expressed here to Japanese-Americans, but we do not know what the attitude would be if a bunch of them were moved into the neighborhood. It is no doubt true that farm help in the middle west is going to be hard to secure this coming summer and the Japanese would take to that sort of work better than the guests we have had at the Hostel... [Iowa] surely would be a better place for some of them than in the desert of Arizona. They could make that little farm at Scattergood 'blossom like the rose' and perhaps produce twice as much as it ever did before. [On a different theme] I think none of us will ever know the far reaching influence which has gone out from the Hostel as it has been conducted or how great a factor such influence may be when it comes time to reorganize the world on a peaceful and sensible basis again... Maybe some day when this dreadful war is ended and we all get on our way back to normal living again, we will better appreciate and be more thankful for the blessings we have enjoyed for so many years but sort of took for granted."

3.) It seems that Friends were acting out of dissonance—on one hand optimistic that their project would find receptive audience yet on the other fearing the opposite. As early as 13 January 1943, for example, Martha Balderston wrote Mary Rogers that "we have all been challenged by the sense of adventure in the Japanese work, at the same time realizing its dangers and difficulties. The neighborhood may be much more violent in its protest against the Japanese than it was against the Germans. But we are willing to investigate further the possibilities. We realize that the Japanese are truck farmers rather than corn-hog farmers."

4.) According to a Scattergood Hostel Report of 12 August 1942, "the work of Scattergood Hostel has brought to the people of Iowa a clearer understanding of the situation in Europe, a new appreciation of friendship, of their responsibility in helping others, a closer contact with Quaker projects, [Civilian Public Service] camps and other work throughout the country. This work is also a practical demonstration of Friends' belief in the value of human personality, of toleration, and an example of living in 'that spirit that takes away the occasion for war.'"

5.) In a letter to the "Dear Scattergood Family," Martha noted: "During the past four years Scattergood has indeed been a home for many of us and we have made rich friendships in that time. As happens in normal life one's family scatters and as a result new centers—homes—are opened and the influence of the home spreads in a widening circle. In a very real sense the same thing happens with our Scattergood family—each individual who goes out into a home of his [or her] own starts a nucleus of love and good will... We are giving serious thought to the next step. Scattergood as a hostel for European refugees has gradually established itself in the minds of the people of Iowa as a living example of understanding and concern for those individuals up-rooted from their homes and background. It is our hope that we can find a project that will carry on as a similar demonstration of the Quaker belief in toleration and responsibility for others." Paul Schwarz' sentiments resonated Martha's image of the diffusion of goodness having been made possible through the now-closing project. On 18 March 1943 he bid : "If this is a farewell letter to the Scattergood Hostel it is not one to the Scattergood ideal. A spark of these ideals lives in each and every one of us who once lived there. Scattergood has fulfilled its wonderful mission once more and 'scattered' those sparks out into the world. The rest is up to us. We shall not fail."

6.) Local opinion was by no means undecided. Over 50 years later Floyd Fawcett— then a Quaker farmer living just outside of West Branch—said that bringing the Nisei to the town "would have been extremely difficult [given] the feeling that I heard in West Branch at the time; that would have been something that have caused a real split within the community... 'We don't want any Japs in our community' was the feeling all over town—pretty predominant, even among some Friends at that time. [Regarding the Europeans,] there'd been so much persecution of the people at that time that were was just a feeling that these were people who needed to be helped. If we'd been involved in the war, that'd have been [different]. But I would have been adamantly opposed to bringing Japanese-Americans into the community because I would have seen such a split in the community." (Interview with AMLT, 17.XI.94)

7.) In a letter she also wrote on 15 March 1943 to Mary Rogers, Martha added : "[The man] wonders if [possessing citizenship] is such a great prilivege [sic] after all! Then [he] goes on to say 'this war is being fought so that every man, woman and child, regardless of race, color or creed...shall enjoy all the rights of freedom... He [sic] shall share in the justices as well as the injustices of the nation to which he has sworn allegiance... If Iowa farmers do not want Japanese on their farms, that is their business. But why don't they make it their business to suggest some useful or constructive method of dealing with the American-Japanese problem, rather than sit back and curse and threaten those who do?' Rather a [sic] interesting thought from such a source, isn't it?"

8.) At breakfast on the hostel's last day someone remarked "well, today Scattergood closes its doors." Reportedly the first-grade boy present "wanted to know how he was to get in when he came home from school that afternoon!"

9.) In reaction to the reactionaries among them, numerous quiet citizens took exception to the way in which their noisiest neighbors had dominated the incident. On 8 April 1943, F.L. Pearson—a cashier at West Branch's First State Bank—wrote to Lynn Zimmerman, who by then was living in Kalamazoo, Michigan and had not been actively involved with the hostel for over 15 months. He explained: "You may be somewhat surprised to receive this letter...but I just wanted to say a word...with reference to the re-location work... When the matter was being discussed with reference to bringing [Japanese-Americans] to Scattergood I took no active part in the proceedings. I did not attend the meetings at the schoolhouse, but at all times have been a good listener, and on a few occasions have expressed my views regarding it. I was very much disappointed in the way the matter was concluded, due to the local opposition. Maybe it was best that it be dropped as it was at that time, but I just want to make this statement, that there is a large number of people in this community who feel that the attitude of the opposition was un-American and that such a race attitude will result in a continuance of world conflict and wars. I think the sentiment in favor of the proposed project has very greatly changed in this community and people are thinking much more kindly toward it now than they did in the beginning, and with the exception of a few very ardent fighters the opposition has quite largely disappeared. It is true there would be opposition. There was opposition when they brought the Jews to Scattergood, and there will be opposition in any community where a like project is started... I ask that you kindly not use my name in connection with it, as, on account of business reasons I need to keep in the background, but I am personally not opposed to giving these unfortunate people a chance, and there is a large number of others in this community who feel the same way."

10.) The refugee names listed here are those used by them in March 1943—often different from the names with which they arrived at Scattergood Hostel and which appear in the records.

APPENDICES

Ia. SCHOLARLY SUMMARY OF QUAKER THEOLOGY

In several respects Quakers were similar to the mainline [Protestant] denominations... Over the years they gradually discarded many of their peculiar cultural patterns. Theologically Quakers continued to be distinctive, but inasmuch as many, if not most, had become "liberal" in respect to their own orthodox historical teachings... [Quakers] shared a common commitment to pacifism, a commitment that derived from their religious principles and was rooted in their historical origins...

Perhaps most basic among the particular tenets of Quakers is that religion, to be valid, must be experiential. Dogmas are relatively unimportant, in fact unessential. Religion, in fact God himself, is experienced through the "Inner Light" reaching into the hearts of men [and women]. Thus there is within every[one] a divine "Seed", or, put differently, God is within every [person]. This holds for all [people], regardless of how much evil may have outwardly seized control of an individual life. Such beliefs have led to an optimistic view of human nature. [A human being] is not essentially evil, but has potential, because of the seed of God within, for goodness...

The conviction that all men have God within gives rise...to a sense of the oneness of mankind. Such views of humanity have led to a respect for all men, nations as well as individuals, thus precluding a resort to violence and war. Their effect is, ideally, a love for all men. Love is an absolute, the only absolute. Love, and goodness, are the means to the creation of a new society, a social order based on justice and righteousness, because men and nations are capable of responding to love as well as goodness.

Tenets such as these have predisposed Quakers to social concern. Indeed, Quakers believe that religious experience and social concern are inextricably related and that the latter is often divinely inspired...[1]

Ib. SOCIOLOGICAL SKETCH OF THE RELIGIOUS SOCIETY OF FRIENDS

The Quakers are in interesting if not a puzzling phenomenon. They worship in silence but publish a continuous stream of books and pamphlets largely about themselves. They are few in number yet you find them everywhere, often in places of considerable influence. They are fearless social reformers and have a very good head for business, some of their leading families being among the richest in England at the time of the Industrial Revolution. They proclaim a great message, yet do it in curiously muted tones. They have never celebrated sacraments nor borne arms. They have never refused to recognize women as ministers and their status as Christians is unquestioned, except by free-thinking members of their own community. They recognize a bond of unity among themselves, but have never appropriated the title of "church", preferring to call themselves a "society" only. The basis of the unity they feel with one another is not doctrine but an attitude which gave rise to one of their earlier names—Friends of Truth.

Quakers are serious people. Rightly so, for their vocation is a serious business. You do not seek to defeat the forces of prejudice, ignorance and cruelty in society unless you are in deadly earnest. Though there is a special off-beat Quaker humour, the belly laugh is not one of their gifts. This makes them introspective—defining the proper "Quakerly" attitude to a multitude of matters is their greatest sport. Seeking to avoid spiritual pride they view with suspicion the use of language, history and theology in any way that might fetter the personal quest of any of their members for truth. They much prefer to travel hopefully than to arrive.

To outsiders, they are frequently annoying. Their kindly, calm and tolerant religion is difficult to convey in words. Those who seek to experience it by worshipping with them tend to end up by becoming Quakers. They seldom answer questions about their faith directly. Some are deeply mystical and have much in common with adherents of other faiths with whom they seem more at home; some are so deeply rooted in biblical faith as to be fundamentalists—one yearly meeting in America going so far as to refuse to recognise all the rest. They are a world-wide fraternity, yet have no central authority. They are so small in numbers that in some countries all the Quakers know all the other Quakers. There are Anglo-Saxon Quakers, Masai Quakers, Mexican Quakers, Eskimo Quakers, Chinese Quakers, Navajo Indian Quakers. A bewildered onlooker might ask, where is the unity in this mass of people as varied as the human race itself?

~ **John Punshon**,
Foreword to *Portrait in Grey: A Short History of the Quakers*

1.) William Edward Nawyn. *American Protestantism's Response to Germany's Jews and Refugee's, 1933-1941.* Ann Arbor: UMI Research Press, 1981, pp. 314-317

Nawyn continues: "Concern often induces service, that is, concrete efforts to reform evil conditions and to help those who are suffering on account of them. The results of such service are incidental, but the service itself must derive from the prompting of God within. Although not the primary goal of service, nevertheless a certain optimism exists that success will attend it because of the basic conviction that God residing within all humans makes them potentially responsive to the sincere application of love and goodness. In implementing such service, Quakers have historically been attracted...to limited pilot projects as a visible way of demonstrating their convictions and goals...in a particular area of concern. Service is also frequently viewed as an alternative to participation in coercive measures prescribed by society, especially military". (p. 317) "Prior to the 1930s, this type of concern had been demonstrated by American Quakers in such areas as the treatment of criminals and the insane, equal rights for women, the peace movement, and...the abolition of slavery." (p. 315)

IIa. LAYOUT OF SCATTERGOOD'S BUILDINGS

These sketches—based on memory—were drawn by Camilla Hewson Flintermann, revised by Lillian Pemberton Willoughby and slightly altered by A.M. Luick-Thrams based on the composite recollections of both women. As Camilla noted, these drawings are not to scale and contain "numerous vague areas". Still, they provide an idea of Scattergood's layout at the time of the hostel's existence.

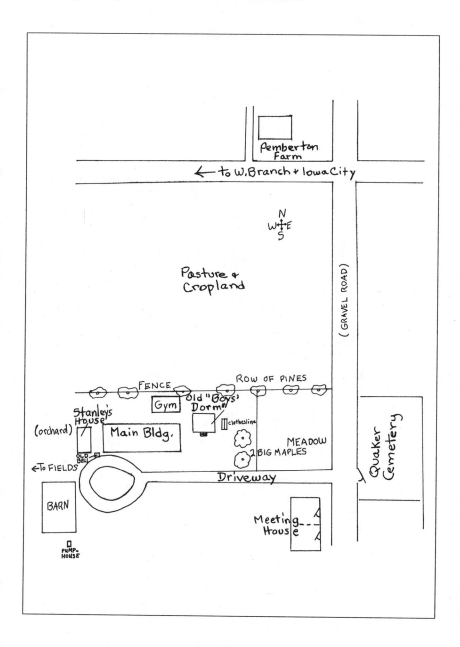

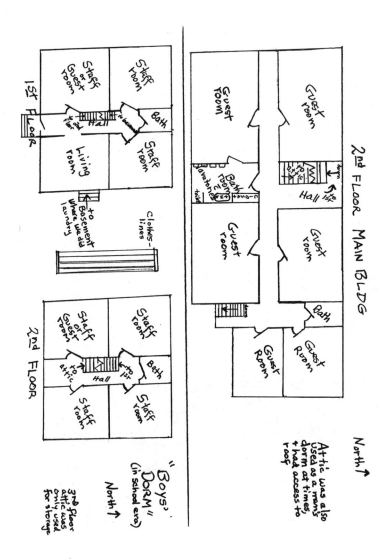

2nd FLOOR MAIN BLDG

Guest room

Guest room

Guest room

Guest room

Bath room lavabories toilet

Hall 1st 2nd

Guest Room

Guest Room

Bath

North ↑

Attic was also used as a man's dorm at times, + had access to roof

1st FLOOR

Staff or Guest room

Staff room

Hall 2nd 1st

Bath

Living room

Staff room

to Basement where we did laundry

Clothes-lines

2nd FLOOR

Staff or Guest room

Staff room

Hall to attic 1st

Bath

Staff room

Staff room

"Boys' DORM" (in school era)

North ↑

3rd floor attic was only used for storage

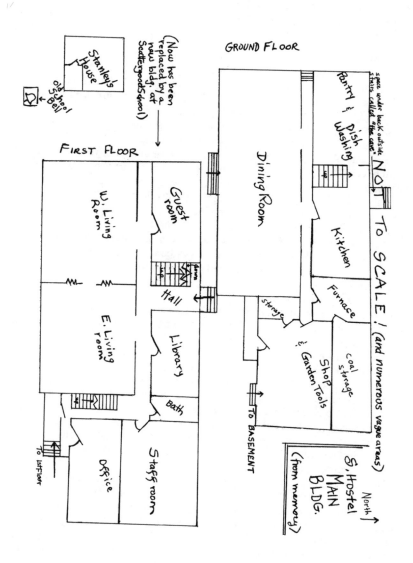

GROUND FLOOR

Stanley's House

old School Bell

(Now has been replaced by a new bldg. at Scattergoods School)

FIRST FLOOR

space under back outside stairs **called "the cave"**

NOT TO SCALE! (and numerous vague areas)

North

S. Hostel MAIN BLDG.
(from memory)

Pantry & Dish Washing

Dining Room

Kitchen

Furnace

Coal Storage

Shop & Garden Tools

storage

To BASEMENT

W. Living Room

Guest room

E. Living room

Library

Bath

Office

Staff room

Hall

down

up

up

To 1st Floor

287

III. CHRISTMAS AT SCATTERGOOD HOSTEL

(Earle and Marjorie Edwards wrote the following article titled "Christmas at Scattergood Hostel" for publication in The Friend on 21 March 1940.)

JANUARY 1, 1940

It is cold in Iowa today and cold at Scattergood, but our hearts are warm enough to compensate for anything the weather-man may bring. At this time Scattergood can look back on a very busy eight months culminating in an exciting and happy two weeks at Christmas, and forward, we hope, to continued creative work as long as there is need for it. The family is larger than ever; the rooms are full to overflowing and that important thing, Scattergood spirit, is flourishing.

The story of the spring and summer is one known to most of you, but have you heard of our Christmas celebration? The activity which brought sixty people at this most sacred time of the year to worship and play together, to be among friends to enjoy the Yuletide festival at that place in this country they most like to call home is, it seems to us, the story that best exemplifies the *esprit de corps* found there and which best shows the place such a hostel can and ought to fill in many lives.

It is a story that begins back in the second week in December, at which time plans were drawn up for the celebration of the 25th. A decoration committee was formed to incorporate work on necessary items with English classes. An entertainment committee met to choose a play for presentation; in another section of the house people discussed the dinner menu, and wondered how we could fit in a few candy-making and cookie-making parties along with the regular schedule. In three days the buildings were humming with activity. A special cleaning schedule had been arranged to insure a spotless house. The decoration committee began making candlesticks, plotting as to which evergreens would be suitable for table ornamentation, consulting with the budget experts on how much could be spent for tree decorations, discussing the problem of mistletoe and other extra things, and also including in their province gift arrangements. The nearby trees were culled for wreath material, the woodpile for pieces for candle holders, and the five and ten for inexpensive decorating materials with which they could manufacture tree ornaments. Silver icicles were purchased and a few shiny balls. The hostel, as a group, decided to ask each person to buy a twenty-five cent gift for another person, the name of his recipient to be drawn from a list of those to be present at the tree festivities.

Then in a corner of the living-room certain persons were to be found day in and day out rehearsing their Christmas play. Within the week they had memorized the parts and mastered the action. "Blessed Christmas" was its appropriate title. In the kitchen we found certain stalwarts working "overtime" daily to prepare quantities of mince pies and other American delicacies. Later in the week the Germans banded together to collect their choicest cookie and candy recipes. They worked on them continuously; then the Wednesday before Christmas the whole hostel gathered in the kitchen to produce many pounds of candy. We ground chocolate, shelled nuts, stuffed figs, transposed grams into ounces and after much labor brought forth a creditable supply of holiday sweets.

By this time the source of the turkeys and the tree had been discovered—a kind donor from a nearby town. The tree was soon brought in and decorated. Then we surely knew that Christmas was coming. To make more certain that knowledge, carol

288

practice started. Then on the 24th the alumni began arriving. A couple came from Kentucky, some from nearer towns. In the evening, thirty strong, we set out to serenade West Branch. It was cold, and Susy, the 1929 Ford, was not feeling at all well, but we made it and surprised the natives besides enjoying ourselves.

Sunday brought more alumni and also brought us all together in the Meetinghouse, over forty this time. A more impressive Meeting few of us have attended. Christmas Eve started with an early supper around long, candle-lit tables. As we came to the end of the meal someone rose to play "Silent Night" on the piano. A few tears on the part of both Germans and Americans followed—almost our only open expression of the solemnity that underlay all of these hours this year, but on which might well have occurred any year and anywhere. Above all, this seemed to be a time to carry on as if nothing were wrong as best we could. After supper we all gathered around the huge tree in the living-room to await Santa Claus's presentation of his many gifts. They had come not only through our exchange system but also from people far and near—personal articles and things for the hostel, old and new, and all welcome.

Christmas morning at 6.30 found two of the hostelites in the kitchen to put the turkeys into the oven. The excellent stuffing was made by a visiting gentleman Friend. For breakfast the whole hostel had been invited to a neighboring farmhouse, but we numbered so many that the excursion had to be made in three shifts. The first one went at 8.30 and from then on "Merry Christmases" could be heard down the road as people passed one another on their way to and from hot rolls, home-made sausages and chocolate. After that came preparations for dinner. Sixty of us sat down to it at one o'clock. Much later one of our visitors from Chicago remarked that of all the things about the week-end which he would remember, most impressive was the spirit exhibited during the preparation, the enjoyment of the meal and the clean-up. It was like that which we generally are accustomed to think of only in terms of family gatherings. It was noticed even by the newcomers who had arrived the previous Saturday and that very morning; all felt completely at home during the whole proceedings.

And this is exactly the spirit which makes Scattergood significant as a current project in aid of humanity. It is exemplified in our general meetings for business held each Monday evening. There we discuss everything from the state of the bath-tubs and techniques of washing to plans for inviting lecturers from the university to spend an evening with us. Hostelites feel free to offer criticisms and suggestions; a friendly give and take prevails. If misunderstandings arise they are more often straightened out by older guests who have caught the spirit of the place than by any staff members. The log for the past week, kept in turn by all residents, is read at this time. Here we discover the informal and the deeper side of group life. There are comments on trips to the movies, the midnight discussions, or an impression of the beauty of the sunrise or of an afternoon, and mention of particularly meaningful morning Meetings. Another aspect of this spirit is apparent in the literary seminars on American authors which are conducted every Thursday evening. All co-operate and the interest shown in the books obtainable from the public or university libraries is thrilling. Or there is the time that these men, who had always considered household tasks the affairs of women, decided almost unanimously to do as much of that type of work as possible to relieve the women of the simpler jobs like mangling, dish-washing, and scrubbing, and allow them to concentrate on the cooking, ironing, and the supervision of the washing. The weekly schedule, apportioning all jobs, does not prevent volunteers turning out to assist on frequent occasions. One sometimes suspects that ordinary American citizens might benefit considerably from such an experience as these refugees enjoy. Last week one of the men disappeared for the afternoon. At nightfall another discovered him trudging up from the Meeting-house. "Where have you been?" came the question. Reluctantly came an answer: "In the Meeting-house." "All afternoon?" "Yes." "Anything wrong?" "Well—come and see." And after that two people had a secret—for the missing member had spent the time cleaning the room and varnishing the benches as a Christmas surprise not to be made known until it was completely finished. After this occurrence it was decided by the whole group that the stove, which occupies an important place in the front-center of the room, ought to be painted to make the place as harmonious and lovely as possible.

This group-feeling is especially obvious at key times in the life of any one member, of course. Recently one of the women was quite upset because she had not received a letter from her parents in central Europe for over three months. When word finally came through the smiles on every face were a moving sign of the mutual concern they felt, both in sorrow and in joy. A real family could hardly be more interwoven in make-up. They share the triumph of each job that is obtained, and we were all proud cooks when one of our numbers attained a prominent spot in a local newspaper with pictures and a recipe for her apfel strudel. Or, again, there was breathless listening to a local radio station both the nights our star pianists gave a concert there. We all knew the compositions. Had we not suffered through his practicing for weeks? But the tense and concentrated atmosphere of the group gathered around the receiving set for that program was as music-lovers hearing Paderewski for the first and only time. And the hostel turn-out when any member or ex-member is to deliver a lecture would warm the cockles of any heart. They can always count on large and most appreciative group of stooges!

Tutoring in English, American government or history is a fascinating experience. No adults can be more enthusiastic, or demanding students than refugees. And no teacher can be too well prepared! Can you think of any more vital subject for discussion than one raised in an English class by a refugee war-resister who, quite conscious of Professor MacIntosh's fate, is looking ahead five years to the time when he must declare his intention regarding the defense of this country in time of war? No one could be either more anxious to be a good citizen, or more opposed to fighting.

The cultural contribution such people make to a community is not to be forgotten when considering the place such a hostel plays in American civilization. Musicians, lecturers, cooks—all add to the life around them in unique ways because of their necessarily different backgrounds. But perhaps more important is the contribution as people that those who have suffered so much and so well make. One is inspired by their equilibrium after these past years of trial; one is rewarded by their friendship and one becomes more rich in the fundamentals of life through working with them and learning to know them better. And here in this particular Iowa spot where roundabout are Danish, German, Welsh, Viennese and Swedish communities, American now but still suggesting their European heritage, it certainly seems meet, right, and our bounden duty to do all in our power for these other Americans-to-be. One refugee guest, urging others to leave New York for Scattergood, said: "I have seen that once you are in Scattergood you are no longer a refugee. You are a man." To the extent that statement is true, the supporters of the hostel may be said to be succeeding in this great task.

IV. Skit Written When Robert Berquist Left Scattergood

(This humorous narrative was written by staff members for a skit presented during the farewell party held for Robert Berquist upon his leaving for Civilian Public Service in November 1941 and provides an "unofficial" look at the life of staff Scattergood Hostel)

Sometimes the account of a person's life makes the most interesting story one could read. On the other hand there are some people in whose lives are such fantastic tales that they are not to believe. The story I will tell you now is a true one. It is an uncensored account of the history of Robert Fletcher Berquist, and it has do with one year of his life—spent at Scattergood Hostel. The more graphic portions of this story will be shown in pantomime with sound effects furnished by people who were personal friends and co-workers of Mr. Berquist at the Hostel.

I ask you to go with me to that country of 10,000 lakes where on a summer evening we find Bob brooding over an article in the *Christian Century*. As you see, he is intensely interested. Suddenly he springs to his feet. He has an idea which, being Bob, he immediately writes down on a slip of paper. What does it say? "Write to Scattergood Hostel and ask if I can spend my two weeks vacation there." After two days of careful consideration of every detail, the letter is sent. Little does he know the part that letter will play in his life from that moment on. The letter arrives at the Hostel and is read by Lynn who passes it on to Martha, commenting, "Some character wants to spend two weeks vacation here. Shall we let him come?" The matter is discussed and a letter is sent back with the result that Bob arrives.

So this is Scattergood. Bob receives a cordial welcome and goes to work immediately. He is delighted with everything and as the two weeks draw to a close he becomes very sad because he must leave. He returns to the 10,000 lakes but always he thinks of Scattergood. He gazes dreamily out the window and says, "Now they are ringing the bell for men's work. I wonder if Rolf and Peter got a job. etc. etc." Finally he could stand it no longer, so the last of October we see him arriving at Scattergood once more, this time as a volunteer staff member.

One of his first duties in this position is to take the Iowa trip. So we see him rushing in from digging the ditch to make out his lists. It's confusing. Lynn tells him the Wednesday trip is on Tuesday this week. No, the Tuesday trip is on Wednesday. What day is this, anyway? Well, it doesn't matter. The list must be made. First, Lillian's butter. That's in West Branch. Marj wants toilet brushes from Woolworth's. Does West Branch have a Woolworth store? Lynn calls through the wall to ask him to stop in West Branch and get the money for allowances. The list grows longer. Don't worry, Bob, it will get much more complicated as time passes.

Well, as we said, time passes, and Bob has enrolled for a course at the University. Night after night he pores over huge volumes and worries about the hours he must stand before his High School class and teach them history. But surely all those papers are not examinations for the children. Oh, no, not long after Bob's migration to Iowa, he went with Giles, Walter, Earle and others to register for the draft. He was pretty lucky—No. 1672. Only Giles did better and he had practiced on slot machines so much. Those papers are questionnaires and since Bob is a CO [conscientious objector] he must study extensively on what will be proper and acceptable answers. Such is his program; breakfast prep, dishes, men's work (the ditch everlasting), and then tuitions which he rushes through at 45 minutes per.

But it's not all work. Christmas approaches. They are being international and are learning Christmas carols in various languages. With benefit of sound we pause to hear the staff struggling with those multi-syllabic German words.

The New Year comes in, but Bob has gone back to the lakes and the Scattergood girls try to satisfy their curiosity about the possible attractions he may have there. Letters held up to the light reveal nothing that could account for it. They can make out only such phrases as "Fellowship of Reconciliation", "the peace group here", "a life of service," "self-dedication," "worthwhile thing to do," "social action." Even a letter from a girl named Frances ends, "Sincerely yours." Elinor tried the direct question method and learned absolutely nothing of significance, so Bob's past remains his own as does his present, and as far as they can see, his future.

Then a crisis is evident. Earle and Marj Edwards are leaving the Hostel and when their will is read, Bob has inherited the bulk of Earle's duties. He rises half an hour earlier to take are of the cars and worries until late at night about the work program. In vain do the girls entreat him to go to the movies. He must work and study. The golden days of youth are passing and Bob is bent over his newest affliction—a correspondence course in 24 lessons. It's summer time and Scattergoodians scatter for moonlight walks and parties. Bob wrestles with his 12th lesson one night but continual interruptions make it most difficult. Lynn and Esther are writing a song for a departing guests and he must censor it. Wearily he goes to Lynn's room and listens with horror to the song. The he goes back to his desk, leaves them to write it all over again, but his trouble is not over. The moonstruck girls are in a playful mood and what can he do when they decide to serenade him.

Sunday was intended for a day of rest, but somewhere along the line that was overlooked. Someone must go for the mail and it seemed a good job for Bob. And since he is driving the car, why not take Doris and Becky to Sunday school? Home for dinner and a nice quiet afternoon to do Lesson 12 again. But it looks like rain; the wind begins to blow and Bob feels a concern for the cars. He dons a raincoat and dashes out to move them away from the trees. Of course Suzy is temperamental and must be pushed, but things like that happen. Visitors appear in spite of the rain and everyone else has disappeared as if by magic, so Bob takes them around trying to explain why this placed is maintained without any people living here. Time passes.

At five o'clock he returns to Lesson 12, but Lynn calls through the wall again to know what to do about the singing. Nothing can be done except to make a list of songs and break the news to Lynn that the West Branch peace group comes here tonight for a meeting at 8:00. Lesson 12 is postponed until after the meeting and Bob must study until late at night. That was his intention, but here's Cornell Hewson come to spend the night, and it isn't polite to keep a light burning when a guest wants to sleep. No study tonight. Time passes. One party stands out in the minds of Scattergoodians. It was the occasion when they played truth and consequences. Bob told the truth, so he said, and confessed he had never kissed a girl. But he got the consequences all the same as the Scattergood girls tried without success to remedy that situation. Time passes again.

One of the most significant instances of Bob's life at this time was the staff meeting. Here the staff members met with long lists of things to be done. There are five additions to be made to the tutoring schedule; the station wagon needs new tires; the meeting house must be painted; something to be done about a lecture course; one room needs bulbs. One by one Martha lists the many emergencies which are received listlessly by all but Bob. One by one he agrees to take over the responsibility and one by one they are added to his list. The last item of business is a speech to be given in Davenport, and Bob sighs as he agrees to address a woman's [sic] club in that city. But he keeps smiling as he drives the station wagon up to the door for Kathe [sic], Rosa and Anny who are going along. The smile grows a trifle strained as he changes both front tires on the car, but at last they are gone. Time passes. At breakfast we greet a haggard Bob who spent most of the night getting the station wagon out of the ditch into which the treacherous ice had deposited it.

Time passes. Suddenly like a belt from the blue comes the summons to a physical examination for Bob and Ernest. They depart, accompanied by Elinor and Esther. Dr. Mosher loses all prestige in our eyes by diagnosing that Bob is a little deaf, but you know our Bob. He passed the examination, so we feel no compunctions about turning over practically all the work to him. What's good enough for the army is good enough for us. Time passes swiftly after that end and Bob brings more and more people from Iowa [City's] bus station. Another Bob arrives as a staff member and the group grows increasingly fond of him, but still Bob B. holds his highest place in the affections of the family unchallenged.

Time passes. Comes the time when most of the staff members go to Chicago to a meeting and Bob drives the station wagon. Everyone comes home inspired to work like mad, but a group of letters drives everything else from their minds. Bob has been summoned to Camp Merom in Indiana. He goes about his accustomed tasks as usual, but no one can forget that there will soon be a vacant chair and their "long Bob" will be gone. Sadly they go their ways, rallying only to prepare a super dinner as a farewell gesture. Sorrowfully, each in his own key and individual pronunciation, they sing the goodbye song.

~ **Esther Smith**

V. An Essay on Daily Life at Scattergood Hostel

I write the following with full recognition of the danger of not being able to see the wood for the trees, that proverbial expression of distrust in the subjective discussion method, of description of events by one whose heart and soul are wrapped up in the events as they occur, yet I feel it is necessary that I share...some of the lights and shadows of life in a Hostel for refugees from war and oppression, and tell you about some of the things that can happen in a place where eleven pacifists from all over the country have come together to serve cooperatively a religious society, a political territory and a band of emigrees [sic]. I say a band of emigrees [sic] because I have heard them sing our Negro spiritual "Go Down, Moses," because I know how they cling to one another and the security of their own group where they find the only fellowship that most of the world allows them...

293

Scattergood is a place where refugees from Germany, direct victims of oppression and war, may find rest and peace and friendship and the beginnings of a better life in a new world. The primary, immediate obligation of Scattergood is service to these people. This service is of necessity so wide in character, making all kinds of demands, that Scattergood reaches out into the general fields of all Friends service, touching vitally our peace testimony, and asking us about resettlement, industrial unemployment, education, insurance, hospitalization, housing, building construction, community living and of course immigration, international relations, tariffs, and postal systems. It has demanded even wider and more divergent considerations from the staff in personal relations, requiring that the American group be all things to all men [and women]: fathers, mothers, sisters, brothers, sons, daughters, friends, barbers, dressmakers, housemaids, legal advisors. Their ministry has been full and unstinting.

Scattergood has established itself in the mind of the middle-west as an experiment in service. There have been constant press notices of the activities of the Hostel, all of them friendly, and thousands of visitors since the Hostel was begun. The effect of these visits has been felt in letters from unknowns who have been among us and write back to offer jobs, furniture, hospitality, turkeys and cranberry sauce.

When you come to visit us you will be awakened in the black dawn of winter by the sound of a bell which used to ring for school in the days when Scattergood was a Friends boarding school, and by the time the sun is up you will be in our cheery dining room, exchanging greetings in Pennsylvania Dutch over quantities of good coffee. If you are tardy you will have to gulp the last cup, because another bell rings, and people have begun to go in twos and threes down the walk by the cedar row that borders the lane to the Meetings House where we gather for worship each day. There is the center of our life, and as you sit around the squat iron stove you will know what it means to be a friend.

As a community Scattergood endeavours to hold its life on a common plane of service and friendly cooperation. Everybody does everything. Nothing is forbidden, work is shared by agreement, no one is forced to work, but everybody does what there is to be done. From eight to ten in the morning brooms and mops and laundry tubs are active, and at ten they are laid aside for pencils and notebooks and a tour into the mysteries of American diplomacy and the pronunciation of an English "r". Here you will learn that America is the land of oppor-r-r-rtunity with jobs and freedom from religious and racial prejudice for all. After two and half hours of mental gymnastics, the bell summons again to food, this time including some of the corn that was picked and canned during a broiling August. In the afternoon men and women scatter to study, write letters, work on building repair, iron, mend, but most beloved of all, learn to drive a car. If you survive one of these driving lessons you will have learned that the very first thing to acquire in America is an automobile. Everybody has one! In the evenings everyone gathers for a Hostel meeting for business in which all matters of policy are freely discussed, or to sing lusty songs in many languages, to participate in a literary seminar,or hear a lecture on some phase of American life. By this time you will probably be tired, for like all our guests you have pitched in and participated in a all the foregoing activity...

These things occur and mean much to all of us everywhere, yet they are but out-

ward evidence of the deeper movings of life among us... Beneath these things one feels a strong will leading through a valley of shadows into a land of light. It has been a humbling experience for those of us who have been to school at Scattergood in this second era. May we have the faith, the courage, and the imagination to carry on.
~ **John Kaltenbach, 1940**

VI. "The Initiation of Elsie, the New Staff Member"
(Transcript of a play presented on 25 December 1940.)

PROLOGUE: The smash hit produced by the Scatterbrain Productions last June has encouraged us to produce another play. The June play dealt with the disillusionment of a new Scattergood guest; this time we shall deal with the disillusionment of a new staff member. This little dramatic gem is purely fiction, and all characters are imaginary. Any resemblance to persons either living or dead is purely coincidental. This play is copyrighted, and may not be produced without permission of the copyright owners. Anyone wishing to reproduce this play, or any portion thereof, must secure the written permission of [Scattergood's beloved cats] Mr. Milquetoast, Mrs. Jane Arden Milquetoast, Mr. Toughy Milquetoast, Miss Sister Milquetoast, and Mrs. Wild Cat, to whom this play is dedicated.

The opening scene is a bus station (just as in the famous play last June). The New Staff Member has just asked the ticket seller for a ticket to "Scattergood, near West Branch", and has been overheard by the retiring staff member who sits wearily on a bench nearby.

Old Staff Member: Pardon me, but I couldn't help overhearing you ask for a ticket to Scattergood, near West Branch. You must be the new staff member. Let me introduce myself. I am Rebecca, the retiring member.

New Staff Member: You have guessed correctly. I am Elsie, the new member. I'm so excited about my new job... I've heard of the wonderful life at Scattergood, and I'm looking forward to my new job. It sounds very easy. I just have to write a few letters, give a few lessons and the rest of the time I'll have for myself.

OSM: Yes, it is a fine life.

NSM: May I ask why you're leaving? I suppose the only reason that anyone would leave would be that they had found an even easier job.

OSM: Well, to tell the truth, I've had a breakdown and have to go away for a six months' rest cure before I can even consider looking for another job.

CURTAIN

The next scene shows Elsie, the new member, sitting at a typewriter, getting her instructions for the day from other staff members who have just had a staff meeting and decided what the new member should do.

DIRECTOR: Now that you've finished the breakfast dishes, Elsie, I wonder if you could write a few letters for me before you clean the living room?

ELSIE: Certainly...how many are there?

DIR: It's an easy day, just 27 without today's mail. Here they are.

ELSIE: But aren't you going to dictate the answers?

DIR: Well, since it's your first day, I'll help you a bit, but usually I am too busy to give you much dictation. Now this is from a man who wants to know all about Scattergood. Two or three pages should fix that up. And this woman has heard of the Fifth Column rumors...just tell her they aren't true, and explain why. Then write to Mrs. Manypennies and tell her we have desperate need for an affidavit and explain what affidavits are and so on. Then will you write to Mr. Rich in Philadelphia and explain why we had to spend $500 too much last month. Then write Mary Rogers a report on why Mr. X lost his job. There here are twelve letters wanting speakers, just find twelve people to make the speeches and schedule the dates. Then write the Scattergood committee to tell them we need a new well and why. After you've finished the letters, won't you please find someone to help out in the laundry because one of the crew members is ill today. And get one of the men on the staff to investigate why there is oil in the water. If they discover that we've struck oil, perhaps we'll be all right. Oh, here's the placement man. He'll want you to do a few letters also.

ELSIE: (still brave about it all) Good morning. What can I do for you?

PM: (hands her a sheaf of letters) Make copies of curriculums to go with these letters, please. Find the men mentioned and check the dates and so on of their employment. Then write all these prospective employers and tell them about Scattergood, and describe the fine professional people we have here. The letters have to be good. I'm just off to make a placement trip, so I can't help you much. You'll find all the material in the files. (He exits in a rush, putting on hat on way)

German guest interrupts: (in German) Elsie, I have a toothache. Please make an appointment for me for the dentist.

ELSIE: (telephoning) I would like to make an appointment for one of our guests... All right... 2:00 will be fine. I'll bring her in.

LILLIAN: (rushing in before telephoning is completed) On your way back from Iowa City will you stop at Verlins [sic] and get some milk—somebody drank it all and stop a Sidwells and get butter and don't forget to pick up the meat...

Elsie starts to type but is interrupted by another German: Will you please help me fill out my application for first papers?

296

Elsie helps her and is interrupted by EARL [sic]: When you go to West Branch, will you please stop at Strattons and tell them that the bath tub is leaking into the living room again and must be fixed before the Executive Committee today. Now if I can find three men to help fix the septic tank, everything will be all right for awhile.

15 minutes later

Another staff member comes in: Elsie, will you copy these affidavits please, and then could you go in to West Branch to pick up Anny...she's at the beauty parlor.

ELSIE: Well, I thought I might finish these letters before lunch.

ASM: Haven't you forgotten the living room?

ELSIE: Oh heavens, yes. Well, I can surely finish them by 2:00.

ASM: That's good, because that is when you start tutoring lessons.

ELSIE: But I have to drive to Iowa City to take someone to the dentist.

ASM: Well, then arrange your lessons for this evening.

ELSIE: Isn't this an unusually busy day?

ASM: Oh, no, they're all like this...you'll get used to it.

ELSIE: (weakly) Ohhhhhhhhhh.

3:00 that afternoon

Elsie with director enters removing her coat and stares at pile of letters still unwritten. "I thought I'd have these finished, but the phone rang so much, and I had to show some visitors around, and hunt up some postage rates, and find out when the next Clipper left, and somehow the time just passed me by.

Enter three Germans: (unison) Elsie, can you give us our lessons now?

ELSIE: OK, I'll try. Can I take you all together (hopefully).

Germans: Oh, no, we get private lessons. You take us all together in the morning when we have classes.

ELSIE: Ohhhhhhhhh.

CURTAIN

3:00 the following morning. Elsie finishes the last letter. "There, that's all the letters. Now I just have to prepare for my class tomorrow morning. Whew! I'm tired. (She starts to get out books to study, changes her mind and inserts another sheet of paper in the typewriter. Types and then collapses on the desk.)

Enter Director and another staff member: Well, Elsie can't take it. She's fallen asleep on the job. This will never do. Wonder which letter she was writing when she passed out. I suppose I'll have to finish it. (She takes it from machine and reads aloud) "Peaceful Valley Sanitarium" That's funny. I didn't give her any letters to a sanatarium, and we don't have any of our guests in sanaitariums [sic], do we?

OSM: No, I don't think so, or do we? I'm a little tired myself and can't remember much.

DIRECTOR continues: Peaceful Valley Sanitarium, Peaceful Valley, Idaho. Dear Sirs: I feel that I'm about to have a nervous breakdown from overwork and want to reserve the cheapest and quietest room you have. Please let me know immediately if you can give me a reservation for next week. I think that I shall not need more than six months to regain my former health. Sincerely yours, Elsie, the New Staff Member.

CURTAIN—next morning.

Two German Women sit sewing or read. One says: I hear an ambulance came and took Elsie away in the middle of the night. She looked so strong and well; I wonder what happened to upset her. It was such a nice, easy job for her. The Americans don't have to work much here; they don't even have to study English or worry about finding a job. They sure are lucky.

Other G.W.: Yes, and do you know, I wonder why they call them American Volunteers...they actually get paid as much as we get for our weekly allowance! And the director's salary is almost as much as the lowest paid person who has been placed from Scattergood! It really isn't fair that their life should be so easy and ours so hard.

GRAND FINALE:
> This is my Scattergood, I found here rest and
>   peace
> This is the place where American volunteers
> Enjoy a life so swell and feel so sweet and well
> As singing birds on our trees
> As singing birds on our lovely trees.

SCATTERGOOD HOSTELITES

Guests 1939-43

Surname, first; [child]; (new name/nickname); nationality; dates of stay; age

1. ADLER, Alfred; (ADLEY); French; 6.XII.41-7.VI.42; 39
2. ADLER, Marta; (ADLEY);German; 6.XII.41-7.VI.42; 34
3. ALES-ADLER, Franticek; (Francis); Czech; 30.I.43-22.III.43; 44
4. ALTMAN, Fred; German; 24.I.42-25.V.42; 56
5. ALTMAN, Marie; Russian; 24.I.42-20.V.42; 36
6. ARNTAL, Doris; [daughter]; German; 28.IX.40-4.VI.41; 4
7. ARNTAL, Rolf; German; 23.VII.40-5.I.41; 37
8. ARNTAL, Tekla; German; 28.IX.40-4.VI.41; 29
9. ASCHKENES, Kaethe; Austrian; 11.VI.41-9.III.42; 50s
10. ASHER, Klaus; German; 17.VII.42-13.II.43; 37
11. BAECK, Grete; (BECK); Austrian; 23.XII.39-8.VII.40; 45
12. BARDACH, Adolf; (Gus); Austrian; 18.III.40-29.IV.40; 40
    2nd x; 6.VII.40-17.X.40
13. BARON, Walter; German; 28.V.42-3.II.43; 38
14. BAUER, Otto; Austrian; 2.XII.40-28.IV.41; 43
15. BAUER, Rosa; Austrian; 2.XII.40-28.IV.41; 41
16. BEAMT, Adolf; (BEAM, Albert); Austrian; 7.XI.39-21.VII.40; 35
17. BEAMT, Lisa; (BEAM); Austrian; 7.XI.39-21.VII.40; 32
18. BENNDORF, Elle; (Elly); German; 8.XII.39-14.III.40; 40s
19. BENNDORF, Oskar; German; 8.XII.39-14.III.40; 43
20. BLUMENKRANZ, Erwin (Irving); Austrian; 10.IX.40-5.XII.40; 20s
21. BRAUN, Andre [son]; (Andrew); Polish; 9.X.42-10.III.43; 3
22. BRAUN, Sonia; Russian; 9.X.42-4.I.43
    2nd x; 1.III.43-10.III.43
23. BRAUN, Stanislaw; Polish; 9.X.42-10.III.43
24. BROESLER, Ernst; (BRESSLER); German; 21.XII.41-14.XII.42
25. BUKOWITZ, Karl; (BUKOVIS, Charles); Austrian; 17.X.41-8.XII.41; 49
26. DEUTSCH, Emil; Austrian; 11.VII.39-20.XI.39; 39
27. DEUTSCH, Hanna; [daughter]; Austrian; 11.VII.39-4.I.40; 6
28. DEUTSCH, Michael; [son]; Austrian; 11.VII.39-4.I.40; 9
29. DEUTSCH, Regina; Austrian; 11.VII.39-4.I.40; 39
    2nd x; 6.V.41-25.VII.41
30. DRAKE, Arthur; German; 5.VII.39-24.X.39; late 30s
31. DRAKE, Ellen; German; 5.VII.39-24.X.39; late 30s
32. DREYER, Otto; German; 6.I.41-13.X.41; late 40s
33. ELIASBERG, Rosa; Latvian; 24.X.41-27.I.42; 37
34. FEIBELMANN, Ernst; German; 24.IX.41-9.II.42; 55
35. FEIST,Wilhelm; (Willi/William); German; 24.I.40-12.VIII.40; circa 50

36. FRANKEL, Theodor; (FRANK, Teddy); Austrian; 3.XI.41-19.I.42
37. FRANKL, Karl; (FRANKLIN,Clarence); German; 18.II.41-27.VII.41; 54
38. FRIEDMAN, Arnold; Polish; 27.VI.42-22.IX.42
39. FRIEDMAN, Mina Barska; Polish; 27.VI.42-22.IX.42
40. FROLICH, Paul; German; 5.VII.41-15.IX.41; 57
41. GAM, Karel; Czech; 15.IV.39-10.VII.39; 26
42. GIDRO-FRANK, Lothar; Hungarian; 1.VII.42-12.VIII.42; 26
43. GRUNWALD, Hans; (GREENWOOD Peter); Austrian; 23.XII.39-
     20.II.40; circa 30
44. GUTTMAN, Richard; Austrian; 28.XI.39-8.II.40; 56
45. HACKE, Ludwig; (Louis); German; 25.I.42-23.VIII.42
46. HACKE, Walter; [son]; German; 26.VI.42-9.IX.42
47. HACKEL, Hedwig; (Omi); German; 19.I42-15.VI.42; 63
48. HACKEL, Nicole; [granddaughter]; French; 19.I.42-25.V.42; 3
49. HACKEL, Nora; [daughter]; Russian; 19.I.42-6.V.42; 40
50. HANSEN, Richard; German; 4.III.42-18.V.42; elderly
51. HARTMANN, Ludwig; German; 20.XII.39-29.I.40; 27
52. HARVEY, Anna; (Anny); Hungarian; 3.VII.41-23.IV.42
53. HARVEY, Francis; Austrian; 3.VII.41-6.IX.41
54. HARVEY, Liselotte; [daughter]; Austrian; 3.VII.41-23.IV.42; 6
55. HAUSEN, Elisabeth; (Lisa); German; 13.V.41-20.III.42; 34
56. HAUSEN, Erich; German; 13.V.41-9.II.42; 41
57. HESSE, Gertrude; German; 25.VI.41-3.X.41; mid-30s
58. HIRSCH, Sabine; Austrian; 1.II.41-6.VI.41; early 50s
59. HOHENADL-PATEK, Klara (Claire); Austrian; 23.XII.39-14.VI.40
60. HOPF, Donald; German; 4.VIII.39-14.IX.39; 21
61. JAFFE, Boris; Russian; 24.I.40-6.IX.40; circa 50
62. JOACHIM, Otto; Austrian; 23.I.40-15.V.40; early 30s
63. JOLLES, Leo; Austrian; 20.VII.39-10.II.40
64. JUCHACZ, Marie; German; 28.I.42-28.IX.42; 62
65. KELLER, Anne-Marie; German; 10.IV.42-17.IX.42
66. KELLER, Annette; [daughter]; German; 10.IV.42-17.IX.42; 2
67. KELLER, Frank; [son]; German; 10.IV.42-17.IX.42; 12
68. KELLER, Leo; Austrian; 20.IX.40-4.VI.41
     2nd x; 25.IX.41-7.X.41
69. KELLER, Robert; German; 10.IV.42-23.VIII.42; 40
70. KELLNER, Frank; Austrian; 18.V.40-23.X.40; late 30s
71. KEPES, Elizabeth; (Elsie); Hungarian; 21.III.41-16.V.41; late 40s
72. KOBYLINSKI, Martin; German; 7.III.41-9.VI.41; circa 50
73. KOESSLER, Thomas; Austrian; 13.XII.39-25.IV.40; 22
74. KOROPATNICKY, Louis; (CROY); Austrian; 28.I.40-28.IX.40
75. KOVACS, Oskar; Austrian; 12.III.41-24.IV.41; circa 30
76. KRAUTHAMER, Ellen; German; 22.V.42-16.I.43
77. KRAUTHAMER, Guenther; [son]; (George); Polish; 22.V.42-16.I.43; 16
78. KRAUTHAMER, Michael; Polish; 22.V.42-13.I.43
79. LADEWIG, Hans Karl; German; 9.VI.39-12.X.39; 53

80.	LADEWIG, Adelheid; (Heid); German; 9.VI.39-12.X.39; circa 50
81.	LANDYCHEFF, Eugenia; Russian; 16.VI.41-24.X.41; circa 60
82.	LEITER, Edith; Austrian; 19.VI.40-29.VII.40
83.	LEITER, Lothar; Austrian; 19.VI.40-29.VII.40
84.	LEITERSDORFER, Hedy; (LAYTON); Austrian; 30.XII.39-17.VIII.40; 30s
85.	LEITERSDORFER, Wilhelm; (LAYTON); Austrian; 30.XII.39-10.VII.40; 40s
86.	LENZBERG, Walter; German; 16.IX.42-13.I.43
87.	LEVINSOHN, Ruben; Russian; 29.I.43-15.II.43
88.	LICHTENSTEIN, Edith; [daughter]; German; 30.X.41-14.VIII.42; 11
89.	LICHTENSTEIN, Elisabeth; German; 30.X.41-14.VIII.42; 39
90.	LICHTENSTEIN, Julius; German; 30.X.41-14.VIII.42; 46
91.	LICHTENSTEIN, Louis; [son]; German; 30.X.41-14.VIII.42; 9
92.	LICHTMAN, Friedrich; (Lister, Fred); German; 3.V.40-17.IX.40; 20s
93.	LIEBMAN, Karl; (LINN); German; 7.X.39-25.V.40; 49
94.	LIEBMAN, Lotte; (LINN); German; 7.X.39-25.V.40; circa 40
95.	LURIE, Heinz; (LAURY, George); German; 16.IV.39-10.VII.39; 26
96.	LUSTIG, Peter; German; 25.VI.41-28.VI.41; 21
	2nd x; 25.VII.42-17.VIII.42
97.	MALAMERSON, Ernst; (van den HAAG); German; 14.III.41-9.VI.41; 25
	2nd x; 4.VIII.41-21.IX.41
98.	MAUTNER, Egon; (MOUTHNER, Joe); Austrian; 3.VIII.40-29.XI.40
99.	MEYER, Guenther; German; 6.VII.39-4.IV.40; 30s
100.	MICHAEL, Walther; (Walter); German; 6.VI.40-30.IX.40; mid-20s
101.	MUELLER, Jan; German; 12.VII.41-18.X.41; 19
102.	NATHUSIUS, Franz; German; 27.I.41-20.VII.41; 50
103.	NEUDE, Hanns; (NORTON, Harry Burnett); Austrian; 1.VIII.41-1.XII.41;circa 60
104.	NEUMANN, Julius; (NEWMAN); Hungarian; 20.IV.42-20.IX.42
105.	OSTROWSKI, Helmut; (WILK); German; 30.III.40-19.VII.40; 38
106.	PEISSEL, Ewald; Austrian; 13.XII.39-25.IV.40; 28
	2nd x; 13.VII.40-23.IX.40
107.	PETERS, Hans; German; 27.X.39-23.IV.40; 33
108, 109.	POLLAK, Friedrich; (Frederick); Austrian; 20.IX.40-12.V.41
	POLZER, Karl; Austrian; 14.IX.42-15.XII.42
110.	POPPER, Hans; (POTTER, John "Jack" H.); Austrian; 25.IV.40-11.X.40; 30s
111.	POPPER, Viktor; Austrian; 14.VIII.41-30.1V.42
112.	REHAKOVA, Jarmila; Czech; 16.I.43-22.III.43
113.	ROSEGG, Kurt; Austrian; 15.IV.39-30.X.39; 30
114.	ROSENZWEIG, Grete; German; 7.IX.40-14.II.41; 45
115.	ROSENZWEIG, Irmgard; [daughter]; German; 7.IX.40-14.II.41; 14
116.	ROSENZWEIG, Louis; German; 7.IX.40-14.II.41; 55
117.	SALIN, Erwin; German; 22.III.41-29.IV.41
118.	SALINGER, Kurt; German; 2.VII.39-29.VII.39; 20s
	2nd x; (?) -17.IV.40
119.	SALMAN, Magdelene; (SALMON); Polish; 12.VI.41-25.VIII.41
120.	SALMAN, Krystine; [daughter]; (SALMON); Polish; 12.VI.41-25.VIII.4; baby

121.	SCHAEFER, Kurt; German; 15.IV.39-30.IX.39; 34
122.	SCHEIDER, Georg; (George); Czech; 3.X.40-13.XII.40; late 30s
123.	SCHEIDER, Rosa Mimi; (Mary); Czech; 3.X.40-13.XII.40; late 30s
124.	SCHEIDER, Wolfgang; [son]; (Walter); Czech; 3.X.40-13.XII.40; 9
125.	SCHICK, Peter; Austrian; 4.III.40-21.IV.40; 18
	2nd x; 28.VII.40-3.IX.40
126.	SCHIFFMAN, Max; German; 19.VIII.40-6.X.40; 52
	2nd x; 27.I.41-12.III.41; 3rd x; 1.IV.41-18.VI.41
127.	SCHIFFMAN, Rosa; German; 19.VIII.40-6.X.40; 50
	2nd x; 27.I.41-12.III.41; 3rd x; 23.IV.41-9.VI.41
128.	SCHIMETSCHEK, Richard; Austrian; 18.III.41-18.VI.41; circa 50
129.	SCHIMMERLING, Hans; Austrian; 18.III.40-3.III.41; 50s
	2nd; 1.VI.41-25.VI.41
130.	SCHLOSS, Frank; Austrian; 20.V.39-7.IX.39; 30
131.	SCHMID, Josef; Austrian; 1.I.43-21.II.43
132.	SCHMIEDL, Marta; (Martha); Austrian; 17.VII.42-28.X.42; 39
133.	SCHNABEL, Karl; Austrian; 23.VII.40-10.I.41; circa 45
134.	SCHOENTHAL, Anne; (Anny); Austrian; 13.X.39-23.VII.40;mid-20s
135.	SCHOENTHAL, Heinrich; (Henry); Austrian; 13.X.39-23.VII.40
136.	SCHORSCH, Fritz; Austrian; 13.I.41-3.X.41; late 20s
137.	SCHRECK, Rudolf; (Rudi); Austrian; 23.II.40-14.VI.40; 28
138.	SCHROEDER, Herta; German; 12.VI.39-4.XI.39; circa 60
139.	SCHROEDER, Gerald; [son]; (G/Jerry); German; 25.V.39-11.IX.39; 20s
140.	SCHUBER, Angela; Austrian; 25.XII.39-25.I.41; 40s
141.	SCHUBER, Erich; [son]; Austrian; 25.XII.39-25.I.41; 14
142.	SCHUBER, Richard; Austrian; 25.XII.39-6.XII.40; 48
143.	SCHUMACHER, Jack; French; 1.VIII.42-8.IX.42
144.	SCHUMACHER, Mariette; French; 1.VIII.42-1.IX.42
145.	SCHUMACHER, Monique; [daughter]; French; 1.VIII.42-1.IX.42; 6
146.	SCHWARZ, Paul; Austrian; 29.XI.39-28.IV.40; 27
147.	SELIG, Ernst; German; 15.IV.40-1.VII.40; circa 50
148.	SELIG, Lucia; (Lucy); German; 16.IV.40-7.I.41; late 40s
149.	SELIG, Werner; [son]; German; 27.V.40-26.I.41; 11
150.	SELIGMANN, Ilse; [daughter]; (SEAMAN, Elizabeth); German;
	17.IX.41-17.I.42; 7
151.	SELIGMANN, Friedl; (SEAMAN); German; 17.IX.41-17.I.42; 45
152.	SELIGMANN, Helmut; [son]; SEAMAN; German; 17.IX.41-17.I.42; 12
153.	SHOSTAL, Claude; [son]; French; 21.VII.42-25.III.43; 2
154.	SHOSTAL, Pierre; [son]; French; 21.VII.42-25.III.43; 5
155.	SHOSTAL, Magda; (Theresa); Hungarian; 21.VII.42-25.III.43; 36
156.	SHOSTAL, Walter; Austrian; 21.VII.42-8.XI.42; 34
	2nd x; 11.XII.42-27.XII.42; 3rd x; 9.I.43-14.II.43
157.	SIEDEL, Peter; (SEADLE); German; 6.VI.40-25.IX.40; 21
158.	SINGER, Paul; German; 15.III.41-16.V.42; late 50s
159.	SOLMITZ, Ernst; (SOMERS); German; 5.V.39-14.IX.39; 17
	2nd x; 30.III.40

160. SPERLING, Eduard; (SPURLING); Austrian; 17.IX.41-16.X.41; 43
161. TRADELIUS, Guenther; German; 3.VII.41-24.X.41; circa 50
162. TREUER, Fritz; Austrian; 15.IV.39-2.VII.39; 44
163. TUERKEL, Theodor; (Ted); Austrian; 13.IV.40-8.V.40; mid-20s
164. TURK, Ernst; German; 1.VIII.42-4.I.43
165. UNTERHOLZER, Kaethe; (UNDERWOOD, Catherine); German; 2.VIII.39-5.X.39; 30s
166. UNTERHOLZER, Ludwig; (UNDERWOOD, Lucas); German; 2.VIII.39-5.X.39; 30s
167. VANDEN BROECK, Alice; [daughter]; Luxembourger; 15.III.41-22.VIII.41; 7
168. VANDEN BROECK, Kaethe; Luxembourger; 15.III.41-22.VIII.41
169. VANDEN BROECK, Paul; [son]; Luxembourger; 15.III.41-11.VI.41; 18
170. VANDEN BROECK, Sylvain; Luxembourger; 15.III.41-9.VII.41
171. VIOLIN, Karl; (VEOLIN); Austrian; 20.IV.40-19.I.41; 50s
172. VOLKMAR, Ernst; Austrian; 4.XI.40-21.IV.41; 40s
173. WEILER, Bertel [daughter]; German; 26.VIII.40-12.I.41; 5
174. WEILER, Gus; German; 18.VII.40-18.XI.40; mid 30s
175. WEILER, Rosl; (Rosa); German; 26.VIII.40-12.I.41; mid 30s
176. WEISS, Margot; (Ellen); German; 7.VI.41-1.X.41
     2nd x; 24.XII.41-5.I.42
177. WEISS, Philip; Austrian; 26.XII.39-8.IV.40
178. WEISZ, Oskar; (Oscar); Austrian; VIII/IX.40- .X.40; 40s
179. WEISZ, Ruth; [daughter]; Austrian; 5.IX.40-30.XII.40; 5
180. WEISZ, Zlata; Austrian; 5.IX.40-30.XII.40; 40s
181. WELTER, Marianne; German; IX.41-29.III.42; 34
182. WERTH, Jean; (John); Austrian; 4.VIII.41-I.XII.41
183. WERTH, Katherine; (Kathryn); Austrian; 4.VIII.41-I.XII.41
184. WINKLER, Jakob; Austrian; 23.IX.41-7.I.42; circa 60
     2nd x; 20.VIII.42-3.X.42
185. WINKLER, Melanie; Austrian; 23.IX.41-7.I.42; circa 60
     2nd x; 9.IX.42-17.X.42

Staff, 1939-43

(Except where noted, all staff were American, Quaker, and in their 20s)
Surname, first; [child]; (assumed name/nickname); nation/relig.; dates of stay; age

1. ANTHONY, Robert; IX.40-early X.40; late 20s
2. BALDERSTON, Martha; 31.X.39-IV.43; 55
3. BALDERSTON, Marydel; VII.41-20.IX.41; 26
4. BALDERSTON, Walter; VII.41-20.IX.41; 28
5. BERQUIST, Robert; Presbyterian; 30.IX.40-6.XI.41; 26
6. CARTER, Ruth; (BURGESS); 1.IV.40-9.VI.40; 27
7. CHARLES, Mary Lane; (HIATT); 20.VI.40-VII.40; late 30s
8. CLAMPITT, Amy; mid V.41-21.VIII.41; 19
9. COPITHORNE, John (Shaun); Irish; 19.IX.41-III.43; 33
10. COPITHORNE, Josephine; Canadian; 19.IX.41-III.43; 39

10a. COPITHORNE, Susan; [baby]; (ROBINSON); early X.42-III.43; SH-born
11. COPPOCK, Ruth; (PALMER); 8.VIII.39-2.IX.39; 20
12. CORY, Robert; 16.IX.41-25.VII.42;26
13. CRAVEN, Roger; 3.X.42- (?) ; 34
14. DANFORTH, Par; 29.XI.41- (?) ; circa 30
15. DeLINE, Joyce; (BALL); Unitarian; 23.I.42-X.42; 22
16. DILTS, Adda; 1.I.41-21.VIII.41; circa 60; 2nd x; 20.VII.42-IX.42
17. EDWARDS, Earle; 29.IX.39-15.IV.41; 23
18. EDWARDS, Marjorie; 29.IX.39-15.IV.41; 22
19. ELLIOTT, Jane; summer 1941; early 30s
19a. ELLIOTT, Becky; [daughter]; summer 1941; 4
20. EMMONS, Ardith; 10.VI.39-early VII.39; 35
21. FOREMAN, Betty; (HUMMEL); summer 1940; 20s
22. GEORGE, Hetta; British; summer 1940
23. GOODENOW, Leanore; 10.VI.39-10.VIII.39; 35
24. HANNUM, Margaret; (STEVENS, Peggy); Episcopalian; 26.IX.41-
      15.VI.42; 29; 2nd x; (?) -III.43
25. HEMINGWAY, Ada Glee; (LEET); (?) - (?) ;20s
26. HEWSON, Camilla; (FLINTERMANN); V.39-VII.40; 16
27. HOLMES, Mildred; (HALE); (?) -VI.40; 20s
28. HUGHES, David; VI.40- (?) ; teenager
29. JENSEN, Marie; (BAKER); 9.VI.39- (?) ; 21
30. JONES, Elinore; (CLOE); V.41-7.XI.41; 18
31. KALTENBACH, John; 15.IV.39-I.VII.40; 22
32. KING, Gertrude; (Trudy); 25.IV.42-18.V.42
33. MARTIN, Albert; 23.V.39-17.VII.39; circa 50
34. MARTIN, Ann; 5.V.39-17.VII.39; late 40s
34a. MARTIN, Joseph; [son]; (Joe); 5.V.39- (?) ; 17
34b. MARTIN, Richard; [son]; (Dick); 5.V.39- (?) ; 11
35. McCOY, Margaret; 11.VII.39- (?) ; circa 30
36. MILLER, Barbara; VII.40- (?); 2nd x; (?) -41
37. PEMBERTON, Beulah; (DeHAVEN); late VI.40-IX.40; 21
38. PEMBERTON/WILLOUGHBY, Lillian; VI.39-VII.41; 24
39. PICKETT, Rachel; (STALNECKER); summer 1939; 20s
40. RICHARDS, Hilde; 3.VIII.42-31.VIII.42; 30s
41. SMITH, Esther; (MEYERDING); Brethren; 20.XI.40-mid XI.41; 25
42. STANDING, Eva; (PLAGMAN); 1.VIII.41-21.VIII.41; 20s
      2nd x; 21.VI.42- (?) ;early 30s
43. STANLEY, Sara; duration; 60s
44. STANLEY, Walter; duration; 60s
45. THORP, George; 31.VIII.42- (?) ; circa 30
46. WILLOUGHBY, George; 1.IX.40-VII.41; 25
47. ZIMMERMAN, Giles; 23.VII.39-early I.42; 25
48. ZIMMERMAN, Lynn; (FRANZEN); Catholic; 18.VII.39-early I.42; 24

REFERENCE NOTES

References are given for most quotations and for curious or debatable items that require a source or about which an inquiring reader might want to know more. Widely-known historical facts or events that can be found in other, standard historical accounts have not been documented. References to quotations from guests or staff at Scattergood Hostel have been given when they seemed important; otherwise, when the source is named in the text, and the work appears in the Bibliography, they have not been cited.

ABBREVIATIONS

AFSC	American Friends Service Committee
AMLT	Aliza Michael Luick-Thrams
CHF	Camilla Hewson Flintermann
CRG	*Cedar Rapids Gazette*
DMR	*Des Moines Register*
EME	Earle and Marjorie Edwards
ICPC	*Iowa City Press-Citizen*
IYMF(C)	Iowa Yearly Meeting of Friends (Conservative)
IYMF(P)	Iowa Yearly Meeting of Friends (Programmed)
MB	Martha Balderston
RB	Robert Berquist
SAN	"Scattergood Hostel News, Special Alumni Number, April 1943"
SH	Scattergood Hostel
SHP	Sara Hinshaw Pemberton
SMNB	Scattergood Monthly News Bulletin
TBOS	*The Book of Scattergood*
WBT	*West Branch Times*
WS	Walter Shostal

NOTE: Page number follows key word. Book titles are listed in abbreviated form and can be found in their entirety in the *Selected Titles* in Bibliography.

Foreword~**A Place of Peace**
PLACE OF PEACE: Rudolph Schreck, Telegram to staff of SH, 18.II.43

Chapter 1~**An Ocean of Light**
REALITY OF GOD: *Portrait*, 11-12.

UPRIGHT WOMAN: *Journal*, 1.
RELIGIOUS SERIOUSNESS: *Portrait*, 41.
THERE IS ONE: *Journal*, 11.
OCEAN OF LIGHT: *Journal*. 19.
TREMBLE AT THE WORD: *Journal*, 58.
TRUE GODLINESS: *Portrait*, 97.

*Chapter 2~*A Holy Experiment
UNDERGROUND RAILROAD: "40 Germans to be Housed in Old School; At West
Branch, Hoover's Home; Where Refugees Will be Brought", DMR, mid January
1939
INDIAN INDUSTRIAL SCHOOL: "Scattergood to Close as a Refugee Hostel March
First; Hostel Has Record of Nearly Four Years Service to Oppressed People of
Many European Countries", WBT, 11.II.43
RECENTLY-FREED SLAVES: Ibid.
CREATE A SCHOOL FUND: "Rush Preparations at Scattergood; History of School
Most Interesting", ICPC, 15.III.39
ANTICIPATION OF THE CAMPUS: Ibid.
WHOLESOME EDUCATION: Ibid.
SOME VERY FINE TALENT: Ibid.
FRIENDLY EDUCATION: Ibid.

*Chapter 3~*In These Dark Hours
SOCIAL AND ECONOMIC PROBLEMS: Leslie Schaffer, Letter to Homer Morris,
1.IX.38
SOME CONCRETE PLANS: Ruth Jones Newlin, Letter to Homer Morris, 24.X.38
PROFOUND SHOCK: AFSC, Open Letter to North American Quakers, 17.XI.38
MUCH INTEREST WAS MANIFEST: Levi Bowles, Letter to Clarence Pickett,
20.XI.38
PERMANENT PLACE IN AMERICAN SOCIETY: Anonymous essay "A New Use
for Scattergood", 29.V.39
PROBLEMS OF READJUSTMENT: Julia Branson, Open Letter to North American
Quakers, winter 1938-39
THESE TWO POINTS: Unsigned and untitled leaflet, circa 1940
JUST SUCH PROBLEMS: Anonymous, undated mimeographed essay "An Ameri-
can Welcome for New Americans"
SIGNIFICANT CONTRIBUTIONS: John Rich, "Americanization Through Quaker
Hostels"
VERY REAL FLAW: WS, Letter to AMLT, 6.VIII.95
FAVORABLE TO THEIR ASSIMILATION: Anonymous Article, "Prejudice",
SMNB, XII.42
HOSTILITY AND DISAPPOINTMENT: Jean Reynolds, Pamphlet "Scattergood
Hostel, West Branch, Iowa", 16.I.40
BECOME TRULY AMERICAN: WS, Unpublished Memoirs "American Begin-
nings", 1994
MOST VALUABLE EXPERIENCE: Homer Morris, Letter to Catherine Williams,

14.XII.38

IN ANY SUCH ENTERPRISE: Ibid.

IOWA FRIENDS WERE UNITED ENTHUSIASTICALLY: "Report on Investigation of the Scattergood School Property at West Branch, Iowa, as a Suitable Place for the Holding of a Refugee Hostel, January 7-10, 1939"

IF THEE WOULD BE INTERESTED: Catherine Williams. Letter to Herbert Hoover, 17.II.39

A VERY WORTHY CAUSE: Wilson Emmons, Letter to SHP, 21.III.39

A FINE THING: James Gable, Letter to Eugene Mannheimer, 18.II.39

THE GERMAN JEW: CRG, late II.39

THIS TRANSFORMATION OF SCATTERGOOD: "IYMF (C) Annual Report, 1939"

RENEWED RELIGIOUS EXPERIENCE: Homer Morris, Letter to Beulah Pemberton, 24.I.39

WHOLLY UNACCUSTOMED TO DORMITORY LIFE: Mary Rogers, Letter to Albert Martin, 11.III.39

COAL BURNERS: Sara and Beulah Pemberton, "News Letter on Scattergood Project", 10.IV.39

DIRECT FROM A MANUFACTURER: SHP, Letter to Jay Newlin, 11.IV.39

KITCHEN POTS AND PANS: SHP, Letter to "Dear Friends", 16.VI.39

PREFERENCES OF THE GERMAN REFUGEES: SHP, Letter to Mary Rogers, 27.III.39

*Chapter 4~*So Much at Home

SO MANY PRESS MEN: John Kaltenbach, Unpublished Log *The Book of Scattergood*, 12.IV.39

LITTLE DANIEL BOONES: Ibid.

AFRICA AND THE MIDDLE EAST: "First Refugees Reach Iowa Haven: Hate Hitler But Afraid to Say So", DMR, 16.IV.39

VIBRATE LIKE A BEE'S WINGS: TBOS, Ibid.

KING OF THE FELATER TRIBE: "First Refugees...", ibid.

I HAVE NOTHING TO SAY: Ibid.

BURST INTO A LECTURE: "Strong Stories Told in Faces of 4 Refugees: Find Iowa Haven After Hitler", DMR, 17.IV.39

AS TO IOWA ROADS: "First Refugees...", ibid.

JANITOR AT RADIO CITY: "Strong Story...", ibid.

ONETIME AUSTRIAN PAPERHANGER: Ibid.

TRAYS OF IOWA FARM FOOD: Ibid.

A MERE 10 REICHSMARKS: "First Refugees...", ibid.

NO OVERTONE OF REVENGE: "Strong Story...", ibid.

WE FEEL AT HOME: TBOS, ibid.

OF THE ORTHODOX RELIGION: "Strong Story...", ibid.

DRIVING EVERYBODY ELSE: Kurt Schaefer, Essay in SMNB, 15.IV.42

JAMMED IN ON THE PIANO: TBOS, ibid.

OUR SPIRITUAL FOREFATHERS: John Kaltenbach, Essay "Scattergood", circa 1940

NEARLY EVERY KIND OF REFUGEE: John Kaltenbach, Letter to Eleanor Slater, Albert and Anne Martin and Reed Cary, 27.IV.39
ANY PARTICULAR SKILLS: Ibid.
WITHALL HE IS DELIGHTFUL: Ibid.
ETERNALLY WRITING AT SOMETHING: Ibid.
PERPETUAL MARVEL: Ibid.
RUDELY AWAKENED: TBOS, 4.V.39
PERPETUAL TONGUE MOTION: Kaltenbach, Letter to Slater..., ibid.
A KIND OF TRAINING EXERCISE: "Erhard Winter", Letter to CHF, spring 1994
A GREASY JEW: "Erhard Winter", Taped Interview with AMLT, 25.X.94
A TIRESOME AFFAIR: "Erhard Winter", Letter to AMLT, 30.VII.94
FOUGHT FOR GERMANY: "Hitler Exiles Happy in Iowa", DMR, 16.VII.39
MOTHERLY, LIKEABLE HEID: CHF, Letter to AMLT, 30.VI.94
MOST BEAUTIFUL SURROUNDINGS: Heid Ladewig, Letter to "Dear S.", circa mid-VI.39
DIFFICULTY ADJUSTING: CHF, Letter to AMLT, 30.VI.94
VERY INEXPENSIVE SUMMER RESORT: Hans Ladewig, Letter to Dear L's", late 1939
A PERMANENT PLACE IN AMERICAN SOCIETY: Unattributed Essay "A New Use for Scattergood", 22.V.39
WOLFING THEIR FOOD: CHF...ibid., plus EME, Taped Interview, 23.X.94

Chapter 5~**A Glimpse of Hope**
SOME OF THE HEARTACHES: Keith Wilson, article in Sunday edition of un-named Omaha, Nebraska, newspaper, 8.V.42
MILITARY BEARING AND AN IMMENSE PRIDE: "Flight from Sorrow", *Washington Post*, 31.V.81
NO ENGLISH WHATSOEVER: Giles Zimmerman, Letter to Mary Rogers, 2.XII.42
OUR MYSTERIOUS RUSSIAN: CHF, Letter to AMLT, 30.VI.94
WALKING BACK AND FORTH: "Flight from Sorrow", ibid.
VERY COMFORTABLE CIRCUMSTANCES: "Our Enemy Aliens", *Goucher Alumnae Quarterly*, May 1942
TRIED HIS HAND AT SEVERAL BUSINESS ENTERPRISES: "Like Discovering a New World: Once Gassed by the Doughboys, Nazi Refugee Befriended Here", DMR, 28.I.40
CONNECTION WITH THE HOMELAND: *Kampf*, 24-28.
RELATIVELY PLEASANT AND BEARABLE: Marie Juchacz, Anonymous Letter, 1945
I WILL COME: Marie Juchacz, Letter to Ida Wolf, early 1948
IT IS NOT EASY: Marie Juchacz, Circular Letter to Friends, 1947
IN THE YEARS OF EMIGRATION: Ibid.
TO BE WITH FRIENDS AND RELATIVES: Anonymous, Notices in SMNB, October-November 1942
HELP PERSECUTED AND EXILED REFUGEES: Irving Blumenkranz, Essay in SMNB, 17.XI.40
REFUGEE FROM NAZI-OPPRESSION: Martin Kobylinski, Transcribed Speech in

SMNB, 17.VI.41

THINGS GOT A LITTLE HOT FOR HIM: "Day by Day", *Davenport Times*, 24.IV.42

THOSE VICTIMS OF HITLER'S INVASIONS: Kaethe Aschkenes, Report in SMNB, 17.VII.41

NEVER FORGET THE LITTLE LONELY FRENCH GIRL: Anonymous, Letter in SMNB, 17.X.41

A GLIMPSE OF HOPE: Mariette Shumaker, Report in SMNB, 15.IX.42

CIVIL DEFENSE WAS NOT WELL PREPARED: Magdalene Salmon, Report in SMNB, 17.IX.41

TO AVENGE THE HONOR OF POLAND: "Scattergood Refugees Can Tell Much: French Army Surprised Pole". DMR, late 1942

GERMAN CITIZENS IN THE FIRST PLACE: Grete Rosenzweig, Unpublished Memoirs "My Life Told for My Grandchildren", 1974

INCREASINGLY CRITICAL SITUATION: Sigmund Seaman, Unpublished Account titled *"Verfolgungsvorgang,"* 5.VI.57

REUNITED ON THE OTHER SIDE OF THE WORLD: "Forced to Flee Germany-3 Refugees Travel 18,000 Miles", DMR, 8.IX.40

I HAD LOST MY NATIONALITY: WS, Unpublished Memoirs, ibid.

IT WAS A VERY SAD CHRISTMAS: Theresa Shostal, Unpublished Memoirs "Through the Occupation of France 1940", 1942

*Chapter 6~*Such Joy

WE SHALL ENJOY HAVING THE CHILDREN AROUND: TBOS, 11.VII.39

MICHAEL AND HANNAH START TO SCHOOL: Ibid., 4.IX.39

FIRST REPORT CARDS FROM SCHOOL: Ibid., 18.X.39

THE YOUTHFUL SPIRITS AND INTEREST WE SO NEED: MB, Report in SMNB, 15.III.40

INNER CONFLICT: Hanna Deutsch Clampitt, Thesis "The Experience of Inner Conflict as Described by Women Between 40 and 60", Center for Humanistic Studies, 1987

THAT MESSED UP SCHOOL: Hannah Deutsch Clampitt, Interview with AMLT, 31.X.94

I WAS TORN: Hannah Deutsch Clampitt, Thesis, ibid

A REAL EXAMPLE OF COOPERATIVE LIFE: *Brothertown*, 88-93.

IT MIGHT MEAN MEETING WILD ANIMALS: Irmgard Wessel, Essay "The Impact of the American Friends Service Committee on My Life", September 1992

DIE ROSENZWEIGEN: Unpublished Song titled "Die Rosenzweigen", February 1941

LOVELY ADDITION TO OUR FAMILY: Kathryn Werth and Fritz Schorsch, Report in SMNB, 17.X.41

A NEW EXPERIENCE FOR MY BROTHER AND ME: Elizabeth Chilton, Letter to AMLT, 1.XI.94

THOUGHTS ON SCHOOL LIFE IN AMERICA: Edith Lichtenstein, Essay in SMNB, 15.VI.42

ALL THE OPEN SPACE: Edith Lichtenstein Morgan, Interview with AMLT,

27.X.95
BE HAPPY IN OUR COUNTRY: Varrell Williams, ibid.
FIRST IMPRESSIONS OF AN AMERICAN HIGH SCHOOL: George Krauthamer, Essay in SMNB, 15.IX.42
FRIDAY WE HAD TO BE INITIATED: George Krauthamer, Report in SMNB, X-XI.42
ONLY SISSIES WORE SNOW PANTS: Pierre Shostal, Letter to AMLT, 16.VII.94
HE STARTED TO TALK AND WOULD NOT FINISH: WS, Unpublished Memoirs, ibid.
WE MISS THEM AS THEY LEAVE: MB, Report in SMNB, 17.IV.41
A LITTLE TOO DOMINEERING: MB, Letter to Mary Rogers, 2.XII.40
MANUFACTURED IN THE WORKSHOP: Unsigned "Scattergood Hostel Report", 12.VIII.42
THEY DO NOT WANT ANYTHING STRENUOUS: Gertrude King, Letter to "Dear Friend", 23.V.42
THE PRETTY WRAPPED GIFTS: Karl Liebman, English-class Essay, December 1939
TO BE A LITTLE LATE: Leo Keller, Report in SMNB, 17.I.41
DISGUISED AS ANGELS AND DWARFS: Anonymous Column titled "Chips from the Yule Log", SMNB, 17.I.42
MANY, MANY GREETINGS: "Helmut, Edith, Ilse, Louis and Lisl", Open Letter in SMNB, 12.XII.41
KEPT US FROM GETTING SENTIMENTAL: Klaus Asher, Report in SMNB, January 1943
QUAKERS DID THEIR BEST TO HAVE THEM SAVED: Anonymous Poem, "SH Report-1941"

*Chapter 7~***Broad Tolerances and Firm Convictions**
TOMATOES FOR BREAKFAST, LUNCH AND DINNER: Lillian Willoughby, Letter to AMLT, 11.IV.95
A CONCERN AND LOVE FOR PEOPLE: Lillian Willoughby, Letter to AMLT, 3.V.95
AT THEIR OWN EXPENSE: Undated "Agreement with the Stanleys", probably early 1939
TENT FOR THE SUMMER: Mary Rogers, Letter to Albert Martin, 11.III.39
SYMBOLS OF AN AMERICA PAST: WS, Unpublished Memoirs, ibid.
WE ARE MUCH IMPRESSED BY YOUR LIST: Mary Rogers, Letter to Anne Martin, 26.V.39
A RATHER UNFORTUNATE CHOICE FOR THE POSITION: Robert Burgess, Letter to Clarence Pickett, 14.VI.39
PLACEMENT WORK SHOULD BE STARTED NOW: SH Meeting for Business Minutes, 16.VI.39
JUST THE SORT OF POSITION: Albert Martin, Letter to Clarence Pickett, 3.VII.39
I THINK OF SCATTERGOOD AS THEY SMALL CHILD: SHP, Letter to Reed Cary, 8.VII.39

WITHDRAW HIM FROM THE PICTURE: Reed Cary, Letter to SHP, 7.VII.39
WE ALL REGRET THE PERSONALITY DIFFICULTY: Reed Cary, Letter to John Kaltenbach, 7.VII.39
WE SHOULD PUT THE NEW LINE-UP IN CHARGE: Clarence Pickett, Letter to Albert Martin, 11.VII.39
A GRAVE INJUSTICE: Reed Cary, Letter to Clarence Pickett, 18.VII.39
WE COULD DO THE HUMAN ACT: Lillian Willoughby, Letter to AMLT, 14.II.95
SELECT SOMEONE FOR SCATTERGOOD WHO IS YOUNG: Albert Martin, ibid.
AN OPPRESSIVE LIST OF SPECIFICATIONS: Reed Cary, ibid.
HUMAN REHABILITATION AND PERSONALITY READJUSTMENT: John Kaltenbach, Letter to Reed Cary, 7.VI.39
ONLY THE DESTRUCTIBLE CAN BE DESTROYED: John Kaltenbach, Tract "The Scattergood Hostel", 10.VIII.39
THEIR SPIRITS ARE KEPT FRESH IN LOVING: John Kaltenbach in TBOS, 15.IV.40
PRISTINE BEAUTY AND SIMPLICITY: "Erhard Winter", Letter to CHF, spring 1994
A PLACE TO ROUND OUR YOUNG YEARS: CHF, Unpublished Memoirs "For Those Who Come After", 1992
IT SURELY HELPED ME GROW UP FAST: CHF, Letter to AMLT, 2.VII.94
I WAS ON THE TEAM: CHF, Letter to AMLT, 10.VI.95
ONE OF THE MOST FORMATIVE OF MY LIFE: CHF, Letter to AMLT, 23.IV.94
SO MUCH TO REMEMBER: CHF, Unpublished Memoirs, ibid.
FIX UP DIFFICULT MANUSCRIPTS: Morrisroe, "The Prime of Amy Clampitt", *New York* Magazine, 15.X.84, 44-48
DREW MANY RAVE REVIEWS: Phil Clampitt, Letter to AMLT, 5.VII.95
IMPRESSIONS OF A SUMMER VOLUNTEER: Amy Clampitt, Essay in SMNB, 17.VIII.41
HER QUAKER ROOTS WENT DEEP: Phil Clampitt, ibid.
THE BURNING CHILD: Clampitt, Amy. *The Kingfisher.* New York: Knopf, 1983, 131-133.
ENGLISH AS RELATED TO FOOD: Lillian Willoughby, Letter to AMLT, 3.V.95
SPECTACULAR AND DELICIOUS: Lillian Willoughby, ibid.
EVEN AT SCATTERGOOD CUPID IS ON THE JOB: Anonymous Article, SMNB, mid-VI.40
ROOMY, OLD, EIGHT-CYLINDER HUPMOBILE: Herb Ettel, "Bound by a Common Humanity: the Willoughbys at 75", *Friends Journal*, September 1990
LOOKED JUST LIKE LIL' ABNER: Hans Peters, Taped Interview with AMLT, 9.XI.94
FAIRLY WORLDLY LADY: CHF, Letter to AMLT, 30.VI.94
THEY LOVED SCATTERGOOD: Sally Weiss, Telephone Interview with AMLT, 9.XI.94
OUR TEMPERAMENT AND EXPERIENCE WERE WELL SUITED: EME, Letters to AMLT; 20.VI., 25.IX. and 7.X.94, and 19.I.95
I BECAME INCREASINGLY DISSATISFIED: RB, Unpublished Essay

"Scattergood Hostel's Influence on My Life", 27.X.94
STRONG, UNSELFISH HAND OF WELCOME: Marcus Bach, Article in *Christian Century*, 3.VII.40
THOSE OF US AT SCATTERGOOD WHO ARE DEEPLY CONCERNED: RB, Unpublished Journal, 27.X.40-21.III.42
I FELT MYSELF LIKE A BROTHER: Paul Frölich, Letter to MB, 12.X.41
AN ALMOST UNBELIEVABLE CHANGE: RB, Article in *Iowa Peace News*, XII.41
ATTENDANCE WAS FAIRLY OBLIGATORY: WS, Unpublished Memoirs, ibid.
WHAT ARE THE PROBLEMS WHICH THE REFUGEE FACES: Margaret Hannum, "Our 'Enemy' Aliens", *Goucher College Quarterly*, May 1942

Chapter 8~The Spirit of the Community
RELIGIOUS SOCIALIST: RB, Letter to AMLT, spring 1994
LIFE IN COMMUNITY: Otto Bauer, Unpublished Prose, winter 1940-41
IOWA FRIENDS SERVICE COMMITTEE: Richard Schuber, Unpublished Essay, 1.III.40
PRESENTATION ON GERMAN PROPAGANDA: Anonymous, Notice in SMNB, IX.40
UNCOMFORTABLE WITH HIS 'FALL FROM GRACE': CHF, Letter to AMLT, 30.VI.94
ITS SPIRITUAL CRYSTALLIZATION: Richard Schuber, Unpublished Essay, February 1940
A QUAKER PROJECT: Lucy Selig, Transcript of a Talk given in the second half of 1940
HOSTEL AS HIS "CHILD": SHP, Letter to Reed Cary, 8.VII.39
LIKE CHILDREN OF A MOTHER: Rosenzweig Family, Unpublished Poem, 22.IV.42
IN HER PROTECTING MOTHERHOOD: Anonymous, Unpublished Poem, 23.IV.42
BEHAVE LIKE NAUGHTY CHILDREN: Rosl "Mimi" Scheider, Letter to MB, 12.I.41
THIS LIVING EXAMPLE OF THE SPIRIT: Vita Stein, Letter to MB, spring 1942
HOMESTEAD: Rose Eliasberg, Telegram to SH, April 1942
SENSITIVE TO THE NEEDS OF OTHERS: RB, Notes written into AMLT's biographical files of SH guests and staff, 31.X.94
THIS DEMONSTRATION OF THE WAY OF LIFE: Mary Middleton Rogers, Letter to SH, April 1941
TRAINING CENTER FOR THE LIFE OF THE SPIRIT: John Kaltenbach, Letter to SH, April 1941
THE SPIRIT IS STILL ALIVE: Hans Peters, Essay in SMNB, 17.I.41
ALL GOOD SCATTERGOOD PEOPLE: Paul Frölich, Letter to MB, 12.X.41
PEOPLE WHO ARE GOOD: WS, Unpublished Essay, 6.VIII.42
INDIVIDUAL HUMAN BEINGS: Regina Deutsch, Letter to MB, 21.IV.42
'MOTHER' TO THE WHOLE WORLD: CHF, Unpublished Memoirs, ibid.
SKINNY, SHY CHILD: CHF, Letter to AMLT, 30.VI.94

IT IS WITH MIXED FEELINGS: MB, Piece in SMNB, 15.III.40
THE LARGEST FAMILY IN THE COUNTRY: Peter Seadle, Essay in SMNB, 17.IV.41
FRIENDS WILL NEVER BE FORGOTTEN: Marianne Welter, Essay in SMNB, 15.IV.42

*Chapter 9~***For the Benefit of All**
TYPICAL SH DAY: CHF, Letter to AMLT, 2.VII.94
THIS GENERAL FRAMEWORK: Ruth Carter, Report titled
"Scattergood—August, 1939"
SINCE THE PREVIOUS WINTER AND SPRING: EME, Report titled "Scattergood Refugee Hostel of the AFSC", August 1940
A WEEK AT SCATTERGOOD: Anonymous Article in SMNB, 17.II.41
SCATTERGOOD'S THIRD BIRTHDAY: Lynn Zimmerman and Esther Smith, Poem in SMNB, 15.IV.42
"VERY GERMAN AND NOT-LAID-BACK: EME, Note written to AMLT, 16.XI.94
ALOOFNESS AND REFUSAL TO COOPERATE: Lynn Zimmerman, Letter to Mary Middleton Rogers and Jean Reynolds, 7.X.40
VERY CRITICAL OF OTHERS: RB, Notes written into AMLT's biographical files of SH guests and staff, 31.X.94
SUGGESTIONS FOR SPRINGTIME WORK: Frederick Pollak, List, spring 1941
THE RIGHT IDEA OF THE QUAKERS: Greta Rosenzweig, Unpublished Memoirs, ibid.
MOST TOOK IT IN GOOD SPIRITS: CHF, ibid.
I WAS FULL OF RAGE: WS, Unpublished Memoirs, ibid.
ASPECTS OF A SMALL FARM: Leo Keller, Essay in SMNB, 17.VI.41
THE HOME SIDE OF HOSTEL LIFE: Sara Stanley, Report in SMNB, 17.VI.41
THE GARDEN IN SPRING: Sara Stanley, Report in SMNB, 15.V.42
SOME 6,000 TOMATO PLANTS: RB, Article in *Northwest Pacifist*, 17.VIII.40
NEVER AGAIN BE INDIFFERENT TO CATSUP: Lynn Zimmerman, Letter to Mary Rogers, 23.V.40
A HOSTEL INNOVATION: Anonymous Report in SMNB, 17.VIII.40
CHARACTERIZED BY THE FOLLOWING: Anonymous Report in SMNB, September 1940

*Chapter 10~***To Accelerate Mastery**
SCATTERGOOD EDUCATIONAL PROGRAM:George Thorp, Article in SMNB, October-November 1942
REPORT OF LECTURES AND FIELD TRIPS: Anonymous Report, January, February, March and April 1941
HINTS FROM THE SCATTERGOOD KITCHEN:Lillian Pemberton, Sections in SMNB, 17.III. and 17.V.41
EDUCATION COMMITTEE HAS COMPLETED PLANS:Anonymous Report in SMNB, 17.IX.41
CENTER OF THE HOSTEL CURRICULUM: WS, Unpublished Memoirs, ibid.

PHONETIC LESSONS AT SCATTERGOOD: Anonymous Report in SMNB, 15.III.42

AMERICAN GOTHIC: Anonymous entry, TBOS, 9.XI.39

TRAPP FAMILY SINGERS: Louis Hacke, Report in SMNB, 15.IV.42

OUTLINE OF ONLY ONE MONTH'S FARE: Anonymous Outline in SMNB, ibid.

WHAT CAN THE TEACHER LEARN: Sabine Hirsch, Essay in SMNB, 17.VI.41

SPEECHES TO DIFFERENT GROUPS: Grete Rosenzweig, Unpublished Memoirs, ibid.

DEAR SCATTERGOOOOOOOOOODIANS: Ruth Carter, Letter to SH, 20.VI.40

ONE OF THE MOST IMPORTANT CLASSES: Hedwig Hackel, Article in SMNB, 15.VI.42

SCATTERGOOD IS UP-TO-DATE: Alfred Adler, Article in SMNB, 16.II.42

MAZE OF POSTAL RULES AND REGULATIONS: Anonymous Report in SMNB, 17.II.41

UNDER FEDERAL ORDERS: Ibid.

UNABLE TO GO TO GRINNELL: Louis Hacke, Report in SMNB, 15.VII.42

RE-EDUCATION FOR DEMOCRACY: Paul Frölich, Essay in SMNB, 15.VIII.42

*Chapter 11~***An Especially Elaborate Celebration**

CULTURAL EXCURSIONS FROM SCATTERGOOD: "The Singers", Article in SMNB, 16.II.42

SEVEN VILLAGES PRACTISING MODERN CAPITALISM: Hans Peters, Article in SMNB, 15.III.40

EXPERIENCE IN COMMUNITY LIFE: Otto Bauer, Unpublished Transcript of a Speech titled "Our Trip to Amana", spring 1941

CANDLE-LIGHT DINNER: WS, Unpublished Memoirs, ibid.

OUR CHILDREN SHOWED THEIR ARTISTIC TALENTS: Anonymous Report in SMNB, 15.V.42

FLASH!! IMPORTANT NEWS: SHF, Report in SMNB, 15.III.40

WE ARE CELEBRATING SARA'S BIRTHDAY: Anonymous Poem in "Scattergood Notes", 17.XII.40

ESPECIALLY ELABORATE CELEBRATION: Anonymous Report in SMNB, 17.VIII.41

A NEW MEMBER TO THE CIRCLE: Anonymous Announcement in SMNB, October-November 1942

AMERICA HAS ITS ROMANCES: Marie Juchacz, Report in SMNB, 15.VIII.42

FAREWELL TO MEMBERS MOVING ON: Anonymous Report in SMNB, 15.IX.42

FAMOUS FAREWELL BANQUET: Anonymous Report in SMNB, June 1940

INTEREST IN A NUMBER OF MEAT LOCKERS: Alfred Dupree, Letter to RB, 26.VI.95

LOSS OF A BELOVED FRIEND: John Kaltenbach, Announcement in SMNB, 17.IV.40

COMMEMORATION OF THE DAY: Anonymous Report in SMNB, 17.II.42

DAY FULL OF LARK AND LAUGHTER: Otto Bauer, Report in SMNB, 17.IV.41

PROBABLY A WORK OF BORNEO: Anonymous Entry in TBOS, 24.II.40

TIME-HONORED AMERICAN CUSTOM: Anonymous Report in SMNB, October-November 1942

ALL SAINTS DAY: Charles Violin, Report in SMNB, 17.XI.40

OH! LOVELIEST DAY: "Ilse Stahl", Essay in SMNB, 12.XII.41

YOM KIPPUR: Anonymous Entry in TBOS, 23.IX.39

HANUKKAH: Edith Lichtenstein Morgan, Interview with AMLT, 27.X.95

NUMEROUS PREPARATIONS: Leo Keller, Report in SMNB, 17.I.41

PREPARATIONS FOR NEW YEAR'S EVE: Hans Schimmerling, Report in SMNB, 17.I.41

EQUIPPED WITH A PENCIL AND A BRAIN: Charles Violin, ibid.

OUR BELOVED "KASPERLE": Tekla Arntal, Report in SMNB, 17.III.41

EXCELLENTLY DONE IN EVERY RESPECT: RB, Entry in unpublished journal, 5.III.41

THIS IS MY SCATTERGOOD: Anonymous Report in SMNB, 15.IV.42

A GOOD THING FOR OUR PURSES: Anonymous Entry in TBOS, 9.VII.39

GOING BACK TO NATURE: Anonymous Report in SMNB, 15.VI.42

SPORT FLASHES: Anonymous Report in SMNB, 15.VII.42

Chapter 12~A New Way of Life

Almost all descriptions of guests' appearance or personalities were provided by CHF in a letter to AMLT on 30.VI.94 and are offered here as a way to better "see" the person being mentioned.

KURT SCHAEFER: "Fred K. Schaefer and the Science of Geography", William Bunge, Association of American Geographers *Annals* , March 1979

FRITZ TREUER: SAN

GEORGE LAURY: TBOS, 15.VI. & 8.VII.39

KURT ROSEGG: TBOS, 30.X.39; "Placement Report Scattergood Hostel July 22, 1940"; SAN

KARL GAM: TBOS, 21.V.39

ERHARD WINTER: "Erhard Winter", Letter to CHF, spring 1994; Interview with AMLT, 25.X.94; SAN

FRANK SCHLOSS: "Ski Expert Prefers Beaded Snow", CRG, winter 1939-40; Frank Schloss, Letters to Robert Berquist & EME, 15.IX.84 &.IV.85, respectively

GERRY & HERTA SCHROEDER: CHF, Letter to AMLT, 30.VI.94; SAN

LOTHAR GIDRO-FRANK: Ibid.

IRVING BLUMENKRANZ: Ibid.

DONALD HOPF: "Prep Student at Drake: Happy to Be in U.S.: Donald Hopf a Refugee", DMR, 15.IX.39

PETER SCHICK: "Placement Report Scattergood Hostel July 22, 1940"; SAN

ERNST van den HAAG: Interview with AMLT, 25.X.95

PETER SEADLE: Lynn Zimmerman, Placement Report, 7.X.40

FRED LISTER: SAN

PETER LUSTIG: Peter Lustig, Article in SMNB, 17.IX. 41;Paul Hegarty, Interview with AMLT, 7.XI.94; SAN

GUNTHER MEYER: "Placement Report Scattergood Hostel July 22, 1940"; "Erhard Winter", Interview with AMLT, 25.X.94; SAN

LUDWIG & KAETHE UNDERWOOD: "Placement Report Scattergood Hostel July 22, 1940"

GRETE BECK: "Placement Report Scattergood Hostel July 22, 1940"; SAN; Keith Wilson, article in Sunday edition of unnamed Omaha, Nebraska, newspaper, 8.V.42

JOE MAUTHNER: SAN

FRED & MARIA ALTMAN: Ibid.

GEORGE & MARY SCHEIDER: "Scattergood Hostel News, Special Alumni Number, April 1943"

WALTER BARON: SAN

SONIA BRAUN: Ibid.

PETER GREENWOOD: Ibid.

JULIUS & ELIZABETH LICHTENSTEIN: Edith Morgan Lichtenstein, ibid; SAN

TED FRANKL: Ibid.

THERESA SHOSTAL: WS, Unpublished Memoirs, ibid; SAN

VICTOR POPPER: Margaret "Peg" Hannum Stevens, Letter to AMLT, 12.III.95; SAN

MARIANNE WELTER: Marianne Welter, Interview with AMLT, 23.X.94; Nicole Hackel, Interview with AMLT, 31.X.95

NORA & OMI HACKEL: Nicole Hackel and Marianne Welter, Interview with AMLT, 23.X.94

HANS & HEID LADEWIG: SAN

HANS PETERS: "Placement Report Scattergood Hostel July 22, 1940"; Letters to AMLT, 30.IV. and 27.VI.94

MARTHA SCHMIDL: SAN

ALFRED & MARTHA ADLER: Ibid.

LUCY & ERNST SELIG: SAN; "Placement Report Scattergood Hostel July 22, 1940"

EUGENIA LANDYCHEFF: SAN

PAUL SINGER: Ibid.

ROSA SCHIFFMAN: Ibid.

GRETE & LOUIS ROSENZWEIG: Irmgard Rosenzweig Wessel, Letter to AMLT, 28.VI.94; SAN

FRANCIS & ANNY HARVEY: Ibid.

MARGOT WEISS: Ibid.

EWALD PEISSEL: "Placement Report Scattergood Hostel July 22, 1940"

ELLY & OSCAR BENNDORF: Ibid.

LEO KELLER: SAN

GUS & ROSL WEILER: Ibid.

JACK SHUMAKER: Ibid.

ERNST TURK: Ibid

OTTO DREYER: Ibid.

ERNST FEIBELMAN: Ibid.

RUDI SCHRECK: "Placement Report Scattergood Hostel July 22, 1940"

MICHAEL & ELLEN KRAUTHAMER: SAN

JULIUS NEUMAN: Ibid.

TED TUERKEL: Ibid.

CLAIRE HOHENADL-PATEK: "Placement Report Scattergood Hostel July 22, 1940"; SAN

ERNST STAHL: Ibid; "Ilse Stahl", Interview with the Edwardses and Willoughbys, September 1994

STAN BRAUN: SAN

KLAUS ASHER: Ibid.

ARTHUR & ELLEN DRAKE: Ibid.

ALBERT & LISA BEAM: "Placement Report Scattergood Hostel July 22, 1940"; CHF, Letter to AMLT, 30.VI.94

GUS BARDACH: "Placement Report Scattergood Hostel July 22, 1940"; SAN

WILHELM FEIST: Ibid; "Placement Report Scattergood Hostel July 22, 1940"

RICHARD GUTTMANN: SAN

OTTO JOACHIM: "Placement Report Scattergood Hostel July 22, 1940"

PAUL SCHWARZ: Ibid; SAN

WILLY & HEDY LAYTON: "Placement Report Scattergood Hostel July 22, 1940"; SAN

GUENTHER TRADELIUS: Ibid.

JAKOB & MELANIE WINKLER: Ibid.

KARL POLZER: Ibid.

CHARLES BUKOVIS: Letter to Josephine and John Copithorne, 16.II.43

FRANZ NATHUSIUS: Robert Berquist, Notes in AMLT's biographical-files notebook, 29.X.94

WALTER & LIESEL LENZBERG: Irmgard Rosenzweig Wessel, Interview with AMLT, 29.X.95; SAN

LOUIS KOROPATNICKY: Ibid.

MARTIN KOBYLINSKI: Ibid.

LOTHAR & EDITH LEITER: Ibid.

MAX & ROSA SCHIFFMAN: Ibid.

LEO JOLLES: Ibid; TBOS, 9.II. 40

HENRY & ANNY SCHOENTHAL: "Placement Report Scattergood Hostel July 22, 1940"

KARL & LOTTE LIEBMAN: Ibid.

WALTER SHOSTAL: Unpublished Memoirs, ibid.

*Chapter 13~***The Melting Pot**

WHAT IS AMERICA: Frye, p. 173.

AMERICA DIDN'T NEED HIM AND HE DIDN'T NEED IT: "Erhard Winter", Letter to CHF, spring 1994

THE REFUGEE AND AMERICAN LIFE: Emil Deutsch, Essay in SMNB, 17.III.41 and 17.VI.41

THE STRANGE AND NEW CULTURE: Ernst Malamerson, Interview with AMLT, 25.X.95

WITH REGARD TO THE MELTING POT?: WS, Unpublished Memoirs, ibid.

*Epilogue~***White Still Nights**
ACTS OF KINDNESS OR SELFLESSNESS: AMLT, "Foreword" of this document.
THE TIME HAS COME: Mary Rogers, Letter to MB, 8.I.43
WE HAVE SEEN THIS SITUATION COMING: MB, Letter to Emery Hemingway, 17.I.43
GREAT NEED FOR A FRIENDS SCHOOL: Scattergood Hostel Executive Committee "Minutes", 23.I.43
BLOSSOM LIKE THE ROSE: Wilson Emmons, Letter to MB, 24.I.43
THE REACTION OF EVERYBODY IN IOWA: MB, Letter to Homer Morris, 25.I.43
CARRY ON FROM HERE: Report on "Des Moines Conference", 2.II.43
HOME FOR MANY OF US: MB, Letter to "Dear Scattergood Family", 10.II.43
AMERICANS OF JAPANESE DESCENT: John Copithorne, Letter to Homer Morris, 12.II.43
OLD GOSSIP IN PANTS: John Copithorne, Letter to Homer Morris, 22.II.43
IMPLICATIONS FROM HERE TO TOYKO: John Copithorne, Letter to Homer Morris, 25.II.43
A PETITION TO CONGRESS: Ibid.
THINGS HAVE BEEN PRETTY HOT IN WB: MB, Letter to Par Danforth, 2.III.43
AS A RESULT OF THIS DECISION: "Press Release", 4.III.43
I WOULD RATHER WORK AMONG FRIENDS: MB, Letter to Mary Rogers, 15.III.43
THE SCENE CHANGED SO QUICKLY: Ibid.
A SPIRITUAL AND UNITING CENTER: MB, "Scattergood Hostel Report, August 1943"

BIBLIOGRAPHY

ABBREVIATIONS

AFSC	American Friends Service Committee
AMLT	Michael Luick-Thrams
CHF	Camilla Hewson Flintermann
CRG	*Cedar Rapids Gazette*
DMR	*Des Moines Register*
EME	Earle and Marjorie Edwards
ICPC	*Iowa City Press-Citizen*
IYMF(C)	Iowa Yearly Meeting of Friends (Conservative)
IYMF(P)	Iowa Yearly Meeting of Friends (Programmed)
LPW	Lillian Pemberton Willoughby
MB	Martha Balderston
RB	Robert Berquist
SH	Scattergood Hostel
SHP	Sara Hinshaw Pemberton
SMNB	Scattergood Monthly News Bulletin
TBOS	*The Book of Scattergood*
WBT	*West Branch Times*
WS	Walter Shostal

PERTAINING TO SCATTERGOOD HOSTEL
Unpublished Material:*

Bauer, Otto. Prose, winter 1940-41

Berquist, Robert. Article in *Iowa Peace News*, XII.41

Berquist, Robert. Article in *Northwest Pacifist*, 17.VIII.40

Berquist, Robert. Essay titled "Scattergood Hostel's Influence on My Life",
27.X.94

Berquist, Robert. *Journal*, 27.X.40-21.XII.59

Book of Scattergood, The, 12.IV.39-15.IV.40 & 16.IV.40-30.VI.40

Deutsch, Emil. Essay in SMNB, 17.III.41 and 17.VI.41

Flintermann, Camilla Hewson. Memoirs titled "For Those Who Come After", fall
1992

IYMF (C) Annual Report, 1939

Kaltenbach, John. Essay titled "Scattergood", circa 1940

Kaltenbach, John. Tract titled "The Scattergood Hostel", 10.VIII.39

Kaltenbach, John (and others). *The Book of Scattergood,*
Kaltenbach, John [attributed to]. Unsigned Tract titled "A New Use for
    Scattergood", 29.V.39
Liebman, Karl. English-class Essay, December 1939
Rosenzweig, Grete. Memoirs titled "My Life Told for My Grandchildren", 1974
Scattergood Hostel [Executive Committee] Meeting for Business Minutes,
    16.VI.23-I.43 *Scattergood Monthly News Bulletin*
Seaman, Sigmund. Account titled *"Verfolgungsvorgang"*, 5.VI.57
Selig, Lucy. Transcript of a Talk given in the second half of 1940
Shostal, Walter. Memoirs titled "American Beginnings", June 1994
Shostal, Magda-Therese. Memoirs titled "Through the Occupation of France
    1940", late 1942
Wessel, Irmgard. Essay titled "The Impact of the AFSC on My Life",
    September 1992

** Articles, letters, reports, poems, et al., are not listed here—only longer docu-
ments. <u>All</u> primary materials used are on file at the AFSC Archives at 1501 Cherry
Street, Philadelphia, Pennsylvania 19102-1479*

Published Material:
Bach, Marcus. "Scattergood Hostel", Article in *Christian Century*, 3.VII.40
Berquist, Robert; Rhodes, David and Treadway, Carolyn. *Scattergood Friends
    School: 1890-1990.* West Branch: Scattergood School, 1990.
Bunge, William. "Fred K. Schaefer and the Science of Geography", Association of
    American Geographers *Annals* ,Vol. 69#1, March 1979
Curtis, Peter. *Palimpsest: A Place of Peace in a World of War.* Iowa City: Iowa
    State Historical Society, 1984.
Griffiths, Louise Benckenstein. *Brothertown.* New York: Friendship, 1941.
Hannum, Peg. "Our Enemy Aliens", *Goucher Alumnae Quarterly*, May 1942
Lemke, Lotte. "Marie Juchacz: Gründerin der Arbeiterwohlfahrt, 1879-1956", from
    Buch Zwei of a series edited by Erich Grassl, *Kampf ohne Waffen—Helfer der
    Menschen.* Donauwörth: Ludwig Auer, 1979
Trachtenberg, Barry. *Voices of Dissent: Christian Rescuers in the United
    States During the Nazi Regime.* M.A. Thesis, University of Vermont, 1993.

Interviews: (recorded, in-person*)
BERQUIST, Robert; 29-31.X.94 and 13.XI.95
CHILTON, Elizabeth (Ilse Seligmann/Seaman); 28.X.95
CLAMPITT, Phil and Hanna (Deutsch); VIII.94 and 10.XI.95
CORY, Robert; 25.X.94
EDWARDS, Earle and Marjorie; 23.X.94 and 1.XI.95
FAWCETT, Floyd and Mary Helen; 30.X.94
FLINTERMANN, Camilla (Hewson); 28.X.94 and 7.XI.95
HACKEL, Nicole; 23.X.94 and 31.X.95
HAUSEN, Lisa; X.94
MORGAN, Edith (Lichtenstein); 27.X.95

PETERS, Hans; 29.X.94
ROBINSON, Susan (Copithorne); 23.X.94
SHOSTAL, Pierre; 26.X.94
SHOSTAL, Walter; 25.VI.94
SOMERS, Ernst (Solmitz); 24-25.X.94
STEVENS, Peg (Hannum); 10.XI.94 and 28.XI.95
THOMAS, Harold; 13.XI.95
VAN DEN HAAG, Ernst (Malamerson); 25.X.95
WELTER, Marianne; 23.X.94
WESSEL, Irmgard (Rosenzweig); 30.X.95
WILK, Harry; 4-5.XI.94 and 18.XI.95
WILLOUGHBY, George and Lillian (Pemberton); 23.X.94 and 31.X.95
* on file at AFSC

(per telephone)
BALDERSTON, Marydel; 30.X.94
BALL, Joyce (DeLine); 6.XII.94
BURGESS, Bob; 30.X.94
CHILTON, Elizabeth (Ilse Seligmann/Seaman); 29.X.94
CLAMPITT, Phil; 29.X.94
CLOE, Elinore (Darwin); 6.XI.94
DEUTSCH, Michael; 29.X.94 and 10.XI.95
LICHTENSTEIN, Louis; 11.XI.94
MAUER, Betty (Balderston); 30.X.94
MEYERDING, Esther; 6.XI.94
MORGAN, Edith (Lichtenstein); 30.X.94
PALMER, Ruth (Coppock); 28.X.94
SEAMAN, Helmut (Seligmann); 6.XI.94
TABARI, Doris (Arntal); 28.X.94
VAN DEN HAAG, Ernst (Malamerson); 27.X.94
WEISS, Sally (Zimmerman); 10.XI.94
WESSEL, Irmgard (Rosenzweig); 24.X.94
ZIMMERMAN, David; 6.XI.94

GENERAL

Benz, Wolfgang. *Das Exil der kleinen Leute: Alltagserfahrung deutscher Juden in der Emigration.* Frankfurt am Main: Fischer, 1994.
Feuchtwanger, *Der Teufel in Frankreich: Ein Erlebnisbericht.* Munich: 1983.
Frye, Alton. *Nazi Germany and the American Hemisphere.* New Haven: Yale University, 1967.
Nickalls, John, ed. *The Journal of George Fox.* London: Religious Society of Friends, 1975.
Pickett, Clarence. *For More than Bread.* Boston: Little, Brown & Company, 1953.
Punshon, John. *Portrait in Grey: A Short History of the Quakers.* London: Quaker Home Service, 1984.
Smith, William Carlson. *Americans in the Making: the Natural History of the Assimilation of Immigrants.* New York: D. Appleton-Century, 1939.
Zuckmayer, Carl. *A Part of Myself.* New York: Carroll and Graf, 1984.